For the Life of the World

The Compass Rose

The emblem of the Anglican Communion, the Compass Rose, was originally designed by the late Canon Edward West of New York. The modern design is that of Giles Bloomfield. The symbol, set in the nave of Canterbury Cathedral, was dedicated by the Archbishop of Canterbury at the final Eucharist of the Lambeth Conference in 1988. The Archbishop dedicated a similar symbol in Washington Cathedral in 1990, and one in the original design in New York Cathedral in 1992, demonstrating that its use has become increasingly widespread. The centre of the Compass Rose holds the Cross of St. George, reminding Anglicans of their origins. The Greek inscription "The Truth Shall Make You Free" (John 8:32) surrounds the cross, and the compass recalls the spread of Anglican Christianity throughout the world. The mitre at the top emphasises the role of the episcopacy and apostolic order that is at the core of the churches of the Communion. The Compass Rose is used widely by the family of Anglican-Episcopal churches. It is the logo of the Inter-Anglican Secretariat, and it is used as the Communion's identifying symbol.

For the Life of the World

THE OFFICIAL REPORT OF THE 12TH MEETING OF THE ANGLICAN CONSULTATIVE COUNCIL, HONG KONG 2002

Compiled by James M. Rosenthal

WITH THE ENTHRONEMENT SERMON
OF ARCHBISHOP OF CANTERBURY
ROWAN WILLIAMS AND TEXTS FROM
THE 2003 PRIMATES MEETING IN BRAZIL

MOREHOUSE PUBLISHING
A Continuum imprint
HARRISBURG • LONDON • NEW YORK

Published for the Anglican Communion Office
Partnership House
157 Waterloo Road
London SE1 8UT
England

Morehouse Publishing
P.O. Box 1321
Harrisburg, PA 17105

Morehouse Publishing is a Continuum imprint.

Printed in the United States of America

ISBN 0-8192-1988-6

Library of Congress Cataloging-in-Publication Data

Anglican Consultative Council. Meeting (12th : 2002 : Hong Kong)

For the life of the world : the official report of the 12th Meeting of the Anglican Consultative Council, Hong Kong, 2002 / edited by James M. Rosenthal. – 1st ed.

p. cm.

ISBN 0-8192-1988-6 (pbk.)

1. Anglican Consultative Council. 2. Anglican Communion – Congresses. I. Rosenthal, James. II. Title.

BX5002.A6326 2002
262'.53–dc21 2003009160

Cover design by Corey Kent

Contents

Theme Song "For the Life of the World"

–Matthew Vernon (English) –Ulfred U

God of Life, God of Joy,
You rouse the weary heart.
God of Hope, God of Justice,
You break the chains that bind.
God of Faith, God of Peace,
You calm the troubled soul.
In You all people shall meet
and find their salvation.

May Your Church, show the way,
to build the Kingdom on earth.
Reaching out to the broken,
the fearful or oppressed.
May our lives, show to all
the Unity You bring,
so that Your Peace and Love may grow
in every nation.

Chorus
Inspire our songs of love for all the world.
A love that breaks all barriers down.
Enrich our stories of the risen Lord,
Jesus, who lived and died, so all may have Life.

Hong Kong Sheng Kung Hui

The history of the Church dates back to the mid-nineteenth century; missionaries were provided by the American Church, the Church of England, the Church of England in Canada, the Church of Ireland, the Churches of Australia and New Zealand. Western missionaries withdrew in 1950. All Churches were closed in 1966 and did not re-open until 1979. Most denominations then joined the China Christian Council. The suppression of the pro-democracy movement in 1989 resulted in stricter regulations for religious groups. Today members of the Chung Hua Sheng Kung Hui (the Holy Catholic Church in China) are found in the post-denominational Church, the Three-Self Movement, except for Hong Kong which returned to Chinese sovereignty in 1997 and in Macao, which was returned to China by Portugal in 1999.

Geographical Area: 1,070 square km.
Population: 6,900,000

Primate: The Most Reverend Peter Kwong
Provincial Treasurer: The Reverend Andrew Chan
Website: Hong Kong Sheng Kung Hui
Eastern Kowloon
Hong Kong Island
Western Kowloon

Preface

—The Most Reverend Peter Kwong, Archbishop and Primate of Hong Kong Sheng Kung Hui

When one sees one's brother and sister Anglican face to face, it is a true joy. The Hong Kong Sheng Kung Hui, the Anglican Episcopal presence in Hong Kong, were amazed at the insights and friendships formed following the ACC-12 Meeting at the Salisbury YMCA Hotel in Kowloon.

The events surrounding the actual meeting as well as the struggles and concerns and joys and hopes expressed throughout the proceedings truly gave those of us in the Hong Kong Sheng Kung Hui a new outlook about what it meant to be part of a global family, part of a family that eats, laughs, talks, argues and debates together.

As the host Archbishop, it was my singular privilege to be able to lead the tributes to Lord and Lady Carey as the former Archbishop's retirement meant that this was his last ACC Meeting. And of course having the 104th Archbishop of Canterbury, designate at that time, The Most Reverend and Right Honourable Rowan Douglas Williams with us for the ACC and Primates Standing Committee was an added joy. The dinner held in his honour certainly was a marvelous prelude to the ACC Meeting itself.

It is always a great privilege to share our ministries with other people and the willingness of the ACC to visit our many social agencies run by the dioceses as well as to participate in worship in St. Mary's Episcopal Church, Hong Kong, and Holy Trinity, Kowloon certainly made a lasting impression on those lively congregations. The services of ordination at the Cathedral and indeed the opening service of the ACC will become part of the permanent historical notes of St. John's Cathedral.

As I write this, Hong Kong faces the unprecedented outbreak of SARS (severe acute respiratory syndrome) and I feel more strong and bold in my prayer knowing that people around the Communion at this and other times are praying for the people of Hong Kong in this strange and difficult moment dealing with this medical emergency.

Being put in isolation from the rest of the world is not a pleasant thing. Wars, anything that divides people, can have the most devastating effect. What a great privilege it is to know that the Anglican family prays together and stays together at these most difficult times.

As this was Canon Peterson's last meeting as Secretary General of the ACC I also join in wishing him farewell as do the other members of the Compass Rose Society in our Church. We are trying our best to be full members and full participants in the life of the Communion and we pray that we continue to be strong contributors in many ways of the programme that is so important to us all.

I assure Archbishop Williams of my utmost support as a fellow Primate as his ministry unfolds and I give grateful thanks to Lord Carey for all he has done for us. I know that the people of the Communion will continue to pray for the witness to the risen Christ that we in the Hong Kong Sheng Kung Hui want to see strengthened and that prayers will be ardent as we look to the future of Hong Kong and China and religious practice in the years ahead.

With my prayers and a blessing.

Acknowledgements

Thanks go to Mrs. Veronica Elks and Marjorie Murphy from the Anglican Communion Office, London. To the Anglican Consultative Council, and for the many individual presenters that contributed to the meeting and who helped in preparing this report. Thanks go to Kenneth Quigley, President of the Morehouse Group, and to Bonnee Lauridsen Voss for their help in publishing this report.

The grace of our Lord Jesus Christ, the love of God, and the fellowship of the Holy Spirit be with us all evermore.

Prayers for the Anglican Communion

—FROM *PARISH PRAYERS,* FRANK COLQUHOUN, EDITOR

The Anglican Communion

O Almighty God, our heavenly Father, who hast called us to be members of the Anglican Communion and to a partnership of churches in all parts of the world: Grant, we beseech thee, that we may understand the mission which thou hast entrusted to us, and our duty to those who are separated from us; that penitently recognizing our failings in the past, we may go forward in unity and love to the fulfilment of our common work; through Jesus Christ our Lord.

—Based on a prayer of the Pan-Anglican Congress, 1908

Almighty God, our heavenly Father, who in thy providence hast made us members of a great family of churches: We pray thee to pour out thy blessing upon the Anglican Communion throughout the world. Grant that we and all its members may be faithful to the trust which thou hast committed to us, and advance thy honour in the cause of Christian unity and mission; through Jesus Christ our Lord.

ANGLICAN CONSULTATIVE COUNCIL (ACC)

Officers and Members of the ACC and Participants and Staff at ACC-12

Officers

President

The Most Reverend and Right Honourable George Leonard Carey
The Archbishop of Canterbury

Chairman

The Right Reverend Simon E. Chiwanga
Bishop of Mpwapwa

Vice Chairman

The Most Reverend John Campbell Paterson
Presiding Bishop and Primate/Te Pihopa Matamuw

Secretary General

The Reverend Canon John L. Peterson
Anglican Consultative Council

Joint Standing Committee
Primates

The Most Reverend and Right Honourable George Leonard Carey
The Archbishop of Canterbury
The Most Reverend Peter Kwong
Archbishop of Hong Kong Sheng Hui and Bishop of Hong Kong
The Most Reverend Bernard Malango
Archbishop of Central Africa and Bishop of Northern Zambia
The Reverend Michael Peers
Primate of the Anglican Church in Canada
The Most Reverend James Terom
Moderator, CNI & Bishop of North India

Anglican Consultative Council

The Right Reverend Riah Abu El-Assal
Bishop in Jerusalem
The Most Reverend Peter Akinola
Archbishop, Metropolitan and Primate of All Nigeria

Mrs. Jolly Babirukamu
Mothers' Union Provincial President
Professor George Koshy
General Secretary, Church of South India & Vice Chair of ACC
The Very Reverend Dr. John Henry Moses
Dean, St. Paul's Cathedral
The Right Reverend John Campbell Paterson
Presiding Bishop and Primate/Te Pihopa Matamua & Chair of ACC
The Right Reverend James Tengatenga
Bishop of Southern Malawi
The Reverend Robert Thompson
Kingston, Jamaica, West Indies
Ms. Fung Yi Wong
Hong Kong, People's Republic of China

Inter-Anglican Finance Committee

The Most Reverend Robert Henry Alexander Eames
Primate of All Ireland & Archbishop of Armagh
Canon Elizabeth Paver
Doncaster, England
The Reverend Robert Sessum
Lexington, Kentucky, U.S.A.
The Most Reverend Peter Akinola
Archbishop, Metropolitan and Primate of All Nigeria
Ms. Fung Yi Wong
Hong Kong, People's Republic of China

Members of the Council

Chief Godwin O.K. Ajayi
Address: Private Mail Bag, 12679, Lagos, Nigeria

The Most Reverend Peter Jasper Akinola
Archbishop, Metropolitan and Primate of All Nigeria
Address: Episcopal House, P.O. Box 212 ADCP, Abuja, Nigeria

The Right Reverend Riah Hanna Abu El-Assal
Bishop in Jerusalem
Address: St George's Close, Box 19122, Jerusalem, Israel

The Right Reverend Samuel Azariah
Moderator, Church of Pakistan & Bishop of Raiwind
Address: 17 Warris Road, P.O. Box 2319, Lahore 3, Pakistan

Mrs. Jolly Hope Babirukamu
Mothers' Union Provincial President
Address: Church of Uganda, P.O. Box 14123, Kampala, Uganda

Mr. Roger Baboa
Address: C/O Diocese of Port Moresby, P.O. Box 6491, Boroko, Papua New Guinea

The Reverend Canon Job Bariira-Mbukure
Diocesan Secretary, Kampala Diocese Church of Uganda
Address: P.O. Box 335, Kampala, UGANDA

Mrs. Margaret Jolly Bihabanyi
Head of Division: Promotion of Craftsmanship, Ministry of Commerce, Industry and Tourism
Address: P.O. Box 73, Kigali, Rwanda

The Very Reverend Michael Andrew James Burrows
Dean Cork Cathedral
Address: The Deanery, Dean Street, Cork Co Cork, Republic Of Ireland

The Most Reverend and Right Honourable George Leonard Carey
The Archbishop of Canterbury
Address: Lambeth Palace, London SE1 7JU, England

Mr. Nicolas Yohesan Casie Chetty
Headmaster St Thomas' Preparatory School
Address: 90 Steuart Place, Galle Road, Colombo 03, Sri Lanka

The Right Reverend Simon E. Chiwanga
Bishop of Mpwapwa
Address: P.O. Box 2, Mpwapwa, Tanzania

Mr. Chang-Jim Chong
Address: 6-101 Daerim Apartment, Eungbong-dong, Sungdong-ku, Seoul 100-120, Republic Of Korea

Ms. Judith G. Conley
Address: 11314 S. Santa Margarita Lane, Goodyear AZ 85338, USA

The Reverend Canon Maurício José Araújo de Andrade
General Secretary Igreja Episcopal Anglicana do Brasil
Address: Caixa Postal 11 510, Porto Alegre, RS 91720-150, RS, Brazil

Professor Adrian DeHeer-Amissah
National Council for Tertiary Education
Address: P.O. Box M28, Stow Hill, Accra, Ghana

The Reverend Govada Dyvasirvadam
General Secretary CSI Synod Secretariat
Address: P.O. Box 688, Royapettah, Chennai-600 014, India

Mr. Robert Fordham
Address: 22 Redgum Court, Newlands Arm Victoria 3875, Australia

Mr. Bernard Georges
Provincial Chancellor, Province of Indian Ocean
Address: Trinity House, P.O. Box 153, Victoria Mahe, Seychelles

Archdeacon Kay Goldsworthy
Address: 2 Mitchell Street, Andross WA 6153, Australia

Mr. Saw Si Hai
National Director of Myanmar Youth For Christ
Address: Bishopcourt,140 Pyidaungsu Yeiktha Road, Dagon P.O. 11191, Yangon, Myanmar

The Venerable Winston Halapua
College of the Diocese of Polynesia
Address: Private Bag 28 907, Remuera Auckland, New Zealand

The Right Reverend Richard Douglas Harries
Bishop of Oxford
Address: Diocesan Church House, North Hinksey, Oxford OX2 ONB, England

The Right Reverend Petrus Hidulika Hilukiluah
Suffragan Bishop of Namibia
Address: P.O. Box 65, Windhoek, Rep. Of Namibia

The Right Reverend Michael C. Ingham
Bishop of New Westminster
Address: Suite 580, 401 W. Georgia Street, Vancouver BC V6B 5A1, Canada

The Reverend Canon Lovey Kisembo
Vicar St John's Church, Kamwokya
Address: St John's Cathedral, Kamwokya, P.O. Box 37, Fort Portal, Uganda

Mr. Amos Kirani Kiriro
Administrator St Paul's Theological College
Address: P.O. Box 43102, Nairobi, Kenya

Mr. Is-Hag Kannidi Kodi Kodi
Diocesan Planning & Development Officer Khartoum Diocese
Address: Episcopal Church of the Sudan, Box 65, Omdurman, Sudan

The Very Reverend Ezekiel Kondo
Provincial Secretary—The Episcopal Church of the Sudan
Address: P.O. Box 604, Khartoum, Sudan

The Reverend Samuel Isamu Koshiishi
The Nippon Sei Ko Kai
Address: #101 2-19-60 Mihara, Asaka-shi, Saitama-ken 351-0025, Japan

Professor George Koshy
Address: B-3 Quanta Annam, 965 24th Street, H Block, Thirumoolar Colony, Annanagar West Madras 40, India

The Right Reverend Bolly Anak Lapok
Assistant Bishop of Kuching The House of the Epiphany
Address: P.O. Box 347, 93704 Kuching, Sarawak, Malaysia

The Right Reverend Carlos López-Lozano
Bishop of Spanish Reformed Episcopal Church
Address: Calle Beneficencia 18, 28004 Madrid, Spain

The Right Reverend Michael Sokiri Lugor
Bishop of Rejaf Episcopal Church of the Sudan
Address: Community Development Programme, P.O. Box 40360. Nairobi, Kenya

Mr. Warren E. Luyaben
Chancellor to the Prime Bishop
Address: Tabuk, Kalinga, Philippines

The Reverend Sunil Mankhin
Address: Village-Ballovepur, P.O. Kedarganj, Meherpur, Bangladesh

The Very Reverend Dr. John Henry Moses
Dean St Paul's Cathedral
Address: 9 Amen Court, London EC4M 7BU, England

The Reverend Canon Dr. Susan Moxley
Parish Priest, Canon of Cathedral Church of All Saints
Address: 5515 Russell St., Halifax, NS, Canada B3K 1X1

The Most Reverend Livingstone Mpalanyi-Nkoyoyo
Archbishop of Uganda & and Bishop of Kampala
Address: P.O. Box 14123, Kampala, Uganda

The Right Reverend Gerard E. Mpango
Bishop of Western Tanganyika
Address: P.O. Box 13, Kasulu, Tanzania

Mr. Ghazi Musharbash
Mirna Industrial Commercial Company
Address: P.O. Box 2001, Amman 11953, Jordan

Mrs. Joyce Luhui Ngoda
Mothers' Union Diocesan Secretary
Address: P.O. Box 35, Korogwe, Tanzania

The Reverend Damien Nteziryayo
Episcopal Church of Rwanda
Address: Kigeme Diocese, BP 67, Gikongoro, Rwanda

The Right Reverend Martin Blaise Nyaboho
Bishop of Makamba
Address: BP 96, Makamba, Burundi

The Very Reverend Dr. David Chidiebele Okeke
Provost All Saint's Cathedral
Address: P.O. Box 922, Awka, Anambra State, Nigeria

Mrs. Lenore Margaret Parker
Address: 4 Bent Street, Maclean NSW 2463, Australia

Mr. Farrukh Marvin Parvez
Director Church World Service—Pakistan/Afghanistan
Address: 74 Garden Road, Karachi, Pakistan

The Right Reverend John Campbell Paterson
Presiding Bishop and Primate/Te Pihopa Matamua
Address: P.O. Box 37 242, Parnell Auckland 1033, New Zealand

Canon Elizabeth Paver
Address: 113 Warning Tounge Lane, Bessacarr, Doncaster DN4 6TB, England

Miss Andrea Candace Payne
Eucharistic Minister, Lay Youth Minister St Leonard's Church
Address: Westbury Road, St Michael, Barbados

The Very Reverend Christopher Potter
Dean of St Asaph Cathedral
Address: The Deanery, 101 Upper Denbigh Road, St Asaph LL17 0RL, Wales

The Reverend Enos Das Pradhan
Provincial Treasurer—Church of North India
Address: 16 Pandit Pant Marg, New Delhi 110 001, India

Mr. John M. Rea
Address: Beaconhill, 58 Main Street, Kirknewton Midlothian EH27 8AA, Scotland

Engineer Antonio Ortega Reybal
Address: Fresnos 37, Fracc.Primavera, Colonia Delicias, 62330 Cuernavaca Morelos, Mexico

The Right Reverend Catherine S. Roskam
Suffragan Bishop of New York
Address: Region Two Office, 55 Cedar Street, Dobbs Ferry NY 10522, USA

The Right Reverend Josias Sendegeya
Bishop of Kibungo
Address: BP 2487, Kigali, Rwanda

The Reverend Robert Lee Sessum
Good Shepherd Church
Address: 533 East Main Street, Lexington KY 40508, USA

Miss Sylvia Scarf
Address: 14 Bridgend Road, Llanharan, Pontyclun Mid Glamorgan CF72 9RA, Wales

The Right Reverend Robert David Silk
Bishop of Ballarat
Address: Bishop's Lodge, 6 Banyle Drive, Ballarat Victoria 3356, Australia

Canon Maureen Sithole
Address: P.O. Box 291, Daveyton 1507 Gauteng, South Africa

The Right Reverend Badda Peter Sugandhar
Bishop of Medak
Address: Bishop's Annexe, 145, MacIntyre Road, Secunderabad Andhra Pradesh 500, 003, India

Mr. Daniel Taolo
Diocese of Botswana
Address: P.O. Box 769, Gaberone, Botswana

The Right Reverend James Tengatenga
Bishop of Southern Malawi
Address: Diocese of Southern Malawi, P.O. Box 30220, Chichiri, Blantyre 3, Malawi

The Reverend Robert Thompson
Address: 14 Ottawa Avenue, Kingston 6, Jamaica, West Indies

Mr. Richard Ian Thornton
Principal Bishop Westcott Boys School
Address: P.O. Namkom, Ranchi-830 010 Bihar, India

Dr. Stephen John Toope
Address: McGill University, 3644 Peel Street, Montréal Quebec H3A 1W9, Canada

Miss Joyce Muhindo Tsongo
Address: ISThA-Bunia, P.O. Box 25586, Kampala, Uganda

Mr. Bernard Selkirk Anderson Turner
Address: P.O. Box N1147, Nassau NP, Bahamas

Miss Kate Turner
Address: 19 Charleville Avenue, Belfast BT9 7HG, United Kingdom

Mr. Luis Roberto Valleé
Morgan & Morgan
Address: Coral Bay Building, 6th Floor, San Francisco, St 77 and 5b Sur Ave, Panama, Republic Of Panama

The Venerable Margaret Brenda Vertue
St Philip's Anglican Church
Address: P.O. Box 5, Gordon's Bay 7151, South Africa

The Right Reverend David Vunagi
Bishop of Temotu
Address: P.O. Box 7, Lata, Santa Cruz Temotu Province, Solomon Islands

The Right Reverend Joseph Otieno Wasonga
Bishop of Maseno West
Address: P.O. Box 793, Siaya, Kenya

Professor Whatarangi Winiata
Address: 22 Te Manuao Road, Otaki, New Zealand

Ms. Fung Yi Wong
Address: Flat 2-B New Wing, St John's College, 82 Pokfulam Road, Hong Kong, People's Republic Of China

The Right Reverend Hector Zavala
Bishop of Chile
Address: Casilla 50675, Correo Central, Santiago, Chile

Consultants/Presenters

The Reverend Canon Ogé Beauvoir
Program Associate, Trinity Grants Program
Address: 74 Trinity Place, New York NY 10006-2088, USA

The Reverend Canon Ted Karpf
Address: St. George's Cathedral, 5 Wale Street, Cape Town 8001, South Africa

The Reverend Dr. Ishmael Noko
General Secretary
Address: Lutheran World Federation, P.O. Box 2100, 150 Route de Ferney, 1211 Geneva 2, Switzerland

The Reverend Canon John Rees
Legal Advisor for the Anglican Communion
Address: 16 Beaumont Street, Oxford OX1 2LZ, England

Archdeacon Fagamalama Tuatagaloa Matalavea
UN Observer
Address: 815 Second Avenue, New York NY 10017, USA

Inter-Anglican Finance Committee

The Most Reverend Robert Henry Alexander Eames
Primate of All Ireland & Archbishop of Armagh
Address: See House, Cathedral Close, Armagh BT61 7EE, Northern Ireland

Primates Standing Committee

The Most Reverend Peter Kwong
Archbishop of Hong Kong Sheng Hui & Bishop of Hong Kong
Address: Bishop's House, 1 Lower Albert Road, Hong Kong, People's Republic of China

The Most Reverend Bernard Amos Malango
Archbishop of Central Africa & Bishop of Northern Zambia
Address: Diocese of Upper Shire, P/Bag 1, Chilema, Zomba, Malawi

The Most Reverend Michael Geoffrey Peers
Primate of the Anglican Church in Canada
Address: 600 Jarvis Street, Toronto ON M4Y 2J6, Canada

The Most Reverend Zechariah James Terom
Moderator, CNI & Bishop of Chotanagpur
Address: Bishop's Lodge, P.O. Box 1, Church Road, Ranchi 834 001 Bihar, India

The Most Reverend Rowan Douglas Williams
Archbishop of Wales & Bishop of Monmouth
Address: Bishopstow, Stow Hill, Newport Gwent NP20 4EA, Wales

Ecumenical

Fr. Donald Bolen
Vatican
Address: Pontifical Council for Promoting Christian Unity, 00120, Vatican City, Italy

The Reverend David Gill
World Council of Churches
Address: Kowloon Union Church, 4 Jordan Road, Kowloon Hong Kong SAR, People's Republic of China

Metropolitan Nikitas of Hong Kong and Southeast Asia
Orthodox Metropolitanate of Hong Kong and Southeast Asia
Address: Universal Trade Center #704, 3 Arbuthnot Road, Hong Kong

Ms. Mandy Tibbey
Associate General Secretary, Christian Conference of Asia

Churches in Communion

The Right Reverend Dr. Joseph Mar Irenaeus
Suffragan Metropolitan—Mar Thoma Syrian Church of Malabar
Address: Hermon Aramana, Adoor—691 523 Kerala, India

The Reverend Dr. Harald Rein
Old Catholic

Bible Study Presenters

The Right Reverend Kenneth Michael James Fernando
Retired Bishop of Colombo
Address: 103 Dampe Road, Madapatha, Piliyandala, Sri Lanka

The Most Reverend Ian Gordon Combe George
Archbishop of Adelaide
Address: 26 King William Road, North Adelaide South Australia 5006, Australia

Dr. Jennie Plane Te Paa
Address: Te Rau Kahikatea, 202-210 St John's Road, Meadowbank Auckland 1005, New Zealand

Dr. Sally Thompson
Co-ordinator International Anglican Family Network
Address: IAFN Office, P.O. Box 54, Minehead, Somerset TA24 7WD, UK

Host Province

The Reverend Dorothy Lau
Address: 1 Lower Albert Road, Hong Kong, People's Republic of China

The Reverend Andrew Chan
Provincial General Secretary
Address: 1 Lower Albert Road, Hong Kong, People's Republic of China

Anglican Communion Office

The Reverend Canon John L. Peterson • Secretary General
The Reverend Canon Eric Beresford • Ethics
Lynne Butt • Travel Office
Mr. Matthew Davies • Communications

Mrs. Veronica Elks • Communications
Mr. Andrew Franklin • Finance and Administration
The Reverend Paul Gibson • Liturgy
The Reverend Canon David Hamid • Ecumenical and Interfaith
Ian Harvey • Computer Network Manager & DTP
Mrs. Deirdre Martin • Executive Assistant to the Secretary General
Miss Marjorie Murphy • Mission and Evangelism
The Reverend Dorothy Penniecooke • Finance and Administration
Canon James M. Rosenthal • Communications and Anglican World Editor
Mr. Christopher Took • Communications & Web Site Manager

Archbishop of Canterbury's Staff

Canon Herman Browne • Archbishop of Canterbury's Office for the Anglican Communion

Support Staff

Miss Fiona Millican • Executive Assistant to Canon Herman Browne
Mrs. Gill Harris-Hogarth • Private Secretary to the Archbishop of Canterbury

Communications Team

Mr. Daniel B. England
Director of Communications, ECUSA
Address: 815 Second Avenue, New York NY 10017, USA

The Reverend Paul Kwong
Address: 11 Weoley Park Rd, Selly Oak, Birmingham B29 6QY, England

Canon Margaret Rodgers
Chief Executive Officer, Media Relations
Address: P.O. Box Q190, Queen Victoria Post Office, Sydney NSW 2000, Australia

The Reverend Canon Alistair Macdonald-Radcliffe
Address: The Rectory, 1 Truro Lane, Fairfax, Virginia USA 22030

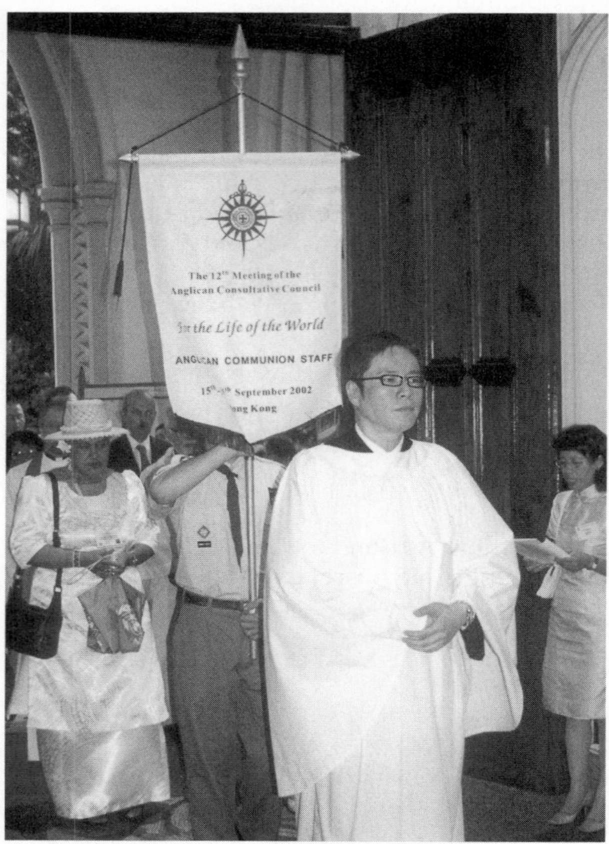

Staff of the ACC Office are escorted to their seats in the Cathedral for the opening service

Young People's Choir joins in a full evening of entertainment for the International Anglican Consultative Council gathering in the Convention Centre

Information session Diocese of New Westminster during ACC-12

All photos: ACNS/Rosenthal

ACC members from South East Asia, Canada, Pakistan, Nigeria and England lead the prayers of the people at the Eucharist

The Australian members

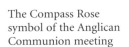

The Compass Rose symbol of the Anglican Communion meeting

Traditional Chinese extraordinary entertainment

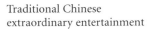

The Ordination of the Revd Dorothy Lau

Archbishop Peter Kwong and his newly ordained deacons process out of the cathedral following the service

Outgoing Chairman Bishop Simon Chiwanga of Tanzania pauses to view the banner of the province of the Anglican Church of Congo, appropriately draped in a black priest stole remembering Father Basimaki who was murdered in his home country on his way to the meeting

Photo of all, at the dinner celebration in the Convention Centre

ACC's new vice chairman, Professor George Koshy, enjoys a traditional Chinese Banquet

Standing Committee meeting, chaired by Archbishop Carey

A warm greeting for staff, speakers and ACC members at local Church

Bishop Martin joins in creating a Chinese masterpiece of food

The Revd Dorothy Lau welcomes guests to the dedication ceremony for the new aged care facility

The Revd Emanuel Adekola (right) and Canon Deaconess Margaret Rodgers work on a media release during the ACC meeting

Please sign in. Hundreds of guests signed a special greetings card to mark the opening of the care facility

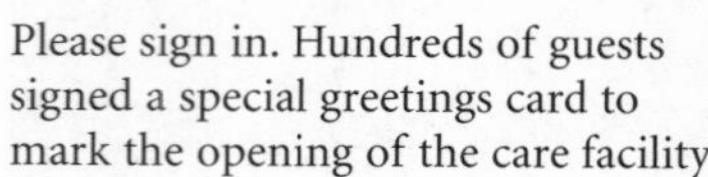

The Gospel of the Lord, the reading is proclaimed in the Nave of Holy Trinity Church

Members of the choir

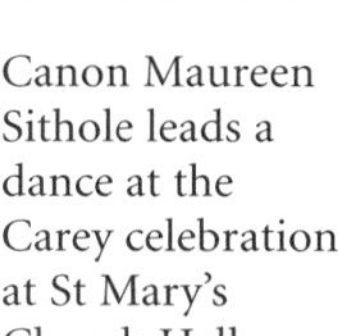

Canon Maureen Sithole leads a dance at the Carey celebration at St Mary's Church Hall

The Church of St John the Baptist, its unique altar, font and sculpture of the baptism of Christ

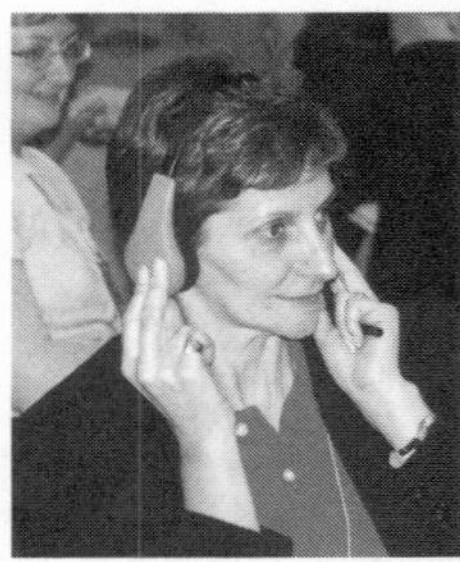

The Very Revd Kay Goldsworthy from Australia uses headphones to hear the translation of the presentation on Francophone provinces by the Revd Ogé Beauvoir

Procession. The choir processes into St Mary's Church

Delegates enjoy Hong Kong hospitality

Antonio Reybal from Mexico listens attentively to the proceedings at ACC-12 in the Salisbury YMCA

Outgoing ACC member Bernard Turner urges ACC to reconsider how voting is accomplished during its meetings

Closing Eucharist at St Mary's Church

14 SEPTEMBER 2002

Sermon at the Ordination Service on Holy Cross Day

—THE MOST REVEREND AND RIGHT HON. GEORGE L. CAREY, ARCHBISHOP OF CANTERBURY

The Cathedral Church of St John the Evangelist, Hong Kong

I am delighted to be here in this wonderful Cathedral with you, Archbishop Peter and so many other delegates of ACC for this Ordination Service. I want to assure Samuel (Tang), Stephen (Hung) and Dorothy (Lau) of our prayers and support at this time.

The image of shepherds and sheep is surely incongruous in Hong Kong. I have no idea as to whether any sheep graze on the hills of the island or if they ever did. Indeed, increasingly, for most of us from urban situations the image in scripture of ministers and priests as shepherds and those we serve as sheep may seem irrelevant and unhelpful. If that is your assumption allow me to disagree and suggest that such a 'shepherd theology' is bang up to date for all those ordained to serve Christ in his Church today.

I want to offer those of you being ordained today three very simple points.

The Shepherd is called to serve Christ's flock.
The Shepherd is called to nourish and defend Christ's flock.
The Shepherd is called to know where the pastures are to be found.

Called to serve Christ's flock. A few years ago you sensed in your spirit and heart a longing and a desire to offer yourself for service in this church. The process of selection, training and examination culminates in what we are doing today as you are set apart for ministry in Christ's Church to serve his people. The Church has discerned in you those special qualities of pastoral care, learning and faith. With confidence today we pray that God's Spirit will fill your hearts and lives with his grace and love.

And grace and love are two of the most crucial elements in the new ministry that is today conferred on you. Grace—because each day you will only survive if you rely on that grace to fill your life with kindness and his Spirit to strengthen and sustain you. And that will only be effective if the outcome is love—love, to care for Christ's people and his flock. In a few moments you will be handed a Bible and told: 'Receive this book as a sign of the authority given you this day to speak God's word to his people.

Build them up in his truth and serve them in his name.' 'Build them up. Serve them.'

But here we come to a theological conundrum, because who comprises God's flock? Swiftly we cry out the answer. 'Of course, it must be those who belong to the Church. Those who are signed up and paid up members of our 'club.' Believers like us.' In a way that is right. We do have a special relationship to those baptised in Christ. But I do so hope that you have a wider view of your ministry than that. I hope you might see all people as embraced by God's love and potentially open to his challenge and grace. Scripture reminds us to draw boundaries as generously as possible and to be as hopeful as the gospel itself in expecting lives to be transformed by the grace of God. So we can see the flock not only as those regular members of the Church, but also the lonely, the drug addicts, that young person who shows no interest in religion, your neighbour in investment banking. You are called to seek and serve all, including the least, the last and the lost. It was one of my predecessors, William Temple, who said famously: 'The Church is the only organisation that exists for the benefit of those who are not yet its members.'

But in order to serve them we must know them and be known by them. You must learn to discern their pains, their aspirations, their hopes and fears; and they must know what you stand for. You may have heard the incident of a woman who approached her local pastor. 'Pastor, pastor, my husband is very ill.' 'Don't say that,' the pastor said. 'All is well in Jesus' name . . . say, he's under the impression that he's ill,' Two weeks later the pastor met the woman and enquired after her husband, 'How is he?' 'Oh him?' the woman replied, 'He's under the impression that he's dead.' In order to serve your people you must, unlike that Pastor, know them well, take them seriously and share in their suffering.

Called to nourish and defend the flock. For this task of service you have had to apply yourself with vigour and determination to the study of scripture and theology. Perhaps it has been hard to find the time in busy lives. Perhaps you have been tempted to think: 'What is the point of all this study? Surely, it's a bit excessive to study history, philosophy, biblical languages and so on when all I shall do is to help in my local church!'

I beg to differ. I hope that the time of learning has been a time of nourishment to you in which your love of our Lord has grown; in which your understanding of the Bible has flowered; in which you have become excited by the wonder of God's salvation and his gospel. And that is what you are required to communicate to those who will listen to you teach and preach the word of God.

You will be required humbly and faithfully to pass to new generations the tradition which we have received as Anglican Christians. But we must so understand the tradition we have received to be in a position to discern when it may have reached the end of its journey. I love the splendid definition of the difference between tradition and traditionalism: 'Tradition is the living faith of the dead; traditionalism is the dead faith of the living.' Traditionalism is when we refuse to move a flowerpot because my great Grandmother placed the church flowers in that very place and pot 70 years ago. Tradition is when we keep godly customs alive because they are as real today as they were 70 years ago. And that is why I have been so delighted to have spent so much of my life in the study of theology.

You are to nourish them with the gospel and defend that gospel in their midst. Sometimes it may mean asking uncomfortable questions of those whose decisions and policies affect adversely the lives of God's people in this place. In doing this, do not flag in zeal. Hold fast to what is good.

A similar challenge arises in our wider society. We live at a time where competing ideologies offer instant gratification to us all. Here in Hong Kong, as in all advanced societies, materialism offers a million and one different choices for the betterment of life. And there are many religious options on offer and so many pseudo-religious claims that may confuse any of us. Does Christ offer a better way? As Christian people we must respect all those who offer a different salvation to that offered in Christ and with the greatest of tenderness and love we can only say with the Psalmist: 'Taste and see how good the Lord is!'. And as you point others to him you will be offering the best defence of all, because the greatest proof of the truth of the Christian way is the difference it makes to our lives.

Called to know where the pastures are to be found. You know, I have often wondered about the theme in the early part of the Bible that Israel is a land flowing with 'milk and honey'! In reality, of course, it is not like that at all. It is one of the stoniest places on earth. Sheep have a tough time finding places to graze. The skill of the shepherd in the time of Jesus was that he knew where the best places were to be found. 'The Lord is my shepherd. he makes me lie down in green pastures.' But this could only be possible because the shepherd had been there time and time again. He knew the way, he knew the best paths and he knew the obstacles and dangers on the way. And that is why your preparation has been thorough and why we want to say to you: keep learning. Make prayer and study your daily delight and your urgent routine.

I like the story of a man who turned up at the Casualty Department of a hospital and asked to see the 'eye and ear' consultant. The Sister on duty said: 'I am sorry we do not have such a specialist. We have an 'ear and throat' specialist but not 'ear and eye.' What is your problem?' He replied: 'Well, you see, it is like this-I can't see what I hear'.

Seeing and hearing may not go together in medical consultancy but they certainly go together as far as the spiritual life is concerned. If you must lead, then people must see in you what they hear from you. If you must 'talk the talk,' then they will expect you to 'walk the walk'. Not only will people—and rightly in my view—expect your deeds to match your words, but you must live amongst them and be a full part of their community. You see, people rarely follow leaders they cannot see. So, if you must lead—and you will—then with confidence lead from the front.

As you grow in the study of God's word so you will become a person who can lead others to the living water. In so doing, it is not so much that you gradually become perfect; or that you acquire the right answers to all the questions that others will throw at you. No. It is not even so much that you will become better at making good decisions, but that you will become better and better at discerning what really matters in reaching whatever decisions you eventually make. Pray for courage. Pray for zeal. Pray for such an abiding love of God's people that you constantly find yourself acting and speaking on their behalf—so that they too can taste and see that the Lord is good.

From my experience I can tell you that the task is never easy, you will sometimes be misunderstood, often lonely and frequently criticised. But the joys of service outnumber the difficulties. And it is service which binds the leader and the led together. Should the leader ever forget that he is first and foremost someone who is always a servant of others and always one on the way as a disciple, he is in danger of confusing leadership with lordship.

In the words of Max Warren, the great Missionary Statesman of the last century: 'Leadership involves discerning what is right, laying a course, and embarking upon the endless business of persuading the rank and file of its rightness. . . . Here is the fearful burden of responsibility . . . however much one may have colleagues for 99% of the way, there will remain the last 1% when one is ahead and alone.' That's true. But I can also say with confidence that you will not be alone, because the Spirit of the Lord will be with you to bear you up as on eagles' wings. The task to which you are called is a tremendous privilege as well as an awesome responsibility. Go forth in the power of God's Spirit.

Amen.

Homily at Early Morning Eucharist, Holy Cross Day

—The Most Reverend Rowan D. Williams, Archbishop of Wales

One of the hidden treasures of Jerusalem is the Monastery of the Holy Cross in a Crescent Hill. If you visit that Monastery and go round the beautiful Monastic Church there, you will see a series of frescos depicting the history of the Holy Cross.

See the story beginning with the funeral of Adam when his son, Seth, places under his tongue a little seed. From that seed grows a tree, the branches of that tree have many strange adventures, they figure in the stories of Abraham and Solomon and goodness knows who else, till at last from that tree is cut the wood on which Christ is hung. It is an extraordinary fantasy. A fantasy which somehow speaks of the very heart of what the cross is about.

The seed of sin lies under the tongue of Adam, out of the sinful speech and imagining of human beings, from the skull of Adam grows this vast tree tangled and knotted upon which the end of the story, the incarnate son of God is killed. Sin grows from the skull of Adam. Sin is like a huge spreading, elaborating bad dream, coming out of the human mind, coming out of the human head, under the human tongue; our speech, our thinking, our imagining, our wanting, all of them somehow doomed to this dream life.

You know what bad dreams are like, you can't just will yourself out of them, they get worse and worse, they become more and more ludicrous and more and more inescapable. The images, the metaphors, the sounds, the sights just spiral on out of control, at the end of the story you wake up.

All I want to say about the gift of the Holy Cross this morning is that the Cross of our Lord Jesus Christ is where we wake up. Awake sleeper and rise from the dead, Christ will give you life. Our sin is like a sleep, like a bad dream, we are locked in ourselves, the mysterious tangled insides of the human mind, the human heart and human speech, trap us more and more. Here the reality of God stands against the unreality of our lives. Awake sleeper, rise from the dead, Christ shall give you life, Christ shall give you reality, Christ shall give you truth.

Church is in the world to issue a wake-up call, to use a much-abused expression. Church says, wake up from unreality. You can get out from inside the skull of Adam; you can get out from under the tongue of Adam.

God will give you life, God will give you reality. You are not locked within yourself. For by God you are called and abled to enter into communion.

Speak with one another, not speak that strange language of sin which talks and talks away inside your head like a bad dream. Just leave it here and to share with one another by the gift of the word of God. And the Church is always tempted like every other human being to slip back inside the skull of Adam. To become trapped in its own fears and fantasies, inside the nightmare, the bad dream of God who is suspicious or hostile towards us. The bad dream of human brothers and sisters suspicious and hostile towards us the bad dream of imprisoning ourselves within ourselves. Yes the Church too [tape unclear] . . . in our midst lifted up over the skull of Adam, as in those great Medieval paintings, the blood of the Cross runs down on the skull of Adam and there is life.

So as we gather to reflect on our own Church life as an Anglican Communion, let us hear the call of God to be awake, to be watchful, to rise out of sleep. Let us remember to be on our guard for all those things that lock us once again inside the skull of sin, all those things which cultivate the growth of nightmare and evil. And what St. James says about that unruly member. We are here to celebrate wakefulness, dawn, because the cross is not the end of the story, but the beginning. The beginning of our walk in daylight and reality, wakefulness in God. The heavens are opened and we see the face of God which is not suspicious or hostile, endlessly light. Where in that light we see each other's faces, or the faces of enemies, faces of those God has given us to make communion with.

Day has dawned: Awake sleeper rise from the dead, Christ is light. One last image there. At the end of the story of transfiguration remember that the disciples had fallen into a trance, wake up, and when they woke up they saw Jesus only. They woke up and saw Jesus only. Seeing Jesus only, we all things, we see God of humanity, we see the world with the light of dawn upon it, we see ourselves truthfully, we see one another truthfully, we see God truthfully. The God who so loved the world that he held up humanity, paying of his own substance, the everlasting Son, to hang on the tree of Adam to cry out to us: Wake sleeper, rise from the dead. His rising, we rise; His life, we live; His light, we shall see it.

15 SEPTEMBER 2002

A Guide to ACC-12 Elections

—John Rea, Chair, ACC Elections Committee

1. THE ELECTIONS: During ACC-12, members must elect to the following positions:

   ACC Chair
   ACC Vice Chair
   ACC Standing Committee (6 vacancies)
   Inter Anglican Finance Committee (IAFC) (2 vacancies)

2. THE PROCESS: The ACC-12 programme has been planned so that there are two occasions when Regional Meetings can, if they wish, consider possible nominations for any of the above vacancies. From the programmer, it will be seen that the Regional Meetings fit into the Elections schedule as follows:

Regional Meeting (consider nominations for Chair and Vice-Chair)	Wed 18 Sept 8 pm (S.13)
Election of Chair	Sat 21 Sept 8 pm (S.22)
Election of Vice-Chair	Mon 23 Sept 4.30 pm (S. 25)
Regional Meeting (consider nominations for Standing Committee or IAFC)	Mon 23 Sept 2.30 pm (S.24)
Election of Standing Committee (6 vacancies) And IAFC (2 vacancies)	Tues 24 Sept 8 pm (S.30)

3. ACC Chair Election

(i) Critical dates:

Nomination papers available	Friday 20 Sept 9 am
Closing date for completed nominations	Sat 21 Sept 4 pm
Voting takes place	Sat 21 Sept 8 pm (S.22)
Result announced	Sat 21 Sept 9 pm (S.22)

(ii) Eligibility:

Open to members whether ACC-12 is their 1st, 2nd or last meeting.

(iii) Likely Attributes:

- ACC and Standing Committee experience
- Wide respect for leadership abilities
- Planning, organization and review experience
- Inclusive working style
- Chairing skills

Ability to represent the best interests of ACC with other Instruments of Unity, in the wider Anglican Communion and externally.

4. ACC VICE-CHAIR ELECTION

(i) Critical dates:

Nomination forms available	Sat 21 Sept 9 pm
Closing date for completed nominations	Mon 23 Sept 1 pm
Voting takes place	Mon 23 Sept 4.30 pm (S.25)
Result announced	Mon 23 Sept 6 pm (S.25)

(ii) Eligibility

Open to members whether ACC-12 is their 1st, 2nd or last meeting.

(iii) Likely Attributes:

- ACC and Standing Committee experience
- Wide respect for leadership abilities
- Planning organization and review experience
- Inclusive working style
- Chairing skills
- Ability to represent the best interests of ACC with other Instruments of Unity, in the wider Anglican Communion and externally.

In terms of balance and perception, it would be advantageous if the Chair and Vice-Chair are from quite differing regions in the Anglican Communion.

5. STANDING COMMITTEE ELECTIONS (6 VACANCIES)

(i) Critical dates:

Nomination papers available	Sat 21 Sept 9 pm
Closing date for completed nominations	Tues 24 Sept 1.30 pm
Voting takes place	Tues 24 Sept 8 pm (S.30)
Result announced	Tues 24 Sept 9 pm (S.30)

(ii) Eligibility

Open only to members for whom ACC-12 is their 1st or 2nd meeting.

(iii) Likely Attributes:

- International experience
- Planning and organization skills
- Creative, constructive approach to issues

(iv) Members finishing in Sept 2002

Ms. Judith Conley	(Lay)	F	USA
Prof. George Koshy	(Lay)	M	S. India
Rev. Dr. John Jae-Joung Lee	(Clergy)	M	S. Korea
Mr. Ghazi Musharbash	(Lay)	M	Jerusalem & Middle East
Mr. John Rea	(Lay)	M	Scotland
Canon Maureen Sithole	(Lay)	F	S. Africa

(v) Balance:

In your nominations and voting, you may like to bear in mind ACC By-Law 2d:

"In electing members of Standing Committee, the Council shall have regard to achieving (so far as is possible) appropriate regional diversity and a balance of representation between clergy and laity and between the genders."

6. INTER-ANGLICAN FINANCE COMMITTEE (2 VACANCIES)

(i) Critical dates:

As for Standing Committee in 5(i) above

(ii) Eligibility:

Open only to members for whom ACC-12 is their 1st or 2nd meeting.

(iii) Likely Attributes:

- Financial and budgetary expertise
- Strategic planning experience

(iv) Membership in Sept 2002:

Ms. Judith Conley
Mr. Ghazi Musharbash

7. NOMINATION PAPERS:

- Specific nomination forms for any of the vacant positions may be obtained from Veronica Elks in the ACC Secretariat after times stated above.
- Completed nomination forms should be returned, by the time stated above, to John Rees, presiding Officer or, in his absence, to Deirdre Martin. Forms received after the time deadline will not be included on the ballot paper.

Sermon at the Opening Eucharist

—The Most Reverend Peter Kwong, Archbishop and Primate of Hong Kong Sheng Kung Hui

The Cathedral Church of St John the Evangelist, Hong Kong

TEXT: "Did you not know that I must be busy with my Father's affairs?" (Luke 2:49)

Welcome to the meeting of ACC-12. Welcome to Hong Kong, the smallest and the youngest Province of the Anglican Communion, and welcome to St. John's Cathedral.

I praise the Lord for calling us to worship Him together here this afternoon. I thank God for making it possible for us coming from different parts of the world to meet here. We are glad to be here. However, may I ask a very naive but important question: "What are we here for?" We may have many different answers to that question. No matter what answer we would give, I hope that all these answers will ultimately be able to focus on the answer that Jesus gave to His parents after their visit to the temple. His answer was, "Did you not know that I must be busy with my Father's affairs?" I pray that we all come here to be busy with our Father's affairs, not just the affairs of the Anglican Church, nor the affairs of yours and mine. It is important for us to take St. Paul's words to the Romans seriously. He says: "Do not conform yourselves to the standards of this world, but let God transform you inwardly by a complete change of your mind. Then you will be able to know the will of God—what is good and is pleasing to him and is perfect. "

In 1991, I was very happy to see the theme of the Assembly of the World Council of Churches which was "Come, Holy Spirit." I thought that this time we would be able to wait for the guidance of the Holy Spirit in moving us forward to serve God and His people. At the end, I was very disappointed because I found that throughout the meeting, people were busy with their own agendas and were preoccupied with their own vested interests. It did not seem to me that we really meant to wait for the Holy Spirit to come.

Similarly, in 1988, all bishops were asked to bring their own dioceses with them to the Lambeth Conference. Many of us did some homework and brought their dioceses with them to the Conference. Only when they got there, they found that there was no place for them to unload their dioceses.

Moreover, I was told that in one meeting, people noticed that the honorary secretary was taking a nap without writing down anything. Nevertheless, after the meeting, he sent out minutes to members attending that meeting. People were amazed and asked him how he could do it. His answer was that every meeting was more or less the same and things would be done routinely as expected.

I have just chosen a few stories reflecting some hidden problems that happen in well-organized international conferences. You all have rich experience in attending conferences. You probably have better stories to share with us. I am sure that we all go to meetings with enthusiasm. We want to make contributions. We would like to get our agendas done. Sometimes we may like to bring in new ideas. We expect our meetings to be efficient and effective. At times, during the course of discussions and debates and with amendments and changes, the outcome would favor those who have louder voices or to those who have more muscle in it. Very often, we forget the real reason why we were in the meeting.

We come to this meeting as delegates, as observers, and as staff. There is a lot of business waiting for us to attend to. We come to review our work in the past and plan for the future of our church. There are plenty of opportunities in front of us. There is so much that we can do. Therefore, we have to choose. We have to screen. We have to talk. We have to listen. We have to discuss and debate. We have to decide. In the process of these, it is very easy for us to substitute our own interest for God's interest without even knowing about it. If we insist on our deliberations, we might be in danger of overshadowing the will of God. Therefore it is important that we cannot lose sight of the fact that, like Jesus, we should be busy with our Father's affairs and not ours. Our Father's will and His concerns should be the focus and the only focus of all our doings in the meeting and nothing else. Søren Kierkegaard says that the purity of heart is to will one thing and one thing only. We should not let any other thing to sidetrack our attention leading to the negligence of God's affairs. Our achievement means nothing if it is only to deal with our affairs and not God's affairs. This is what Edward Norman in his book "Secularisation" is trying to warn us about, the secularisation of the church.

Brothers and sisters, I think that there are a few things we have to keep in mind in order to do our Father's affairs. Jesus tells us that if we want to follow Him, we have to deny ourselves. To deny ourselves means that we have to empty ourselves. If we really mean to deny ourselves, we would not exert ourselves. Only when we empty ourselves we may be able to accommodate others. Consequently, we would not insist on our own views to be entertained. In the Council of Nicea, so many church leaders gathered together at a time when there were so many heresies, they were able to give up their own views and came to a common mind to formulate the

Nicene Creed which is good for so many generations. This is a very good example about how people deal with our Father's affairs.

Then Jesus asked us to carry our cross. To be the servants of Jesus Christ, just like Him, we have to be suffering as well. To suffer also means to sacrifice. If one is really happy to I sacrifice for Christ's sake, that person certainly would not care for success in the world. If one can be in such a state of giving up everything for God, that person must have room for others. In this case, the process of gives and takes will lead to the Truth instead of only wanting to take but not to give which will lead to bias, pride and prejudice. Hence to sacrifice does not mean just to give up something material. It is more important to give up just ourselves including our bias, prejudice and pride.

One of the tests that we can use to see if what we are doing is really doing our Father's affairs is to see what kinds of fruits that it bears. If it is our Father's affairs, the fruits must be the fruits of the Spirit which are love, joy, peace, patience, kindness, goodness, faithfulness, gentleness, and self-control. It is obvious. It is easily understood. It is difficult to understand how we can treat war, hatred, curse, indulgence, exploitation and greediness as the business of our Father. It is no good just to say that we are serving God if we are not producing the fruits of the Holy Spirit. It is not helpful just to say that we are doing all these for Christ if we are not mindful of the affairs of our Father.

If we are mindful of the affairs of our Father rather than ours, at the end of our meeting, we will see all of us come out from the conference room with smiles, relaxation, and an easy mind. We can see hopes in delegates' eyes. We can sense the peace surrounding us. We will enjoy the fellowship among us. We can feel the strength or unity pushing us forward. Just like the Psalmist says: "How good and pleasant it is when brothers and sisters live together in unity." This is the fruit of the Spirit. This is the concern of our Father. This is the purity of our hearts.

Dear delegates, the agenda for the meeting is just the skeleton of the meeting. We need to put the spirit into it. If we always keep God in mind for every item on the agenda, we certainly will be able to transform every thing into Christ-like rather than secularizing every thing that the church would be doing.

May God bless each one of you to be able to produce the fruits of the Holy Spirit. May God bless us to have a fruitful meeting so that God's will be done.

Guidelines for ACC Meetings

General

1. All arrangements for the conduct of the business of the Council shall be made under the general direction of the President.

Arrangements for Meetings

2.1 The Standing Committee:

2.1:1 shall make all detailed arrangements for meetings of the Council, and

2.1:2 shall settle the agenda and determine the order in which business shall be considered by the Council at its meetings, and

2.1:3 may delegate any of its functions relating to such matters to member(s) or Officers(s) as it shall see fit

2.2 In settling the agenda, the Standing Committee shall pay particular regard to:

2.2:1 The role of the Council as one of the instruments of unity in the Anglican Communion, and

2.2:2 Specific issues referred by the Archbishop of Canterbury, by the Lambeth Conference, by previous meetings of the Council, and by the Primates' Meeting, and

2.2:3 The need to inform members about the ongoing work of the Council, its Standing Committee and its Officers, and

2.2:4 The finances of the Council

2.3 In its preparation for each meeting of the Council the Standing Committee shall give opportunity to members at the first business session of every meeting (which shall take place within the first three days of assembling) to comment upon the settled agenda and to request the inclusion of additional material

2.4 The Chairman after consultation with the President shall have power to direct the addition to the agenda at any time of such urgent or specially important business as shall seem to them desirable

Chairing of Meetings

3.1 The Standing Committee shall appoint persons to chair each session of the Council who shall be either the President, the Chairman, the Vice-chairman or such other member of the Council as the Standing Committee shall think fit

3.2 It shall be the duty of the chair of each session to maintain order in debate, to ensure so far as possible that discussion of matters is broadly representative of the full range of views of members of the Council as a whole, and to encourage the Council to reach general assent on matters under discussion

3.3 The chair of each session may with or without the request of any member of the Council after such consultation as the chair shall think fit suspend debate on any topic under discussion for a specified period or impose any speech limit or direct that any matter under discussion shall be put to the vote or give any other direction as shall seem to the chair to be conducive to the proper despatch of business

Speakers

4.1 In their contributions to discussion members shall pay proper respect to the chair of the session and in particular shall have regard to the duties of the chair under 3.2 above

4.2 All members of the Council shall qualify to be called upon by the chair of the session to speak in any session of the Council, and Primates, ecumenical participants or other persons present at the invitation of the Council may address the Council at the invitation of the chair of the session

4.3 The chair of any session may request that Members wishing to speak on any particular subject be asked to submit their names in writing to the chair of the session in advance with a general indication of their particular interest or expertise in relation to the matter under discussion

4.4 Members may not speak unless called upon to do so by the chair of the session and, if called upon to speak, shall address their remarks through the chair

4.5 Upon being called upon to speak, a member shall first announce his or her name, province or church

4.6 Subject to any other direction by the chair of the session, a speaker introducing a report or moving a motion may speak for up to 10 minutes and all other speakers may speak for up to 5 minutes

4.7 The chair of the session shall call a member to order for failure to address remarks through the chair, irrelevance, repetition of previous arguments, unbecoming language, discourtesy, or any other breach of reasonable order of debate, and may order a member to end any speech

4.8 The person moving a motion (but not an amendment) shall have a right of reply limited to 5 minutes at the close of the discussion, but no member may otherwise speak more than once in the same discussion except with the express permission of the chair

Motions and Amendments

5.1 In so far as daily business shall not have been dealt with in the main agenda relevant motions shall be made available in writing to members in such form as the Standing Committee shall determine as soon as possible after receipt from the person proposing the motion and in any event not later than the commencement of the session in which it is proposed to be presented or discussed, unless the chair of the session shall permit otherwise

5.2 Motions for consideration by the Council shall be presented:

5.2:1 in the case of motions forming part of the main agenda, by a member of the Council nominated by the Standing Committee; and

5.2:2 in the case of motions formulated by a regional or other group set up for a specific purpose as part of the work of group of sessions, by a member of such group; and

5.2:3 in the case of any other motion to be brought to a plenary session designated by the Standing Committee for such business, by any member of the Council with a written indication of support signed by ten other members;

and in the case of motions under 5.2:2 and 5.2:3 above the full text of such a motion shall be submitted in writing not later than the time directed by the Standing Committee in advance of the relevant discussion in order that the full text may be made available for consideration by all members unless the chair of the session shall permit otherwise

5.3 Members wishing to submit any amendment to an existing motion shall submit the full text of such motion or amendment in writing, signed by the mover and ten other members, not later than the time directed by the Standing Committee in advance of the relevant discussion in order that the full text may be made available for consideration by all members unless the chair of the session shall permit otherwise

5.4 An amendment shall not be accepted for discussion if in the opinion of the chair of the session it repeats an amendment which has already been withdrawn or disposed or would negate the motion to which it relates

5.5 Amendments will normally be considered in the order in which they first affect the motion under discussion but may be considered in some other order at the discretion of the chair of the session and the order in which amendments will be taken shall be announced at the commencement of the session

5.6 A main motion shall not be put finally to the meeting until all amendments shall have been carried, withdrawn or otherwise disposed of, and in the event that an amendment shall have been carried, the chair of the session will read to the Council the motion as amended before further discussion on the motion or any outstanding further amendment may proceed

5.7 When all amendments shall have been dealt with, the motion, subject to any agreed amendments, shall be put to the Council

Decisions on Business

6.1 Only members of the Council shall be entitled to vote on business before the Council

6.2 The chair of each session shall put the motion under discussion to the Council for its general assent which may be indicated in such manner as the chair shall think fit

6.3 If the chair of the session shall so direct, or if upon the chair requesting general assent any member shall request that a vote be taken, and such request has the support of not less than one-third of the members present and entitled to vote, then a vote shall be taken by show of hands or on ballot papers as the chair of the session shall decide

6.4 In the event of a vote being taken a simple majority shall be required unless the President after consultation with the Standing Committee shall direct that some other majority shall apply

General

7.1 The chair of a session may after consultation with the Standing Committee suspend the application of these Guidelines for part or all of the relevant session if the chair shall think it conducive to the better despatch of the business then before the Council

7.2 The Council may at any time with the consent of the Standing Committee revoke, amend or supplement these Guidelines or any part of them for the better conduct of the business of the Council

16 SEPTEMBER 2002

Archbishop of Canterbury's Presidential Address

"Re-Imagining The Anglican Communion"

It is with mixed emotions that I stand to give my last Presidential Address as Archbishop of Canterbury. It is my fourth and last ACC. I think of ACC-9 in Cape Town in 1993 where the issue of Apartheid was so prominent; ACC-10 in Panama in 1996 where the shocking genocide in Rwanda occupied our minds; ACC-11 in Dundee in 1999 where we focused on mission; and now ACC-12 in Hong Kong in 2002 where the terrible events of Sept 11th 2001 form the backdrop to our common life. Each ACC has been special and different; each has made a distinctive contribution to our identity and life.

So at the outset of this address let me say from the heart 'thank you' for your support and for the privilege to share in the leadership and service of our great Communion with you. A particular thanks to the Chairs of ACC I have served with over the years. Canon Colin Craston, Bishop Simon Chiwanga and vice-Chairman Archbishop John Patterson and the two Secretary-Generals with whom I have worked very closely, Canon Sam Van Culin and Canon John Peterson.

I want to begin with a statement from an unusual source:

'Inspired by no earthly ambition, the Church seeks to do one thing only; under the lead of the Holy Spirit, to carry forward the work of Christ himself, who came into the world to give witness to the truth, to save and to judge; to serve and not to be served.'

Those inspiring words written some forty years ago come from the Preface of ***Gaudium et Spes***, the Second Vatican Council's Pastoral Constitution on **The Church in the Modern World**.

That sentence is immediately followed by the Introductory Statement:

'To carry out such a responsibility, the Church has always the duty of scrutinising the signs of the times and of interpreting them in the light of the gospel. . . . We must, therefore, recognise and understand the world in which we live, its expectations, its longings, and its often dramatic characteristics. . . .'

It goes on to say: *'Today the human race is passing through a new stage of its history. Profound and rapid changes are gradually spreading around the whole world. Hence we can already speak of a true social and cultural transformation, one which has repercussions on our religious life as well.'*

For the purposes of this Address I wish to take up the challenge of some of the ideas in that powerful statement—to '*scrutinise the signs of the times and interpret them in the light of the gospel, and to understand the world in which we live.*' As I mused on the passage I began to re-imagine the Anglican Communion which we represent here at ACC-12. What kind of Communion does Our Lord wish us to become? What is the vocation to which we are called?

Although written so long ago the words from ***Gaudium et Spes*** are equally relevant to the times in which we live. How difficult it is to make sense of the confusing world in which we live and interpret it. We have only to consider four great contrasts to realise the ambiguities of our world.

First, **the tension between globalisation and fragmentation**. 'One man's meat is another man's poison' is an English saying. It is very true when it comes to today's great buzzword 'globalisation.' For some it is the way to a promised land of plenty for all; for others it is a new form of slavery leading to fragmentation and the death of local businesses.

A Christian response to the challenges of globalisation will want to focus more on the moral than the supposedly imperial, I suspect. But it will certainly not shy away from the economic impact of globalisation. Indeed when the bishops of the worldwide Anglican Communion met for the 1998 Lambeth Conference, it was globalisation of the market economy that they identified as 'the greatest single new force shaping the world.'

So what should we make of this new force? Well, we should certainly be cautious about concluding that globalisation is irredeemably and fatally flawed. Indeed, it has already brought many benefits to some of the poorer nations—for example, through direct foreign investment. Nevertheless, we have to recognise that rich and poor nations are not competing on a level playing field. Indeed, the very interconnectedness that globalisation offers through the liberalisation of trade, the power of the Internet and free movement of currency may lead to new forms of fragmentation and exclusion.

Poor nations with inadequate infrastructures and limited educational and health resources are likely to struggle to compete in sophisticated and rapidly moving market conditions. That goes some way to explaining why an estimated one-third of the world's population is so far reaping no tangible benefit from globalisation. I know that for many of us in the Anglican Communion the benefits as well as the negative effects of globalisation are experienced by us. It challenges our notion of what it is to be a Communion.

Secondly, **the tension between our longing for peace and the threats that undermine it**. My time as Archbishop began with the collapse of Communist Russia. What heady times they were! Who can ever forget that picture of

Boris Yeltsin in 1991 atop a tank in front of the Russian Parliament defying the coup that had just ousted Gorbachev! Equally dramatic was the picture of thousands of ordinary Russian workers streaming out of their factories the following day and marching to the Palace Square where one of the leaders exclaimed: 'The people can no longer be forced to their knees.' The collapse of Russia as a super power gave us all hope for a more peaceful world.

The irony is that we live in more perilous times as the events of September 11th clearly show. Certainly we do not have time to go into the reasons for terrorism and suicide tactics as part of it although equally certainly the fact and impact of globalisation are factors involved. However, the events of Sept 11th did not simply arise from desperate and very poor people reacting against an evil West but were part of a deliberate campaign of a powerful and wealthy network aiming to de-stabalise another part of the world. And we in Europe know all about this through the bloody work of the IRA and Basque separatists in Spain. The sad reality is that many Christians today have to live out their faith in the context of shocking violence. The presence of the Bishop Riah is a reminder of the difficulties faced by our Church in Palestine as the sad standoff between Israelis and Palestinians continues. While we pray for peace in the Holy Land we do not assume that violence is limited to it. Tragically one of the delegates to ACC from Congo, the Reverend Basimaki Byabasa was hacked to death on his way to us. It is a shocking reminder of the perils that face many of the people we represent.

Thirdly, **the tension between an inter-faith world and the clash of religions**. On the one hand we can point to encouraging developments in convergence of faith in our world as dialogue deepens among different faith communities. We shall have reports to that effect later in our Conference. I myself have been involved in a number of international dialogues and will continue to be interested in making a contribution in the future. But there is another reality as at local levels minority faith communities face dangers and difficulties that belie the rhetoric of international inter-faith gatherings. We have only to look at our Communion; Pakistan, where in recent month there have been three attacks on Christian churches and hospitals; Sudan, where Christians are persecuted in the north. Nigeria, where the imposition of Sharia law in a number of northern States threatens the existence of Christian communities. In India Muslims and Hindus have clashed with extreme violence leading to many deaths; in Indonesia minority Christian communities live in daily fear of violence. The list is long and getting longer as each year passes.

Finally, I point finally to another 'dramatic characteristic' which is **the tension and clash between cultures**. Again there is nothing new about this. There is often a 'strangeness" and an 'alienness' about cultures when they first meet that can lead to a clash or to a sympathetic alignment. Each nation has varying shifts of culture between tribes, communities and isolated gatherings which manifest themselves in language, dialect, religion, custom and creed. When we join the Christian Church, whoever we are and wherever we are from, we identify with a body which has its own distinctive culture manifested in belief and practice and mediated to us through the bible and the church.

The journey we have made from the first Lambeth Conference of 1867 and right up to the present represents an increasing understanding of the importance of the Communion, with an awareness that disconnectedness between the independent Provinces cannot be the future of the Anglican Communion. Indeed, I have said on many occasions that, in a sense, we are not yet a Communion because we are still too separate, still too ignorant of one another and, more importantly, in danger of allowing our national and local cultures to pull us apart.

So, here are just some of the characteristics of our world which form the backcloth of our mission. How do we respond to *Gaudium et Spes'* challenge that *'the Church seeks to do one thing only; under the lead of the Holy Spirit, to carry forward the work of Christ himself '*?

In my re-imagining of the Communion I think of four aspects through which we carry forward Christ's mission and fulfill our mission as a Communion.

First, we are called to 'carry forward the work of Christ'. I was struck by one phrase in that Catholic statement. It says 'one thing only.' It reminded me of the conversation which Jesus had with the sisters Mary and Martha. He said to the ever-busy Martha who was jealous of Mary spending so much time with Jesus: 'Martha, only one thing is necessary'. That is the real business of the Church of Jesus Christ; to spend time with him and to promote his mission. Everything else—all the fine work we do and everything else we shall say—is nothing but the outworking of presenting Jesus Christ as Lord and Saviour.

However, as most of us know, to proclaim Christ is not the easy thing that some claim. As faiths jostle side by side in all our communities, we are constantly challenged by the question, What is the basis on which we present him as Lord when others may wish to make similar claims for the object of their devotion? Are we compelled to abandon our claim that Jesus Christ is the only Saviour?

I would answer without hesitation: 'No, But it all depends on *how* we say it.' To draw back from the firm tones of New Testament Christianity that Jesus is way, the truth and the life, would be a betrayal of the faith itself and an abandonment of historic Christianity. As the Primates of the Communion said in Canterbury this year: We believe that God the eternal Son became human for our sake and that in the flesh and blood of

Jesus of Nazareth God was uniquely present and active. All claims to knowledge of God must be brought to Christ to be tested.'

Nonetheless, we have to find ways of putting this truth across in the context of respecting other faiths and understanding their value systems and strengths. William Carey, that great Baptist missionary to India two centuries ago, learned eight different languages and waited 14 years before he began his ministry of preaching and church building. I have enjoyed the story told of Barbara McClintock, a geneticist who won a Nobel Prize. She was once asked how her new science was done. She replied: 'You have to have a feeling for the organism.' The reporter didn't know what to make of that reply so pressed the question: 'Now, really, how is this new science done?' Dr McClintock pondered for a while and said: 'I guess the only way I can answer it is, you have to lean into the ear of the corn.'

I find that an attractive idea—leaning into the ear of the corn. And today we have to do something similar as we lean into the ear of the culture in which we live and find new ways of connecting with our cultures. May I say how much I admire the missionary energy of our churches in many parts of Africa for their unafraid witness and joy in preaching Christ. They have so much to teach us and share with us all. I welcome the report of the Inter-Anglican Standing Commission on Mission and Evangelism, which is in our papers for this conference. How much I endorse one Resolution which states: 'The structures of the Church should be orientated towards mission as the Church's first priority.' It is vital that we heed that call and find new ways of offering Christ to our needy world. Indeed, for churches in first world countries the imperative must be to focus on children and young people. Healthy plants propagate; healthy churches communicate joyful faith to their young and encourage them in their growth.

One way we Anglicans have leaned into the ear of the corn takes me into my second point. **As I re-imagine our life as a Communion I urge that we do not waver in our commitment to mission in action.**

And that leads me to believe that the Christian imperative to look first and foremost to the needs of the very poor must be a focal point of the mission of the Church in responding to the changes that globalisation and fragmentation bring.

In my time as Archbishop I have seen many examples round our increasingly globalised world of that challenge being met—examples that should inspire and give hope for the future. Let me offer you just two examples of the Church in action on behalf of the most vulnerable.

First, I recall a visit to Brazil where I was shown a huge rubbish tip in the city of Recife. In that awful environment, hundreds of destitute people—children as well as adults—had been living off whatever they could find, including, I was told, human remains dumped there from a nearby hospital.

An Anglican priest stirred by the plight of these people moved her home there and started a small church among the 'rubbish people' as they were called. Over the years she has helped them reclaim their dignity; she has brought them education and health care—in fact, during my visit I was asked to dedicate a dentist's chair! That woman priest has also helped them to find homes and jobs—indeed some 400 people work in the recycling business that she helped to set up.

I think too of South Africa where grinding poverty combined with the frightful scourge of HIV/AIDS is causing such human devastation. We visited a Church-run orphanage in Durban, caring for babies and children under five with the AIDS virus. There we held in our arms lovely looking babies, many of whom had just a few months to live. It was the only home of its kind in the city. The Province of the Church of South Africa under the leadership of Archbishop Ndungane is doing a most excellent job.

Illustrations like these and so many more that I could give bear out the story of the young man training to be a Rabbi and burning the midnight oil. His tiny baby was crying incessantly. In the end his father goes up to the nursery and comforts the baby. As he passes his son's study on the way down he quietly said: 'You can't be studying the Word of God if you can't hear the cry of a child.'

Hearing the cry of children and responding to their distress and those most vulnerable has been characteristic of the incarnational ministry in our Communion. We care for people and that means our concern for their eternal well being takes in the conditions under which they live today. But this does not mean that we are there simply there to help pick up the pieces. Sadly, too often in the past this has been our attitude. But I note with great satisfaction that are beginning to play our part in representing the very poor and speaking up for Christian values.

We are beginning to work in critical solidarity with the international institutions tasked with regulating global capitalism instead of simply writing them off as irretrievably serving the interests of the rich nations. I recall the President of the World Bank telling me that the World Bank began to take the Churches seriously when a team visited Tanzania and discovered to their amazement that the Christian Churches were providing nearly half of the social services need of the country—hospitals, clinics, education and homes for orphans and the elderly. They found similar proportions in other poor countries too and it changed the relationship between the World Bank and religious organisations.

Much more could be done however. I encourage us all to seek ways of getting alongside the opinion formers and political leaders. We have nothing to lose and much to gain. In this connection let me remind you of the significant work of Archdeacon Faga, our Observer at the UN. She is there for us. Get to know her this week.

There is one thing that greatly concerns me. One of the reasons why I have said we are not yet a Communion but becoming one is my sad conclusion that the richer parts of the body are not doing enough for fellow Anglicans in greatest distress. We ought to be horrified and deeply ashamed and concerned that in many parts of the Communion devoted servants of the Church are not paid adequately, if anything at all. In many African Provinces no pension provision are at present made and for the foreseeable future unlikely to be offered. During my time as Archbishop I have endeavoured to help assist bishops and clergy in Sudan, Uganda, Rwanda and elsewhere. But such discretionary help cannot address the urgent need of clergy, particularly in Africa. I call on the rich Pension Funds of first world Provinces to assist by offering advice and by finding ways of sharing what previous generations have given us. We can and must do better.

I re-imagine furthermore a **growing Communion honouring our heritage of faith**. With all great bodies and churches there lies the danger that growth may lead to separation. This is what I was getting at with my comments on culture earlier. Diversity, also a great buzzword in our world, is only a positive element if it is secondary to a fundamental unity in spirit and purpose. Where do we find the marks that identify us as Episcopalians and Anglicans wherever we are from? We immediately think of worship. Yes, indeed, there is a family likeness in the way we worship-whether we be Chinese, American, Australian or Zambians. However, unity in worship is not enough because it will not long survive serious rupture in matters of faith and order. Of far greater importance, then, must be our doctrinal unity which has been expressed in our self-understanding as a Communion which is Catholic and Reformed. That is to say, we cherish those traditions and creeds that unite us with Catholic and Orthodox branches of the Church and with the mainstream historic Reformation churches in their acceptance of the primacy of scripture.

Of course, we accept that the Bible is a complex book, and is capable of many interpretations. I love St. Augustine's description of the Bible as a 'vast ocean in which infants can play in safety in the shallows and elephants can wallow to their hearts' content!' It has room for us all. We are committed to thoroughness in study of scripture and are indebted to generations of scholarly research which has made us aware of how much we don't know of the intricacies of the text as well as reaffirming what we do know of God's will for us. Nonetheless, this has not led to vagueness of belief. Our doctrinal commitment to the Triune God made known to us in Christ is as firm as any other church and our obligation to live out that faith in holy living is equally as clear.

However, honouring that legacy of faith means that we are constantly challenged to nourish the bonds of affection between us and to confront all issues that divide us in a spirit of love and understanding. It is easy to love those who agree with us; how we handle disagreement is much more taxing but is at least as important for our identity as Anglicans. In that great missionary Bishop Stephen Neill's phrase, "We are a learning church as well as a teaching church", and learning demands patient listening to one another's insights.

It is at this point as the outgoing Archbishop of Canterbury that I must point to my greatest worry. I would be failing in my duty if I recoiled away from it out of an assumption that silence is the safer option.

In short, my concern is that our Communion is being steadily undermined by dioceses and individual bishops taking unilateral action, usually (but not always) in matters to do with sexuality; and as a result steadily driving us towards serious fragmentation and the real possibility of two (or, more likely, many more) distinct Anglican bodies emerging. This erosion of communion through the adoption of 'local options' has been going for some thirty years but in my opinion is reaching crisis proportions today.

We have seen the formation of AMiA in the United States and scarcely a week goes by without some report reaching me of clergy teetering on the brink of leaving the Anglican Communion for that body. I have been clear in my condemnation of the schism created by AMiA and the actions of those Primates and other bishops who consecrated the six bishops. Sadly, I see little sign of willingness on the part of some bishops in the Communion to play their part in discouraging teaching or action that leads some conscientious clergy to conclude that they have no option other than to leave us for AMiA.

It is not my intention to address now the issue that has led some clergy in the diocese of New Westminster to rebel against their own bishop and their diocesan Synod. I respect the sincerity of Bishop Michael Ingham and his diocesan synod, and I do not doubt that they believe that they are acting in the best interests of all, as they see it.

But I deeply regret that Michael and his synod, and other bishops and dioceses in similar situations in North America, seem to be making such decisions without regard to the rest of us and against the clear statements of Lambeth '98. And, on the other hand, as I have said, it is disappointing to note the steps that have been taken in reaction by a number of clergy, bishops and even Archbishops in our Communion, equally in disregard of carefully thought-out Lambeth Conference resolutions.

It is for this reason that I have submitted to this ACC a resolution that I hope you will strongly support. In short the Resolution calls upon all dioceses that are considering matters of faith and order that could affect the unity of the Communion to consult widely in their provinces, and beyond, before final decisions are made or action is taken. We cannot insist that they do so, but as a Consultative Body we can urge them to do so.

And let me remind you that this resolution is not novel. Indeed, it was the unilateral action of one bishop, Bishop Colenso of Natal, that led to the first Lambeth Conference of 1867. The fourth resolution of that first Lambeth Conference in fact called upon all dioceses to submit to 'superior synods.' This constant emphasis on interdependence and mutual responsibility towards one another—especially in those matters upon which we disagree—is a recurrent, and highly characteristic, theme of our life together.

Of course, the issue is far more than a matter of internal discipline, though it is certainly that. It affects our mission, and relationships with other churches. Let me say clearly that I believe far too much energy is going into fanning the flames of argument on these matters that divide us taking our attention away from the critical needs of evangelism and mission.

But it also has serious ecumenical implications. I have had countless conversations with leaders of other Churches who have spoken gently but sternly of our internal disorderliness on issues such as this. It is viewed as a major stumbling block to the unity we claim we seek with the universal Church.

And let me make quite clear that the resolution is not merely about handling issues to do with sexuality, but it applies to all sensitive matters that threaten our common life. That is to say, it entreats the diocese of Sydney on the issue of Lay Presidency to submit the matter to its Province, and to have regard to the effect of any decision it makes on the wider Communion to which it belongs, just as much as it applies to a diocese contemplating the official introduction of services in relation to same-sex unions. Likewise the resolution is as relevant to the deposition of Fr. David Moyer by Bishop Charles Bennison in the diocese of Pennsylvania, which has consequences not only for that diocese but also for the entire Communion.

The issues we face in our time are as demanding and painful as any our forebears have had to wrestle with; and there are lessons we can learn from them, as to how we too may find ways to discern God's will for us by listening to one another, carefully considering the impact of our actions on one another, and above all praying for one another. I hope my Resolution will receive your clear endorsement, and so send out a strong signal that it is not enough to carry on talking about being a Communion while we take actions that contradict our words.

My fourth and final comment arises from the rapid and profound changes spreading around the world in **the matter of inter-religious conflict and the urgent need to deepen inter-faith dialogue**. Again, the Inter-Anglican

Standing Commission on Mission and Evangelism speaks of the urgency of this. Since September 11th last year more than half of my time has been spent in this area of work. I shall be speaking about this later in the week so I need not now say any more. But I flag it up as an issue on which we must spend time because it is of the greatest of importance to our brothers and sisters in areas where persecution is a daily reality for them and where our mission for Christ is under the greatest attack. I am more than confident that we can and will meet this urgent challenge.

So I wish to end where I begin with a word of deep gratitude from Eileen and myself. The last eleven and half years have been deeply rewarding for us both in which we have made so many friends. It has been our joy to serve our Communion. We leave with much unfinished but thank God that he has called Archbishop Rowan Williams to carry on this work. We are confident that he will and he knows he has our support and friendship.

Therefore I end on a note of thanksgiving to Almighty God who chooses unworthy people to serve him. As I re-imagine our Communion I am confident that as long as we focus on strengthening the bonds of affection and deepen out mission to the most vulnerable, the very poor and those without hope in Christ, we shall grow stronger and fulfil the enormous potential of which we are capable. So I repeat again those words with which I began:

Inspired by no earthly ambition, the Church seeks to do one thing only; under the lead of the Holy Spirit, to carry forward the work of Christ himself, who came into the world to give witness to the truth, to save and to judge; to serve and not to be served.'

Surely, that is our objective too.

Report of the Standing Committee of ACC-12

1.00 Membership

The Right Reverend Simon Chiwanga, Tanzania, Chairman
The Most Reverend John Paterson, Aotearoa, New Zealand and Polynesia, Vice Chairman
The Most Reverend Peter Akinola, Nigeria
Ms Judith Conley, United States of America
Professor George Koshy, South India
The Reverend Dr Jae-Joung Lee, Korea
Mr Ghazi Musharbash, Jerusalem and the Middle East
Mr John Rea, Scotland
Canon Dr Maureen Sithole, Southern Africa

The Standing Committee meets with the Standing Committee of the Primates, and the membership of that group is comprised of the following:

1999–2000

The Most Reverend & Right Honourable Dr George Carey, England
The Most Reverend Livingstone Mpalanyi-Nkoyoyo, Uganda
The Most Reverend Michael Peers, Canada
The Most Reverend Vinod Peter, North India
The Most Reverend Sir Ellison Pogo, Melanesia
The Most Reverend Dr Rowan Williams, Wales

2001–2002

as above with the addition of
The Most Reverend Peter Kwong, Hong Kong

.1 In Memoriam

In November 2000 The Most Reverend Vinod Peter, Moderator of the Church of North India, was killed in a motor vehicle accident, and a letter of condolence was sent to the Church of North India. The Joint Standing Committee gives thanks for his life and witness, and his contribution to the life of the Communion.

During the year 2000, two former Presidents of the Anglican Consultative Council died. The Joint Standing Committee remembered with prayerful thanksgiving the lives and work of Lord Coggan of Sissinghurst and Canterbury, who had been Archbishop of Canterbury from 1974 until 1980, and Lord Runcie of Cuddesdon, Archbishop of Canterbury from 1980 to 1991.

The contribution of both Archbishops to the life and vitality of the Anglican Communion, and particularly the Lambeth Conferences and ACC meetings over which they presided, will long be recalled with gratitude and affection.

In April 2001 Bishop John Howe, the first Secretary General of the Anglican Consultative Council, died. A Memorial Service had been held in London in September, at which tributes were paid for his outstanding service to the Anglican Communion.

2.00 Meetings

The Joint Standing Committees have met at Aylesford Priory in Kent, England in October 2000, at Kanuga, North Carolina, USA in February 2001, at Dublin in the Irish Republic, February 2002, and immediately prior to ACC-12 at Hong Kong, October 2002.

Staff of the Anglican Communion Office attend each meeting, and we have also had in attendance on a number of occasions The Reverend Canon John Rees, Legal Adviser to the Anglican Communion, and the member of the Archbishop of Canterbury's Staff with responsibility for Anglican Communion matters—The Reverend Andrew Wheeler, and latterly his successor in that post, The Reverend Canon Herman Browne.

At every meeting the members of the Committee are given an opportunity to speak about their own lives and the important events in the life of their own Church. This gave rise to a Resolution of support for the people, clergy and bishops of the Anglican Church of Canada, who have been facing grave difficulties and much litigation in recent years arising from the former residential schools of that land. The Standing Committee expressed appreciation of the commitment to the goals of healing and reconciliation and assured that Church of our prayers for its on-going life, work and mission.

3.00 Finance

The Members of the ACC Standing Committee also act as Trustees of the Anglican Consultative Council, and on each occasion, careful consideration is given to the Report and Accounts presented by the Inter Anglican Finance Committee. Approval was given for the Reports and Financial Statements for the periods ending 31 December 1999, 30 September 2000 (following a change in the Financial Year) and 30 September 2001. These matters are the subject of a separate Report to ACC-12.

Bye-law 4 of the ACC provides for the IAFC to be comprised of three representatives of the ACC and two Primates. The ACC is responsible in law to see to the proper application of the IAFC funds, and to lay before each meeting of the ACC duly audited accounts including full financial reports on the Inter Anglican Finance Committee, the Primates' Meetings, and where necessary the Lambeth Conference.

During the period in review, Mr Michael Nunn resigned as Treasurer of the Inter Anglican Finance Committee, and Director of Finance and Administration in the Anglican Communion Office, and the Joint Standing Committee expressed its deep appreciation for his service in these roles. Mr Andrew Franklin has now been appointed as Director of Finance and Administration.

The Inter Anglican Finance Committee has been chaired for a number of years by The Most Reverend Robin Eames, Archbishop of Armagh, and he has signalled his intention to step down as Chairman of the IAFC following the meeting in Hong Kong. His has been a notable contribution in this role, and the Communion has good cause to be grateful to Archbishop Eames.

3.1 Endowment for the Anglican Communion

The Joint Standing Committee expressed pleasure at the news of the stated intention of the Compass Rose Society to raise funds for an Endowment for the work of the Anglican Consultative Council in its many and varied aspects, and resolved to work with the Compass Rose Society to that end. The work of the Secretary General, Canon John Peterson, in this regard has been outstanding and this was acknowledged by the Committee. The Joint Standing Committee also expressed its concern that there was an increasing reliance on special fund raising efforts to finance various aspects of the work of the Communion. This cannot continue indefinitely and it is important to draw to the attention of the Provinces the critical significance of their continuing to meet their contributions to the Inter Anglican Budget.

3.2 Budgets

The shortfall in contributions from the Provinces has meant that some of the work requested by various parts of the Communion is unable to be carried out. In 2001 the Joint Standing Committee had requested an increase of 4% from the Provinces for this purpose, but this had not been forthcoming. The Budget for 2002 was approved, and the Joint Standing Committee noted the projections for 2003 and 2004 which contained unacceptable deficits. It was noted with gratitude that the Archbishop of Canterbury and the Secretary General had found funding from sources other than the Inter Anglican Budget to allow the Primates' Meeting to be held on an annual basis, and the Joint Standing Committee resolved to ask the Primates' meeting as the members reflect on the frequency of their meetings, to give attention to how they might be financed from sources other than the Inter Anglican Budget.

3.3 Anglican Communion Sunday

ACC-12 is to be asked to debate a suggestion that a second offering from parishes and congregations on a suitable Sunday, perhaps designated anew as Anglican Communion Sunday, might be made available to the Anglican Communion Office for additional funding for the Inter Anglican Budget.

3.4 Strategic Meetings

The Inter Anglican Finance Committee has been asked by the Joint Standing Committee to provide for face to face meetings with key people in the member Churches with a view to a higher priority being given to the needs of the Anglican Communion and its Budget in their budget-setting processes.

3.5 Priorities

The Inter Anglican Finance Committee has always been conscious that budget priorities might dictate other means of setting priorities in the work of the Communion. A good deal of work has now been done on the matter of priorities and the way they are established, and this work continues with a view to putting recommendations to ACC-12.

4.00 Evaluation of ACC-11

The evaluation forms following the meeting at Dundee were considered carefully. 75% of those present who had returned the forms expressed general satisfaction with arrangements and content and design of the meeting. Particular problems were identified with lack of space for small group work, and allowing individuals to feel that their story had been heard and understood. In preparation for ACC-12 the following matters were noted:

- Member Churches should be asked well in advance for items they would like to see included;
- Reports with financial implications should be given before the approval of the Budget. In this regard it might be necessary to present the financial overview early in the meeting and delay the approval of the Budget until later in the meeting;
- Allow reasonable time for feed-back from the floor following major presentations.

The following members were elected to serve as the Design Group for ACC-12:

> The Most Reverend John Paterson—Chair, Mr John Rea, Canon Maureen Sithole and Ms Fung Yi Wong.

5.00 Anglican (Congress) Gathering 2008

Following ACC-11 the Archbishop of Canterbury appointed a Design Group to investigate the feasibility of holding a Congress 'in association with' the Lambeth Conference in 2008. Canon Maureen Sithole and Mr Albert Gooch and Archbishop Peter Kwong, as members of that Design Group, have reported on their investigations to the Joint Standing Committee, and have recommended that planning proceed for an "Anglican Gathering" in 2008. This will be the subject of a separate Report to ACC-12. The Group has stated its preference for the terminology of 'Gathering' rather than 'Congress' so as to make it less legislative and more of an event which will bring Anglicans together to express their identity.

The Joint Standing Committee received the report of the Design Group with gratitude, and reaffirmed its commitment to the holding of such a 'Gathering' in 2008, and encouraged the Design Group to continue its work in this regard.

6.00 Staff Reports

The Standing Committee gives consideration to the reports from the various departments within the Anglican Communion Office, and these always begin with a report from the Secretary General. It was noted that Canon Peterson's initial contract ended on 31 December 2001 and the Committee recorded its pleasure at the achievements made during his term in office and agreed to extend his appointment for two years until 31 December 2003. Initial steps for a process to replace Canon Peterson will be announced during ACC-12.

6.1 Communication

At the October 2000 meeting Canon Rosenthal submitted a written report but was unable to be present to speak to the recommendations in person. This addressed communications in general, an advisory committee for 'Anglican World' and a policy for translation. In February 2001 these matters were further debated, and the Committee resolved to establish a Task Force to draw up policy for communication and communication strategy along with terms of reference for an Editorial Board. The Secretary General was asked to identify people to serve on this Task Force. A report was also received from the April 2000 Inter Anglican Consultation on Telecommunications funded by Trinity Church, Wall Street, New York City. The Joint Standing Committee gave initial encouragement to the development of a written proposal for a Commission on Telecommunication, and it is expected that further information will be available to ACC-12. Canon Rosenthal also reported in very positive terms on the Intern Programme and the experience of having Siphiwe Sithole in the Communication Office as an intern.

6.1.1 Anglican Cycle of Prayer

Canon Rosenthal has reported on discussions with *Forward Movement Publications* on matters concerning this publication and particularly the format. It has now been suggested that it will revert to a one year cycle in which each of the 38 Provinces would be assigned one Sunday in the year. Other aspects of the life of the Communion would feature on the remaining Sundays. It is also possible that it will become available as a CD-ROM and by on-line subscription.

6.2 Ecumenical

The Reverend Canon David Hamid reports regularly on the work of the Ecumenical Department, and the initial work undertaken by the Inter Anglican Standing Commission on Ecumenical Relations, along with the work he undertakes as Secretary of the Inter Anglican Theological and Doctrinal Commission. Up-dated information was given on the Baptist-Anglican Relations, Lutheran-Anglican Relations, Old Catholic-Anglican Relations, Oriental Orthodox-Anglican Relations, Orthodox-Anglican Relations, Roman Catholic-Anglican Relations, Relations with New Churches and Independent Christian Groups and Multilateral Relationships.

6.3 Anglican Observer at the United Nations

The work undertaken by Bishop Herbert Donovan as interim Observer was greatly appreciated, and particularly so in preparing for the appointment of Archdeacon Taimalelagi Fagamalama Tuatagaloa-Matalavea from Samoa, as Anglican Observer from September 2001. Full reports on the work of the Office, and the matters attended to by the Advisory Council were received by the Joint Standing Committee. Archdeacon Matalavea is a former member of the Anglican Consultative Council, and has made a very good start to her work in New York. A report in person will be made to ACC-12.

6.4 Ethics and Technology

Canon Eric Beresford is seconded for 1/5 time by the Anglican Church in Canada to work in the area of Ethics and has reported on his efforts to develop a database of contacts on environmental issues and ethics and technology concerns. A particular concern has been intellectual property rights and the Patenting of life forms, and the impact of technology and environmental change on communities. Canon Beresford is exploring the possibility of arranging a Consultation on Colonialism, Post Colonialism and the Environment. Likewise he will be reporting on the establishing of a possible Environmental Network for the Communion.

6.5 Liturgy

Dr. Paul Gibson has continued as Coordinator for Liturgy, and has reported regularly to the Joint Standing Committee in this role, as well as serving as Chaplain to many of the Anglican Communion meetings. In particular he has brought to the attention of the Standing Committee those matters arising from the work of the International Anglican Liturgical Consultation. A matter of particular concern has been the use of substances other than bread and wine at the Eucharist. The Joint Standing Committee considered this at length, because of the theological, doctrinal and ecumenical implications of any departure from standard practice. It is a matter that needs to be considered by both the Inter Anglican Theological and Doctrinal Commission and the Inter Anglican Standing Committee on Ecumenical Relations. It was agreed that a survey be undertaken of practices in relation to the elements of Holy Communion in the Provinces of the Anglican Communion and of the grounds stated for any departure from traditional usage.

6.6 Mission and Evangelism

Marjorie Murphy has carried responsibility for coordinating the work of the Mission and Evangelism Department, and in particular has organised the Provincial Mission and Evangelism Co-ordinators Conference in Kenya on behalf of the Anglican Communion Office. Much work has been done in establishing the Inter Anglican Standing Commission on Mission and Evangelism (IASCOME). Canon Maureen Sithole has acted as Liaison person between the Joint Standing Committee and IASCOME. Marjorie has reported regularly to the Standing Committee on matters affecting her portfolio, and the work involved in setting up the Anglican Mission Organisations Conference. Much of this has grown out of the MISSIO Report and a Review of the Decade for Evangelism.

6.7 Travel Department

Ms. Lynne Butt has reported on the activities of the Anglican Communion Travel Office, a service which is much appreciated by the Joint Standing Committee and those who travel to various Anglican Communion events and meetings.

7.00 Membership of the Anglican Consultative Council

7.01 Church of Tanzania

The Standing Committee expressed pleasure that growth in church membership in Tanzania had produced a request that Tanzania be moved from Schedule (c) to Schedule (b) allowing three representatives rather than two.

7.02 Primates' Standing Committee and Membership on the ACC

The matter of membership on the ACC of the five Primates who make up the Primates' Standing Committee was debated at length. The Joint

Standing Committee resolved to advise the Primates' Meeting that it wished to regularise the position of those five Primates within the Anglican Consultative Council and asked that appropriate constitutional amendments be prepared for ACC-12 to consider. These would allow for the inclusion in the membership of the ACC and its Standing Committee of those Primates who were members of the Primates' Standing Committee.

8.00 Review of the See of Canterbury

The Joint Standing Committee met with the Group of people established to carry out a Review of the See of Canterbury, and were able to present a range of views from across the Communion. We were then sent a copy of the initial findings of the Review Commission, and subsequently were able to comment on the published Report of the Review Group. The Standing Committee was grateful to have been given this opportunity.

9.00 Office Accommodation

A good deal of time has been spent in considering the possibility of different accommodation for the Anglican Communion Office, in view of the need to find more space than is currently available at Partnership House. One particular possibility has been examined at length, and the Legal Adviser has been very much involved in the negotiations over the lease and the relationship with the Charity Commissioners in terms of a possible change in the use of the property in question. This matter has not been an easy one for the staff members who currently work at Partnership House, due to the distances and times involved in commuting to work in London, and related issues. A Project Group was established to work through this issue, and it is hoped that a full report will be available for ACC-12.

9.01 Anglican Communion Office Archives

A related matter was the need to store the archival material carefully and in a suitable location where it could be properly catalogued, accessed and used. The Joint Standing Committee resolved to establish a Working Group on Archives, Records Management and Cultural Heritage. The Terms of Reference of the Working Group are attached as Appendix A to this Report.

10.00 Liability of Trustees

Consideration has been given to the risk of personal liability carried by members of the Standing Committee, and in order to minimise this, the Legal Adviser has been investigating the possibility of establishing a Limited Liability Company, the membership of which might be restricted to members of the Standing Committee, with those other members of the Council belonging to some other category of membership, which would not require attendance at an annual meeting.

11.00 Networks

The Standing Committee appoints one of its members to act in a liaison capacity with each of the Networks of the Anglican Communion, and these members present a report as appropriate at each meeting.

11.01 International Anglican Family Network
[Liaison—Mr John Rea]

The Network has continued to produce Newsletters on specific topics which are published in *Anglican World* and evoke very good responses. Dr. Sally Thompson has continued to act as Secretary. Financial viability has been greatly assisted by the generosity of a private donor, introduced by the Secretary General. The President of the Network had been Dr. Richard Holloway, Primus of the Scottish Episcopal Church, and on his retirement, The Right Reverend John Paterson of New Zealand had accepted appointment as President. A continuing challenge is to find the ways and means of printing the Newsletters in French and Spanish. The Children's Society had been very helpful for a number of years in supporting the work of the Network, but was now having to withdraw as host agency after 2001. In this regard the Network was very grateful to Mr. Ian Sparks of that Society who has been the Chair of the Network.

11.02 Peace and Justice Network
[Liaison—The Rev Dr Jae Joung Lee]

The Network always publishes a full report of each meeting, and it last met in November 2001 in Auckland, New Zealand. Much of the work is co-ordinated by The Reverend Brian Greaves of ECUSA, working from 815 Second Avenue in New York. Both the Anglican Observer at the United Nations and Canon Eric Beresford were present at the meeting in New Zealand, and it is important to note the strategic importance that Network places on the UN Observer's role.

11.03 Anglican Indigenous Peoples Network
[Liaison—Ms Judith Conley]

The Standing Committee has received an informal indication of the wish of this Network to be granted observer status at meetings of the ACC and the Standing Committee, but this has not yet been notified officially. The Reverend Malcolm Chan of Hawaii is the Secretary of the Network.

11.04 Network for Inter Faith Concerns
[Liaison—Mr Ghazi Musharbash]

Canon John Sargant retired as Co-ordinator of the Network in December 2000. Three Presidents have been appointed, viz. The Rt. Rev Kenneth Fernando of Sri Lanka, The Rt. Rev Michael Nazir-Ali of England, and The Rt. Rev Josiah Idowu-Fearon of Nigeria. NIFCON news was appearing regularly in *Anglican World* and assistance with funding had come from the Archbishop of Canterbury's Anglican Communion Fund, from a member of the Compass Rose Society, and from the Bishop of New York.

11.05 Refugee and Migrant Network
[Liaison—Mr John Rea]

Archbishop Ian George of Adelaide, Australia is the Co-ordinator of the Network, which has also been greatly assisted by a grant from the Archbishop of Canterbury's Anglican Communion Fund. Effort has gone into establishing a correspondent or agent in each Province for receiving and disseminating information. A conference or active workshop on refugee and migrant issues is being considered in an appropriate part of the world.

11.06 Women's Network
[Liaison—Canon Maureen Sithole]

The Network struggles to find funds to enable a meeting to be held. Planning is taking place to establish a database. A Mission Statement has been suggested, to be ratified by women in the Communion, in two parts:

1. Values:
   Inclusivity—age, race, culture, language, education, economic
   Informative
   Rooted in prayer
   Serving and strengthening the Communion
   Solidarity

2. Purposes:
   Communicate
   Affirm and encourage the role of women in the Church
   Support the awareness of needs
   Share resources
   Respond to issues from a woman's perspective
   Be a resource to the Anglican Consultative Council.

Eight women had registered as participants under the auspices of the ACC at the 44th Session of the Commission on the Status of Women, held in New York February 2000. It is hoped to bring together a meeting of people occupying women's desks.

11.07 Youth Network
[Liaison—Deirdre Martin]

Constant turnover in Youth Officers in the Provinces causes difficulties for this Network to operate efficiently. It is felt that another meeting of Youth Officers is necessary to breathe fresh life into the Network.

11.08 International Anglican Urban Network

The Secretary General has provided the liaison in the early years of establishing this Network. The Standing Committee was visited by The Rt. Rev Roger Sainsbury, The Rt. Rev Laurence Green and The Rev Andrew Davey, who presented updated information on the work, which resulted in the Standing Committee voting to approve the formation of the Network as an officially recognised Network of the Communion. Provinces have been asked to nominate official representatives, funding has been obtained, and the work is under way.

12.00 The Unity of the Anglican Communion

The Standing Committee gave careful consideration to the issues surrounding the unity of the Communion, and in particular the irregular ordination of bishops. Attention was given to the way the Primates' Meeting in Oporto in 2000 had dealt with these matters and a four part resolution was adopted as follows:

> The Standing Committee welcomes the statement of the Primates' Meeting in Oporto as a collegial and pastoral statement which offers teaching which may be useful in the churches at every level as we seek a common mind on controversial matters and encourages Provinces to include the laity in discussion and prayer about these issues and about the nature of the unity we share;
>
> endorses the position outlined in the letter of the Archbishop of Canterbury to the bishops of the Communion dated 17 February 2000 regarding the damage to the life of the Communion that may result from irregular actions undertaken without due consultation and regard to the integrity of the life of the Provinces;
>
> expresses its support for the ongoing efforts of the Archbishop of Canterbury and the Primates to resolve the underlying issues of sexuality and theology which divide us, however long it takes, and to maintain the highest degree of communion among the churches of the Anglican Communion;
>
> encourages the Inter Anglican Theological and Doctrinal Commission to give priority attention to the issues of communion, unity and diversity within the Anglican Communion.

13.00 The Archbishop of Canterbury's Anglican Communion Fund

Three representatives of the ACC were appointed as Trustees of the Anglican Communion Fund, viz Mr Bernard Georges, Professor George Koshy and Ms Fung-Yi Wong. It was noted that the principal objectives of the Fund are:

- to provide assistance for the Provinces or dioceses of the Anglican Communion at times of crisis;
- to support strategic initiatives to assist the Anglican Communion; and
- to provide official representation at international institutions and consultations including the Office of the Anglican Observer at the United Nations.

The Standing Committee also appointed Ms Fung-Yi Wong as the representative of the ACC on the Executive Committee of the Fund. It was noted that the Primates' Standing Committee had similarly appointed The Most Reverend Michael Peers.

14.00 Mrs Deirdre Martin

The Standing Committee in 2001 recorded its deep appreciation for the ministry of Mrs Deirdre Martin over 25 years in work for the Anglican Communion.

15.00 Completion of Terms of Office

A number of members of the Standing Committee will complete their ordinary terms of office at ACC-12. These will include The Reverend Dr Jae-Joung Lee of Korea, Mr John Rea of Scotland, Professor George Koshy of South India, Canon Maureen Sithole of Southern Africa, Ms Judith Conley of USA, and Mr Ghazi Musharbash, Co-opted Member representing the Laity of the Church in Jerusalem and the Middle East. The Right Reverend John Paterson finishes his term as Vice Chairman, and The Right Reverend Simon Chiwanga steps down as Chairman of the Council after a distinguished period of membership representing the Anglican Church in Tanzania, two meetings of the Council as Vice Chairman, and now two meetings of the Council as Chairman. The Council will also mark the retirement of our President, The Most Reverend and Right Honourable Dr George Carey, Archbishop of Canterbury.

John Paterson
Vice Chairman

Appendix A

Working Group on Archives, Records Management and Cultural Heritage

Terms of Reference

(a) To draft and recommend appropriate policy for the permanent preservation of the documentary and related heritage resources in all media of the Anglican Consultative Council;

(b) To assess the current archives and records management needs of the ACC offices including the London Office, the United Nations Office and the offices of non-residential staff;

(c) To survey options and recommend solutions for the care, custody and control of the permanent archives of the ACC consistent with its role within the synodical structures of the Church;

(d) In co-operation with administrative staff, to devise appropriate records management procedures, that ensure the maintenance of all records on the principles of a lifecycle management system;

(e) To recommend policies and procedures for the management of electronic records and record keeping systems;

(f) The Working Group will be made up of 6–10 members who will represent

   i) the interests of the ecclesiastical leadership in the cultural resources of the ACC

   ii) those individuals who possess expert knowledge of professional practice and standards in the context of Anglican polities and traditions; and

   iii) those with special insight or historical knowledge of the Communion and/or the ACC;

(g) The Working Group will relate to the officers and staff of the ACC and will report regularly to the Standing Committee;

(h) The mandate of the Working Group will extend until the ACC-13 meeting and may be renewed.

17 SEPTEMBER 2002

Address

—THE RIGHT REVEREND MICHAEL LUGÖR, THE PROVINCE OF SUDAN

Warm greetings in Christ. My first task is to register my profound gratitude to our Chairman for having given me this opportunity to say a word on behalf of the delegation of the Province of the Episcopal Church of the Sudan.

My second task is to draw the attention of the members to hear these words in Isaiah 18:2. "Go, swift messengers, to a people tall and smooth-skinned, to a people feared far and wide, an aggressive nation of strange speech whose land is divided by rivers."

Honourable members, perhaps some of you are not aware of the meaning of the word 'Sudan'; virtually it means the country of 'black people for black people.' Perhaps this is why my fellow Sudanese present here and I are dark due to our ethnic tribal grouping. Therefore Isaiah's words should not be overlooked.

Indeed, it is a pity to speak about the war-torn Sudan, because the current war has caused thousands and thousands, otherwise over four million people to flee to our neighbouring countries of Uganda and Kenya, and as far as to America, Canada and Australia (only to mention a few countries). Nearly two-thirds of these people are living in the jungles of Uganda and Kenyan borders, and they need your prayers.

They have lost all their property and over two million have been killed or died as the victims of the war between 1972 and 2000, let alone those who were killed or died between 1955 and 1972, numbering one million people!

Therefore, due to all this political unrest in the Sudan, peace is inevitable. In other words, peace and the issue of self-determination for the people of the Southern Sudan and Nuba Mountains, including other marginalized people of the Sudan is needed most urgently.

Of course, we in the Church do recommend very strongly that self-determination is a 'Human Universal Right' and that it is *the right* of the people of the South Sudan and those from the Nuba Mountains and others to exercise that right through referendum. I repeat, it will be the choice of the people if they want the Sudan to remain one or they may apply the philosophy of Ibrahim and his cousin Lot in Genesis 13:8. Such I believe will also solve the problem of Religion and the State.

As regards religious persecution, I believe Human Rights Watch and other humanitarian organisations have already recorded several violations; e.g., there is a concern that certain people otherwise the Government in the North may apply a licensing scheme for teaching religion and the manipulation of funding to favour one religious community.

However, in regards of wealth-sharing, which is one of the burning issues, especially the oil, which is now being used by the present regime to fuel the war in the Sudan; it is advisable that this must be negotiated by an international body, otherwise it must be stopped until peace is achieved. Of course, this issue of wealth-sharing includes all the assets of the Sudan and should not focus only in oil alone!

It is only very unfortunate to hear that Sudan peace talks agreed upon by the two warring parties had to come to a standstill after the capture of Torit town in Eastern Equatoria by the SPLA, which angered the Government delegation and caused them to pull out from the talks under the chairmanship of President Daniel Arap Moi of Kenya in the town of Machakos, Kenya.

Hence with this background, it is my pleasure and humble duty as one of the least of the servants of Christ to urge the members of this Council to please adopt the proposed resolutions already submitted to this Assembly for approval and to pass; i.e., for ACC-12 to adopt the proposed resolution on the Sudan as follows:

1. (a) that ACC-12 urges the Government of the Sudan to return to the peace negotiations in Machakos, Kenya;

   (b) that ACC-12 urges the Government of the Sudan and the SPLM/A to agree to a just and comprehensive ceasefire leading to a just and durable (everlasting) peace in the Sudan;

2. that ACC-12 urges all Provinces of the Anglican Communion to note with concern the flight of all involved in the conflict, in particular the Christian community (and those who are refugees outside the Sudan) who are suffering from the result of over 20 years of the civil war.

Mr. Chairman, with these words, I believe this gathering of ACC-12 will take seriously the issue of peace for the Sudanese people who are now scattered like sheep without a shepherd. Presumably that might have been one of the reasons God sent messengers to a people tall and smooth-skinned, to a people feared far and wide, an aggressive nation of strange speech whose land is divided by rivers (Isaiah 8:2 f).

Thank you very much indeed in anticipation.

Chairman's Address

—The Right Reverend Dr. Simon E. Chiwanga

The Joint Standing Committee of the ACC and the Primates has asked me, as retiring Chair and longest serving member, to reflect, before you, on my experience of the ACC in the last eighteen years. I boarded the ACC Ship as an ordinary member of the Province of Tanzania in 1984, at its 6th Meeting in Nigeria, and I have remained in it since then.

Collin Craston, my immediate predecessor, and I could possibly have been the victims of a too generous interpretation of the ACC Constitution. That is why I am most grateful to the lawyers present at this Council Meeting for seeking to clarify the relevant clauses in our Constitution in order to be consistent with the spirit of the Constitution as we seek to maintain a reasonable balance between the need for continuity and the need to have new leadership for fresh vision and ideas.

I will begin with a brief history of the birth of the Anglican Consultative Council. The Anglican Congress of 1963, held in Toronto, Canada, was a watershed for the contemporary Anglican Communion. This meeting of Anglican lay people, priests, and bishops from every corner of the Globe were gripped by a far-reaching vision: "Mutual Responsibility and Interdependence in the Body of Christ" (MRI). MRI proposed a radical reorientation of mission priorities and stressed mutual responsibility for mission between all Anglican Churches as equal partners. It stated in part:

> In our time the Anglican Communion has come of age. Our professed nature as a worldwide fellowship of national and regional churches has suddenly become a reality. . . . The full communion in Christ, which has been our traditional tie, has suddenly taken on a totally new dimension. It is now irrelevant to talk of 'giving' and 'receiving' Churches. The keynotes of our time are equality, interdependence, and mutual responsibility. (E. R. Fairweather, ed., *Anglican Congress 1963: Report of the Proceedings,* n.p.: Editorial Committee of the Anglican Congress, 1963, 118).

The real question for Anglicans then and today is how can this mutual responsibility and interdependence be lived out in reality in a community of, now, 38 equal, and autonomous Churches? As is the case for our human family life, for the family to stay together its members must talk together in a properly understood way.

The Anglican Consultative Council, born out of the 1968 Lambeth Conference Resolution, was seen to be one way, perhaps the most effective way, of achieving the necessary and regular consultations, in which "Anglicans may fulfill their common inter-Anglican and ecumenical responsibilities in promoting the unity, renewal, and mission of Christ's Church." (Lambeth Conference Report 1968, p145). A quasi-synodical structure of laity, clergy and episcopal should enable the Anglican family to talk together, and therefore remain together. Its first meeting was in February 1971 at Limuru, Kenya.

It has been argued that the theological basis of the shared leadership between the three orders is that "the authority of Christ over his Church is devolved to the whole people of God. Hence the Anglican way has well been described as episcopally led and synodically governed. There is a rightful authority residing in the episcopate, singly and collegially, but that is to be balanced by the authority of a 'bishop in council' with laity and clergy. If the balance is not kept, trouble ensues. Anglican experience of Episcopal leadership and synodical government is a distinctive contribution to the universal Church," (Collin Craston, Anvil Vol. 11, No.2, 1994).

The one thing of which I have been the most proud is the general orientation of the ACC toward mission, constantly reminding the Church to be a Church turned inside-out: outwardly-focused, transformative, prophetic. The world is longing for the redemption of Christ, and only such a mission-focused Church can bring that message to the world. I think the ACC will go down in history as developing the theology of mission more than any Anglican body. I have in mind here the work done by ACC 6, as part of preparations for Lambeth 1988. "Mission from everywhere to everywhere" is now the accepted model and expectation. Human and economic development is now seen as a part of our mission imperative, especially in the developing world provinces. We've been very consistent, and I hope that continues.

It is absolutely important that we sustain our efforts in mission because, as we all know, the Church, as the Body of Christ in the world, is called and uniquely empowered by the Holy Spirit to participate with God in God's mission of justice, compassion and reconciliation. Jesus demonstrated in word and deed that the Reign of God, realized in the sending of God's son, must continue to expand to the ends of the earth. "As you have sent me into the world, so have I sent them into the world," (John 17:18).

I have been most inspired by the ACC's emphasis on ecumenical and inter-faith approach to mission. It was the South Indian theologian S. J. Samartha who said:

> In a religiously plural world, Christians, together with their neighbors of other faiths, are called upon to participate in God's continuing mission in the world. Mission is God's continuing activity through the

> Sprit to mend the brokenness of creation, to overcome the fragmentation of humanity, and to heal the rift between humanity, nature and God. (*One Christ—Many Religions: Towards a Revised Christology*, Maryknoll, NY: Orbis Books, 1995, p.149).

As it has been repeated several times at this Meeting, in these difficult times, and following the death and destruction of September 11, it becomes particularly important that we as Anglicans recognize and lift up our commonality, not just with other Churches, but also with the other great Abrahamic faiths, especially Islam, in what Presiding Bishop Frank Griswold has called 'God's project' of mending the brokenness of creation and healing the rift and fragmentation between humanity.

I would like to say a word about the shift from a white, predominantly English speaking church of the West to a Church, predominantly in the Southern Hemisphere, which encompasses vast differences of culture, geographies, and languages. Anglican mission scholar David Barrett has documented that in the year 1900, 77% of the 558 million Christians in the world lived in Europe or North America. Today only 37% of the close to two billion Christians live in that same area. Dr Barrett further predicts that in less than three decades, in the year 2025, fully 71% of the projected 2.6 billion Christians worldwide will live in Asia, Africa, Latin America and the Pacific.

With regard to the Church in Africa south of the Sahara, Dr Barrett says, in 1960 (after 150 years of Western missionary activity), the number of Christians in Africa was approximately 50 million. From 1960 until 1990, the Christian population in sub-Saharan Africa increased from 50 million to 300 million! That change represents a five-fold increase in one fifth of the time. These figures refer to Christians as a whole, not just Anglicans. The total figure for Anglicans worldwide is estimated at 75 million.

What are we, particularly those of us from the South, to make of this transformation in the global Body of Christ, in particular, Anglicanism, which has been transformed into a truly global Christian community? In the last eighteen years I have sometimes been very depressed to see two things happening in some areas of the South:

- A growing dependency and inferiority complex which leads to failure to meet our obligations in maintaining the Instruments of Communion and an emulation of archaic ecclesiastical structures of the 19th Century Western Church;
- A 'congregationalist' ecclesiology, by which Church members do not see the need to support and pay for their Diocese, or Province, and consequently the worldwide Anglican family.

With regard to mission programs, it's interesting what we don't do now that was once right at the centre of the work of ACC. We no longer have

PIM consultations. From the early 1970s until the mid-80s ACC staff were key part in running them and monitoring follow-up. The world has changed. The combination of the availability of air travel and telecommunications contact means that grass roots people—clergy and laity, not just bishops and or a privileged few—get involved in Inter-Anglican visits. But we may need an audit of who's left out in this brave new world. What is certain it will be the poorest of the poor will be among them.

It's also interesting what we do more of. Even by the middle of the 1980s responsibility for serving the Ecumenical Dialogues was very dispersed and some of us were concerned that Anglicans could be saying things in one Dialogue that contradicted what we said in another. Now all the Dialogues are managed under one roof. And the range has been much expanded to include Pentecostals and Baptists as well as Roman Catholic and Orthodox, which seemed all important in earlier days.

In 1984 ACC embarked on the telecommunications project in partnership with Trinity Church Wall Street, New York. At the time there were people who thought we were crazy. Time has shown this was a farsighted move and it's evolved as a very important means of keeping in touch in the Communion. Trinity's sustained commitment to the Communion via this project needs to be applauded. We have already heard of the proposed Commission on Telecommunication. I urge this Council to approve the formation of this crucial organ to the life of the Communion.

The mid-1980s were the years when the Networks came into their own. This way of relating together has radically changed and expanded the range of contacts that happen in the life of the Communion. It is important to remember that the ACC expects a Network to have been in existence and actually operating, before it applies for recognition by the Council. The main reason for this expectation is that it allows for the Council, when considering recognition of a Network, to see whether it bears the marks of global Anglicanism.

There has been a re-branding of the Anglican Consultative Council Office. It was Archbishop Ted Scott of Canada in the early 1980s that observed the need to distinguish between the ACC as the Assembly of Representatives of the Churches and the ACC as an on-going office that served the Anglican Communion. Hence our letterhead now says 'Anglican Communion Office, serving the Lambeth Conference, the Primates Meeting, and the ACC.' This is a development that I have not been able to understand. Probably because of this shift a number of organs that were serving all of the other Instruments of Communion while remaining with the ACC label now want to be known as 'Inter-Anglican Something!' Is it a search for status? Could the ACC view itself as the 'Deacon' among the Instruments of Communion?

The Archbishop of Canterbury has done his best to enhance relationships between the ACC and other Instruments of Communion. In 1988 ACC members were invited, for the first time, to attend the Lambeth Conference as observers. In view of the fact that ACC 6 and 7 Meetings devoted a great deal of time to preparing for Lambeth 1988, the participation of ACC members was received with mixed feelings. The situation was a lot better at the 1998 Lambeth, with Archbishop George Carey making the historic and daring move of inviting the Chair of ACC to preach at the Opening Eucharist.

There was a joint Primates-ACC meeting at Cape Town in 1993. It helped us realize that both bodies needed to find ways of relating to each other in a more enriching way. The experiment has not yet been repeated. On the other hand, Lambeth 1998 passed on to ACC a resolution that was discussed in Dundee and may come back again at this Council meeting, seeking a structure that will integrate all the Primates with ACC. The Standing Committees of the Primates and ACC have successfully met together since 1992.

Collin Craston says if the balance between orders is not kept, trouble ensues. This reminds me of a meeting I attended where those who attended Lambeth 1998 were reporting back.

> "The experience of Lambeth has stirred in me, as it has in many others, a storm of urgent questions. Should we ever again leave the bishops to represent Anglicanism alone, without the presence of the laity and the other orders of ordained ministers? Isn't this gathering of bishops a theological anachronism? Isn't it obvious how the hegemony of men in the church is distorting its public witness with typically male obsessions and anxieties? Don't we have to forge new forms of public theology that are not driven by the needs to produce political-style resolutions or hampered by the ludicrous mechanisms of parliamentary procedure? How are we going to raise up leaders who can really interpret in the Spirit chaotic and complex forces of our post-modern world?"

When I asked at that meeting whether they knew of the ACC, which would meet their longing, very few participants were aware of it. The ACC has impressed me as a functional body, not just a talking shop. This spirit has continued, even intensified, and grown. I have consistently observed it in my seven Council meetings. I admired the working relationship of the ACC members—that they worked together regardless of the boundaries of status, tenure, position, ordination, gender, nationality, etc. There was a blurring of the ranks of which we are so aware in the rest of life. Especially, I was impressed that the chairmanship could be held by anybody, irrespective of these kinds of differences. In fact, the outgoing chair at ACC 6 meeting was John Denton, a very able layperson from Australia. I was moved that the elections committee worked deliberately with the Provinces to nominate ACC members, ensuring a mixture of women and men, lay, clergy and bishops. This was not a matter of coercion but simply an expression of a widespread conviction that such was good for the functioning of the ACC.

I was also impressed with the consultative nature of the Council, as opposed to the legislative nature of a synod or parliament. In a parliament the deliberations are secondary to the votes, the decisions; in fact, at times they can hardly be called deliberations, being rather mere posturing by the members. Even a government Cabinet—such as the Cabinet of Julius Nyerere where I served for five years—has as its main task decision-making and administrative implementation, and its deliberations serve that purpose. But with the ACC, the deliberations are the thing. The conversations are as important as the ends. The resolutions are simply the product, or distillation, of the consultations as they have taken place. The emphasis, as our legal adviser Canon John Rees said at the first session of this Meeting, is always to reach a consensus: Talk till you agree (Democracy under the Mango Tree); Consensus fidelium.

There's one challenge I want to issue to the members and provinces, and that is to keep the communication flowing between the ACC and the provinces. Some provinces do this well, but others seem preoccupied with domestic concerns. Some members are not given good opportunities to report ACC deliberations to their provinces, and some provinces do not give good input to their ACC representatives so that their concerns can be well articulated to the ACC. So I call on the Provinces and members to work more closely together.

From the ACC I learned for the first time the nature of the authority of such a consultative body. It's moral rather than constitutional. It's persuasive rather than coercive. It depends entirely on the quality of the resolutions and papers, as they are perceived to be helpful to their recipients throughout the Communion. That, and only that, saves us from being irrelevant. Such authority preserves the autonomy, freedom, and diversity of members of the communion—Provinces, organizations, and individuals. Such authority wields the power of powerlessness—the same power that Christ has in our lives—the Christ "who, though he was in the form of God, did not regard equality with God as something to be exploited, but emptied himself . . . and became obedient to the point of death—even deal on a cross" (Phil 2:6–8).

From the ACC I also learned the art of listening, the art of maintaining a conversation between people of different opinions. This is one of the greatest gifts I personally take away from my ACC experiences. I have grown as a person in the area of reconciliation, in appreciating and managing constructive tension, in balancing unity and diversity. This has been especially true in my role as Chair, when I was immersed in a number of tensions and crisis situations.

I would like to use this opportunity to thank the Archbishop of Canterbury and the Presiding Bishop of the Episcopal Church, USA, for appointing me to serve on the twelve-member 'Conversation Group on Human Sexuality,' as a follow up to the 1998 Lambeth Conference discussions on the subject. That was a very eye-opening experience for me. I learned there how far one can be moved in Christian charity without necessarily compromising your mind about your own convictions. Two members of a Public Conversation Project from Massachusetts, USA, facilitated the Conversation. The Public Conversation Project is a secular NGO in the United States that teaches the art of mediating highly conflicted conversations. This may be something we can share within the Provinces. Being called upon to speak at various Anglican gatherings has required me to work out a message that will reach all kinds of people, all sides in the prominent debates of the day, in a way that I never had to before.

In our Communion, we are still wrestling with the tension between two seemingly contradictory directions: the first, to pin down and define the theology, doctrine, discipline, or power structures of the Church, and the second, to live in the world with the ambiguities, contradictions, and varieties of interpretations and practices that a church of many cultures—and cultures in the midst of rapid, profound change—is bound to have.

It is very tempting, especially when we do not seem to adopt a self-imposed discipline in honoring our consensus, to want the instruments of unity—not only the ACC but also the Primates, the Archbishop of Canterbury, and the Lambeth Conference—to take stands on every issue and to enforce such positions on each member Province. But our job as the ACC is to listen, not only to political opinions, but also to experiences of Anglicans worldwide. To respect the stands taken by individuals or groups. To discuss. To reflect. To pray. To articulate what we have seen and heard and deliberated to the rest of the Communion. To witness clearly to what we have seen and heard. To articulate where we see the Spirit moving in global Anglicanism. But it's the responsibility of individuals, particularly leaders in the Church, to make constructive, critical use of what we say. To take it or leave it, as seems best to them, in the local situations they find themselves in.

We do want unity. We do recognize the Anglican Communion as a body, where no member can say, "I have no need of you." The way to greater Anglican unity is not tighter doctrinal definitions or centralized authority structures—it is first, a recommitment to the missio Dei, God's mission, God's project in the world, in solidarity and companionship with our brothers and sisters from other parts of the Communion. Second, a contextual and disciplined approach to our respective lives and ministries that respects the worldwide family.

I have seen over and over again how true hospitality, encounter, companionship and friendship breaks down barriers between people, whether they are barriers of culture, nationality, gender, status, or political views. The small "table fellowship" groups for Bible study at ACC and Lambeth Conferences, which are intentionally mixed as to orders, gender, and diocese, have consistently proven to be extremely transformative, not to individuals but also to the tenor and mood of the larger meeting. Is this the future of Anglican unity? Drawing closer to one another by working side-by-side with our neighbours—neighbours near and far, those like us and those profoundly unlike us—in order to further the mission of God, in order to usher in the Kingdom of God on earth?

When I mentioned to a friend of mine that I have been on the ACC for eighteen years continuously, he asked, "What crime did you do to deserve such a punishment?" My response was that it has not been a punishment, but rather a fascinating pilgrimage of deep spiritual and intellectual growth about my own faith, my worldwide Anglican family, the universal Church, God's world and His mission to the world, because of at least four unique growth-opportunities:

First, the opportunity to work with several Bishops and Archbishops from around the Anglican Communion, such as one sees at this very Meeting. In particular, to work with the Archbishop of Canterbury, the President of the ACC. For twelve, out of eighteen years of my work with the ACC, I served with The Most Reverend and Right Honorable Dr. George Carey. One person recently made the comment, "What has transpired during his time as Archbishop of Canterbury is staggering!" Yes, our Father in God, George, and, as we say in Africa, Mama Eileen, I want to express my deepest thanks for your friendship in matters personal and pastoral, global and local. Your visit to our Province and Diocese is a priceless memory, especially in consecrating our roofless cathedral; in Mrs. Eileen Carey laying for us the St. Luke's Clinic Foundation Stone; and now the relocation of your vast library to our Cathedral School for Ministry, will ever remain a further cause of deep rejoicing for us.

As a family, we in the Anglican world have realized that your commitment to us was beyond what we could expect or imagine, from a person, a leader, with a portfolio as scattered and encompassing as yours. We will say thank you collectively over these days, but from me, as Chairman, privileged to sit alongside you as President, and from my wife Gladys, we say ASANTE SANA SANA! Thank you very much indeed. When I consider the rock from which I was hewn, I truly want to join the Psalmist in praising God who **"raises the poor from the dust and seats them with the princes of their people"(Ps 113:7)**.

Second, the opportunity to visit Churches in different situations and in different countries: Nigeria, Singapore, Wales, South Africa, Panama, Scotland, and now Hong Kong, not to mention England, USA, Canada, Ireland, Australia, New Zealand, where we visited for either the Standing Committee or something else to do with the ACC. In all the places we have been for ACC Meetings, the Church and people have been extremely generous in their hospitality and welcome. They have tirelessly arranged exposure events for our learning and growth.

For my last ACC Meeting to be held in Hong Kong I feel I have been given a wonderful parting gift! The generosity of the Hong Kong Sheng Kung Hui has deeply touched and challenged me. We can never thank Archbishop Peter and Mrs. Kwong, and their whole Church, sufficiently enough for the marvelous support for the work of ACC and this Meeting. I was informed that Hong Kong has the second largest number of Compass Rose Society Members who are keen to support the work of the Anglican Communion.

We have no better words in which to express our gratitude to you Archbishop Peter and to your Church, but these simple ones: THANK YOU MOST SINCERELY!

I want to humbly offer my plea to every Province, but particularly to the Third World Provinces, to follow Hong Kong's good example. We have a saying in Swahili, "It is the heart you have, not your wealth, that makes you a generous giver." It can be tempting for some of us to jump to conclusions and say that Hong Kong is giving so generously because of its rich resources. In my eighteen years on the ACC I have seen the work of the Communion adversely affected due to the failure of some Provinces to pay their dues.

Third, the unique opportunity of meeting wonderful friends from every corner of the world—at meetings of the Council, at the Standing and the Finance Committee Meetings. Archbishop Peter Kwong was very kind to observe that he has seen me smiling most of the time as if nothing bothers me at meetings. I have enjoyed working with every kind of member at all the meetings I have chaired. In advising political leaders against eliminating every difficult character, President Julius Nyerere of Tanzania used to give the analogy of a driver and a mosquito. Never wipe off every mosquito from the car, but to leave one or two to keep the driver awake when driving, especially at night. Sometimes I have entered into night driving as chair and those who have labeled themselves as trouble shooters/makers have kept me awake! I THANK ALL OF YOU FOR TRAINING ME IN THE CHAIR.

Fourth, the wonderful opportunity of enjoying the service of dedicated Staff at the Anglican Communion Office, which includes the Office of our Observer at the United Nations. It goes without challenge that the work accomplished in our name, actually us, the ACC, is managed by a sincere, dedicated often overwhelmed staff, led by the Secretary General, Canon John L. Peterson. Some are long-serving members: Deirdre Martin 25 years, Jim Rosenthal 12 years, Marjorie Murphy 15 years; others only recently joined the staff, such as Andrew Franklin, Dorothy Pennicook, and Christopher Took; others are very young in their age, such as Matthew Davies.

I have a few words to say about our Secretary General. Well, this is not quite true. I actually have volumes but I don't want Deirdre's bell to go off in the middle of a chapter. I would be remiss if I didn't express some of my deep appreciation to the man John L. Peterson, who happens to be Secretary General of the Anglican Communion.

John is, and has been, a friend in the fullest sense of the word; a confidant when I need an ear to listen, a guide to cheer me when I need direction, but above all a brother in Christ with whom I can pray. Most of you don't know that the calm and serene man whom you see seated at the dais spends most of his waking hours tirelessly paddling with both oars in the water in order to keep the Communion moving forward.

His work goes far beyond securing necessary funding to maintain the mandates of our budget. John, in his role as Secretary General, is our constant communicator within the Communion and attempts to be a presence whenever called upon. John, I thank God for this gift he has given to me and to our Anglican Communion.

I mentioned Deirdre Martin earlier in jest, but I cannot tell you how much it has meant to have her support and care for me, and our Church. Her work and witness have blessed us for the last twenty-five years. I wish her a longer service, and I thank her husband, my old and dear friend John Martin, for letting her serve the Communion.

The sum total of this long answer to my friend's question is that in the eighteen years of time with the ACC, I have witnessed this Instrument grow from strength to strength and become a body that can offer anyone aboard this ship unique opportunities for growth and transformation. If you finish your term of office as a member or staff more impoverished rather than more enriched than you came, then you have reason to examine how you made use of the various opportunities offered to you by ACC.

Finally, I leave this Council with mixed emotions. On one hand, I am absolutely convinced that, even if the Constitution allowed me, it is to the best interest of the ACC I love so much that I should retire. On the other hand, I find it hard to leave such dear friends. On the whole, I feel I really need to sing the Song of my name's sake, old Simeon, joined by my African brothers and sisters attending this Council Meeting:

Lord, now lettest thy servant depart in peace,
According to thy word;
For mine eyes have seen thy salvation,
Which thou hast prepared before the face of all people,
To be a light to lighten the gentiles,
And to be the glory of thy people Israel.
Glory to be to the Father, and to the Son, and to the Holy Ghost;
As it was in the beginning, is now, and ever shall be,
World without end. AMEN.

GOD BLESS YOU ALL, AND GOODBYE!

Report by the Secretary General

—THE REVEREND CANON DR. JOHN L. PETERSON, SECRETARY GENERAL OF THE ACC

Thanks to Hong Kong Sheng Kung Hoi

What a great privilege it is for the Twelfth Council Meeting of the ACC to be meeting here in Hong Kong, the youngest of all Provinces in the Anglican Communion and yet a Province that is rich in history. The hospitality and the support which have been given to this Council meeting by the Provincial Office of the Church in Hong Kong have been absolutely outstanding. Certainly I know I express your gratitude when we thank Archbishop **Peter Kwong** for inviting this Council meeting to be held in Hong Kong. There are a great many people to thank as well, including all seven hundred volunteers from the Church of Hong Kong, and yet I can name only four today. The Revd Dr. **Dorothy Lau**, ordained priest last Saturday, and her assistant **Sally Law** have given countless days working with our office. At the same time, the Reverends **Andrew Chan** and **Paul Kwong** have also been very much involved. I know I express the gratitude of the entire Council to you all for your outstanding contributions.

September 11

Since our last meeting in Dundee, we have all experienced an event from which all other events over the next few years will be measured. That, of course, was September 11, 2001 and the attack in New York, Washington and Pennsylvania.

The impact of September 11 came home visibly to me at the Joint Standing Committee Meeting when we met in the Province of Ireland in February. This morning I would like to share with you two snapshots from that meeting. The Revd Dr. **Jae-Joung Lee**, the representative from Korea, who believes his role as priest and politician is important, spoke eloquently about the negative impact that President Bush's State of the Union Address has had on the peoples of both North and South Korea. The President had named three countries that he described as the "axis of evil," Iraq, Iran and North Korea. The Anglican Church in Korea has been diligent in seeking reconciliation and reunification between both countries. Jae-Joung pointed out that the United States' "war on terrorism" was in itself terrorism as it impacted the efforts to bring reconciliation and understanding between the peoples of North and South Korea.

The second snapshot from that Standing Committee is of **Judy Conley**, the representative of the Episcopal Church in the United States. Judy shared with us the impact that September 11 had on her. She had three friends working in the Twin Towers that day. Fortunately all three were able to escape, but the fear and the trauma had definitely affected her. Judy is a strong person who has dedicated her life to social justice issues. But as she shared her experience that day, she was in tears as she relived the horrors of the attack in New York.

The reason I share these two snapshots with you is because each of us carries our own memories of that day. The impact that day has had on the global community cannot possibly yet be known. The impact that day has had on the Anglican Communion cannot possibly yet be known. It is within this context that much of this report is given.

Tribute to Bishop John Howe

Since our meeting in Dundee, two Archbishops of Canterbury and one Secretary General have died. In a tribute written to Bishop **John Howe**, the first Secretary General of the Anglican Communion, Canon Sam Van Culin wrote, "Bishop John Howe was responsible for bringing the Anglican Consultative Council into being." as a result of a resolution which was passed at the Lambeth Conference in 1968, which approved the constitution for the Anglican Consultative Council. It ultimately came to fruition when Bishop Howe organised the first meeting of the Council in Limuru, Kenya in 1971. As we gather here today in Hong Kong, we are indebted to John Howe, for his vision of what a synodical body would mean to the Anglican Communion.

Tribute to Archbishop Coggan

Lord Donald Coggan died on 17 May 2000 at the age of 90. At his memorial service, eulogies referred to Archbishop Donald's passion for mission and evangelism, his preaching based on biblical exposition, his concern for the unity of the church, as well as his commitment to Jewish-Christian relations.

One of Archbishop Coggan's lasting legacies was his inauguration of the Personal Emergencies Fund for the Anglican Communion. So far just this year, 23 people from 11 countries around the Communion have received £28,000 from the Personal Emergency Fund.

Tribute to Archbishop Robert Runcie

The last time I saw Archbishop Robert Runcie was on December 17, 1999, some six months before he died in July 2000. I asked him, "How are you doing?" and his response to me was, "John, I am dying gracefully." That comment, "I am dying gracefully was so Robert Runcie and so reflects the person he was: graceful.

Robert Runcie raised the profile of the Office of Archbishop of Canterbury in the Anglican Communion by his international travels. The first visit the Archbishop made after his enthronement in 1980 was to Ghana, which began his many visits throughout the Communion, perhaps highlighted by his famous visit to Rome as he searched for visible unity with our brothers and sisters in the Roman Catholic Church. Archbishop Runcie had an enormous capacity for friendship, a marvelous sense of humour, and a wit that endeared him to world leaders, church people, and ordinary folk.

Tribute to the Revd Canon John Rye

This last month The Revd Canon John Rye, formerly a World Mission Partner Officer for the Anglican Church of Canada, died. I would like to recognize his special ministry to the Communion during the Lambeth Conference in 1998, when he distributed the bursary funds fairly and with a great deal of integrity. We give thanks for John's life and for the important support he gave to us.

Visits in the Anglican Communion

Cuba

In June 2000, members of the Compass Rose Society visited Cuba. We experienced a country that has faced the brutality of an embargo, an embargo which has had a devastating impact on the life of the country as well as the church. But what is absolutely remarkable is that the embargo has not "broken" the people. Recently the Cuban Government has been more open to the Church and as a result the Church is experiencing new growth with young and energetic clergy and lay people.

Every church we visited was packed. But the Church has no Prayer Books, people have no medicine, people have no medical supplies, children are in need of shoes, hospitals do not even have sheets for their beds.

The needs of the Church in Cuba are many. We are asked to reach out to them. But I hope they will reach out to us as well because they can teach us an important lesson. They can teach us what it means to live under an embargo. As a Communion this is an important lesson as we struggle with all of the embargos which enslave us.

Jerusalem

At the beginning of the second Intifada, the Archbishop of Canterbury and the Presiding Bishop of the Episcopal Church inaugurated the Jerusalem 2000 initiative. This initiative has been extremely successful. In England alone, over a million pounds has been raised for different projects within the Diocese of Jerusalem.

Jerusalem, of course, has been very much in our thoughts and prayers since our Dundee Meeting. Many of you have made pilgrimages to stand in solidarity with the Church in Jerusalem, particularly as it faces discrimination and economic pressures. The Archbishop of Canterbury made an historical Pastoral Visit to Jerusalem in July 2001. The purpose of that visit was to stand in solidarity with the Church in Jerusalem, but that visit also laid a foundation stone for a peace initiative which the Archbishop would make some six months later. The Archbishop visited President Arafat in Gaza and Prime Minister Sharon in his Jerusalem Office. Such high level initiatives are really important because the Church in Jerusalem is living more and more in a minority position in its homeland. Soon there will be very few Christians remaining in Jerusalem, in Palestine and in Israel. Jerusalem must be one of our concerns. We need to support the Christian community in Jerusalem and this must be a priority. During this Council Meeting we shall have an opportunity to hear from **Bishop Riah** of Jerusalem.

Australia

Last July I was invited to participate in the second **National Anglican Conference in Australia**, sponsored by the General Synod of that Church. The theme of the Conference was "Making Connections." Australia has its own unique issues concerning "Making Connections" and how a church that is so provincially run relates to the national church as a whole.

The organisers of the Conference invited me to address the issue of making connections in interfaith relations within the Anglican Communion. This topic has taken on new dimensions since September 11. One of the important vehicles we have in the Anglican Communion for making connections with our interfaith family is NIFCON, the Network for Interfaith Concerns, but also initiatives which have been taken by the Archbishop of Canterbury. This topic will be discussed during this Council Meeting and it is my hope that we will be able to receive the report of NIFCON as well as two important initiatives which have been initiated by the Archbishop of Canterbury, the al-Azhar Agreement and the Alexandria Declaration.

Kenya

This last May when the Inter Anglican Mission and Evangelism Commission met in Nairobi, the Archbishop of Kenya at that time, **David Gitari**, invited me to participate in the inauguration of KAMA, the Kenya Anglican Men's Association. Today I want to acknowledge the important initiative that KAMA represents in the Church of Kenya. That Saturday morning at St. Stephen's Church in the Diocese of Nairobi, some 620 men, individually, become members of KAMA. Two of the reasons for KAMA are to help men live a faithful Christian life as well as encourage Anglican lay men and women to play a positive role as Christians in the political, social and economic life of the nation.

Archbishop David Gitari

While I am speaking about Kenya I would also like to recognise the recent retirement of Archbishop David Gitari, a Primate who has been fearless in his struggle for social justice in Kenya. One of the great Anglican prophetic voices of our time, David has served the Church in Kenya with distinction. Just this last week David was once again subjected to a threat on his life when a police car rammed his car. Thank God David was not hurt seriously.

Reports From The Communion Anglican Observer at the United Nations

Since our Dundee meeting, the Anglican Communion has appointed a new Anglican Observer at the United Nations in the person of **Archdeacon Taimalelagi Fagamalama Tuatagaloa-Matalavea**. One of the criteria of the Selection Committee was that the new Observer would be very much involved in "knocking on the doors" at the United Nations, which would support the different Provinces in the Communion when particular needs arise.

Geneva Advisory Committee

One of Faga's initiatives has been to start a Geneva Advisory Committee like the Advisory Council she has in New York. Much of the work of the United Nations takes place in Geneva, particularly with regard to UNAIDS, World Health, Social Development, the International Labor Organisation and the Human Rights Commission. Faga asked the Revd Canon **Samir Habiby**, priest-in-charge of Christ Church, Lausanne, Switzerland to put together a Geneva Committee to respond to the social needs that have been identified in the Anglican Communion. The Geneva Advisory Committee has met on five different occasions and has enabled us to make significant introductions, particularly to UNAIDS. As soon as the Provincial structures are put in place in Africa, and in other parts of the Anglican Communion as well, we will be able to apply for grants from UNAIDS to support the work of the different dioceses and parishes within the Communion which are doing grassroots work with this pandemic.

Anglican Observer's Advisory Council

I would also like to recognise the significant work that is done by the Advisory Council because they have basically accepted the responsibility to find funding for that office. The Archbishop of Canterbury has been tireless in his support and the UN Advisory Council has done a tremendous job enabling the Anglican Observer's Office to exist. It is my hope, however, it will not have to continue to be a hand-to-mouth operation, but that we can get substantial Endowment funding to enable the office to do its work.

HIV/AIDS

At the Primates Meeting at Kanuga in 2001, the Archbishop of Cape Town offered a challenge to the Communion regarding HIV/AIDS. One of the presenters at that Primates Meeting was the Revd **Gideon Byamugisha**, a priest living with AIDS from Uganda. His eloquence and his depth of spirituality moved the Primates to make HIV/AIDS a top priority in the Anglican Communion. Out of that meeting came a Conference in Johannesburg in August 2001 that has changed the face of our Communion with regard to the HIV/AIDS pandemic.

Canon **Ted Karpf**, from the Province of Southern Africa and the co-ordinator of the HIV/AIDS programme in Southern Africa, will be giving a report to this Council meeting on the initiatives which have been taken, both by the Primates on the continent of Africa as well as by the local churches in Africa.

One thing I must say, however, is that I am bitterly disappointed how slowly this whole process has unfolded. To be honest we were promised funds to establish this programme in each one of the African Provinces, but the promised funds never came through. It is only because of a generous grant which we were given last week by the Parthenon Trust that at long last this programme will be established. This programme will enable the Provinces in Africa to apply for grants so that the Provinces can have an effective programme to combat AIDS. In Africa AIDS will not be defeated by the Governments, but by the Church.

St. Andrew's House

When ACC-11 met in Dundee we reported that the Anglican Communion had been approached by the Sisters of St. Andrew's and the Tavistock Trust who wished to give their building in Westbourne Park, London, to the Anglican Communion so an Anglican Communion Centre could be established. Over the last three years we have been in conversation with the Sisters and the Trust, and a decision was taken by the ACC Standing Committee last February in Ireland that the ACC should accept the generous offer of St. Andrew's House. We have been given St. Andrew's House for a "peppercorn rent" with a lease for 20 years.

St. Andrew's House will provide the Anglican Communion with a Centre which will include sufficient office space not only for our present office staff, but also the Lambeth Conference staff who will join us in 2005. In addition, it will also provide accommodation for temporary staff members as well as some rooms for visitors from around the world. I would like to acknowledge the hard work of **Canon John Rees** as he has been working with the Tavistock Trust, **Andrew Franklin**, our Financial Officer, who has been dealing with many of the financial and personnel issues concerning St. Andrew's House, and an Anglican Communion Office team headed by Marjorie Murphy who has been looking at space utilisation.

Endowment Fund—Compass Rose Society

In my tribute to the Archbishop of Canterbury in the latest edition of *Anglican World*, I wrote that the Compass Rose Society was born out of a vision and dream that Archbishop George Carey had for the Anglican Communion. That vision was that we would communicate more effectively with each other as well as putting the structures of the Anglican Communion on a more stable economic footing.

Out of this dream came the Compass Rose Society. The Society now has members from Canada, China, England, Hong Kong, Japan, Switzerland, United States, Uruguay and hopefully soon, Australia.

This last year the Compass Rose Society committed itself to raise a $20,000,000 Endowment for the Anglican Communion. The interest from this Endowment will enable the Communion to be financially viable in relation to new initiatives and special projects.

It is my hope that you will reaffirm the decision of the Joint Standing Committee by giving your support to this Endowment initiative for the Anglican Communion. My goal is when ACC-13 meets in 2005 it will be reported to you that the 20 million dollar endowment has been raised.

Because of the importance of the Compass Rose Society's $20 million Endowment campaign and the need to put this Endowment in place within the next two years, the Anglican Communion has received a generous grant from the Parthenon Trust which will enable us to hire a retired diplomat to help support my work in the Anglican Communion Office. His coming will free me so I can be more involved in the Endowment campaign. To this end we have invited the recently retired British Ambassador to the Holy See, **Mark Pellew**, to assume this responsibility. Not only is Mark well versed in the international scene, but he also has a keen interest in ecumenism.

Inter Anglican Finance Committee

This morning I would like to recognize the important work that is being done by the Inter Anglican Finance Committee, which is Chaired by Archbishop **Robin Eames**. Working with Archbishop Eames on the Committee are Archbishop Peter Akinola, Judy Conley, Gahzi Musharbash, Fung-Yi Wong and Bishop Simon Chiwanga, an ex-officio member as the Chair of the ACC. This Committee works diligently to examine ways to utilize the resources available to it to fund the programmes of the Communion.

While we are all appreciative of the generous support of the Compass Rose Society and Trinity Church, Wall Street, the major source of income for the Anglican Consultative Council and therefore for the work and witness for our Communion family is, and must remain, the Provinces of the Anglican Communion and the United Churches. The Joint Standing Committee has recognized over the last eight years that many of the new initiatives which it has been given, either by the Council itself, the Primates, or the Lambeth Conference, are not provisions that have been within the budget of the Communion.

For example last year the Joint Standing Committee requested an additional 4% from each Province to pay for new ecumenical initiatives and the Inter Anglican Theological and Doctrinal Commission. Only two Provinces responded. The Joint Standing Committee recognizes the economic problems many Provinces are facing.

We only need to look at the economic pressures facing the Church of England and the fact that they are freezing their 2003 and 2004 commitment to the Inter-Anglican Budget at their 2002 level. We all know the difficult time that South Africa is having as the Rand loses its value, as has been the case in New Zealand with their dollar as well. We must also face the difficult reality that the Diocese of Sydney does not pay a portion of their budget to the General Synod of the Australian Church and therefore the Church in Australia contributes only 58% of their asking every year to the Inter Anglican Budget. Regardless of the reasons, these shortfalls have a devastating effect on the ministry of the Communion and our inter-relatedness to each other.

If we are going to be responsible to each other as a global family, if we are truly going to be inter-dependent, then we will have to be more financially responsible to each other as a Communion. The Inter Anglican Finance Committee has looked seriously at our finances and will be challenging us to remember that the member churches are the major source of income for the ACC. If each Province contributed its due share, there would not be a deficit—and at the same time the Council would be able to serve the Anglican Communion in the way it is requested to do by the ACC, the Lambeth Conference and the Primates.

Four New Networks

During this Council Meeting you will receive a recommendation from the Joint Standing Committee that the Anglican Communion accept four new Networks as official Networks of the Communion. They are the Colleges and Universities of the Anglican Communion, the Network of Francophone Dioceses in the Anglican Communion, the Anglican Communion Environmental Network and the Legal Advisers of the Anglican Communion. It is my hope you will support these Networks by giving them official recognition in the life of the Communion.

The Francophone Dioceses in the Anglican Communion are the second largest language group and they have established outstanding programmes to support each other. Our support to their network initiative will affirm what is already a reality in the Communion.

This last July I had the opportunity to attend the meeting of the Colleges and Universities of the Anglican Communion in Tokyo. In discussing their application to the ACC to become an official Network of the Anglican Communion, there was much enthusiasm amongst the members. The potential here is enormous. One of the things I urged CUAC to consider was establishing continuing education programmes for laity, clergy and bishops within their local provinces. That suggestion was well received and I believe that we have here yet another significant route for theological continuing education.

The Anglican Communion Environmental Network has its roots both in the commitment of individual provinces to environmental stewardship, and in the Lambeth Conference, which in 1998 requested the formation of a Commission on the Environment with staff support. The proposal before you is an attempt to respond to these initiatives in ways that are consistent with the structural and financial capacities of the ACC. It also reflects the urgency of the issues before us. Anglican delegates from 21 Provinces met near Johannesburg immediately prior to the World Summit on Sustainable Development and they gave resounding support to this network. They asked that this ACC give the Environmental Network official status.

I was present for much of the Legal Advisers Consultation at Canterbury in March 2002. It was held at the initiative of the Archbishop of Canterbury, and drew together principal legal advisers from 17 Provinces of the Communion. Its report and recommendation went to the Primates Meeting in April, and will be brought to the ACC by our Legal Adviser, John Rees. The Consultation made a number of important findings about the things that unite us as a Communion, as well as identifying a range of legal problems that face individual provinces.

Your support of these Networks to become official Networks of the Council would be very much appreciated.

Decade to Overcome Violence

The decade to overcome violence began in 2001. Throughout this period, 2001–2010, the World Council of Churches encourages churches and Christian World Communions to acknowledge and address all aspects and issues of violence in their own contexts, and to work together for peace, justice and true reconciliation. The Anglican Communion must continue to embrace efforts to fight against all forms of violence and abuse. We must reflect on biblical and theological perspectives that affect our attitudes and behaviours in our daily lives.

Staff Reports

Ecumenical

The ecumenical and studies department of the ACO is one of the busiest sections of our office in London, and there has been significant progress in a number of areas since ACC-11.

The formation of the Inter Anglican Standing Commission on Ecumenical Relations will help us present a coherent face in conversations with all our ecumenical partners.

Among the several bilateral relationships which we support, I would like to point out the significant new developments in three areas. First of all, as a result of the historic meeting of Anglican and Roman Catholic Bishops and Archbishops in Mississauga Canada in 2000, the International Anglican-Roman Catholic Commission for Unity and Mission has been formed, which will complement the theological dialogue carried out by ARCIC. The establishment of the Unity and Mission Commission signifies that Anglican-Roman Catholic relations have reached a new level, when leaders of our Churches are now committed to finding ways to make our Communion in Life and Mission more visible.

Our relations with the Lutheran World Federation have also reached a new milestone. The Anglican-Lutheran International Working Group has completed its task of reviewing all the regional dialogues which have taken place or which are currently taking place around the world.

Our dialogue with the Baptist World Alliance is now in full swing, and will produce a report which will be ready for ACC-13 in 2005.

Remarkable progress continues to be made in our dialogue with the Orthodox Churches, and a new commission with the Oriental Orthodox Churches will have its first meeting this November.

Each year there are more than a dozen ecumenical international consultations or meetings. These meetings include interchurch relations, department staff meetings as well as the Inter Anglican Theological and Doctrinal Commission, which has just had its second meeting. The commissions of dialogue and the Doctrine Commission undertake careful, technical and sensitive work on behalf of the Communion as a whole.

I urge the members of the ACC to help promote and support the ecumenical and doctrinal work of the Communion in your home Churches, particularly encouraging bishops, clergy and lay leaders to become better acquainted with the dialogues and particularly with the fruit of many years of patient work.

Tribute to David Hamid

For almost six years Canon David Hamid has been the Ecumenical Affairs and Studies Officer of the Anglican Communion. David has served in that position with distinction. Therefore, the announcement on July 19 that David had been appointed the Suffragan Bishop in Europe, was a cause for rejoicing. Although his appointment is a tremendous loss for the Ecumenical Desk in the Anglican Communion Office, David's outstanding gifts will certainly serve the Diocese in Europe well.

No single Diocese in the Anglican Communion covers more countries, a larger geographical spread, more languages, more ethnic traditions and more national churches, than the Diocese in Europe. David is a gifted linguist and he will bring to that office not only his language skills, but also a deep commitment to ecumenical work. I know all of you will want to join me in extending our appreciation to David for his outstanding work as the Ecumenical Officer of the Anglican Communion and our prayers as he assumes his new responsibilities in the Church of England.

I would like to announce to the Council that Bishop **John Baycroft**, retired Bishop of Ottawa, and recently the Director of the Anglican Centre in Rome, has accepted our appointment as Interim Director of Ecumenical Affairs and Studies until June 2003.

Liturgics

The International Anglican Liturgical Consultation completed its long-term project on baptism, eucharist, and ministry (the agenda of the 1982 Lima Conference of the Faith and Order Commission of the World Council of Churches).

The Consultation based its concluding work on ministry and ordination to ministry on a theology of the baptismal nature of the church, emphasizing that the people of God are revealed in baptism to be a holy people ministering to the world, to whom a variety of gifts have been given to build up the body of Christ and enable its mission.

The Consultation also engaged in a lively discussion of the elements of the Eucharist and recommended that a survey be conducted to discover current practice in the Communion. The recommendation also suggested that the ACC form a small working group to study the data and draft a report with Guidelines for further consideration by the Consultation and the ACC Standing Committee. The Joint Standing Committee subsequently agreed and recommended that in the light of such a survey, it should establish a working group to study the data and present a report with suggested guidelines to the Committee.

Might I extend your thanks to the Revd **Paul Gibson** for all that he does as the Liturgical Officer of the Anglican Communion.

Mission and Evangelism

Since our meeting in Dundee, the new Inter Anglican Commission on Mission and Evangelism has met on two different occasions, earlier this year in St Andrew's, Scotland and last year in Johannesburg, South Africa. There are 21 persons on this Commission, representing all of the different Regions in the Anglican Communion.

One of the major concerns of the Mission and Evangelism Commission is equipping the Communion for ministry. Theological education has been identified as one of the major mission concerns of the Commission, both in the training and formation for mission in the Communion. When the report of the Standing Committee on Mission and Evangelism is given, the Anglican Consultative Council will be asked to endorse the Commission's role in its work on leadership training and the formation for Mission. Might I add that the Commission sub-committee for theological education wants to work closely with the Primates' initiative in theological education.

The interim report you have been given is entitled "Traveling Together in God's Mission" and in that report there are six broad areas of mission which are being given to the different Provinces of the Anglican Communion for consideration and comment. It is important for me to mention the six points here:

- Islam and Islamisation
- Developing Anglicanism: A Communion in Mission
- The Journey towards Wholeness and Fullness of Life
- Mission as Justice Making and Peace Building
- Money, Power and Christian Mission
- Evangelism

Please give consideration to these six points so the Council will be able to support wholeheartedly the work that has been done by the Mission and Evangelism Commission.

Statement on Marjorie Murphy

Over the last few years Marjorie Murphy has carried the title of Executive Assistant to the Secretary General for Mission and Evangelism. During that time for all effective purposes, Marjorie has been the Director of Mission and Evangelism, fulfilling her responsibilities extremely well. When the Mission and Evangelism Commission met earlier this year in St. Andrew's, Scotland they recommended that Marjorie should become the permanent Director of Mission and Evangelism. I was more than happy to regularise what in fact had already become "the reality on the ground" for the last several years. I know the members of this Council will want to recognize Marjorie in appreciation for her dedication to Mission and Evangelism as well as her willingness to take on the responsibility as Conference Co-ordinator here at ACC-12.

Communications

Over the last several years the Communication programme under the direction of Canon **Jim Rosenthal** has been strengthened enormously because of support from Trinity Church, Wall Street and the Compass Rose Society. Today the Anglican Communion is able to provide a real service to the many Churches in the Communion that have no other means of telling their story except through instruments like *Anglican World*, the Anglican Communion News Service and our new Telecommunications programme which includes our web site. The Communication Department provides an important service for the all the Provinces in the Anglican Communion. It is my hope that *Anglican World* will be supported and numbers increased in each one of the Provinces of the Anglican Communion. Also a new format for the Anglican Cycle of Prayer will be launched in 2003.

During this Council meeting you will be presented with a new Telecommunication concept, totally funded by Trinity Church, Wall Street. For the last four years we have been working to put this Telecommunications programme together as well as an Inter Anglican Commission on Communications. Within the last nine months this dream has been moving towards reality. We look forward to welcoming the Reverend Canon **Ogé Beauvoir** next Monday, along with Jim Rosenthal, who will be presenting this important new initiative to the Communion.

One of the recommendations from the first telecommunication group that met and recommended a Commission two years ago was that we hire a full time Web Manager. This has now come to fruition in the appointment of **Christopher Took** who has joined the staff in London full time for the next two years. However, he is not new to the Anglican Communion Office having worked part-time for us from Ireland "online." The web pages for the Anglican Communion are being developed by the introduction of a web portal, which will enable the Churches in the Communion to share their news. The design and appearance of some of the new web pages will be presented to the Council next Monday.

We have already written to the Primates and the Provincial Secretaries to solicit names of people who could serve on the new Inter Anglican Commission on Telecommunications. It is anticipated at the next meeting of the Joint Standing Committee of the ACC and the Primates that this Commission will be named.

This Commission will support the important ministry of the Department of Communications as it looks forward to serving the Communion in the future. Indeed, we are grateful to Trinity Church and the Compass Rose Society for their strong commitment to excellence in communications.

It was announced at the Joint Standing Committee that met last week that Jim Rosenthal will be taking a sabbatical to do some writing from October through December this year. We have invited Bishop **Onell Soto**, retired Bishop of Venezuela, to act as the Director during Jim's sabbatical. Onell comes to us after years of communication work in the Anglican Communion. His main task will be to formulate a translation grant request.

Travel Office

The Travel Office is now in its fifth year of operation, and 2002 has been the busiest so far (excluding, of course, the 1998 Lambeth Conference). A number of new meetings in Mission and Evangelism and the annual meeting of the Primates have considerably increased the work of the department. Travel is arranged throughout the year for regular Ecumenical commissions and consultations as well as for the extensive global travel of the Secretary General, the Director of the Ecumenical Department, and the Director of Communications.

The Travel Manager also helps to administer the Compass Rose Society and organises the Annual Meeting of the Society in London for members and guests. **Lynne Butt** also accompanies the Secretary General on Mission Visits with society members and frequently writes accounts of the experiences for *Anglican World* and the Compass Rose Society publication, the *Communicator.*

ACO Staff Changes

Since ACC-11 in Dundee numerous changes have taken place on the staff at the Anglican Communion Office. Earlier this year we said good-bye to **Mike Nunn** who had been the Financial Officer of the Communion since 1994. Replacing Mike is **Andrew Franklin** who for many years worked for Kawasaki.

In the few months that Andrew has been on the Anglican Communion Office staff he has been able to grasp the nettle and he is doing an outstanding job. In Andrew we have been blessed with excellent continuity as well as another fine Financial Officer for the Communion. **Graeme Smith**, who for many years was Mike Nunn's assistant, accepted a missionary appointment with the Salvation Army to serve in Eastern Europe. After a long search The Revd **Dorothy Penniecooke** joined the staff and once again we have received a great gift in Dorothy. A priest in the Church of England, Dorothy not only does her job as the assistant to the Financial Officer extremely well, but she has become the Chaplain in the Anglican Communion Office.

Shortly after ACC-11, **Ann Quirke** resigned as the Travel Officer of the Anglican Communion and she was replaced by **Lynne Butt**. Lynne was immediately thrown into the depths of the job, but she has done an outstanding job in the Travel Office.

Replacing **Jon Williams** as the Sales Officer for *Anglican World* is **Matthew Davies**, who has also taken on some responsibilities for the Anglican Communion News Service as well as working as an assistant to Canon Jim Rosenthal. *Anglican World* is produced with a very small staff and Matthew is becoming an important person in that process.

Responsible for the database today is **Michael Ade** who replaced **Helen Bates** who left the employ of the Anglican Communion Office after 14 years of service. Michael brings an extensive knowledge of the database and our records are being kept well today under his care.

During ACC-11, **Frances Hiller** was the receptionist in the Communion Office, but since that time she has taken on the responsibilities of Information Officer as well as a member of the Ecumenical team. She has been an enormous support to Canon David Hamid's ministry.

Thanks to the Parthenon Trust NIFCON, the Network of Interfaith Concerns, now has a part time administrator, **Susanne Mitchell**, who is directly responsible to Clare Amos, the Co-ordinator of NIFCON, and already in the few months that Susanne has been in post, there is a greater awareness of different interfaith concerns throughout the Anglican Communion.

I would also like to share with you some news about other staff members. This year **Deirdre Martin** celebrated her 26th anniversary in the Anglican Communion Office. I personally find her an invaluable executive to me and I am grateful for the enormous support she gives to the Office of the Secretary General and to the Communion as a whole.

I also want to acknowledge other support staff in the Anglican Communion Office for the outstanding work that they do. In Administration and Finance, **Rosemary Palmer**; in Ecumenical Relations, **Christine Codner**; in Communications, **Veronica Elks**; and in Information Technology, **Ian Harvey**. Both Veronica and Ian are also working in the Secretariat here at ACC-12. I would also like to mention my wonderful secretary, **Barbara Stanford-Tuck**, who works with me and all my myriad tasks and correspondence. The Anglican Church in Canada has seconded Canon **Eric Beresford** to the Anglican Consultative Council to co-ordinate our efforts in Technology and Ethics and we look forward to receiving Eric's report during this Council meeting.

Tribute to the Standing Committee Members Who Are Retiring

At this meeting of the Council six of the seven members of the ACC

Standing Committee will be retiring. This Standing Committee has been a very active Committee and I would like to say a few words of appreciation about each person. I have already spoken about **Judy Conley**, but I would also like to mention that she has been an excellent liaison person between the Inter Anglican Finance Committee and the Joint Standing Committee. Judy was also very helpful in dealing with St. Andrew's House.

Professor **George Koshy** was for many years the General Secretary of the Church of South India. He brought to the Joint Standing Committee a passion for the poor and the oppressed and a new awareness for many of us in the Anglican Communion of the sub-continent.

The Revd Dr. **Jae-Joung Lee** from Korea has not been able to be an active member on the Standing Committee because of his position in the National Assembly in the government of Korea. However, when Jae-Joung has been present, he has always made significant contributions to the life of the Council representing well the interests of Southeast Asia.

Mr. **Ghazi Musharbash** was put on the Council as an At Large member from Jordan. Ghazi has served as the liaison for NIFCON and he has always been willing to accept responsibilities to Chair different sub-committee groups, including the group which reported on membership to ACC-11 in Dundee.

Mr. **John Rea** from Scotland has had an influential voice on the Joint Standing Committee. He has been very much involved in the Office of the Anglican Observer at the United Nations. John has served on each one of the Council Design Groups for both the Dundee as well as the Hong Kong meeting and he has recently been serving on the St. Andrew's House Committee.

Canon **Maureen Sithole** has also been an active member of the Standing Committee, most recently serving as one of the co-Chairs of the Lambeth Conference/Gathering 2008 Committee which was formed as a result of an ACC resolution from Dundee. Maureen has also been the liaison person from the Standing Committee to the Inter Anglican Commission on Mission and Evangelism.

It has been a great pleasure working with each member of the Standing Committee and each in his/her own right has represented you well as members of the Standing Committee. Please take a few moments to say your own personal thanks to each one of these members because they have given much time to represent you on the Standing Committee.

Tribute to Presiding Bishop John Paterson

Since Panama the ACC has been served brilliantly by our Vice Chair, Presiding Bishop John Paterson. Only those of us who have had the privilege to work closely with John on a day by day basis know how much time he has given to all aspects of the life of the ACC. John really believes in the ideals of the ACC and this is evident in John's dedication to this Instrument of Unity. We all thank you, John, for everything you have done for us.

Tribute to Bishop Simon Chiwanga

For the last 18 years Bishop Simon Chiwanga has served the ACC with distinction. Simon served three meetings as a clerical member from Tanzania. In 1990 Simon was elected Vice Chair and then in Panama, Simon was elected the Chair of the Council. While most of us know Simon for his work in the ACC, which has indeed given him an international profile, I have had the privilege of making two Mission Visits with the Compass Rose Society to Tanzania and to the Diocese of Mpwapwa.

It is when one visits Simon's diocese that one is able to see the very fibre of our Chair. Simon's diocese is a rural diocese. There is only one paved road, and as Simon travels to his different parishes he can never go more than five minutes before hitting gravel and frequent potholes. During the rainy season Simon can be blocked off from his diocese for days at a time because the roads become impassable.

Tanzania is the third poorest country in the world yet I have never experienced such enormous generosity. The generosity of Spirit, the absolute sharing of everything. The commitment to improve the quality of life is at the core of life in the Diocese of Mpwapwa. One certainly sees in this Diocese the face of Jesus in the people of God there. The priest and people, those who lead and serve, those who receive from others and are fed are the true body of Christ.

Simon has brought a Tanzanian experience to the life of our Anglican Communion. Those of us who have had the privilege of working with him over the years have grown enormously as we have witnessed his commitment for the work of the Communion. Simon even taught me how to take a shower with one bucket of water, but he has also taught me what Jesus meant when he spoke about the "poor in spirit." Such poverty as described by Jesus in the Sermon on the Mount shows that we need to be fully conscious of the poverty of all human resources, and knowing our need and desire for God. The ACC has been blessed by you, Simon, for you have truly been one of the "founding fathers" of its work. We are all indebted to you for your love and support that you have shown to the Council and to us all. We are all going to miss you, but we are grateful that you have shared so richly with us from the very depth of your personhood and your priesthood.

Tribute to Archbishop George Carey

For nearly eight years I have had the privilege to be your Secretary General. No one could have given me a greater gift in the church than the privilege to serve our global family in this office. Also during this time I have had the honour to assist the Archbishop of Canterbury, George Carey. Therefore it is only fitting that I conclude this Address by extending my deepest thanks and gratitude to the Archbishop for his eleven years as the President of the Anglican Consultative Council. While there will be many public words of gratitude spoken during this meeting, I would like to make my remarks personal.

When I became Secretary General, the Archbishop of Canterbury made a commitment to me during our very first meeting. I remember the day well. It was a Saturday. I had not yet assumed my office, but I had come from Jerusalem for the first meeting of the Design Group for the 1998 Lambeth Conference. I arrived at Lambeth Palace at 9:30. I had no idea where your office was and I was lost in the corridors of Lambeth when all of a sudden you appeared in "mufti" coming down the steps from your residence.

As we began our hour's meeting you said to me, "John, I want you to have total accessibility to me." Throughout our nearly eight years together you have been absolutely true to your word.

Please let me mention but two outstanding gifts you are leaving to us.

The support and encouragement you have given to the Compass Rose Society has been phenomenal. As a result, the Society is strong and on October 9 when we hold our Annual Meeting in London, 104 members from every corner of the world will be coming to say thanks to you and to Eileen. Now we have the responsibility to help the Compass Rose Society "come of age" as we raise the $20,000,000 endowment for the Communion so future generations will be able to grow in independence as they join hands together.

As I travel around the Anglican Communion today there is a far greater awareness of our independence and that we are a family. During your eleven years as Archbishop you have travelled endlessly throughout the Communion sharing our stories. You had prophetic courage when you were in the Sudan, you grieved with the people of Rwanda as you witnessed the horrors of the genocide, you cried with the victims of the Twin Towers in New York, you rejoiced with the people of Hong Kong when they became a new Province. You have had a ministry of presence. You have been the voice of the voiceless. You have walked the corridors of power urging decision makers to honour the right of every human being.

My last words in this address can only be: thank you for being yourself during these last eleven years, thank you for your gifts, thank you, Archbishop, thank you, Eileen, for your love and care, for your dedication, for your passion as you have supported our great family of Churches, the Anglican Communion. God bless both of you.

Report on the Political Situation in Burundi

—THE RIGHT REVEREND MARTIN BLAISE NYABOHO

Introduction

Next month the country of Burundi will mourn again its people who have been killed (and continue to be) during the past nine years. The political crisis which started on 21 October 1993 has caused so much damage: internally displaced people living in camps, the infrastructures destroyed, vehicles burnt out, an increase of poverty, the inflation of our local currency, etc.

Despite the inauguration of a three-year interim/transitional government on 1 November 2001, the conflict between rebel forces and the army is still claiming the lives of innocent people in the country. The proliferation of arms has not yet stopped. People live in fear and despair.

Is Burundi Heading Towards a Ceasefire?

Under the chairmanship of former President Nelson Mandela, the political negotiations, which have taken over two and a half years, climaxed in the inauguration of an interim/transitional government on 1 November 2001. The rebel groups who are fighting were not invited to be part of the negotiations in Arusha (Tanzania). Therefore, there was no ceasefire.

As I share this with you today, both the rebels and the Government are negotiating in Dar es Salaam. As far as I know, their negotiations will not end tomorrow while people are still being kidnapped, killed and their properties destroyed.

One American asked me in June 2000 during a trip I made to New York City (14 months before the September 11th tragedy), "Does Burundi have diamonds, gold or oil, Bishop Martin?" I answered him frankly that we don't have any of them, but that we have suffering human beings created in the image not of gold but of God. He was astonished by my answer.

That is why the international community doesn't care of what is taking place in our country. As a Church leader, I concluded by telling him that one day God will ask the international community where their brothers and sisters are.

Requests

On behalf of the Province of Burundi, which I represent here, I wish to invite ACC-12 to:

1. Pray with the Church of Burundi for current negotiations to give hope and a durable peace to our people;
2. Help the Church to speak louder to those involved in the conflict in Burundi to stop the killing of people and the destruction of their properties;
3. Join the Church's voice of the international community to discourage the proliferation of arms in the Great Lakes Region in general, and Burundi in particular;
4. Participate in the repatriation, reconstruction and rehabilitation programme which is ahead of us once peace has been restored.

Report by the Department of Ecumenical Affairs and Studies

—The Reverend Canon David Hamid, Director

Contents

Introduction

At the heart of the constitution of the Anglican Consultative Council can be found explicit reference to tasks pertaining to the ecumenical and doctrinal life of the Communion:

> *To keep before national and regional Churches the importance of the fullest possible Anglican collaboration with other Christian Churches.*
>
> *To encourage and guide Anglican participation in the Ecumenical Movement and the ecumenical organisations, to co-operate with the World Council of Churches and the world confessional bodies on behalf of the Anglican Communion; and to make arrangements for the conduct of pan-Anglican conversations with the Roman Catholic Church, the Orthodox Churches and other Churches.*
>
> *To advise on matters arising out of national or regional church union negotiations or conversations and on subsequent relations with united Churches.*
>
> *To keep in review the needs that may arise for further study, and where necessary, to promote inquiry and research.* (Anglican Consultative Council Constitution 3.2)

The Department of Ecumenical Affairs and Studies is the body within the secretariat of the Communion that is responsible for these aspects of the Council's work. This report highlights the work of the department since ACC-11 in Dundee, Scotland.

The report is divided into two major sections.

Section one contains an *update* on each official ecumenical dialogue or inter-church relationship in which the Anglican Communion is engaged at the world level, and includes comments on regional ecumenical developments within each relationship as appropriate. Also in this section is information on relations with Churches in Communion with the Anglican Communion.

Section two contains a *summary* of the work of the two Commissions for which this department is responsible: the Inter Anglican Standing Commission on Ecumenical Relations (IASCER), and the Inter Anglican Theological and Doctrinal Commission (IATDC).

Appendix A is the final report of the Anglican-Lutheran International Working Group (ALIWG) which is being circulated for information at this stage, as it will be dealt with in detail by IASCER (not included in this volume). Appendix B is the Statement and Action plan resulting from the historic meeting of Anglican and Roman Catholic Archbishops and Bishops in May 2000 (not included in this volume).

Appendix C is the Communion-wide study of the ARCIC report *The Gift of Authority* which was mandated by ACC-11 and prepared by IASCER (not included in this volume). Appendix D provides a complete report of the work of the first two meetings of IASCER and includes a list of acronyms (not included in this volume).

The staff of the department consists of the Director of Ecumenical Relations and Studies, the Revd Canon David Hamid, a Personal/Programme Assistant, Mrs Christine Codner and a Programme/Research Assistant, Ms Frances Hiller. On occasions as the workload has demanded we have been grateful for the assistance of Ms Rosemary Palmer and Mr Matthew Davies.

The work of ecumenical or theological dialogue is by nature collaborative. Close co-operation and co-ordination is thus maintained with the Archbishop of Canterbury's Officer for Ecumenical Affairs, with the Ecumenical Officers throughout the Communion, and with colleagues of other Churches and Communions. Work related to the Doctrine Commission is in collaboration with the Revd Dr Philip Thomas, who assists the Chairman of that Commission, the Rt Revd Stephen Sykes.

The work that is undertaken by the department is wholly dependent upon the contributions of the experts, theologians, church leaders and volunteers who participate in the commissions and dialogues. The Communion is indebted to the many gifted leaders whose dedication to the ecumenical and doctrinal work of the Church is rooted, not in a mere intellectual interest, but in a conviction that the visible unity of the Church (and the unity of the Communion, which is the particular concern of the Doctrine Commission) is necessary for the Church to fulfil its mission faithfully: that such unity is God's plan.

A former president of the Vatican's Pontifical Council for Promoting Christian Unity, Cardinal Johannes Willebrands, said in a visit to Toronto Canada, "Ecumenism is not an effort, generous but short-sighted, to reunite divided Christians *at all costs.* Its specific purpose is not "reunion" resulting from human efforts, mainly political or sentimental. It is something very different; it is *the unity which God wills.*"

Ecumenical and Inter-Church Relations

Anglican-Baptist Relations

Anglican-Baptist International Conversations (ABIC)

Following the Lambeth Conference Resolution IV.15 which mandated a formal international dialogue with the Baptist World Alliance (BWA), the Anglican-Baptist International Conversations were established in 2000. The goal of the ABIC is not visible unity or full communion as with other international dialogues, but is more limited for this initial stage of international talks. The objectives are: to enable Anglicans and Baptists to learn from each other and to deepen mutual understanding of the relationships between the two Communions; to share understandings of the faith and to work towards a common confession of the Apostolic Faith; to identify issues of doctrine and of the nature of the Church to be explored in possible future conversations; to seek ways to co-operate in mission/community activities and increase common witness to the Gospel. The design of the conversations permits a wide sharing in regional meetings. A continuation group of 3 aside plus the secretaries has met or will meet in a total of 5 regions of the world, in each place calling together a larger gathering of local Anglicans and Baptists. The Anglican co-chairman is the Revd Dr Bruce Matthews. At end of the 5 years of conversations the continuation group will draft a report for the BWA Congress and the ACC of 2005. Issues for future formal theological dialogue may emerge from the regional meetings.

The European round of the ABIC was held at Norwich Cathedral from 21–24 September 2000. Baptists and Anglicans from England, Germany, Ireland, Italy, Scotland and Wales took part. Europe is the birthplace of both the Anglican and Baptist traditions, so much of the focus was on the historical ecclesiological self-understanding of the two churches. Questions related to continuity/apostolicity, the place of statements of faith or confessions, Christian initiation, Eucharist, recognition/reconciliation, the meaning of "local church", the nature of oversight, and approaches to mission, evangelism and pastoral care were explored.

The Asia/Oceania round was held from 18-21 January 2001 in Yangon, Myanmar at the Myanmar Baptist Convention headquarters. The continuation committee was joined by Anglicans and Baptists from India, Myanmar, Korea, Hong Kong, and Australia. Anglican and Baptist representatives gave an overview of the life of their respective communions in Asia revealing their missionary nature. Presentations were given on Baptist identity and issues that define Asian Baptist life, and a reflection on *The Virginia Report* from an Australian perspective. Papers on *episcope* and Christian initiation from representatives of the Church of North India brought a valuable dimension to the conversations.

The significance of holding the meeting in Myanmar was clear from the opening dinner to which came over 100 church leaders from throughout the country. The group was also able to attend the opening worship of the Week of Prayer for Christian Unity which was held at the Anglican Cathedral in Yangon.

The African round was hosted by the Kenya Baptist Convention in Nairobi, Kenya from 24–26 January 2001. in Norwich (for Europe) in 2000 and Yangon (for Asia/Pacific) in 2001. Participants from Ghana, Kenya, Nigeria, South Africa, Tanzania, Uganda and Zimbabwe and joined the members of the continuation group. Presentations were given on aspects of baptism, local Anglican-Baptist relations, and mission and ministry in the African Church. The plenary discussion drew together some rich insights from the African context into the themes which emerging from previous regional conversations, namely: continuity and story; recognition and acceptance; contextual mission and ministry; baptism and Christian initiation; membership and community; oversight and episcope; and confessing the faith. Many common concerns from Baptists and Anglicans were shared with regard to the experience of "partnership" with overseas Churches. In reflecting on the story of Baptist and Anglican life in Africa, many perspectives were shared on the place of the ancestors in the faith, on the prophetic role of the Church in society, and on Church growth, evangelism and Church planting. A special presentation was given on a joint Baptist-Anglican programme "Kids to Kids" which provides for approximately 60 of Nairobi's street children every day.

The next phases of the conversation will take place in the Latin America region (Chile), the Caribbean region (Bahamas) both in 2003. In 2004 the final regional consultation for North America will take place. A report will be drafted for submission to the authorities of the two Cmmunions in 2005.

The BWA is a fellowship of 192 Baptist unions and conventions comprising a membership of more than 42 million baptised believers and a community of more than 100 million Baptists world-wide.

Anglican-Lutheran Relations

Lutheran World Federation (LWF)

Since the last meeting of the ACC in Dundee, closer working relationships have been nurtured between the LWF and the Anglican Communion.

The Anglican Communion was represented at the historic signing of the Joint Declaration on the Doctrine of Justification between the Lutheran World Federation and the Roman Catholic Church which took place in Augsburg, Germany, on 31 October 1999. Anglicans have been present at follow up consultations hosted by the LWF and the Roman Catholic Church looking at the wider ecumenical implications of this Joint Declaration.

Bishop Christian Krause, President of the Lutheran World Federation, visited the Archbishop of Canterbury, at Lambeth Palace in October 2001. The two leaders were reviewed developments in world-wide Anglican-Lutheran relationships and noted the particular progress made in Europe, the USA and Canada, together with the initiatives in Africa, Australia and Brazil. In addition, the Archbishop and the President were able to reaffirm their churches' commitment to the global south where both Communions are growing significantly.

As a result of a recommendation from the Anglican-Lutheran International Working Group (see below) annual joint staff meetings have been instituted between the ACO and the LWF. Representation at the other communion's meetings are now a common feature of our life, underlining the strong links between the two church families.

Anglican-Lutheran International Working Group (ALIWG)

As a result of resolution IV.16 of the 1998 Lambeth Conference the ALIWG was formed in 1999. Three meetings have been held: in Alexandria, Virginia USA (2000), Sk·lholt, Iceland (2001) and Porto Alegre Brazil (2002). The working group has completed a report which is found in Appendix A.

It is a report of a rather technical nature, examining in particular the consistency among the various regional Anglican-Lutheran Agreements. Some specific recommendations to both Communions are contained therein. The Inter Anglican Standing Commission on Ecumenical Relations will review this report and its recommendations and present any items for action by the Anglican Communion to the next meeting of the Joint Standing Committees of the ACC and the Primates.

All Africa Anglican-Lutheran Commission (AAALC)

A series of Anglican-Lutheran consultations and preparatory meetings held in Harare 1992, Johannesburg 1993 and 1997 and Harare in 1999, sponsored by the Anglican Communion and the LWF have led to the establishment of the AAALC. This initiative has been stimulated by the progress in ecumenical relations between Anglicans and Lutherans globally, as well as by a conviction by Church leaders that common service and a visibly united Christian Church will strengthen witness to the Gospel in the African continent.

The inaugural meeting of the commission was held in Nairobi, Kenya from 1–4 April 2001 which agreed a **plan of action**:

1. that in countries where Anglican-Lutheran cooperation is already experienced this should be intensified and nurtured towards official relationships of communion;

2. that in countries where Anglicans and Lutherans coexist but where there are no bilateral relationships between the two churches, that immediate contact be encouraged between the appropriate authorities at the national level to consider ways of cooperation;

3. that in both these cases, the following steps be taken by the churches involved:

a. to undertake education at grass-roots level to bring about knowledge and understanding of each church as to history, liturgy, doctrine, church order and polity;

b. to exchange visits, extend mutual invitations to each other's synods, hold discussions, and engage in other forms of getting to know each other;

c. to plan and carry out together joint theological education, lay training, women's and children's programs as a way of deepening cooperation between the two churches;

d. to take action in these matters at provincial/synodical level at the appropriate time.

The plan of action is designed to address the fact that in many places on the continent, Anglicans and Lutherans are not aware of each other's churches and contact at every level needs to be nurtured. In addition, official commitment by the authorities of the churches is being sought to broaden the ownership for this ecumenical dialogue beyond interested individual church leaders.

The next meeting of the Commission is scheduled for Addis Ababa, Ethiopia in 2003.

Anglican-Lutheran Developments in Other Regions

Although not directly involved in the proposals in Canada, the USA, Europe and Australia, the Anglican Communion Office has been communicating regularly with the Ecumenical Officers of the relevant Provinces and providing support when requested. The report of ALIWG outlines the progress in these regions in more detail.

THE UNITED STATES OF AMERICA—CALLED TO COMMON MISSION

The General Convention of ECUSA in 1997 gave overwhelming approval to ECUSA to the *Concordat of Agreement* with the Evangelical Lutheran Church in America (ELCA). The Church Wide Assembly of the ELCA subsequently failed to approve the agreement by six votes short of the required two-thirds majority. A new drafting team then presented a revision of the Concordat, *Called to Common Mission*, which was approved by the ELCA in August 1999. The agreement was celebrated on the feast of the Epiphany 2000 in the National Cathedral in Washington DC. At the heart of this agreement is a recognition by Lutherans and Anglicans on the doctrine of "apostolic succession"—an ongoing faithful proclamation of Christ. Anglicans bring to the relationship the "historic episcopate,"—a succession of bishops as a sign of apostolicity.

Small pockets of opposition to the historic episcopate in ELCA persist, resulting in a decision by that Church to allow ordination by pastors only "in unusual circumstances". ECUSA has expressed clear opposition to this development as contrary to the agreement. There have been no ordinations in the ELCA by pastors only, to date.

CANADA—WATERLOO

The Waterloo Declaration was overwhelmingly approved by the National Convention of the Evangelical Lutheran Church in Canada (ELCIC) and the General Synod of the Anglican Church in 2001. Full communion was inaugurated at a Eucharist celebrated on 8 July 2001 in Waterloo, Ontario. A Joint Commission has been established which will nurture the new relationship and report regularly to the governing bodies of both churches.

EUROPE—PORVOO

The Porvoo Contact Group continues to oversee the implementation of the Porvoo agreement signed by the 4 Anglican provinces in Great Britain and Ireland and 6 Lutheran Churches in the Scandinavian and Baltic region. It is now 10 years since the agreement was reached and this anniversary will be celebrated in October in Helsinki. Relationships are deepening through diocesan twinnings (over 50 Anglican and Lutheran dioceses have active links) a common prayer cycle, a hymn collection, mutual participation in episcopal consecrations, and consultations of Primates and Church Leaders. *A Contact Group* fosters implementation of the Porvoo agreement. The Church of Sweden is planning a Porvoo youth encounter in 2004. In 2000, the *Igreja Lusitana* (Portugal) and the *Iglesia Episcopal Reformada de España* (Spain) were deemed to be included in the agreement by virtue of their metropolitan being the Archbishop of Canterbury.

EUROPE—MEISSEN

The *Meissen Common Statement* is an agreement between the Church of England and the Evangelical Church in Germany, (which includes Lutheran, Reformed and United Churches). A fourth Meissen Theological Conference, was held in March 2001 but was unable to resolve differences about the historic episcopate. The Church of England is to do further work on this issue and on Anglican requirements for the full interchangeability of ministers. Papers from the third and fourth conferences will be published this year in a bilingual volume to initiate a period of study and reception before the next round of dialogue. The Meissen Commission has produced a report on the second quinquennium of its work in implementing the Meissen Agreement, together with recommendations for 2002–2007.

EUROPE—REUILLY

Conversations between the British and Irish Anglican Churches and the French Lutheran and Reformed Churches have lead to an agreed text

The Reuilly Common Statement. This agreement is more of a "Meissen" rather than a "Porvoo" type since it does not entail full interchangeability of ordained ministers. (The Lutheran and Reformed Churches involved are not episcopal churches). Public celebrations were held last summer in Canterbury and Paris to mark the approval of the *Reuilly Common Statement* by all four French Lutheran & Reformed Churches and by the Anglican provinces of Britain and Ireland. A Contact Group has been appointed to oversee implementation, and held its first meeting in May 2002.

AUSTRALIA—COMMON GROUND

The Anglican Church of Australia and the Lutheran Church of Australia are considering a report of their bilateral dialogue: *Common Ground: Covenanting for Mutual Recognition and Reconciliation.* The approach in Australia is to set realistic goals and enable national covenanting processes between Anglican and Lutheran Churches, allowing more concrete negotiations to take place under this umbrella in areas where that is possible. The proposal distinguishes "national covenant", "local agreements" and "regional agreements". The text recognises that the goal of full communion is held in view for the long term. The Lutheran Church in Australia is an associate member (not a full member) of the LWF. It is not an episcopal church. IASCER has done an analysis of *Common Ground* at the request of the Anglicans in Australia.

Anglican-Methodist Relations

Since the publication in 1996 of the report of the Anglican-Methodist International Commission (AMIC) *Sharing in the Apostolic Communion* there has been little formal Anglican-Methodist activity at the international level. The 1998 Lambeth Conference recommended the establishment of a Joint Working Group with the World Methodist Council (WMC). This recommendation was considered by the last meeting of IASCER which agreed to approach the WMC with a view to establishing a preparatory phase of an international dialogue which will prepare the agenda and clarify the questions for such a working group.

Regional dialogues with Methodists can be found in England (with the Methodist Church of Great Britain), Scotland (a multilateral dialogue), Wales (multilateral), South Africa (multilateral) and New Zealand. Talks are being considered in Canada with the United Church of Canada, and in the USA with the United Methodist Church. (ECUSA has a multilateral conversation which includes Methodists, through the "Churches Uniting in Christ" (CUIC) process).

The Anglican-Methodist in England has published a report *An Anglican-Methodist Covenant* which, has now been received and commended for study and response throughout the respective congregations of the Church of England and the Methodist Church Great Britain authorities.

Anglican-Oriental Orthodox Relations

Anglican-Oriental Orthodox International Commission (AOOIC)

Under the co-chairmanship of His Eminence Metropolitan Bishoy of Damiette of the Coptic Orthodox Church, and the Rt Revd Dr Geoffrey Rowell, Bishop of the Church of England diocese of Gibraltar in Europe, Anglican and Oriental Orthodox representatives, delegated by their churches, met in Midhurst, England from 27–30 July 2001 to consider the recommendations of the Lambeth Conferences of 1988 and 1998 and decisions of Oriental Orthodox Churches that the Anglican-Oriental Orthodox dialogue be upgraded from a Forum (1985–1993) to a Commission.

At this preparatory meeting delegates noted that the Churches of the Anglican Communion and the Oriental Orthodox Churches have enjoyed a long history of cordial relations and pastoral contact in many regions of the world. They received information on scholarship and exchange programmes aimed to encourage contact between Oriental Orthodox and Anglican Churches and expressed their appreciation for the ways these programmes enrich mutual understanding.

The delegates affirmed that the time is now right to seek agreement in faith by addressing theological issues of common interest and concern, as part of the response to our Lord's great intercessory prayer, that His disciples might be one as He and the Father are one "that the world might believe". It was thus agreed to establish the Anglican-Oriental Orthodox International Commission. The delegates also established the agenda, and clarified matters related to the membership, procedures, methodologies and timetable for the new Commission.

The agenda for the Commission includes topics related to Christology and Pneumatology, authority in the Church, Holy Scripture and Holy Tradition, ecclesiology, sacraments, moral issues, the place of women in the Church and matters of concern to the Churches in their mission and pastoral care. The Commission will begin to work immediately on Christology in the hope of preparing an agreed statement, so that Anglicans and Oriental Orthodox may be able to proclaim formally a common faith in the Incarnation of our Lord Jesus Christ.

The first plenary meeting will be held in Armenia from 5–10 November 2002, at the invitation of the Catholicosate of All Armenians.

The family of Oriental Churches includes: The Coptic Orthodox Church, the Syrian Orthodox Church, the Armenian Apostolic Church, the Ethiopian Orthodox Church and the Malankara Orthodox Syrian Church. In many countries Anglicans and members of these Churches experience a close pastoral and ecumenical relationship and several national bilateral dialogues are flourishing.

Anglican-Orthodox Relations

International Commission of the Anglican-Orthodox Theological Dialogue (ICAOTD)

The present work of the ICAOTD dates from 1989 when a reconstituted commission met in Finland and drew up a work plan, commonly referred to as the "New Valamo" scheme which sets before the commission a series of topics related to the doctrine of the Church. A 1987 joint communiqué from the Archbishop of Canterbury and the Ecumenical Patriarch affirmed that "the dialogue is aimed at nothing less than that visible and sacramental unity which Christ wills for his One, Holy, Catholic and Apostolic Church".

Good progress is being made on the New Valamo workplan, on some very complex and potentially divisive subjects for both Communions. Several interim agreed statements have completed: *The Trinity and the Church, Christ, the Spirit and the Church and Christ, Humanity and the Church (Parts 1 and 2); Episcope, Episcopos and Primacy; and Priesthood, Christ and the Church.* The Commission is now in the midst of discussions on the ordination of women to the priesthood and the episcopate, and continuing its exploration of non-priestly ministries in the Church. Issues still to be addressed include reception by the Church of new ideas and practices, and questions regarding heresy and schism in the Church.

The Commission hopes to complete the agenda set in New Valamo and publish the agreed statements for study in the churches before the next Lambeth Conference.

Anglican/Orthodox Informal Talks

Annual informal talks continue to be held with representatives of the Ecumenical Patriarchate and the Anglican Communion. These are vital meetings which allow both Communions to share concerns of a pastoral and practical nature, and which monitors the progress of the theological dialogue.

Anglican-Roman Catholic Relations

Anglican/Roman Catholic International Bishops' Consultation

An Anglican-Roman Catholic International Bishops' Meeting took place in Mississauga, Canada, 14–20 May, 2000, under the presidency of Cardinal Cassidy of the Pontifical Council for Promoting Christian Unity and Archbishop Carey. This unique meeting has moved the official relationship between the two Communions to a new plateau, reflected in the title of the bishops' statement *Communion in Mission.* An action plan was also approved. Bishops or Archbishops were present from Churches in Aotearoa New Zealand, Australia, Brazil, Canada, England, Ireland,

India, Nigeria, Papua New Guinea, Southern Africa, Uganda, United States and the West Indies.

The meeting was the result of a proposal which arose out of the Archbishop of Canterbury's visit to the Pope in 1996. One result of the Mississauga meeting is the establishment of the International Anglican-Roman Catholic Commission for Unity and Mission (IARCCUM) to complement the work of the Anglican-Roman Catholic International Commission (ARCIC), which, since 1970, has been engaged in the official theological dialogue between the two Communions. A booklet containing the key addresses, papers and outcomes of the Mississauga meeting will be published in the near future.

International Anglican-Roman Catholic Commission for Unity & Mission (IARCCUM)

The inaugural meeting of this high-level group, established as a result of the Mississauga Meeting of Bishops, was held from 20–24 November 2001. Conversations with the Archbishop of Canterbury and Pope John Paul II were key moments in the meeting which began in London and continued in Rome. Archbishop Carey shared his vision for the work of the new Commission: to support further progress towards visible unity between the Anglican Communion and the Roman Catholic Church, in order to strengthen the mission of the Church of Christ. The Pope similarly urged the Commission to intensify the efforts to deepen the communion we now share and to be led by the Holy Spirit in our journey towards full visible unity.

Cardinal Walter Kasper, the President of the Pontifical Council for Promoting Christian Unity explored with the Commission the proposal for the preparation of a joint declaration which would formally and publicly express the degree of agreement that exists between Anglicans and Roman Catholics and consolidate the results of more than thirty years of dialogue. The Cardinal also underlined the key role this Commission will play in guiding and promoting the response and reception of the ARCIC agreed statements throughout the Churches. The Commission began intensive work on these priority areas as well as on the development of strategies to translate the degree of spiritual communion that has been achieved into visible and practical outcomes. Three subgroups have undertaken work throughout the past year on: (a) the preparation of a common statement; (b) reception of and response to agreements; and (c) ways to enhance visible and practical co-operation.

One possible avenue for greater co-operation which was explored during the meeting in Rome is in the field of inter-faith relations, which was emphasised in a consultation with Bishop Michael Fitzgerald, the Secretary of the Pontifical Council for Inter Religious Dialogue. Amidst the tensions and conflicts which make our present world context so fragile, the members affirmed the importance of deepening our joint commitment to work together in social and cultural spheres for the defence of human dignity and the promotion of justice and peace.

The sessions included extensive time of prayer and reflection, along with the renewal of baptismal vows.

Anglican-Roman Catholic International Commission (ARCIC)

ARCIC continues its study on the place of the Blessed Virgin Mary in the life and doctrine of the Church. This is the last remaining item on its agenda from the original mandate agreed by Pope Paul VI and Archbishop Michael Ramsey in 1966. The Commission in this study has undertaken a comprehensive survey of matters related to Mary in the Scriptures, Patristic though, Medieval, Reformation and post-Reformation periods, including much material from Anglican authors of the 16th and 17th centuries. A preliminary draft of an agreed statement has been prepared and redrafting is underway to bring this work to a more mature stage.

ARCIC also produced a background paper, highlighting key elements from the past 30 years of its work, as a resource for the international meeting of Anglican and Catholic bishops which took place in May 2000.

In 1998, ARCIC completed a report called *The Gift of Authority: Authority in the Church III* which was published in 1999. ACC-11 passed a resolution on this report and the Inter Anglican Standing Commission on Ecumenical Relations has accordingly prepared a study packet which has been circulated to provinces and churches. (The study packet originally appeared as Appendix C but is not included in this volume.)

Anglican/Roman Catholic Informal Talks

Annual informal talks continue to be held between the Vatican and the Anglican Communion to share concerns of a pastoral and practical nature which arise from time to time in various places around the world. These talks also provide an opportunity to co-ordinate the complementary activities of ARCIC and IARCCUM.

World Council of Churches (WCC)

Joint Working Group (JWG)

The director is a consultant to the JWG which, since 1965, has been the principal instrument for co-operation and joint work between the WCC and the Roman Catholic Church. The WCC fellowship includes over 342 Anglican, Orthodox, Old Catholic, Protestant and Pentecostal Churches, including 34 Anglican Churches. The Roman Catholic Church, the largest Christian body is not a member. There are annual plenary meetings of the JWG, and studies are presently under way on the "ecclesiological consequences of baptism", "theological anthropology", "national and regional councils of churches", and "the nature and purpose of ecumenical dialogue", as well as ongoing monitoring of issues of pastoral concern such as mixed marriages.

Relations with Evangelical and Pentecostal Churches

The director has been part of the continuation committee which is carrying forward the proposal to establish a "Forum of Christian Churches and Ecumenical Organisations". The idea of a Forum, first suggested in the mid-1990s, grew out of a concern that has been growing in different parts of the Church to bring more voices into the search for the reconciliation and cooperation of Christians and their churches. The Forum is understood as a process of bringing Christians from around the world to a common table in an informal atmosphere; it is not to be another organization. Its stated purpose is "to create an open space in which representatives from a broad range of Christian churches and interchurch organizations, which confess the triune God and Jesus Christ as perfect in His divinity and humanity, can gather to foster mutual respect, to explore and address together common challenges".

At the last consultation at Fuller Theological Seminary, two members of IASCER represented the Anglican Communion: Archbishop Drexel Gomez (West Indies) and the Revd Sarah Rowland Jones (Wales). Among the concerns that surfaced and were frankly discussed were the following: the problems of different approaches to the Scriptures; the place of tradition, often unacknowledged, in the different churches; the need to understand each other's use of Christian vocabulary; the movement of the Spirit in today's world; proselytism and religious freedom; and the new cooperation between churches who are in dialogue with each other or are together suffering persecution. Panels and plenary discussions addressed two issues: one session looked at evangelisation from a variety of perspectives; another focused on breakthroughs to interchurch relationships, as well as barriers to reconciliation.

Churches in Communion

Old Catholic Churches of the Union of Utrecht

A relationship of communion has existed for a number of years between the Churches of the Anglican Communion and the Old Catholic Churches of the Union of Utrecht, by means of the 1931 Bonn Agreement. Both families of Churches continue their commitment to deepen the communion between them, including ways of taking counsel and making decisions together.

The Old Catholic Bishops' Conference has sent a participant to be part of the Anglican-Lutheran International Working Group, to be part of the

Anglican team, thereby demonstrating the importance of holding together existing relations of communion as new relationships develop. A similar arrangement has been suggested regarding the possible participation of an Old Catholic theologian in the Anglican-Orthodox dialogue, particularly as that dialogue is reaching a crucial stage of discussions on the ordination of women to the priesthood and the episcopate. (The Department of Ecumenical Affairs and Studies co-sponsored the translation into English of the Old Catholic-Orthodox dialogue *Bild Christi und Geschlecht* which has made some remarkable progress towards agreement on the ordination of women. The translation will appear shortly in *Anglican Theological Review*).

In recent years the Union of Utrecht has experienced some strain as some member Churches move to ordain women. The Germans, Austrians, Dutch and Swiss Churches now ordain women priests but the Polish National Catholic Church (PNCC) has made it clear that it is not in communion with Old Catholics who do so, but it nevertheless remains in the Union of Utrecht. Several years ago, the PNCC broke communion with the Anglican Church of Canada and ECUSA on similar grounds, but has not declared any alteration in relationships with the Church of England nor with any other Anglican province.

The number of Old Catholics faithful is about 300,000.

Anglican/Old Catholic International Co-ordinating Council (AOCICC)

ACC-9 mandated the formation of an Anglican-Old Catholic Co-ordinating Council specifically to deepen the relationship formed through the Bonn Agreement. It has a three-fold mandate: (1) to nurture the growth in communion between the Churches of the Anglican Communion and the Union of Utrecht; (2) to address questions of co-operation and growth in mission and pastoral care; and (3) to ensure that theological questions of continuing and mutual concern are addressed and studied by joint meetings of Anglican and Old Catholic theologians.

Annual meetings have been held since 1998. The AOCICC has surveyed existing co-operation between Anglican and Old Catholic congregations in continental Europe; monitored the discussions towards addressing the anomaly of overlapping jurisdictions; discussed relations with Roman Catholics, including reflecting on the ARCIC report *The Gift of Authority* (many Old Catholic jurisdictions date from the time that Papal Infallibility was defined by Vatican I in 1870); and the ways that our churches are facing fresh challenges of human sexuality and mission in secular societies. A booklet aimed at informing Anglicans about Old Catholic Churches will be ready for publication shortly.

In 2006 Anglicans and Old Catholics will be seeking ways to celebrate the 75th anniversary of the Bonn Agreement of 1931.

Mar Thoma Syrian Church of Malabar

This Church is rooted in the Syrian Orthodox tradition in South India. Under the influence of CMS missionary activity in the 19th century, a group undertook a conservative revision of its liturgy, although retaining its Orthodox form and ethos. It has been in communion with most Anglican provinces since 1974. Episcopal succession derives from the Patriarchate of Antioch. The Inter Anglican Standing Commission on Ecumenical Relations has requested that a theologian from the Mar Thoma Church participate in its meetings for the next two years, to underscore the importance of this relationship of communion as other ecumenical dialogues are reviewed.

The Mar Thoma Syrian Church of Malabar has from 700,000 to 1,000,000 members.

The Mar Thoma Church is itself in communion with another smaller Church (about 10,000 members), also of Syrian Orthodox origin and tradition, the Malabar Independent Syrian Church of Thozhiyoor. This church originated from in the late 18th century when a Syrian prelate consecrated a local monk as bishop who was not accepted by the Malankara Metropolitan. Mar Basilios the present Metropolitan visited the UK recently and is seeking to establish closer relations of communion with Anglicans.

Iglesia Filipina Independiente (IFI)

The IFI is also known as the Philippine Independent Church, and originated in a struggle in the Philippines against Spain at the end of the 19th century. It was formally established in 1902 and is thus celebrating its centenary this year. The IFI received episcopal succession from ECUSA, and full communion was established with Churches of the Anglican Communion, on the basis of the Bonn Agreement, in the 1960s. The IFI has 30 dioceses and over 6,000,000 members. There is presently no formal body to co-ordinate Anglican-IFI relations, but IASCER intends to invite a theologian from this Church to be part of its meetings from 2004–2006.

Inter Anglican Commissions

Inter Anglican Standing Commission on Ecumenical Relations (IASCER)

IASCER reviews and discusses all the present international dialogues involving Anglicans, and receives information on, and advises churches on provincial and regional initiatives towards unity with other Christians. Two meetings have been held, in Nassau in 2000 and Cape Town in 2001. Three working groups carry forward detailed study on some general issues which touch upon several dialogues: Communion with and within the Anglican Communion; Holy Orders; Ecclesiology and Communion and Anglican identity and coherence in dialogue. The members of the Commission are drawn from each international dialogue involving Anglicans, including the multilateral dialogue of Faith and Order. Additional consultants bring particular regional or theological expertise. Cross appointments from the Doctrine Commission and the Liturgical Consultation ensure coherence with the work of these bodies.

The Inter Anglican Theological and Doctrinal Commission (IATDC)

The Archbishop of Canterbury set up a new Inter Anglican Theological and Doctrinal Commission in 2001. This body is comprised of prominent theologians from around the Anglican Communion. The chairman of the Commission is the Rt. Revd Professor Stephen Sykes, Principal of St John's College, Durham, England.

The Commission was given the mandate to study themes related to the nature and basis of *communion* and the implications of membership in a fellowship of Churches in communion with the See of Canterbury. The work will thus deepen and extend the findings of the previous Commission that produced *The Virginia Report* for the 1998 Lambeth Conference.

The first meeting was held from 14 to 18 September 2001 in Wimbledon, England. It was originally scheduled to be held at Virginia Theological Seminary (VTS), in Alexandria Virginia, on the outskirts of Washington DC. The devastating events of 11 September 2001 required a transfer of the venue to England, as many members were either passing through London *en route* to the USA, or beginning their journey in the United Kingdom. Due to the disruptions in air travel, and the pastoral commitments of those based in the United States, the Commission had to proceed in the absence of some members. This was far from ideal conditions for the inaugural meeting of the new Commission, but work began with as many as could be present.

The study will involve analysis of the limits of diversity within a communion of Churches, some further reflection on collegiality and interdependence, and the implications of being in communion with the See of Canterbury. At the Wimbledon meeting the Commission was able to identify the key questions that will need to be faced in the study of "communion", and to outline the processes and resources that might enable us to move the study forward when the full complement of members are together.

Among the highlights of the first meeting were: an assessment of the way the Churches of the Communion and individual theologians are evaluating

The Virginia Report (1997) of the previous doctrine commission; an analysis of the main proposals in *To Mend the Net*, a volume prepared for and presented to the Primates' Meeting in 2001 and referred by that meeting to the IATDC; the consideration of the concept of "the fundamental articles" of Christian faith

Four key questions which will give direction to the work were identified and these have been circulated to provinces and theological centres around the Communion for response.

The IATDC recognises that complementary work on "communion" is being undertaken by IASCER and relevant papers and study material will be shared between IASCER and IATDC to ensure coherence in the respective studies.

The second meeting of the Commission was held at Virginia Theological Seminary, Alexandria Virginia, USA, from 5–11 September 2002. At the time of preparation of this report, details from the second meeting were not available.

Anglicans and Communion: Six Propositions from the Inter-Anglican Theological and Doctrinal Commission

—+ Stephen Sykes (Chairman)

When the Commission began its work we posed four questions to Anglicans world-wide. A summary of the answers received can be found in *The Communion Study, 2002* (which can also be seen on www.anglicancommunion.org.uk) and our discussion has continued in response to what has been said. A summary of the conversation so far—in deliberately non-technical language—has been expressed like this:

- Communion is God's gift—and it is good for you. Human beings are not meant to exist on their own. It is in fellowship with God and neighbour that we find lasting fulfilment and real life.
- This 'communion' is offered to everyone in the Gospel, to be received by faith, sealed in baptism, and sustained by faithful participation in the family of God's thankful people.
- It is not easy to love your neighbour. In our world it is difficult enough to even meet one. And at times disputes and controversies can threaten to disrupt even the most Christian communities.
- What enables Christian people to walk together in the footsteps of Jesus is their common Faith, which is intimately linked with their shared calling to a corporate life of holiness.
- You cannot often specify in advance what distortions of belief or behaviour could disable the Christian fellowship, but listening to God's Word together, entering in to the story and actions of His salvation, and keeping in touch with other parts of the family, helps sensitise it to things which could be really damaging.
- Anglicans share a 'family likeness' with other families around the world. They do not look much like each other, but when they do happen to get together they realise how much they have in common.
- They all face different problems—although even the same problem can look different when it is viewed from another angle. Some communities are especially worried about personal issues, like homosexuality or whether gender determines who is competent to lead the churches. Most are more concerned about how their fellow Christians

and fellow citizens possibly survive under the threat of prejudice, poverty, violence or the enormity of human suffering.

- Each church has to face its own problems, but in a communion there must always be ways for them to help each other with their tasks. After all, communion is God's gift—and no one church has ever unearthed the full extent of all his promises!

- What many people are wondering at the moment is whether there might be some better ways for Anglican churches to support each other as they discover the significance of their life together. It is not just a matter of money (although that can certainly make a difference). The biggest help we can offer each other is the chance see *ourselves* in a new way. We can learn from each other about good things that God offers his people. We have insights, ideas, convictions to share that can help us on the way, and clarify our sense of common purpose in God's service together. (Philip Thomas, England)

To continue the study process the Commission would like to test SIX PROPOSITIONS, arising from these discussions, which follow. We want to encourage churches, theologians, and individual Anglicans to share something of their own experience, and tell us as frankly as possible how they see the theological issues confronting the Anglican Communion today. Details of how you can do this can be found overleaf.

In the following pages you will find:

- **Six propositions** which summarise essential issues from the Commission's discussions so far;

- **A passage of Scripture** related to each issue;

- **A comment** on the six propositions from individual members of the Commission; and

- **A series of questions** to which we would especially like your reaction.

We are seeking to do our work, not in splendid academic isolation but as an act of positive collaboration with the whole Communion. That is at least one aspect of what is meant by *koinonia*, communion! What we would value is your comments on this material. We will appreciate however much you care to offer to our deliberations. Reaction to the whole approach will be welcomed; responses to each statement would be excellent; but comment on particular issues will be valued too.

From the questions we will particularly value insight into the concrete, everyday experience of your church—Province, diocese, congregation—in celebrating and sustaining the gift of communion. Please send your contribution by 30th June, 2003 to:

The Rt Rev John Baycroft
The IATDC Secretary
Anglican Communion Office
157 Waterloo Rd
London
England SE1 8UT

The Rev Dr Philip Thomas
Assistant to the Chairman
The Vicarage
Heighington
Co Durham
England DL5 6PP

Or by e-mail to: Philip.Thomas@durham.anglican.org

Proposition 1: The koinonia of the Anglican Communion is both greatly enriched, and at times challenged and confused, by the variety of ways of encountering scripture. We bring our whole lives, in our different cultural and personal contexts, to scripture, and from those places open ourselves to 'being read by' scripture.

A passage for reflection: Luke 24. 13–35

As particular members of the Anglican Communion, we bring our contextual, cultural, and personal situations to bear upon the task of 'reading in communion' with others across space and time. Private reading and study of scripture takes place, by implication, within the larger framework of the church's praise of God and proclamation of the Word in common prayer and eucharist.

The Anglican tradition of reading the Bible carries an historic deep respect for biblical scholarship, taking seriously the integrity of the canon, historical contextuality and original languages of the Bible. 'Historical' studies are well complemented by 'theological' interpretations and 'literary' readings. In addition, theologians in many parts of the world have called attention to issues of power and privilege in biblical interpretation and the need for Christians to listen to one another across cultural differences and economic divisions.

The rich variety of material within the canon resists all human attempts to reduce it a flat or uniform agenda. At the same time, the biblical writings are consistent witnesses to the trustworthiness of the triune God and, for all their differences of style, content, and opinion, they are clearly part of one conversation that intends to be open to hear the Word of that one God. A Ghanian parable of individuals and community within the village helps us here: from a distance one sees the people of the village like a forest; only in closer proximity does one see the particular features of each tree. So the art of reading and living under a scripture which is both unified and diverse is an organic part of the vocation to live together within our single, yet richly variegated, Communion. It is within this context that our ongoing and vital debates about the 'authority' of scripture must take place.

A. Katherine Grieb (U.S.)
Esther M. Mombo (Kenya)
N. Thomas Wright (England)

How does the Bible function as a source of authority in setting priorities and resolving disputes in your church?

Proposition 2: Dividing doctrine from ethics not only creates the possibility for serious mistakes in Christian thinking but also diminishes the coherence of the life of holiness which is the Christian vocation.

A passage for reflection: Ephesians 4. 1–6

> In our initial questions to the churches, we asked in what way Christian teachings about moral behaviour are integral to the maintenance of communion. The answers we received were overwhelmingly affirmative. And this indeed is our view. What we call ethical teachings are woven into the fabric of Christian doctrine. Christians are called to die to sin and to rise again with Christ into newness of life (Romans 6.4). The doctrines of the resurrection and of baptism contain a teaching about personal transformation. Indeed the very idea of communion is inseparable from holiness of life, a sharing in the very being of God (II Peter 1.4). It belongs to the integrity of the Church that it teaches the truth that is in Christ Jesus, which is a new way of life (Mark 10.21). That life is no easy option. It involves personal struggle against temptation and a commitment to freedom from oppression. It is taken up truly as a taking-up of the cross (Ephesians 4.20–24). It is simply a mistake to think that 'core doctrine' does not include such teaching (as apparently the Righter Judgement of 1994 does).
>
> + Stephen Sykes (England)

Where do you see Christian doctrine informing or challenging ethical questions arising in your own situation?

Proposition 3: The reality of the incarnation implies that the Gospel is always proclaimed in specific cultures. Inculturation always runs the risk of syncretism, in all cultures without exception. One of the gifts which comes from membership of the Anglican Communion is that other Provinces hold up a mirror to each of us, enabling us to question whether the gospel has bee compromised among us.

A passage for reflection: Acts 17. 16–34

> The Incarnation of Jesus Christ is God's Self-revelation to the world. Jesus' ministry on earth included both the acceptance of a particular culture and a moral confrontation with elements in that culture. When Jesus in turn commissioned his disciples, they too were to pursue the mission, which the Holy Spirit would give them by relating to their society incarnationally. The theological concept of inculturation denotes the process whereby the church becomes incarnated in a particular culture of a people.

Inculturation occur when dialogue is sought at the level of trust between Christian message and praxis *vis-à-vis* local beliefs and values. Thus, as Christianity carries the structures and theology of the church into the conversation, so the same must grow out of local symbols, and, in so doing maintain the cultural and spiritual integrity of the local people. Inculturation, well understood, is openness to a process whereby the Christian gospel is interpreted and reinterpreted in an ongoing process of faithful reciprocity among peoples in the different contexts and cultures of the global church.

However, inculturation is not limited to religious cultural beliefs and practices. In its broadest sense, it includes all endeavours aimed at making the Christian message relevant to the local context. It is also an interaction and integration of the Christian message and socio-political and economic reality. True inculturation entails a willingness to incorporate what is positive, and to challenge what is alien to the truth of the Christian faith. It has to make contact with the psychological as well as the intellectual feelings of the people. This is achieved through openness to innovation and experimentation, an encouragement of local creativity, and a readiness to reflect critically at each stage of the process—a process that, in principle is never ending.

Victor Atta-Bafoe (Ghana)
Luke Pato (South Africa)

What are the issues in your own cultural situation which need to be reconsidered in the light of the gospel?

Proposition 4: Since the beginning of Christianity disputes have arisen in which the truth of the Gospel is seen to be at stake. Not all disputes are of such significance, but some are. In a Communion made up of many different churches, discernment is required to identify what in any particular context are the crucial issues for the life of the Church.

A passage for reflection: Acts 15. 1–35

The Scriptures themselves bear witness to varieties of understanding within the people of God. This diversity of interpretation has sometimes given rise to lively disputes: for instance, in the Hebrew Scriptures, about the obligations of the covenant, both for God and for Israel, or in the New Testament about the demand that Gentile converts to faith in Christ should be circumcised in accord with the Law. In some such conflicts, fidelity to the covenant, or to the Gospel, was seen to be at stake. In others, legitimate diversity of interpretation is reflected in the diversity of Scriptural witness: for instance, in the Hebrew Scriptures there are two versions, with differing emphases, of the pre-Exilic history of Israel, and in the New Testament there are four Gospels, which give four distinctive perspectives on Jesus and the

Gospel. We can therefore expect diversity of practice and of theological interpretation to continue within a communion of churches, especially when the individual churches are reading the Scriptures and practising the Christian faith in hugely different contexts and circumstances. Even within the New Testament, it is clear that some Christians thought others were not being faithful to the Gospel and, on the issue of circumcision, a council was held at Jerusalem to resolve the issue. From the beginning, conciliar processes and conciliar decision making have enabled the Church to identify those issues on which unity must be maintained and to reaffirm its faith in Father, Son and Holy Spirit, often in innovative ways. Within the conciliar process, an openness to the fresh reading of Scripture and of Christian tradition, together with a willingness to listen to one another and so to what the Spirit may now be saying to the churches, has been vital to the faithful proclamation of the Gospel in changing circumstances.

+Paul Richardson (Papua New Guinea and England)
Nicholas Sagovsky (England)

In what ways can church councils, synods, bishops and theologians be seen to maintain a balance between faithfulness to common belief and effective engagement with changing local circumstances?

Proposition 5: Disputes in the Church may be on many issues. Issues of discipline, such as Church teaching on sexuality or the recognition of ministerial orders may be important in some contexts: specific issues of poverty, justice and peace in others. Attention to the concerns of other churches within the Communion is important for putting those of each local church into a proper perspective.

A passage for reflection: II Corinthians 1. 23–2.11

We recognise the importance of addressing together the issue of human sexuality, and of homosexual practice in particular. It has become for many a church-dividing issue. For others the ordination of women to the priesthood and episcopate still lingers as a crisis of faith. For still others, the persistence of white supremacy stifles the spirit of Communion.

We also weigh the importance of the world-wide distribution of wealth, issues of justice in varying contexts, and the goals of peace and the cessation of violence. Often the developed world puts its own hot-button issues in the forefront and misses other equally important issues, such as global warming. Our Communion serves us when it puts all the issues on the table, omitting none.

Paul Zahl (U.S.)
Kortright Davis (West Indies)

How far can membership of a Communion of churches help a local church to discern what are the crucial issues in its own situation?

Proposition 6: At every level, the practice of koinonia requires that there are those who have the responsibility to arbitrate in disputes and conflicts vital to our shared life. Such arbitration gains its force from the ties that bind us together in a voluntary communion. The church then, needs to develop structures for testing, reconciliation and restraint.

A passage for reflection: Matthew 18. 15–17

We should not be surprised when conflicts and disputes occur in the church. Such things arise for many reasons, for example, failure of communication, misunderstandings, jealousy etc. Conflict also occurs because of the sheer richness of the gospel of Christ and the difficulty of deciding amidst a number of possibilities what is the faithful way forward in a particular situation.

In a voluntary society like the church we rely heavily on the ties that bind us together as the body of Christ as a way if resolving our differences and disputes. The church places a high premium on face-to-face relations as the natural means through which it tries to discern what is right, test disputed practices and exercise discipline. Conflict resolution and the kinds of sanctions exercised in the church are thus primarily persuasive compared with those of a coercive and judicial kind.

However, this does not mean that arbitration can be avoided in disputed areas at a level appropriate to the strength and extent of the disputed. Indeed, the church would be failing in its duty if it did not work hard at all levels of its life—parish, diocese, province, region and beyond—to deal with disputed matters, striving for reconciliation and implementing appropriate sanctions when necessary.

The church needs those who will exercise a ministry by which disputes are resolved and structures which allow such arbitration to take place. These structures will be both formal and informal and involve face-to-face relations as befits the community of Jesus Christ.

Stephen Pickard (Australia)
+ Matthew Owadayo (Nigeria)
Bruce Kaye (Australia)

How are disputes addressed and conflicts resolved in the practice of your church?

Please let the IATDC have your comments on the Propositions, and especially tell us how the experience of your church throws light on the accompanying questions. Every contribution, no matter how brief, or comprehensive, will be welcome. Addresses for replies, especially valued before by 30th June, 2003, are given above.

18 SEPTEMBER 2002

InterAnglican Standing Commission on Mission and Evangelism (IASCOME) Interim Report to ACC-12: "Travelling Together in God's Mission"

List of Contents

Executive Summary

A. Introduction

This is an interim report summarising work undertaken by the 21-person Commission at its two meetings since their appointment in 2000.

B. Mandate and Summary of Action so far

This summarises how the Commission has addressed the six aspects of the Mandate given to it by the Council.

C. Major Meetings held and forthcoming with reports on three Conferences

- Encounters on the Road'—Provincial Mission and Evangelism Co-ordinators Conference (Nairobi, Kenya, May 2002). **This very significant Conference, the first of its kind, highlighted a number of mission themes (e.g., the significance of encounter with Islam) identified elsewhere in the Communion. The report and recommendations of this Conference are in Appendices II and III.** The ACC is asked to support a follow-up Conference in 2004.
- **'Transformation and Tradition in Global Mission' Cyprus 12–18 February 2003.** This will be a major gathering of representatives of voluntary and synodical mission organisations from across the Communion, the first since Brisbane 1986.
- **All-Africa HIV/AIDS Consultation, Johannesburg, August 2001.** The AIDS pandemic had been identified as one of the major mission issues facing the Communion. A member of the Commission contributed to the planning of the Conference. The Conference statement 'Our Vision, Our Hope' is in Appendix IV.

D. Tasks Remitted to IASCOME reports on specific issues on which the Commission has been asked to comment

- **'Mission 21'**—The church growth programme developed by the Scottish Episcopal Church.
- **Proposal from the GEM Network** for a network of Anglican Dioceses in Global Mission.
- **NAME**—a network of bishops in mission and evangelism formed at Lambeth 1998.
- **The South to South Movement**—a network of representatives of

Churches in the south that emerged after the Brisbane 1986 Conference.

- **The Anglican Gathering** proposed for 2008.
- **CWME—The ecumenical Commission for World Mission and Evangelism**.
- **The Partners in Mission process**—IASCOME noted that new forms of associating for mission are emerging, taking over from the PIM consultation process.
- **Companion Diocesan Links**—the Commission keeps a watching brief on these connections and how they can be encouraged to develop.

E. Equipping and Formation for Mission

Theological education, training and formation for mission has been long identified as a priority. This section reviews the history of recent discussions, the remit given to the Commission, suggests ways forward and reports that comments have been made to the Primates Strategic Working Party on their initial report. **The ACC is asked to endorse the Commission's role in its work on leadership training and formation for mission.**

F. Some Areas of Concern and Continuing Work

Six broad areas of mission are listed and interim recommendations made for consideration and comment by provinces:

- **Islam and Islamisation**. The theme of encounter with Islam (often in very difficult situations) has run through reports to the Commission of Mission and Evangelism across the Communion. This section focuses particularly on areas of conflict and the challenge to dialogue in such contexts. **The recommendations call for gatherings of those caught up in such situations for mutual support and learning.**
- **Developing Anglicanism: A Communion in Mission**. The section suggests that Anglican identity is to be found in its calling to be a Communion in mission, in which the quality of relationships (koinonia) are key characteristics of the effectiveness the Church, the pilgrim people of God, and of its structures. **ACC is asked to affirm the Commission's developing this thinking**.
- **The Journey towards Wholeness and Fullness of Life**. Reports from around the world identify many threats to life and of the forces of death. Jesus calls us to life—but life through the cross. The section focuses on the role of healing ministry, liturgies of healing, healing of the psyche and the soul (individual and

communal) alongside programmes of peacemaking and conflict resolution. **The recommendations suggest ways the Commission and others might take these forward**.

- **Mission as Justice-Making and Peace-Building**. Based on reports of the role of Anglicans in working for peace and reconciliation, the section looks at violence and the ways Christians in mission express their calling to live in opposition to a culture of violence. **The recommendations to provinces suggest ways in which justice-making and peace-building can be taken forward**.
- **Money, Power and Christian Mission**. Based on reports of how money and power can be used positively but can also be abused and corrupt, the section comments on four aspects of the relationship of wealth and power in the life of the Church and in Christian mission. **Recommendations to provinces highlight the importance of the Global Reporting Initiative Standard as a guide to ethical investment and address issues of corruption in the Church**.
- **Evangelism**. The Commission notes that it has evangelism as a major item for its future agenda.

G. Resolution

A. Introduction

The Inter Anglican Standing Commission on Mission and Evangelism (IASCOME) is unique in that its 21 members are drawn on the nomination of provinces from all regions of the Communion, according to detailed criteria and provide a very wide range of experience of mission and evangelism as well as life within Church and Society. There has been a depth of understanding and fellowship as well as, at times, frank but loving differences of opinion among the members that has proved greatly enriching and supportive—a microcosm of life in communion.

The following report summarises work undertaken at the two meetings held so far—in Johannesburg (South Africa) and St. Andrews (Scotland). In each place we have been warmly welcomed by our host provinces and given vital experience of the life and witness of the Churches through weekend and other visits. We endorse the view of the previous Mission Commission that such on the ground experience is essential to the Commission's work.

In our report:

- we give account of how we have addressed our mandate and report on tasks remitted to us,

- we report on three important Conferences to which we have contributed or organised,
- we highlight our concern about the mission focus at the heart of theological education
- we identify a number of areas of concern and continuing work,
- we list in ***bold italics*** our interim recommendations for comment and endorsement by the ACC and resolutions.

In particular we would draw attention to the reflection that is developing on being a 'Communion in Mission' (Section F2) and our concern to see the thinking found in other documents of the Communion (e.g., the Virginia Report) developed in a more earthed and mission direction.

B. Our Mandate and Summary of Action So Far

In this section we list our Mandate (in bold type) and provide a summary of action taken since the last ACC meeting.

B1. Reporting

- **To report to and receive reports and tasks from the Anglican Consultative Council.**
  We table this interim report.
  We received a report from the Primates Special Working Party on Theological Education established by the Primates, on which two of our members sit. Action arising from this is reported below (Section E).

B2. To oversee mission relationships

- **To facilitate companion diocese and other companionship links throughout the Communion, in accordance with the guidelines for such links.**
  We affirmed the value of this programme and appointed our member from Canada to organise a more intentional promotion and facilitation of this programme, in support of the Lambeth 1998 resolution and in accordance with the guidelines for such links.
- **To work with Anglican networks for mission and evangelism as they currently exist or might emerge in the future.**
  See section below on 'Tasks remitted to IASCOME' (Section D).
- **To facilitate the sharing of resources, both human and financial, throughout the Communion.**
  Conferences that have either taken place or will do so enable connections to be made and complement resource lists published and on the world-wide web.

- **To link, share and critique experiences of capacity building for mission and evangelism.**
  The main contribution has been made through Conferences.

B3. Reflection

- **To engage in theological reflection on mission.**
  See the sections below on Justice-Making and Peace-Building, Wholeness and Fullness of Life, Islamisation, Money and Power (Section F).

- **To be a forum where the provinces and the voluntary and synodical agencies of the Communion share and reflect.**
  IASCOME meetings themselves are such forums. In addition we have convened one conference for Provincial Mission & Evangelism Co-ordinators, with a conference for Mission Organisations to be held in February 2003. One other conference is under consideration.

B4. Priority of Mission & Evangelism

- **To continue the momentum of the Decade of Evangelism.**
  We have convened a conference for Provincial Co-ordinators of Mission & Evangelism (see Appendix III). We intend to reflect further on the nature of evangelism and its place within the mission of the church.

B5. New Structures

- **To encourage the emergence of new and appropriate structures for mission and evangelism.**
  We have encouraged the GEM proposal, and received reports from NAME (Sections D2 and D3). IASCOME has also been in correspondence with the International Fellowship of Parish Based Missiologists and a Consultation of Anglican Contextual Theologians.

- **To liaise with the South-to-South Movement.**
  We have discussed a report from our member from Singapore.

B6. Ecumenical Expression

- **To encourage, monitor and learn from ecumenical expressions of mission.**
  Our Canadian member sits on the Commission for World Mission & Evangelism of the WCC, and reports on and circulates the documents from that body. Our Indian member brings perspectives from the united Church of North India (CNI). The WCC staff person for Evangelism, Carlos Ham, was a theme speaker at our Nairobi Conference (see below). Our members from Ghana and Sudan are employed by ecumenical councils of churches in their own countries. Other members of IASCOME are involved in a myriad of ecumenical conversations and memberships in their own countries.

C. Major Meetings and Conferences Held and Forthcoming

In this section we report on major Communion-wide events organised by the Commission, or in which members have contributed to planning.

C1. 'Encounters on the Road' Nairobi, Kenya, May 6–13, 2002

Sponsored by IASCOME this was the first ever **Consultation of Provincial Co-ordinators of Mission and Evangelism** within the Anglican Communion. It brought together forty representatives from provinces in Asia, the Pacific, Australasia, the Middle East, Central, West, and Southern Africa, North America, the Caribbean, Britain and Ireland. Over two-thirds had never attended an international Anglican Communion consultation before. It was a deliberate follow-up to the Decade of Evangelism. The Conference was funded by special gifts from individuals, congregations, agencies and provinces of the Communion.

There was much exchange of stories, ideas and encouragement in a conference that was full of energy and vitality. A full report of the Consultation is under preparation. **Appendix II** provides a summary report. **Appendix III** lists the major findings and recommendations. These have been circulated to Primates, Provincial Secretaries etc. They have also been considered by the Commission which has agreed how the recommendations should best be taken forward.

An email network has been established to pursue the connections made at the Consultation. Participants have expressed a strong desire to maintain momentum by meeting again and plans are being put forward for a second meeting early in 2004.

C2. 'Transformation and Tradition in Global Mission' Cyprus 12–18 February, 2003

This Conference was recommended by the previous Commission and will be the first gathering of representatives of mission organisations of the Communion since Brisbane 1986. Its aim is to explore new dimensions of our common mission. This Conference is being arranged and organised by IASCOME.

Objectives of the Conference

- To bring together diverse forms of Anglican mission agencies and organisations that express the comprehensive nature of world mission today;
- To bring together the current generation of lay and ordained mission leaders in the worldwide Anglican Communion, to share their experiences;

- To gain a better understanding of contemporary mission issues and changing patterns in mission (for example, outreach to immigrants and web-based evangelism);
- To renew our vision for mission through biblical and theological reflection, worship and prayer;
- To be challenged by new church models in mission and evangelism;
- To encourage the development of new networks among mission organisations, dioceses and parishes in the Communion.

The planning group has prepared a detailed programme. Speakers have accepted. Invitations to mission organisations are in the process of being sent out. It is anticipated that about 150 representatives of voluntary mission agencies, organisations and synodical boards of the Anglican Communion will be present both to look back, learning and reflecting on the past and consider the emerging mission movements and organisations.

The Conference is self-funding but because of problems of funding in parts of the world, a programme of bursaries will be offered.

C3. All-Africa HIV/AIDS Consultation

Along with many other parts of the Communion, the Commission, at its first meeting in Johannesburg identified the HIV/AIDS pandemic as one of the major challenges to the mission of the Communion and so strongly supported the Primate of Southern Africa's initiative, supported by the Primates, to call a conference in South Africa in August 2001 on HIV/AIDS. A member of IASCOME was a member of the planning committee of the conference as well as representing IASCOME at the conference. The report of the conference was tabled at our meeting and discussed.

The Conference had two distinct tracks. Track One for Anglican Communion representatives from all levels of the Anglican Communion across Africa, as well as a delegation of People Living With Aids (PWAs) from a number of African countries.

Delegates participated in sessions to:

- Focus on their own experiences of the HIV/AIDS pandemic
- Articulate a vision around key issues facing their church communities in relation to HIV/AIDS
- Indicate how they believe the worldwide Anglican Communion can best intervene and contribute to addressing the unfolding pandemic.

Track Two was for representatives from partner organisations and included international donor agencies, AIDS service organisations, civil society groups and representatives from government departments. They too were asked to:

- Focus on their own experiences of the HIV/AIDS pandemic
- Articulate a vision of key issues facing their church communities and church partners in relation to HIV/AIDS
- Indicate how they believe that the worldwide Anglican Communion can best intervene and contributed to addressing the unfolding pandemic.

The main purpose of the Conference was to engage the Anglican Communion in a process of strategic planning to guide its response to HIV/AIDS in Sub-Saharan Africa. The outcome of this process was a model of planning that the delegates could adapt and use at parish, diocese or provincial level.

At the end of this conference the Primates from Africa met and commended the work done and resolved to create an AIDS Board in the Council of Anglican Provinces in Africa (CAPA) with the Archbishop of Southern Africa, as chair to ensure that the strategic planning process is implemented in all the dioceses in Africa.

Strategic planning workshops have been run in every diocese of the Church of the Province of Southern Africa. **Appendix IV** consists of the Statement **'Our Vision, Our Hope'** made by the Conference.

D. Tasks Remitted to IASCOME

We list here our action on particular issues remitted to the Commission in its Mandate or by the ACC, Primates Meeting or Joint Standing Committee.

D1. 'Mission 21'

This programme has been developed by the Scottish Episcopal Church to encourage the growth of existing congregations. It has been in use in the Church since 1995. It differs from catechumenal courses like Alpha and Emmaus, which are basic introductions to the Christian faith. One of its unique features is that trained facilitators accompany, support and encourage congregations as they develop programmes of welcome and implement them. The programme was warmly welcomed by ACC-11. It is being piloted in the Church of Ireland and there are plans and funding for it to be used in Uganda. The Commission has received presentations at both its meetings.

D2. Proposal from the GEM Network

The Global Episcopal Mission [GEM] network is a voluntary network of dioceses of the Episcopal Church in the USA committed to international (global) mission. The Joint Standing Committee referred to the Commission a proposal from the Network to accept in principle that a network of dioceses committed to global mission ('Anglican Network of Dioceses in Global Mission') be formed as an official network of the Communion. It also made proposals about acting as the 'enabling agent' for a number of possible initiatives.

The Commission noted that the GEM network is currently solely a network of American Dioceses. It encouraged the network to act as an 'enabling agent' to take soundings among the dioceses of the Communion (e.g., by holding a Consultation) to see whether there was wider support for such a network and what together dioceses across the Communion might set as an agenda, to see what might develop and to keep in touch with the Commission.

Official recognition as a network of the Communion might be considered at a later date.

D3. Network for Anglicans in Mission and Evangelism (NAME)

NAME was formed initially by bishops in Section Two (Mission) of the 1998 Lambeth Conference to seek to support and resource each other in diocesan mission initiatives. Although it applied to ACC-11 for recognition as a formal network of the Communion, ACC-11 decided to defer a decision until a more worked out proposal came forward and the Commission was asked to remain in touch with NAME in the interim.

The Commission at its first meeting received a formal report from NAME and subsequently informally through connections between some of its members and members of NAME. The network has now bedded down and carries out significant practical initiatives with a number of provinces and dioceses of which the following is a key example. Assisting the Council of Anglican Provinces in Africa (CAPA) in its conference with the World Bank on 'The World Bank and the Churches'.

The Commission will continue to remain in touch.

D4. The South to South Movement

The Commission keeps in touch with the 'South to South Movement' through the Bishop of Singapore (a member of the Commission). The movement came out of the 1986 Brisbane Conference to enable representatives of mission work in churches of the Global South to encourage and support each other. Two meetings ('Encounters in the South') have been held—Nairobi (1992) and Kuala Lumpur (1997).

The officers of the Movement had changed and in December 2001 the Chairman (the Most Revd Peter Akinola, Primate of Nigeria), the Treasurer (the Rt Revd Dr Mouneer Anis, Bishop in Egypt) and the Secretary (the Rt

Rev John Chew, Bishop of Singapore) led a review meeting of the movement in Cairo.

The meeting reviewed the two 'Encounters in the South' and noted the positive opportunities for those from the 'non-Western' world to interact. It also noted the organisational inadequacies in terms of follow up and implementation. It was unanimously agreed to broaden contact with Primates and diocesan bishops of the South to gain their views on the continuance of the South-South Encounter and whether to hold a third meeting in 2003 or 2004. After these soundings have been taken a more definite vision and objectives of the South-South movement will be drawn up and presented.

D5. The Anglican Gathering

The Commission has received regular reports of developments in thinking about the gathering proposed for 2008. It has reiterated its concern that the mission of the Communion be the theme of the Gathering. It welcomed the Nairobi Mission and Evangelism Co-ordinators affirmation of the Commission's call for inclusion of mission representatives on the design group.

Recommendation

IASCOME recommends:
that two of its members are members of the Planning Group of this Gathering.

D6. CWME—Conference for World Mission and Evangelism

One of IASCOME's members is a member of the Standing Committee of CWME and keeps the Commission briefed on ecumenical developments in mission as seen through CWME. In particular the Commission has received the draft statement on *Mission and Evangelism in the Modern World* the successor statement to the seminal document *Mission and Evangelism: an Ecumenical Affirmation* and of 1982. It has also heard of plans for the CWME Conference (the latest in the line of world Conferences on Mission since Edinburgh 1910) in February 2005 and will ensure that Anglicans who are invited to that Conference meet together during its course.

D7. The Partners in Mission process—a comment

PIM Consultations—their preparation and their follow up—were important practical bonds of holding together and developing the relational life of the Communion during the 1970s, 1980s and early 1990s until overtaken by the Decade of Evangelism.

The previous Mission Commission commented that 'the Partners-in-Mission process of consultations appears to have slowed to a virtual halt' and provided some reasons for that development. It stressed that the lessons learned should be developed and carried into the new context of the twenty-first century (*Anglicans in Mission: A Transforming Journey*, pp. 66–7).

That slowdown has continued. There has not been a formal provincial Partners in Mission (PIM) Consultation since 2000, although a few informal consultations on specific issues or around specific areas of work have been held.

We observe that new forms of association for mission are beginning to emerge which while not taking over the role of the Partners in Mission process do, in fact, provide networks of connection that flesh out the principles of partnership and companionship identified in previous Mission Commission reports. These networks and consultations are distinct from the 'official' networks of the Communion and do not have nor necessarily require the formal endorsement of the ACC, but the Council needs to be aware of them. The Commission is in touch with them all.

1. **Networks and Consultations initiated through ACC Mission Commissions**
   - The South to South Movement
   - The Provincial Mission and Evangelism Co-ordinators Consultation (2001)
   - The Mission Organisations Conference (2003)
2. **Initiatives independent of the Commission, but with which the Commission is in touch**
   - Network of Anglicans in Mission and Evangelism (NAME)
   - Emerging networks of Anglican Communion Mission Agencies
   - Fellowship of Parish Based Missiologists
   - GEM network proposal to develop a network of dioceses in mission
   - Network of Anglican Contextual Theologians
   - The Global Anglicanism Project

D8. Companion Diocesan Links

The development of formal links between two or more dioceses has been a major feature of the developing koinonia in mission of the Communion over the last twenty years. IASCOME has taken note of the Lambeth Conference 1998 Resolution II: 3 on Companion Dioceses particularly the encouragement to all dioceses to have another diocese as a companion by the time of the next Lambeth Conference. Through its staff in the Anglican Communion Office a list of companion links is maintained and advice offered to dioceses. The Commission has observed that better briefing on companion diocese links could be provided to new bishops and appointed our member from Canada to organise a more intentional promotion and facilitation of this programme, in support of the Lambeth resolution and in accordance with the guidelines for such links.

E. Equipping and Formation for Mission

At the first and second meeting of IASCOME, significant attention was paid to the concerns of equipping and forming God's people for God's mission. We reviewed the background and the work of past mission commissions that referred to theological education and the work proposed in the Action Plan of the Primates' Meeting (Kanuga 2001). We believe that IASCOME has a significant contribution to make to inter-Anglican conversations concerning theological education.

At our first meeting in South Africa (May 2001) we sought clarification about what is meant by theological education, mission formation, and clerical preparation. To assist the Primates Special Working Party on Theological Education, called for in the Action Plan, we articulated the following definitions:

- **Theological education** as an overarching term to describe the study of God in service to the church, the academy and also for public discourse.
- **Mission formation** as the empowering of the people of God in holiness, truth, wisdom, spirituality, and knowledge for participation in God's mission in Jesus Christ through the Spirit. As such mission formation includes leadership training.
- **Clerical preparation** as the specific training of the current and future ordained ministers (bishops, priests, and deacons) for service in and for the church.

IASCOME rejoiced that the Anglican Communion is growing rapidly and changing, especially in the Global South. Anglican Mission and other Commissions over the last two decades have noted that this change has brought about challenges and opportunities for theological education. These realities have led us to ask questions about changing paradigms in theological education that force us to look beyond clerical preparation towards mission formation. This Commission is prepared to ask hard questions about church and theological education because God's mission is larger than promoting Anglicanism.

The Commission recognised that there is a range of theological education models in the Anglican Communion today that are specifically orientated towards the preparation of clergy, often in difficult circumstances. These models need to be supported and encouraged as an important contribution to theological education. Whilst appreciating this tradition, we recognise that this approach does not prepare the whole people of God for mission. And even within the preparation of clergy, the emphases on contextual and local theological understandings of mission and mission practice are rarely present or fully embraced.

We can imagine that some of the current theological education centres and models could be broadened to be centres for mission formation primarily for all God's people including the ordained. And secondarily these centres could offer clergy preparation for the furtherance of mission. If this is to happen effectively, theological education needs to be refocused around a formation that is more than just in-formation. Theological education for mission formation is grounded in and shaped by local contexts, and must be about both personal holiness and the affirming of life in wider society and the world. Such centres might form mission educators who could then advance other formation models. We learned of similar mission educators in such diverse contexts as Scotland (Mission 21) and Papua New Guinea.

We heard about emerging efforts across the Communion to advance theological education committed to mission formation. The Commission commented on and encouraged the development of the consultation for Anglican Contextual Theologians and an International Fellowship of Parish Based Missiologists. We believe that these and other ventures across the Anglican Communion will advance theological education and with strong missiological commitments. We will be inviting others to inform the Commission about similar initiatives.

At our second meeting in Scotland (June 2002) we reviewed recent developments in the Anglican Communion's concern for theological education with particular attention to mission formation. We noted the following:

- Mid-point Review of the Decade of Evangelism held in Kanuga USA in 1995, in their report to Missio, *The Cutting Edge of Mission,* contains a major section on ministry to the whole church, ministry of laity and empowering the whole people of God.

- Missio, (the Mission Commission of the Anglican Communion) in their final report to the Anglican Consultative Council 11, 1999, *Anglicans in Mission: an Transforming Journey,* acknowledged that the Decade of Evangelism highlighted the need for training and formation for leaders in mission and called for a Communion-wide review of such.

- Anglican Consultative Council 11 (Dundee, 1999) accepted the recommendation from Missio in their resolution 11.

- The Chair's Advisory Group to the new Inter-Anglican Standing Commission on Mission and Evangelism in September 2000 suggested a process for the new Commission to follow in fulfilling the Missio generated ACC resolution.

- The Primates Meeting at Kanuga, (March 2001) called for a Special Working Party to analyse and give advice to the Primates on theological education around the Communion. IASCOME was noted as a resource for this work.

- IASCOME produced a communication to the Primates Special Working Party of its priorities for mission formation at its meeting in South Africa (May 2001).

- The Primates Special Working Party met in October 2001 and a report was produced for the Primates Meeting that proposed five recommendations on theological education.

- IASCOME sponsored the Anglican Communion's Provincial Mission and Evangelism Co-ordinators Consultation in Nairobi (May 2002) that noted the strategic priority for training in evangelism.

- IASCOME at its meeting in Scotland (June 2002) heard reports from affiliated networks and projects with related interest in mission formation including: the International Fellowship of Parish Based Missiologists, The Anglican Contextual Theologians Network, and the Global Anglicanism Project.

- Concern for mission formation will be given top priority at the Mission Organisations Conference in Cyprus (February 2003) sponsored by IASCOME.

- On the basis of this review and consideration of the report of the Primates, the Commission made a number of proposals to the Primates Special Working Party on Theological Education about an additional term of reference on Mission Formation and membership of the Action Groups.

Recommendation

IASCOME therefore recommends:
that ACC-12 re-affirms IASCOME's mandate to continue fulfilling the initiatives begun with Missio and ACC 11 with respect to leadership training and formation for mission.

F. Some Areas of Concern and Continuing Work

In the course of our work and the reports we have received from across the Communion we have identified a number of mission issues on which we have begun to reflect. We list them below as an interim summary comment on what we hope to include in our final report. The sections contain a number of recommendations.

F1. Islam and Islamisation

In our review of the relations with people of other faiths, the issue of relations with Muslims was the most widely expressed concern. We heard from the Philippines, Indonesia, Malaysia, Tanzania and in particular Nigeria and Sudan of how Christians experienced their relations with the Muslim community and in particular the effects of growing Muslim presence and Islamisation, often funded from Saudi Arabia, Libya or Iran. The events of September 11 and evidence of international networks of radical Islamist groups, often with strong political, economic and violent agendas, has changed the scene very significantly.

We recognised that the situation is complex and contexts vary greatly. For example in the West where Islamic communities are in a minority the situation is very different from parts of the Middle East where the Church is very small and often overlooked. Situations in Africa where Christianity and Islam often seem to be in competition significantly differ, for example, from Pakistan and South East Asia, where Christian communities are much smaller than Churches in Nigeria and Sudan.

Care needs to be taken to consider each situation on its own terms rather than generalising or drawing universal principles from very particular experiences.

We heard that examples of the practical expression of Islamisation included the increased building of mosques, social and economic institutions and the restriction of construction of churches; discrimination against Christians in employment and in legal cases, the forced marriage of Christian girls by Muslims. There was particular tension for Christian communities in situations where Shariah law has been imposed. There was also reference to political radical Islamist movements and expressions among them of desire for domination of the Christian world-particularly in Africa.

At the 1998 Lambeth Conference the first guideline recommended by the Bishops on the approach of Christians to relations with people of other faiths was:

Commitment to working towards genuinely open and loving human relationships *even in situations where co-existence seems impossible.*

We have heard of situations in which the possibilities of dialogue (a word with which those in such situations found increasing difficulty) were severely constrained by the nature of the Muslim presence. Dialogues at the national or international level, important and welcome as they are, seemed often to have little effect at grassroots level.

We give two examples:

Nigeria. The process of Islamisation has continued since we last met with more states declaring Shariah law. Churches have been burnt and people killed. The introduction of Shariah law is evidence of an on-going process of Islamisation in spite of repeated calls for dialogue, tolerance and peaceful co-existence.

Sudan. The question of Islam and Islamisation in the Sudan has been a serious concern to Sudanese Christians for over four decades ever since Sudanese independence.

It is believed that there is a deliberate effort to Islamise and Arabise Sudan. This is seen in the consistent trends undertaken by successive Sudanese government policies of Islamisation and Arabicisation of the Sudanese populace at all costs. Islamic schools and Islamic Universities have been set up. Arabic is enforced as the official language of the country, and there is a comprehensive programme of what is known as Islamic orientation. The whole educational curriculum for the Sudan has been Islamised. The media, especially radio and TV, are used as tools of Islamisation. The country has been declared an 'Islamic country' with Arabic as the official language. *Sharia Islamia* (Islamic Law) has been introduced and the whole constitution of the Sudan is Islamic in complete disregard of the non-Muslims in the Sudan.

As if all these were not enough, Islam has taken a prominent and almost central place in the civil war that has lasted over four decades in the Sudan. 'Jihad' has been invoked by Islamic leaders as a way of perpetuating the cause of Islam in the Sudan.

This leaves the Sudanese Christians with very limited or no options for dialogue. Sudanese Christians see Islam as being used by the government as a threat. They feel a very high sense of persecution. Is there a way for others to share their pain and agony?

Recommendations

In responding to such situations IASCOME recommends:

1. ***that the priority of appropriate witness and service among Muslims be raised to a higher place on the Primates' and ACC agendas.***
2. ***that there be gatherings of people living in situations of Muslim presence to share accounts of Christian living and witness for encouragement and learning. We heard with appreciation that one such gathering sponsored by USPG and CMS had already been held, but we recommend others to be planned in which the active participation of women and men; lay people and clergy alongside bishops be ensured.***

3. ***that particular attention be paid to ensuring children are included in gatherings and their voice and their hopes are heard.***

4. ***that there be such a gathering specifically for those living under Shariah law.***

5. ***we recognised that there needs to be action on many fronts, for example the Archbishop of Canterbury's Al-Azhar initiative is to be greatly welcomed. We encourage all such initiatives at all levels.***

6. ***that out of the gatherings clear guidelines be prepared on how to respond to Islamisation in a Christian way.***

7. ***that the cry and pain of those Christians and Churches suffering or under pressure in the face of Islamisation be acknowledged with great sensitivity and understanding.***

The Commission discussed and warmly welcomed the report of the 'Agreement for dialogue between the Anglican Communion and al-Azhar al-Sharif'. It placed on record its warm support for the initiatives taken, the visits made and the commitment given by the present Archbishop of Canterbury in developing relations with leaders of Muslim communities in many parts of the world.

F2. Developing Anglicanism: A Communion in Mission

The Anglican Communion has grown out of the vision for world mission. The Decade of Evangelism highlighted this founding perspective and encouraged Churches of the Communion to explore what this might mean for a new era. Today we see signs of many different kinds of mission in the Communion leading to growth and developments in terms of both the size and nature of Anglicanism.

One way of expressing this emerging perspective is to say that we are a family of Churches who find their Communion in Mission. Within this Communion we find structures which express our unity, marks which identify our mission, and relationships which create our fellowship. We are a Communion in Mission in so far as our identifiable mission is relational and our structures serve those mission relationships.

As a Communion in Mission, being led forward by the Holy Spirit, we acknowledge (with other sister Churches) that we are God's pilgrim people, and therefore whilst affirming the patterns and traditions of our past we realise that these are provisional and that our Communion is developing as it is being transformed in Christ.

Indicators of Mission

The various issues addressed in this report can also be seen as indicators of mission. We have identified a number of these:

i) *The missio Dei*, the mission of God, is grounded in the Trinitarian affirmation of a Communion in Mission (see above). One way of understanding the mission of God, in which the church is called to participate, "is to restore all people to unity with God and each other in Christ".

ii) The Church finds its vocation as it expresses and serves a restored, reconciled and redeemed creation.

iii) The new creation brought forth by the mission of God embodies wholeness and life abundant in the pains and possibilities of our daily experiences.

iv) A Communion in Mission is characterised at one and the same time by a celebration of commonality and difference. Our commonality and difference is sustained by apostolic truth and the promise of the unity of all things in the worship of God.

v) The evangelistic imperative draws the Church into a movement to both proclaim and live out a restored, reconciled and redeemed new creation.

These indicators of mission challenge us to see Anglican identity as developing historically over time through an engagement with a variety of contexts. The variety of contexts push us to give priority to *relationships* as fundamental to a Communion in Mission.

The Quality of Mission Relationships

A Communion in Mission is characterised by the quality of its relationships engendered by God's own relational life in mission (*koinonia*). These characteristics include:

- interdependence
- integrity
- honesty
- transparency
- laughter
- acceptance
- openness
- vulnerability
- sharing
- brokenness
- compassion
- solidarity in pain

Structures of Communion

The structures of the Communion in Mission express God's mission when they:

- seek to serve and not to be served
- offer effective leadership
- nurture relationships
- effect reconciliation, freedom, justice and peace
- are alive and moving
- are flexible, available and accessible

Recommendations

1. ***ACC-12 is asked to affirm IASCOME's concern to give priority to the development of and reflection about Anglicanism as a Communion in Mission.***

And specifically to:

1. ***Support ventures in the Church that serve relationships in mission, e.g., the Anglican Gathering and the emergence of new networks;***
2. ***Lift up and celebrate the stories of mission relationships across the Communion;***
3. ***Live more deeply into the local-global nature of the Anglican Communion today;***
4. ***Address questions of authority and truth in relation to the life of the Church as a Communion in Mission.***
5. ***The Commission recognises that there is still further work to do on new ways of being Church and new forms of evangelism.***

F3. The Journey towards Wholeness and Fullness of Life

Listening to reports from many parts of the world we are aware of so many serious threats to life—not just of individuals, communities and nations, but also to the life of the planet. For example we heard accounts of:

- The unfolding consequences of the HIV/AIDS pandemic on families and, in particular, children across sub-Saharan Africa.
- The traumatic effects of exploitation of children, child soldiers, internal displacement of families and child abuse in countries like Sri Lanka and parts of Africa on the emotional growth and social development of children from whom leaders of the future are likely to emerge.
- The effects of environmental degradation in situations of war and conflict, for example in the Sudan, has brought about desertification caused by the cutting down of trees and the effects of the oil industry.
- The internal displacement of millions of people in the Sudan and many more becoming refugees outside the country divides families and deprives children of education and development of skills for the future quite apart from the emotional impact upon them.

- War between nations and within countries (for example, the thirty-six-year war in the Sudan, conflict in Sri Lanka, Democratic Republic of the Congo, Israel/Palestine) has lasting physical and emotional effects on those involved and tears the social fabric of civil society apart.
- Poverty in many areas has a crippling effect.
- Slavery and terrible physical abuse of captives in war situations, forming part payment for unpaid government troops.
- In northern nations where material wealth might be greater than in other parts of the world there are many areas of poverty and the effects of dysfunctional families and relationships, the pressures and stress of life can all prove wounding and death dealing.

So many of the tragic situations in the world today are evidences of the work of forces of death and destruction that contradict the desire of God expressed in Jesus' words that 'all people should have life, life in all its fullness.' (John 10:10)

It is the Christian witness that God is a God of Life expressed in the working of God's Spirit throughout the created universe to bring life and to counteract the forces of death. The universal life-giving work of God's Spirit is focused in human form in the person of Jesus. 'In the beginning was the Word . . . in him was life, and the life was the light of all people. . . . the Word became flesh and lived among us.' (John 1:1–14) Jesus is described as 'the Bread of Life'; 'the Way, the Truth and the Life'; 'the Water of Life'. Through his death on the Cross he entered into the pain and evil of the world, taking on the forces of death and destruction and rising after they had done their worst into a new resurrection life.

The Bible speaks of the Spirit of Jesus carrying on his ministry of bringing life and pressing all people to join in the journey into life which will culminate in the new heaven and new earth.

Our response to the forces of death is to analyse causes, develop programmes to take action to prevent, provide alternatives and to heal, in other words to pursue Jesus' Nazareth Manifesto (Luke 4:18–19). In this section we focus specifically on the call to heal, to make whole those wounded physically and emotionally as individuals and communities by the death dealing trends in the world. The prophet Isaiah speaks of God's servant not breaking 'the bruised reed' and not quenching 'the flickering flame' but of binding up and healing wounds and helping all people on the journey to wholeness that is God's calling and all people's need.

- In relation to HIV/AIDS there is a ministry of care, counselling and support both for People living with AIDS and for their families and those who support them, both before and after their death—a ministry of support, accepting and holding.

- Destruction of the environment calls for a healing of the wounds inflicted on the earth.
- Communities that have suffered trauma and displacement need reconciliation and healing.
- The ministry of healing, which takes the form of prayer, the laying on of hands and anointing with oil, is frequently practised in some and being rediscovered in other parts of the Communion as a form of ministry to Christians and those outside the Christian faith alike.
- The healing of children who have suffered abuse and need emotional and social healing is a skilled and demanding work of love.

Recommendations

IASCOME therefore recommends:

1. ***that Liturgies for cleansing and healing in communities where terrible things have happened be researched and listed/collected for sharing more widely.***
    - ***This should include liturgies for environmental healing.***
    - ***Connection with representatives in provinces on liturgical committees or on the International Anglican Liturgical Consultation.***
    - ***Liturgies from Anglican and other Church sources.***
    - ***New liturgies for healing and the laying on of hands that are being developed in some parts of the Anglican Communion.***
    - ***Any reports on healing produced within member Churches of the Communion.***
    - ***Examples of the work of circles of prayer, healing and reconciliation.***
2. ***that the ways in which the ministry of healing and reconciliation, including its psychological elements, are part of the theological and ministerial formation of Church and youth leadership be researched.***
3. ***that some assessment be made of how the Church in each country plays its important role in the preparation of leaders for the future in the light of the huge threats posed by HIV/AIDS and the consequences of war to the present and next generation of leaders within many countries.***
4. ***that stories be collected and shared (in an appropriate way) of the effects of the forces of death and of life-giving responses being made as the basis for analysis. People's stories have proved so valuable in awakening awareness.***

    ACC-12 is asked to affirm the Commission in undertaking these tasks and encouraging others to do so.

F4. Mission as Justice-Making and Peace-Building

At both the first and second meetings of IASCOME, we listened to members describe the mission work of their various churches, and were struck by the powerful stories of committed Anglicans challenging injustices in their own contexts and also working to bring about peace and reconciliation in areas of conflict. In many parts of the Anglican Communion the mission focus of the church at this time is justice-making and peace-building in contexts of poverty, abuse of power and violence.

We noted **two types of violence**, visible and spectacular violence against individuals and communities, and systemic, structural violence.

These are characterised as follows:

- **Visible and spectacular violence:**
    - Wars arising from ethnic, religious, political conflicts and from socio-cultural practices are funded through external sources and often fought using outside personnel.
    - Domestic violence within the family.
    - Violence against children, including child trafficking, child labour and child soldiers.
- **Systemic and structural violence:**
    - Poverty perpetuated by oppressive and exclusionary systems.
    - The abuse of power in and by both secular and religious institutions.
    - Globalised capitalism, including unethical biotechnology practices.

Based on the stories we heard, we make the following observations about how Christians in mission behave:

- Christians in mission live out the values of the gospel: love, justice, peace and preferential option for the poor, powerless and weak. They respect and affirm the dignity of each person, looking for and honouring the Christ in each child of God.
- Christians in mission affirm those structures and value systems that are life-giving, and seek to transform cultural practices that oppress, discriminate and are contrary to the gospel.
- Christians in mission have a richness of spirit that leads them to repent, forgive, reconcile and restore.
- Christians in mission are engaged in the political and economic life of the/their world in a non-partisan way. They challenge unjust structures

and value systems in institutions, especially the church, in groupings in society such as tribes, clans and social movements, and in the economic and political systems at local, national and international levels of the world.

- Christians in mission are prophetic risk-takers.
- Christians in mission are actively involved in peace-making as part of building a safe world. They find ways to hold safe spaces where opposing forces can listen and talk to each other.

We believe the imperatives for this behaviour are firmly grounded in the teaching of Scripture and the faith of the practitioners, which we heard articulated as follows:

- Jesus said, "Love one another as I have loved you." His life is the example of how we are to love.
- Jesus said, "Love your enemies." The challenge is to hold our enemies accountable in the hope of bringing change, without destroying them.
- All people are created in the image of God, irrespective of race, class, gender, age, sexual orientation.
- God continues to redeem humanity, and Christians in mission are called to be instruments of this redemption in their own cultures.

IASCOME affirms the good work done by the Anglican Peace and Justice Network (APJN) and encourages provinces to support those in their midst engaged in the mission work of justice-making and peace-building.

Recommendations

To expand and strengthen this work, IASCOME makes the following recommendations:

1. ***that provinces examine their health and educational institutions to ensure that there are appropriate policies and monitoring mechanisms to protect the vulnerable, and as much as possible, to guarantee fair access to services.***
2. ***that provinces examine their cultural practices, affirming those that liberate, and transforming those that contradict and deny the liberating message of the gospel.***
3. ***that provinces, dioceses and parishes include in their various cycles of prayer, prayers for peace-makers and those involved in the work of reconciliation.***
4. ***that provinces gather and submit to IASCOME resources being used in peace-building, so that these can be made available to assist in the training of peace-makers.***

F5. Money, Power and Christian Mission

During the course of our first two meetings, the members of IASCOME have listened to stories of the benefits which a healthy local economy, financially self-sufficient churches, and the compassionate exercise of power can bring to the furtherance of Christian mission. But we have also heard how poverty, financial dependency, and financial corruption coupled with the abuse of power can obstruct and distort God's mission. Based on these stories, we make the following observations:

- Jesus came to offer abundant life to everyone (John 10:10). This means the material basis of life as well as the spiritual. The Good News has no credibility if people remain poor and powerless while the rich thrive.
- Love of God is false unless there is a genuine love of neighbour through mutual respect and service. We are accountable to God for the gifts we have received and for the welfare of our neighbours (Matt. 25).
- Wealth is a gift from God requiring honesty, transparency and vigilance in financial management and accountability. Financial scandals tarnish the image of the church and diminish the credibility of the gospel.
- Power must be exercised in the service of the powerless, as exemplified by Jesus. Failure to follow Jesus' example of empowering the powerless makes a mockery of the liberating message of the gospel.

Those engaged in Christian mission need to include the following tasks in their work:

- **Economic analysis**. People need to be equipped to seek answers to their concerns about their local economic situations. This means paying attention to the economy at the global as well as the local level, since the two are so closely intertwined. Information and basic tools of analysis need to be provided so that people can make informed economic decisions.
- **Sharing financial resources**. Financial resources need to continue to be shared across the Communion, but capacity must also be built in wealth generation and financial management. The sharing of resources should be seen as a stepping stone to financial self-sufficiency. To this end, we need good ethical teaching in Christian stewardship that leads to accountability and tithing.
- **Participation in civil society**. People need help in becoming involved in civil society. This requires building dignity and self-confidence, and teaching organisational skills, as well as finding ways to both share power and exercise it in compassionate and responsible ways.

- **Ethical financial behaviour**. Christian values apply at all levels, local, and global. Financial corruption and mismanagement need to be challenged, as do unethical investment practices.

It is important that Christians in mission challenge the abuse of power and financial corruption and mismanagement in the wider society. At the same time, these sins continue to be present within the church and need to be corrected.

Recommendations

IASCOME recommends:

1. ***that provinces examine their entire investment portfolios, including pension funds, to ensure that they meet the Global Reporting Initiative Standard (see Appendix VI)*** *(website http://www.globalreporting.org)*, ***especially in relation to the arms trade and the environment.***
2. ***that provinces examine their governance structures to ensure transparency in decision-making processes and financial management.***
3. ***that provinces seek ways to train creative administrators who are also strategic thinkers.***
4. ***that provinces put in place measures to deal with corruption in the church at all levels, and make these measures known to the membership.***
5. ***that each province affirm its commitment to the Anglican Communion by a renewed endeavour to fulfil its financial obligation to the Inter-Anglican Budget.***

F6. Evangelism

Evangelism has run as a theme through many of the Commission's discussions and presentations, but a sustained reflection on evangelism across the Communion has been identified as a major piece of work for future Commission meetings. We look forward to continuing to encourage and support the significant efforts in evangelism that are emerging in the Communion.

G. Resolution

Resolves

1. ***To receive with thanks the Interim Report 'Travelling Together in God's Mission' from the Inter Anglican Standing Commission on Mission and Evangelism (IASCOME)***
2. ***To give thanks for the successful Nairobi Consultation for Provincial Mission and Evangelism Co-ordinators 'Encounters on the Road'; to receive the report of that Consultation; to encourage dissemination of its report and***

to support plans for a follow-up conference, funded outside of the budget of the ACC

3. ***To look forward to and pray for the mission organisations Conference planned for February 2003***

4. ***To take note of action taken on matters remitted to the Commission***

5. ***To note that comments on the Primates Strategic Working Party on Theological Education have been sent direct to that working party***

6. ***To encourage the Commission to develop its mandate, reflection and work particularly in the areas of***

   - ***Leadership Training and Formation for Mission***
   - ***Islam and Islamisation***
   - ***Developing Anglicanism: A Communion in Mission***
   - ***The Journey to Wholeness and Fullness of Life***
   - ***Justice Making and Peace Building***
   - ***Evangelism***

7. ***To circulate the interim report to provinces, other Commissions and networks and more widely for comment and discussion.***

APPENDIX I

Members of the Commission

The Revd Canon Maurício J. Araújo de Andrade	Porto Alegre, Brazil
The Rt Revd Joseph Akinfenwa	Ibadan, Nigeria
The Rt Revd Dr Sebastian Bakare	Mutare, Zimbabwe
The Rt Revd Dr John Chew Hiang Chew	Singapore
Mr John Clark	London UK
The Revd Canon Tim Dakin	London UK
The Rt Revd Dr Harold Daniel	Kingston, Jamaica
The Revd Joseph William Kofi deGraft-Johnson	Accra, Ghana
The Revd Dr Ian T. Douglas	Cambridge, USA
Mrs Joy Kwaje Eluzai	Khartoum, Sudan
The Rt Revd Armando Guerra-Soria	Guatemala
The Very Revd Muhindo Ise-Somo	Congo
Dr Ellie Johnson	Toronto Canada
The Revd Joseph K. Kopapa	Popondetta, Papua New Guinea
The Rt Revd Edward P. Malecdan	Mountain Province, Philippines
Ms Pat McBryde	Edinburgh, Scotland
Ms Shirley Moulder	Johannesburg, South Africa

Sister Chandrani Peiris	Moratuwa, Sri Lanka
The Ven Te Kitohi Pikaahu	Auckland, New Zealand
The Revd Pearl Prashad	Lucknow, UP, India
The Revd Fareth S N Sendegeya	Dar-Es-Salaam, Tanzania
The Revd Canon Richard Naramana	Honiara, Solomon Islands

Others

The Revd Canon John L. Peterson	ACO Secretary General
Miss Marjorie Murphy	ACO Director for Mission and Evangelism
Dr Maureen Sithole	ACC Standing Committee Liaison person

APPENDIX II

A Report of the Anglican Communion Provincial Co-ordinators Mission and Evangelism Consultation

Resurrection Gardens, Nairobi, Kenya, May 13–18, 2002

"Mission at the Heart of the Church"

'Mission is at the heart of the life and calling of the Church. God's mission of love and life is universal in scope—to all people in all situations (John 3:16)'

This was the central affirmation of the first-ever Consultation of Co-ordinators of Mission and Evangelism within the Anglican Communion meeting in Nairobi, Kenya from 6–13 May.

Representatives from Anglican provinces in Asia, the Pacific, Australasia, the Middle East, Central, East, West and Southern Africa, North America, the Caribbean and Britain and Ireland met for the first major gathering on mission and evangelism in the Anglican Communion since the end of the Decade of Evangelism.

They were joined by representatives from the world mission agencies–the Mothers' Union, Church Army (Africa), CMS and USPG.

(Mr.) John Clark, Chief Secretary for Mission of the Church of England, chair of the Consultation commented: 'This has been an invigorating and spiritually refreshing experience. I sense a great energy and vitality amongst those present and within the Communion, and a renewed commitment to make evangelism and mission a priority within the life of our church. The Consultation has helped us appreciate the rich variety of the Communion and to be deeply challenged by those amongst us who are seeking to forward the gospel in situations of great suffering and hardship.'

The majority of those attending had never participated in an international Anglican Communion gathering before. So there was much sharing of accounts of how the churches from which they had come were carrying out God's call to mission. Churches are growing often in situations of conflict and poverty, among displaced people, in many cases threatened by HIV/AIDS. The challenge of life and witness in Islamic contexts and under Shariah law was identified as a major concern. Co-ordinators also shared from experience on how best to carry out their jobs and began to prepare a list of guidelines for new co-ordinators.

There was a particular focus on church planting, evangelism in the context of affluent nations, like the USA, co-operation between provincial structures and mission agencies and work with other denominations. Dr. Carlos Ham, Executive Secretary for Evangelism in the World Council of Churches, challenged the consultation with insights drawn from beyond the world of Anglicanism.

Archbishop David Gitari, Primate of the Anglican Church of Kenya, spoke on the role of a bishop in mission and evangelism, drawing from his years of experience in Kenya and emphasising the bishop's role as a missionary, called to lead in the work of evangelism.

Particular attention was given to the importance of the witness of lay people and the provision of training for evangelism. Clergy and Bishops in particular were challenged to exercise their role of leadership and encouragement in mission and evangelism.

Co-ordinators exchanged details of how they carried out their work and agreed to form an email network as initial step in continuing to support, challenge and stimulate each other.

Daily worship beginning with a Eucharist and including mid-day, evening and night prayers drawn from liturgies across the world enriched the meeting and provided a framework for discussion. A half night prayer vigil was held during which all Churches within the Communion were prayed for.

Bishop Mano Rumalshah, former Bishop of Peshawar, Pakistan, and now General Secretary of the United Society for the Propagation of the Gospel (USPG) presented daily Bible studies on encounters that Jesus had with people during his ministry and the lessons they provided for mission and evangelism today.

The Rt. Rev Michael Nazir-Ali, Bishop of Rochester (England) provided a theological and historical framework for the Conference with a presentation on 'Evangelism and the Wholeness of Mission'.

Much of the work of the Consultation took place in group discussion. Conclusions laid stress on the importance of prayer and worship and the

Christian community in mission and evangelism. The importance of local contexts leading to a diversity of approaches to mission and evangelism was emphasised but attention was also drawn to the influence of global trends e.g., in globalisation, urbanisation, HIV/AIDS and the growth of Islam.

Training in mission and evangelism was identified as a priority. The role of bishops and clergy not just in setting a lead but also in encouraging others was stressed. There was a call for greater sharing of ideas, experiences, people and finance across the Communion and for all provinces and dioceses to appoint a mission and evangelism co-ordinator.

The Conference, hosted by the Anglican Church of Kenya (ACK), concluded with Sunday visits to parishes and congregations in and around Nairobi to give participants an inspiring experience of the Church in Kenya at worship.

The Consultation was an initiative of the Inter-Anglican Standing Commission on Mission and Evangelism (IASCOME) which will hold its second meeting in St. Andrews, Scotland from 16–25 June. There is to be a similar consultation for mission agencies of the Communion in Cyprus in February 2003.

APPENDIX III

A Report of the Anglican Communion Provincial Co-ordinators Mission and Evangelism Consultation

Resurrection Gardens, Nairobi, Kenya, May 13–18, 2002

"ENCOUNTERS ON THE ROAD"

Conclusions and Recommendations

The following points have been prepared immediately after the Consultation as a report of the major findings to remind Consultation members of the basic findings and to report to the Inter Anglican Standing Commission on Mission and Evangelism (IASCOME).

These notes list basic principles in **bold** text with recommendations in italics.

I. FOUNDATIONS

1. **There are many ways of describing and expressing God's mission.**
2. **All mission is fundamentally God's mission, most clearly expressed in the sending of Jesus Christ and the Spirit.**

3. **The Church is called to participate in God's mission and so has an essentially missionary character. ("As the Father has sent me, even so send I you" John 20:21)**
4. **Mission is universal in scope—to all peoples in all situations. (John 3:16)**

   1. *The Anglican Communion needs a renewed vision for mission and evangelism.*
   2. *This requires continual, deliberate, prayerful and intentional reflection on how the Communion is both engaging and called to engage in mission.*

II. PRAYER AND WORSHIP

1. **The Anglican Communion is part of a living Church in which the Spirit of God is moving.**
2. **We need always to be open to how the Spirit is working in the Church and the world.**
3. **We must remain in touch with God.**
4. **In mission and evangelism we particularly need to take seriously the call to prayer:**

   - **for each other**
   - **for guidance**
   - **for inspiration**

   following the example of Jesus.
5. **We often spoke of the importance of worship as a way of sharing the gospel and making Christ known.**

   1. *All our practice of mission must be rooted in prayer, worship and reflection on scripture.*
   2. *Provincial mission and evangelism co-ordinators need to connect with the liturgical committees and groups of their provinces to ensure that liturgy is rooted in God's call to mission.*

III. CONTEXTS

1. **All mission must fit local situations and contexts. So mission and evangelism will be expressed differently in different places.**
2. **We need to know and understand the different contexts in which we do mission and evangelism, and formulate appropriate strategies and ways of working.**

3. **We recognise and accept that this will lead to a diversity of approaches and models in our Communion.**

4. **In each situation, mission and evangelism needs to relate to the particular context, culture and people.**

5. **In looking at situations/context we need to take account of:**

   - **the historical context**
   - **the socio-political situation**
   - **the internal context of the Church**
   - **global concerns and pressures**

6. **We need to celebrate and learn from the diversity of approach to evangelism and mission within the Anglican Communion, as we have at this Consultation.**

   1. *The Consultation identified a range of specific situations and issues. Those involved in these situations need opportunities to share together their stories, experiences and insights so mission and evangelism might be taken forward. We call for opportunities to be created for that sharing.*

   2. *Situations and issues include:*

      - *Islam and Islamisation (particularly living under Shariah Law)*
      - *conflict and war*
      - *youth*
      - *poverty and abundance*
      - *trade*
      - *marginalised peoples*
      - *HIV/AIDS*
      - *people who do not yet know Christ*
      - *globalisation and urbanisation*

IV. PARTNERSHIP

1. **If all mission is God's mission, then mission must always be in partnership with God.**

2. **In the same way, all mission should be open to partnership with all others in God's mission.**

3. **In many situations, particularly of conflict and poverty, solidarity is one way in which partnership is expressed.**

   1. *We encourage an openness to partnership in mission:*

      - *among provinces, dioceses, individuals*
      - *with mission agencies*

- *with other Christian Churches and Communions*
- *all who share our common purpose*
- *through international mission teams going from and to each diocese*

2. *We commend the Anglican Communion's 'Ten Principles of Partnership' [found in 'Anglicans in Mission: a Transforming Journey', p 126; and in the booklet "Guidelines and Principles for Mission and Evangelism" available at the Consultation.]*

V. THE MINISTRY OF THE WHOLE PEOPLE OF GOD

1. **All Christians are called to be witnesses to Christ and to share in his mission and ministry.**

2. **The Church is missionary by its very nature because this is the nature of God.**

3. **All ministry, lay and ordained, shares in the missionary task. We have a shared ministry, and must have a shared vision of mission.**

4. **It is vital to help and encourage lay people to be effective in witness and mission.**

5. **We recognise the important role of clergy and bishops in leading and encouraging the witness and mission of all Christians.**

6. **Clergy and lay people need to work together in the mission task.**

7. **Bishops have a particularly important role in affirming the priority of mission and evangelism through their leadership, example and encouragement of others.**

    1. *We call for each province and diocese to review training in mission and evangelism and ensure that it fits the local situation.*

    2. *We call for mission and evangelism co-ordinators to ensure that there is effective lay training in mission and evangelism in their provinces.*

    3. *We encourage the sharing of courses of lay training across the Communion.*

    4. *We call for a rethinking of the orders of ministry and their role in the light of our missionary calling and situation. This includes:*

        - *the role of the Bishop in mission (see Lambeth Conference 1998, Report Section II)*
        - *the role, ministry and mission of priests and deacons*
        - *the role and recognition of other ministries/orders e.g. evangelists, catechists, readers, etc.*

5. *We call for bishops to reflect on how they are leading in mission and evangelism, and encouraging others.*

6. *We call for the priority of mission and evangelism to be considered when making appointments at provincial, diocesan and parish level.*

VI. RESOURCES FOR MISSION AND EVANGELISM

1. **Resources do not just mean money. They include people, ideas, experience, prayer, spiritual gifts and insight, practical materials (e.g., literature, pictures, films, etc).**

2. **Since mission is at the heart of the Church, resources are held in trust for mission.**

3. **Across the Communion there is rich diversity of these resources.**

4. **But there is also a disparity and inequality in sharing resources across the Communion. There are often limited financial resources for mission and evangelism.**

5. **We need to find ways of sharing resources (particularly money) to support mission needs and opportunities within the Communion.**

    1. *We call for provinces and dioceses to examine their budgets and funding for mission and evangelism to ensure that it reflects the priority of mission and evangelism.*

    2. *We call for guidelines to help in sharing finances for mission across the Communion.*

    3. *We call for practical action to direct resources to those in frontier situations of conflict, oppression and poverty (particularly Sudan, Myanmar, Congo, Palestine).*

    4. *We encourage greater sharing of people, ideas, materials, etc. across the Communion, in order to assist and strengthen mission and evangelism. We ask for practical ways to enable this to happen (for example, through a regular video documentary and/or through printed news about mission and evangelism).*

    5. *We call for creative use of the Internet to help share resources (for example, an Internet site and web editor for Anglican mission and evangelism).*

    6. *We recommend that every diocese should have a diocesan evangelist and/or evangelistic team.*

VII. TRAINING

1. **We identified training and encouragement as an important priority.**

2. **Telling our faith story is a vital way of witnessing, but people may need help to know and tell their story.**

3. **Training is important, but effective witness depends much on the integrity, Christ-likeness and authenticity of Christians.**

    1. *We call for a greater sharing of what is actually happening (courses, ideas, stories, materials and insights) in training for mission and evangelism, and for practical ways to enable this to happen.*

    2. *We affirm the work of organisations like the Church Army, the Mothers Union and others in equipping people for evangelism.*

    3. *We call for the further development of programmes and training centres to equip lay people and evangelists.*

VIII. MISSION AND EVANGELISM CO-ORDINATORS

1. **Mission and Evangelism Co-ordinators in dioceses and provinces have a vital role in sharing information, encouraging people and parishes, training others, advising bishops and clergy, co-ordinating action, and developing initiatives and strategies in mission and evangelism.**

    1. *Every Church/Province/Diocese of the Communion should be encouraged to appoint a co-ordinator for Mission and Evangelism.*

    2. *We recommend that guidelines be developed for the work of Mission and Evangelism co-ordinators. These will include an outline of their roles and tasks (our Consultation already has begun a list).*

IX. NETWORKS

1. **Meeting and sharing in mission is vital for exchanging news and ideas, developing initiatives, for prayer and worship, and for encouraging each other.**

2. **Networks need to include provincial structures, mission agencies and other denominations.**

    1. *We recommend that the network of those at this meeting (and their regional equivalents) continue to work and meet. We intend to set up an e-mail network among ourselves as part of this process.*

    2. *We recommend that opportunities (conferences and consultative meetings) at various levels (diocesan, regional and world levels) be organised on a regular basis.*

3. *We encourage the development of diocesan mission teams to work across boundaries (geographical, cultural etc).*

4. *In particular we encourage development of networks to share insights about mission and evangelism in multi-faith situations and in the area of church planting.*

X. ANGLICAN CHURCH STRUCTURES

1. **The structures of the Church should be orientated towards mission as the Church's first priority.**

   1. *We recommend that provinces rethink their provincial, diocesan and local structures in the light of the mission and evangelism priority. We recommend that mission and evangelism co-ordinators assist in this process.*

   2. *We call on provinces to continue the process of consultation we have so valued at this meeting.*

   3. *We affirm the importance of maintaining a Co-ordinator for Mission and Evangelism for the Communion within the Anglican Communion Office (see tasks listed in 'Anglicans in Mission: A Transforming Journey').*

   4. *We strongly re-affirm the Mission Commission's call for the inclusion of mission representatives on the design group for the 2008 Anglican Communion Congress. We affirm the Mission Commission's call for "mission" to be the theme of the Congress.*

APPENDIX IV

'Our Vision, Our Hope, The First Step'

Statement from the All Africa Anglican HIV/AIDS Planning Framework

Johannesburg, August 2001

1. Our Vision

We, the Anglican Communion across Africa, pledge ourselves to the promise that future generations will be born and live in a world free from AIDS.

2. God's call to transformation

We are living with AIDS. As the body of Christ, confronted by a disaster unprecedented in human history, we share the pain of all who suffer as a result of AIDS. Faced by this crisis, we hear God's call to be transformed. We confess our sins of judgement, ignorance, silence, indifference and denial.

Repenting of our sin, we commit ourselves to:

- Breaking the silence in order to end all new infections
- Educating ourselves at every level within the Church
- Confronting poverty, conflict and gender inequalities
- Ending stigma and judgement, and
- Holding ourselves accountable before God and the world.

Only then can we live out the Good News of the all-embracing love of Christ.

3. Our mission

Our mission is to respect the dignity of all people by:

- Securing the human rights of those infected by HIV/AIDS, and giving unconditional support
- Improving the health and prolonging the lives of infected people
- Accompanying the dying, those who mourn and those who live on
- Celebrating life
- Nurturing community, and
- Advocating for justice.

We acknowledge that we cannot do this alone. We are sustained by the love of God and emboldened by the Holy Spirit. We are inspired by the compassionate efforts of the faithful in attending to those affected by HIV/AIDS. We accept the responsibility of our leadership. We invite the wider community into creative, life-giving partnership.

4. Our commission in the context of AIDS

We believe we are created, in the image of God, as physical and spiritual beings. We are created to be in relationship to God, the community and ourselves. We believe that we are given the freedom to make choices, to love, to celebrate, to live in dignity and to delight in God's creation. We believe that suffering and death are neither punishment from God nor the end of life and that we are called to an eternal union with God.

Stigma is a denial that we are created in the image of God. It destroys self-esteem, decimates families, disrupts communities and annihilates hope for future generations. We commit in all our efforts—personal and corporate, programmatic and liturgical—to confront it as sin and work for its end.

Given who we are, and who we are called to be by God, we have defined and embraced a six-fold commission of ministry in response to AIDS.

These six calls in our commission are:

4.1 Prevention

The Church's commitment to prevention recognises that all life is sacred. Because we love our children, we speak and act to protect them from infection. Sex is a gift from God. We are accountable to God and one another for our sexual behaviour. Christian communities have a special responsibility and capacity for encouraging and supporting loving, just, honest relationships.

4.2 Pastoral Care

Pastoral care supports spiritual growth with the aim of sustaining whole and holy relationships with God, each other and community. This is achieved by affirming the dignity and worth of each human being and making clear the claim of God in our lives.

4.3 Counselling

Christian counselling equips people to live into God's invitation to wholeness, freed of the burdens of the past, and capable of moving in freedom toward the perfection promised in Christ's example with confidence and determination.

4.4 Care

In caring for all who suffer, we fulfill God's purpose by restoring dignity and purpose to people's lives. Christian care, therefore, seeks the fullness of life, in the context of the community, by the restoration of body, mind and spirit.

4.5 Death and dying

Death is a rite of passage in our spiritual journey and into eternal life. The call of all Christians is to uphold the dying by our love, as well as those who live on and those who mourn.

While death brings suffering and loss, our faith can make it a time of enhanced relationship and growth for individuals and communities. We are a resurrection people and our relationship with God does not end with the death of physical bodies.

4.6 Leadership

All authority is accountable before God. All people of the church are stewards of God's creation. We have a unique responsibility to speak truth to power, to act without fear, and to embody Christian values of love, compassion and justice.

5. Our Response

5.1 Prevention

Out of love for our children, one another and our communities, we commit to speak openly and with moral authority about responsible sexual behaviour, and to support one another, embracing and adopting behaviours that avoid the transmission of HIV.

5.2 Pastoral Care

As the embodiment of the merciful Christ in a suffering world, we commit to equip our clergy and laity to support all people, especially those living with HIV, in life-sustaining relationships with their God and their community.

5.3 Counselling

We commit to promote voluntary counselling and testing for HIV by our own examples and as a ministry of the Church. We call for the establishment of support groups and other counselling services for those who are orphaned, ill, afraid, dying or bereaved.

5.4 HIV Care

We commit to being central to networks of community support, to meet the health care and basic needs of those who are orphaned, ill or excluded due to HIV, freeing them to productive life as long as their health permits.

5.5 Death and Dying

As death transforms the body, AIDS calls us to transform those traditions and practices, by which we care for the dying and honour our dead, that consume scarce resources and contribute to denial.

We commit to:

- Training the Church to provide holistic care for the dying and prepare families for living on
- Offering rituals that honour the dead and promote the well-being of those who survive

- Training the clergy to counsel and protect the rights of those who survive, especially women and children.

5.6 Leadership

Silence permits inaction and is the breeding ground of stigma. We call for bold, compassionate community and institutional leadership at every level, to prevent infection and care for the ill and dying. We invite similar leadership by government, and all sections of society and international partners.

Because leadership must address power, culture and morality, we call on our government leaders to be accountable for health expenditures and to declare an 'HIV state of emergency', in order to combat AIDS and mobilise resources. We further declare that all people have the right to health, which includes access to basic health care.

HIV calls for bold and creative approaches by our leaders, which recognises the reality of power and gender patterns at community levels, and mobilise resources and facilitate development of new models of leadership, particularly among laity and women.

5.7 Education and training

Nothing in our educational systems equips us to deal with this catastrophe. In achieving the strategies outlined in this document, it is essential to assess needs and establish education and training capacity, in order to assure that sufficient numbers of clergy and laity:

- Have current and accurate basic information on the science of HIV, standards of home-based care, and the rudiments of treatment.
- Have both the technical information and the interpersonal communication skills to effectively teach and counsel regarding human sexuality.
- Are knowledgeable of local laws and practices regarding inheritance and equipped to impart that information.
- Receive practical training in community organisation and development, so that they may assist in establishing care and support which is needed.
- Are trained and available to meet exploding demands for pastoral care necessitated by HIV/AIDS.

5.8 Theological reflection

As the Church, it is uniquely our task to gather for study, for prayer and for worship. Therefore we must engage in constant theological reflection, seeking discernment on the issues of sin, guilt, grace, judgement and forgiveness. To this we commit ourselves, our families and our friends.

APPENDIX V

Mission Focus Expressed by Commission Members

Commission Members have been asked to summarise the mission focus of their Church, province or mission agency. This list is provided for the interest of ACC members.

1. The Church in the Province of the West Indies is committed to be and to become more and more God's agent of reconciliation within the complex network of relationships in the Caribbean Society. (Harold Daniel)

2. The focus of the Province of South East Asia is to equip and mobilise the whole people of God in our diocese/province through total mission and evangelism to make Jesus Christ known and confessed as Saviour and Lord in our region and beyond. (John Chew)

3. The Mission of God is the mission of the Episcopal Church in the Philippines. It is the proclamation of Jesus Christ and what he has done for us in his passion, death and resurrection. This is expressed in various mission programmes, such as,

   - children's ministry
   - nurture of members, etc.

   The most prominent programme where this mission is expressed is in the prophetic ministry of the church in relation to poverty, which is endemic in the country. This is based on the ministry of Jesus, which was actively a ministry in favour of poor people.

   Our struggle, therefore, is how to do the Mission of God in a country that is suffering from hunger, unemployment and other social evils resulting from poverty and its causes. (Edward Malecdan)

4. The Scottish Episcopal Church carries out its mission through Mission 21, which is an emphasis of all seven dioceses. We aim to increase the spiritual vitality of the congregations through helping congregations to discern their vocations and God's future plans for them. In doing this, the Church seeks to serve God's reconciliation with creation in Scotland. (Pat McBryde)

5. In the Anglican Church of Tanzania, there is a constant challenge to rethink and re-evaluate the traditional "Empire-like" Parishes, Deaneries and Dioceses. The cry of many is to have ministry brought as close to the grass-root peoples as possible. Thus the need to create and re-create smaller more "manageable" Parish Churches, Deaneries and Dioceses. (Fareth Sendegeya)

6. The mission of the Church of the Province of Southern Africa is to actively witness and be God's presence in the ministry of healing and reconciliation, to speak Truth to Power and continue to challenge injustice. (Shirley Moulder)

7. The mission focus of the Church of Central Africa is to preach the gospel and uphold its values of justice, peace and love in an environment that is hostile to human dignity and freedom. (Sebastian Bakare)

8. The mission focus of the church in Sri Lanka is on our solidarity in our common humanity and faith in Jesus Christ, and the renewal of our commitment to share the good news of Jesus Christ to our fellows in the region and beyond. Encouraging practical encounters and people exchange programmes in order that churches in the Province to closer partnership in mission and evangelism and bring about the healing to our nations. (Sister Chandrani Peiris)

9. The focus of the mission of the Church in Brazil includes three challenges, service, transformation and celebration. (Mauricio Andrade)

10. The Church in Papua New Guinea is focusing on the training and equipping of church leaders as well as the whole body of Christ in building up a strong healthy church, based upon small Christian (faith) communities. (Joseph Kopapa)

11. The mission focus of the Anglican Church in Central America is the consolidation of the work and the planting of new congregations in the main cities of its five countries. (Armando Guerra-Soria)

12. The mission focus of the Church in the Province of Melanesia is justice making and peace building—reconciliation, transformation and nurturing. (Richard Naramana)

13. The focus of the Church of Nigeria is on Evangelism and church planting, with investment in projects that are of great benefit to the people, and to be self-sustaining.

14. The focus of the Church of North India is to make Jesus and his gifts of forgiveness and everlasting life to be known through witness, service and unity. (Pearl Prashad)

15. The Church in the Province of West Africa is focused on the need to reflect on and to design strategies to minister to people in the context of

    - conflict and civil strife amidst political instability;
    - increasing presence of HIV/AIDS;

- increasing rate of abuse and neglect of the vulnerable; and
- newly emerging structures and their leadership requirements (Joseph Kofi deGraft Johnson)

16. The current mission focus of the Anglican Church of Canada is to work towards building right relationships between Indigenous and non-Indigenous people in our church and in our nation within the wider of goal of working for healing and reconciliation between all the various groups in Canadian society. (Ellie Johnson)

17. The Church of England seeks to be **outward-looking** (sharing in the mission of God for the world and working for God's justice and peace for all); **united** (growing together in the love of God); and **confident** (living and proclaiming the good news of Jesus Christ). This will be reflected in four priorities—all undergirded by worship and the call to the visible unity of all Christians:

    - Engaging with social issues
    - Equipping to evangelise
    - Welcoming and encouraging children and young people
    - Developing the ministry of all (John Clark)

18. The mission agencies of the Church of England, (as in other provinces) have developed and enacted a world mission mandate for the Church. These agencies have acted on behalf of and as part of the Church in seeking to share the gospel with all peoples that all may be drawn into fellowship with Christ. This mandate now consciously includes mission to the European context. (Tim Dakin)

19. The mission of the Episcopal Church, USA, especially in light of the horror of September 11, 2001, is to participate in God's project of reconciliation, seeking to restore all people to unity with God and each other in Christ. (Ian Douglas)

20. The focus of the Church in the Democratic Republic of Congo is to seek lasting peace, justice and reconciliation and also to fight the silent enemy, which is HIV/AIDS. (Muhindo Ise-Some)

21. In Sudan, where the context is dominated by conflict, civil war, Islamisation, poverty, uprootedness and displacement, the main aim of the Church is to bring about the reconciliation of all the peoples of the Sudan (the different tribes and races) under the Cross of Jesus, to preach the message of the good news of Jesus Christ, and to work for justice, peace and reconciliation. (Joy Kwaje Eluzai)

APPENDIX VI

The Global Reporting Initiative (GRI)—A Background Overview

A Common Framework for Sustainability Reporting

Overview

Timely, credible, and consistent information on an organisation's economic, environmental, and social performance is a key element in building sustainable societies. Communities, investors, governments, and businesses need reliable information to effectively address the development challenges of the 21st century.

The Global Reporting Initiative (GRI) was established in late 1997 with the mission of developing globally applicable guidelines for reporting on the economic, environmental, and social performance, initially for corporations and eventually for any business, governmental, or non-governmental organisation (NGO). Convened by the Coalition for Environmentally Responsible Economies (CERES) in partnership with the United Nations Environment Programme (UNEP), the GRI incorporates the active participation of corporations, NGOs, accountancy organisations, business associations, and other stakeholders from around the world.

The GRI's Sustainability Reporting Guidelines were released in exposure draft form in London in March 1999. The GRI Guidelines represent the first global framework for comprehensive sustainability reporting, encompassing the "triple bottom line" of economic, environmental, and social issues. Twenty-one pilot test companies, numerous other companies, and a diverse array of non-corporate stakeholders commented on the draft Guidelines during a pilot test period during 1999-2000. Revised Guidelines were released in June 2000.

By 2002, the GRI will be established as a permanent, independent, international body with a multi-stakeholder governance structure. Its core mission will be maintenance, enhancement, and dissemination of the Guidelines through a process of ongoing consultation and stakeholder engagement.

A Steering Committee with a membership drawn from a diverse mix of stakeholders has guided the GRI thus far.

Vision

The GRI seeks to make sustainability reporting as routine and credible as financial reporting in terms of comparability, rigour, and verifiability. Specifically, the GRI's goals are to:

- Elevate sustainability reporting practises worldwide to a level equivalent to financial reporting;

- Design, disseminate, and promote standardised reporting practises, core measurements, and customised, sector-specific measurements;
- Ensure a permanent and effective institutional host to support such reporting practises worldwide.

A generally accepted framework for sustainability reporting will enable corporations, governments, NGOs, investors, labour, and other stakeholders to gauge the progress of organisations in their implementation of voluntary initiatives and toward other practises supportive of sustainable development. At the same time, a common framework will provide the basis for benchmarking and identifying best practises to support internal management decisions.

Opportunity

Improved disclosure of sustainability information is an essential ingredient in the mix of approaches needed to meet the governance challenges in the globalising economy. Today, at least 2,000 companies around the world voluntarily report information on their economic, environmental, and social policies, practises, and performance. Yet, this information is generally inconsistent, incomplete, and unverified. Measurement and reporting practises vary widely according to industry, location, and regulatory requirements.

The GRI's Sustainability Reporting Guidelines are designed to assist organisations publish reports:

- In a way that provides stakeholders with reliable and relevant information that fosters dialogue and inquiry;
- Through well-established reporting principles, applied consistently from one reporting period to the next;
- In a way that facilitates reader understanding and comparison with similar reports;
- In a form that provides management across different organisations with valuable information to enhance internal decision-making.

Learning

A broad array of stakeholders interested in sustainability reporting came together to fashion the March 1999 exposure draft Sustainability Reporting Guidelines.

Twenty-one companies, representing diverse countries and multiple industry sectors, tested and provided comments on the draft Guidelines. At the same time, hundreds of additional comments were provided by external stakeholders, representing perspectives from human rights, accountancy, government, business, labour, and multi-lateral, international, environmental, and religious organisations.

Reflecting the feedback gathered through this process, the June 2000 Sustainability Reporting Guidelines incorporate the following:

- Flexibility in the order in which reporters present information, while assuring information is easily located by users;
- Guidance to reporters on selecting generally applicable and organisation specific indicators, as well as integrated indicators that span multiple aspects of sustainability;
- Incremental application of the Guidelines (e.g., "environmental only "reports, or "headquarters country" reports);
- Forward-looking indicators; including strategy, management indicators, trend information, and targets for future years;
- Articulation of reporting principles adapted from financial accounting.

The Future

The GRI vision is bold. It has brought together disparate reporting initiatives into a new multi-stakeholder, global process with long-term implications for disclosure, investment and business responsibility. Its success will lead to:

- Expanded credibility of sustainability reports using a common frame work for performance measurement;
- Simplification of the reporting process for organisations in all regions and countries;
- Quick and reliable benchmarking;
- More effective linkage between sustainable practises and financial performance.

On the basis of this vision, the United Nations Foundation awarded a $3 million partnership grant to CERES and UNEP to support GRI activities. From 2000–2002, the GRI will pursue:

- Creation of a permanent, independent host institution for the GRI;
- Continued periodic revision of Sustainability Reporting Guidelines developed through the efforts of a global, multi-stakeholder process;
- Extending the reach of GRI to all regions of the world to enlarge its reach and ensure continual feedback to enhance the quality of the Guidelines.

The GRI is uniquely positioned to bring standard reporting guidelines to a global audience. The GRI's engagement of multiple stakeholders across regions and nations distinguishes the GRI from numerous other reporting initiatives. At the same time, the GRI continues to build bridges to such initiatives in pursuit of its vision of a generally accepted sustainability reporting framework.

APPENDIX VII

Recommendations and Resolutions

Recommendation page 143
IASCOME recommends:

> ***that two of its members are members of the Planning Group of this Gathering.***

Recommendation page 147
IASCOME therefore recommends:

> ***that ACC-12 re-affirms IASCOME's mandate to continue fulfilling the initiatives begun with Missio and ACC 11 with respect to leadership training and formation for mission.***

Recommendations page 149

In responding to such situations IASCOME recommends:

1. ***that the priority of appropriate witness and service among Muslims be raised to a higher place on the Primates' and ACC agendas.***
2. ***that there be gatherings of people living in situations of Muslim presence to share accounts of Christian living and witness for encouragement and learning. We heard with appreciation that one such gathering sponsored by USPG and CMS had already been held, but we recommend others to be planned in which the active participation of women and men; lay people and clergy alongside bishops be ensured.***
3. ***that particular attention be paid to ensuring children are included in gatherings and their voice and their hopes are heard.***
4. ***that there be such a gathering specifically for those living under Shariah law.***
5. ***We recognised that there needs to be action on many fronts, for example the Archbishop of Canterbury's Al-Azhar initiative is to be greatly welcomed. We encourage all such initiatives at all levels.***
6. ***that out of the gatherings clear guidelines be prepared on how to respond to Islamisation in a Christian way.***

7. *that the cry and pain of those Christians and Churches suffering or under pressure in the face of Islamisation be acknowledged with great sensitivity and understanding.*

Recommendations page 152

1. *ACC-12 is asked to affirm IASCOME's concern to give priority to the development of and reflection about Anglicanism as a Communion in Mission.*

And specifically to:

1. *support ventures in the Church that serve relationships in mission, e.g., the Anglican Gathering and the emergence of new networks;*
2. *lift up and celebrate the stories of mission relationships across the Communion;*
3. *live more deeply into the local-global nature of the Anglican Communion today;*
4. *address questions of authority and truth in relation to the life of the Church as a Communion in Mission.*
5. *The Commission recognises that there is still further work to do on new ways of being Church and new forms of evangelism.*

Recommendations page 154

IASCOME therefore recommends:

1. *that liturgies for cleansing and healing in communities where terrible things have happened be researched and listed/collected for sharing more widely.*
    - *This should include liturgies for environmental healing.*
    - *Connection with representatives in provinces on liturgical committees or on the International Anglican Liturgical Consultation.*
    - *Liturgies from Anglican and other Church sources.*
    - *New liturgies for healing and the laying on of hands that are being developed in some parts of the Anglican Communion.*
    - *Any reports on healing produced within member Churches of the Communion.*
    - *Examples of the work of circles of prayer, healing and reconciliation.*
2. *that the ways in which the ministry of healing and reconciliation, including its psychological elements, are part of the theological and ministerial formation of Church and youth leadership be researched.*

3. that some assessment be made of how the Church in each country plays its important role in the preparation of leaders for the future in the light of the huge threats posed by HIV/AIDS and the consequences of war to the present and next generation of leaders within many countries.

4. that stories be collected and shared (in an appropriate way) of the effects of the forces of death and of life-giving responses being made as the basis for analysis. People's stories have proved so valuable in awakening awareness.

ACC-12 is asked to affirm the Commission in undertaking these tasks and encouraging others to do so.

Recommendations page 156

To expand and strengthen this work, IASCOME makes the following recommendations:

1. that provinces examine their health and educational institutions to ensure that there are appropriate policies and monitoring mechanisms to protect the vulnerable, and as much as possible, to guarantee fair access to services.

2. that provinces examine their cultural practices, affirming those that liberate, and transforming those that contradict and deny the liberating message of the gospel.

3. that provinces, dioceses and parishes include in their various cycles of prayer, prayers for peace-makers and those involved in the work of reconciliation.

4. that provinces gather and submit to IASCOME resources being used in peace-building, so that these can be made available to assist in the training of peace-makers.

Recommendations page 158

IASCOME recommends:

1. that provinces examine their entire investment portfolios, including pension funds, to ensure that they meet the Global Reporting Initiative Standard, (www.globalreporting.org) especially in relation to the arms trade and the environment.

2. that provinces examine their governance structures to ensure transparency in decision-making processes and financial management.

3. that provinces seek ways to train creative administrators who are also strategic thinkers.

4. that provinces put in place measures to deal with corruption in the church at all levels, and make these measures known to the membership.

5. *that each province affirm its commitment to the Anglican Communion by a renewed endeavour to fulfil its financial obligation to the Inter-Anglican Budget.*

Resolution Page 158

Resolves

1. *To receive with thanks the Interim Report 'Travelling Together in God's Mission' from the Inter Anglican Standing Commission on Mission and Evangelism (IASCOME)*
2. *To give thanks for the successful Nairobi Consultation for Provincial Mission and Evangelism Co-ordinators 'Encounters on the Road'; to receive the report of that Consultation; to encourage dissemination of its report and to support plans for a follow-up conference, funded outside of the budget of the ACC*
3. *To look forward to and pray for the mission organisations Conference planned for February 2003*
4. *To take note of action taken on matters remitted to the Commission*
5. *To note that comments on the Primates Strategic Working Party on Theological Education have been sent direct to that working party*
6. *To encourage the Commission to develop its mandate, reflection and work, particularly in the areas of*
    - *Leadership Training and Formation for Mission*
    - *Islam and Islamisation*
    - *Developing Anglicanism: A Communion in Mission*
    - *The Journey to Wholeness and Fullness of Life*
    - *Justice Making and Peace Building*
    - *Evangelism*
7. *To circulate the interim report to provinces, other Commissions and networks and more widely for comment and discussion.*

IASCOME PowerPoint Presentation

Mandate

- To report to and receive reports and tasks from the Anglican Consultative Council.
- To facilitate companion diocese and other companionship links

throughout the Communion, in accordance with the guidelines for such links.

- To work with Anglican networks for mission and evangelism as they currently exist or might emerge in the future.
- To facilitate the sharing of resources, both human and financial, throughout the Communion.
- To link, share and critique experiences of capacity—building for mission and evangelism.
- To engage in theological reflection on mission.
- To be a forum where the provinces and the voluntary and synodical agencies of the Communion share and reflect.
- To continue the momentum of the Decade of Evangelism.
- To encourage the emergence of new and appropriate structures for mission and evangelism.
- To liaise with the South-to-South Movement.
- To encourage, monitor and learn from ecumenical expressions of mission.

Major Meetings and Conferences Held and Forthcoming

Provincial Mission and Evangelism Co-ordinators Conference

> 'Encounters on the Road'—
> (Nairobi, Kenya, May 2002)

Strategic Recommendations:

- Guideline for Provincial Mission and Evangelism Co-ordinators
- Networking through email for Provincial Mission and Evangelism Co-ordinators
- Regional and provincial evangelism consultations
- Appointment of Mission and Evangelism Co-ordinators in all Provinces, dioceses and parishes
- Share training resources in evangelism, mission, leadership and spiritual formation
- A second Provincial Mission and Evangelism Consultation in 2004

The ACC is asked to support a follow-up Conference in 2004.

Mission Organisations Conference

'Transformation and Tradition in Global Mission'
Cyprus 12–18 February 2003

Objectives of the Conference:

- To bring together diverse forms of Anglican mission agencies and organisations that express the comprehensive nature of world mission today;
- To bring together the current generation of lay and ordained mission leaders in the worldwide Anglican Communion, to share their experiences;
- To gain a better understanding of contemporary mission issues and changing patterns in mission (for example, outreach to immigrants and web-based evangelism);
- To renew our vision for mission through biblical and theological reflection, worship and prayer;
- To be challenged by new church models in mission and evangelism;
- To encourage the development of new networks among mission organisations, dioceses and parishes in the Communion.

Tasks

- The Anglican Gathering
- The Partners in Mission process
- Companion Diocesan Links

Equipping and Formation for Mission

- Theological education
- Mission formation
- Clerical preparation

The ACC is asked to endorse the Commission's role in its work on leadership training and formation for mission.

Some Areas of Concern and Continuing Work

- Islam and Islamisation

The recommendations call for gatherings of those caught up in such situations for mutual support and learning.

- Developing Anglicanism: A Communion in Mission

ACC is asked to affirm the Commission's developing this thinking

- The Journey towards Wholeness and Fullness of Life

The recommendations suggest ways the Commission and others might take these forward.

- Mission as Justice-Making and Peace-Building

The recommendations to provinces suggest ways in which justice-making and peace-building can be taken forward.

- Money, Power and Christian Mission

R*ecommendations to provinces highlight the importance of the Global Reporting Initiative Standard as a guide to ethical investment and address issues of corruption in the Church.*

- Evangelism

A major item for future agenda to build on the momentum of the Decade of Evangelism.

Resolution

Resolves

1. *To receive with thanks the Interim Report 'Travelling Together in God's Mission' from the Inter Anglican Standing Commission on Mission and Evangelism (IASCOME)*
2. *To give thanks for the successful Nairobi Consultation for Provincial Mission and Evangelism Co-ordinators 'Encounters on the Road'; to receive the report of that Consultation; to encourage dissemination of its report and to support plans for a follow-up conference, funded outside of the budget of the ACC*
3. *To look forward to and pray for the mission organisations Conference planned for February 2003*
4. *To take note of action taken on matters remitted to the Commission*
5. *To note that comments on the Primates Strategic Working Party on Theological Education have been sent direct to that working party*
6. *To encourage the Commission to develop its mandate, reflection and work particularly in the areas of*
    - *Leadership Training and Formation for Mission*
    - *Islam and Islamisation*
    - *Developing Anglicanism: A Communion in Mission*

- *The Journey to Wholeness and Fullness of Life*
- *Justice Making and Peace Building*
- *Evangelism*

7. *To circulate the interim report to provinces, other Commissions and networks and more widely for comment and discussion.*

IASCOME Report: Questions for Discussion

For all groups:

i) What does the group consider are the two most important issues the Commission is addressing and why?

ii) Are there mission issues that the group feels the Commission should address and why? [Name no more than two.]

iii) Are there any general comments the group has on the report?

For:	
Group I	Do you have any comments on section D especially D5, D7, D8?
Group II	Do you have any comments on section E?
Group III	Do you have any comments on section F1?
Group IV	Do you have any comments on section F2?
Group V	Do you have any comments on section F3?
Group VI	Do you have any comments on section F4?
Group VII	Do you have any comments on section F5?
Group VIII	Do you have any comments on Appendices II and III? *[Conclusions of the Nairobi Conference?]*
Group XI	Do you have any comments on Appendices II and III? *[Conclusions of the Nairobi Conference?]*

Each group is requested to write up their findings as comments on the forms to be given to each group to be passed on to the Mission Commission. Please hand in your response to Miss Marjorie Murphy, Director for Mission and Evangelism.

Strategic Recommendations

- To gather material and put together a booklet of Guidelines for Provincial Mission and Evangelism Co-ordinators.

- For Provincial Mission and Evangelism Co-ordinators to continue communicating, encouragement, the sharing of stories, resources and news through email net working based at the ACO.

- To hold a second Provincial Mission and Evangelism Consultation in 2004 to report back to each other on the recommendations and for mutual encouragement.

- To encourage regional and provincial evangelism consultations to strengthen and encourage mission and evangelism locally.
- To encourage the appointment of Mission and Evangelism Co-ordinators in all the Provinces of the Anglican Communion and in the dioceses and parishes.
- To share resources, especially for training of laity and clergy in evangelism, mission, leadership and spiritual formation.

HIV/AIDS Presentation and Resolves

—The Reverend Canon Ted Karpf, Provincial Canon Missioner for HIV/AIDS, The Province of South Africa

I greet you on behalf of the Most Reverend Njongonkulu Ndungane, Archbishop of Cape Town and Metropolitan of the 3.5 million members of the Anglican Church of the Province of Southern Africa, and as spokesperson for the Worldwide Communion on HIV/AIDS.

I greet you on behalf of all of us living with HIV/AIDS in Southern Africa.

And finally, I greet you in the language of the Zulu people, one of the dozen distinct languages spoken in South Africa, with these words *Sawubona.* This means, because I have seen you and acknowledge you, I exist as a human being. Your response is *Yebo.* This means: because we have seen you and acknowledge you as a person, we exist. Therefore, *Sawubona, Yebo.*

Background: What is Happening Today?

Today there are some 30 million people in the grip of this pandemic on African soil, and more than an estimated 47 million worldwide. Living in South Africa I work in the very heart of the holocaust. I come among you, bringing a witness to what we are facing in the hope that your understanding and compassion will extend to us.

HIV/AIDS in Africa reached the level of a pandemic within a decade of its discovery in 1982. What is it about a pandemic that sets it apart from other catastrophic human experiences? We seem able to accommodate ourselves quickly to the losses inflicted in wartime or to react with lightening speed when we lose thousands to a natural catastrophe. A pandemic, however, is different. The losses may be as many or more than any disaster imaginable. But the way humans respond is different because it is about disease and death and these events take time to manifest and take their toll.

For a nation, a pandemic means facing the serious risk of the loss of two productive generations, and with them, the slow but inexorable erosion of the fabric that knits together stable societies and nations. Teachers, clergy, doctors, miners, farmers, hospital workers, administrators, mothers and fathers begin to disappear, but things seem to be the same. With these losses social stability, institutional memories, and productivity diminish and eventually disappear. For nations struggling with transformation such as the nations comprising the Church of the Province of Southern Africa, a pandemic means the potential and actual loss of the promised future.

On the level of an individual or family, a pandemic is most different from other human events in the way individuals experience it.

- For a 50-year-old grandmother, a pandemic means that two of her five children are already dead, eight grandchildren need care. Three to five of them will die from the effects of AIDS, too. Who will care for her in her old age? Who will care for these grandchildren when she is no longer able?
- For a ten-year-old head of household with three younger siblings, HIV/AIDS means that he alone is responsible. Who will pay his school fees? Where will food be found? Who can be turned to for comfort? When he is 14, will he become infected, too?
- For an economically active woman in her 30s, the crisis means supporting her family of three in addition to her sister's family of five children orphaned by the disease. If she becomes infected by her HIV-positive husband who works as a truck driver, what will happen to those who rely on her?
- For all individuals now living with HIV in the geography encompassing the Province of Southern Africa, it is estimated that there are as many as 10 million of us. Who will remember our names when we have died?

Here are some updated statistics to give you a clear sense of the global crisis: (slides follow with the numbers appearing in sequence of severity—Africa is at 30 million).

But what do these figures mean to people living in Africa? To help you frame the reality of this nightmare, think of it this way: In sub-Saharan Africa we experience the same number of losses every single day, seven days a week, 52 weeks a year, that the world experienced in one day on 9/11. Every day in Africa is another 9/11. Yet if you listen carefully to the world, you will note that there is a peculiar silence.

- Every day 1,500 more persons in Africa become HIV-positive. Every minute of the day another child dies from AIDS.
- In South Africa alone, half of the 15-years-olds today will not reach their 25th birthday because they will die from AIDS.

- Think about this: The life expectancy of Africans is set to reach one of its lowest levels ever. By the year 2005, most Africans will die before they reach their 48th birthday.

Individual countries fare even worse. In Botswana, for instance, you will be lucky to see your 37th birthday, while in Zimbabwe most people will die by the time they're 43 years old. In stark contrast, life expectancy in Hong Kong, for instance, is 83.9 years if you're a woman and 78 years for men. In China, most people will live to be 72, while in India the average life expectancy is 62. In South America it is 67.

These statistics speak volumes and highlight where your intervention is needed most. It would be a sin to behave as if these figures had no bearing on your life or the life of our Church.

Church's Response to HIV/AIDS

For our Anglican Communion, this pandemic means confronting the relentless progression of a crippling social force, and assisting people in making spiritual sense of what is often beyond human control. After 20 years of silence, our own worldwide Anglican Communion through its Primates has declared, **"HIV/AIDS is not a punishment from God."**

Nonetheless, we are still challenged to interpret the will of God when so many have died of a preventable sexually transmitted infection. How can we embody the love of Christ when we are challenged by increasing numbers of funerals to be performed and increasingly fewer people and even scarcer resources to mobilise?

To this question, the Church does have a response. Archbishop Ndungane has committed us to a mission of hope with these words:

- No one should die alone.
- No one should care alone.
- We are all living with AIDS, whether infected or affected.

In the past the Church in South Africa and the rest of the continent focused on fighting the evils of apartheid and other injustices: AIDS is the new struggle. Failing to the meet the challenges posed by it means there will be no one to left to worship in our churches, attend our schools or take up the challenges of the future. We must act now!

What Have We Done?

In March 2001, the Archbishop of Canterbury tasked Archbishop Ndungane with the responsibility of developing a Communion-wide understanding of the scope of the AIDS pandemic in Africa.

The Archbishop's first task was to convene the leadership of the African Churches through the Council of Anglican Provinces in Africa (CAPA) to determine the breadth and scope—as well as the potential responses—of this pandemic. To this end, the All-Africa Anglican Conference on HIV/AIDS was held in Boksburg, South Africa in August 2001, sponsored by the Compass Rose Society, Christian Aid of Great Britain, UNAIDS, US Agency for International Development and the Pharmaceutical Research and Manufacturers Association.

At this All-Africa Anglican Conference, the voices of Africa spoke, and a vision statement to guide the Communion's response to HIV/AIDS across the globe was formed.

Such a vision promises that future generations will be born and live in a world free from AIDS. This pledge is guided by God's call for transformation, for "We are living with AIDS."

As the body of Christ, confronted by a disaster unprecedented in human history, we share the pain of all who suffer as a result of AIDS. We confess our sins of judgment, ignorance, silence, indifference and denial. Stigma fuels the fire of HIV/AIDS across the world stage, and denies that we are created in the image of God.

Through our communal vision of future generations living in a world without HIV/AIDS, we have committed all our efforts—personal, corporate, programmatic and liturgical—to confront stigma as sin and work for its end.

Most importantly, this vision is a call to action that embraces a commitment to an HIV/AIDS ministry through a six-fold commission made up of:

- Prevention
- Pastoral Care
- Counselling
- Care
- Death and Dying
- Leadership

The Boksburg conference served as a much-needed catalyst to find ways of tackling HIV/AIDS within faith communities. So urgent was the task that the proceedings document from the Boksburg conference was published as a ready-to-use planning manual, *Planning Our Response to AIDS: A Step-by-Step Guide to HIV/AIDS Planning for the Anglican Communion.* It provided a template for planning an AIDS ministry response to the expanding crisis.

Since the conference, the response of the CPSA Office of HIV/AIDS Community Ministries and Mission has been to lead strategic planning efforts in the dioceses of the Church of the Province of Southern Africa. Since mid-November 2001, nearly every diocese has participated in planning activities, setting and adopting its own strategic plan for meeting the challenges of the HIV/AIDS pandemic. All plans have been characterised by local, community-driven solutions.

Worldwide Communion Response

The response to the Strategic Planning process and the early results it is producing across Africa has been striking. In April 2002, after reporting to his fellow Archbishops at a meeting in Canterbury, Archbishop Ndungane not only received praise and support from the Primates of the Anglican Communion but was also re-commissioned to continue leading the worldwide Communion in responding to this catastrophe.

From Canterbury came a pivotal statement which will inform our way forward. Here is a short extract from this memorable document.

- We raise our voices to call for an end to silence about this disease—the silence of stigma, the silence of denial, the silence of fear.
- We confess that the Church herself has been complicit in this silence. When we have raised our voices in the past, it has been too often a voice of condemnation.
- We now wish to make it clear that HIV/AIDS is not a punishment from God.
- Our Christian faith compels us to accept that all persons, including those who are living with HIV/AIDS, are made in the image of God and are children of God.

The Primates also commended to the Communion the six-fold commissions regarding HIV/AIDS. And endorsed the planning framework to churches beyond Africa, urging strategic planning and policy development to confront the HIV/AIDS crisis. Finally, they called on the whole church to minister among all affected by the disease.

Stories from the Provinces

With regard to the pandemic and its impact on our lives, I want to say that across the Anglican Communion in Africa, our Church has moved forward. One of the major steps since last year is that every Province has is using the "Our Vision, Our Hope" Vision Statement to formulate ministry responses to AIDS. Additionally, every Province has used the six focal concerns as a way of identifying and reporting their ministry. Here is a quick run-down of what has been happening across Africa since last year.

For example:

• In Uganda, the Church is leading the way in ending discrimination and stigma, people with HIV/AIDS are welcomed by the Church. The success of the Church in de-stigmatising people living with AIDS was significantly advanced by HIV-positive Canon and Priest, Gideon Byamugisha, who has travelled the world telling the Uganda story.

• In Nigeria, the Church is sensitising the clergy and Bishops in the area of Pastoral Care and Support. Because AIDS is the new "growth-industry" of Nigeria, it is critical that the Church has the latest, best and most accurate information among its people, to correct local myths and profiteering. To model the role of the Church in the larger community, an AIDS Clinic has been established at the Provincial Office of the Archbishop of Nigeria.

• In Tanzania, the Church has openly discussed the efficacy of condom use and endorsed such use in order to save lives. Home-based Care and Living with Hope seminars enable clergy and laity to care for the sick and dying. Discussions are underway to create and Voluntary Counselling and Testing programmes through the Church.

• In Boga/Democratic Republic of Congo, a difficult war is still going on despite efforts to bring peace from the new African Union. Nonetheless, AIDS work goes on. The Church is engaged in hands-on care-giving and Voluntary Counselling and Testing. While efforts have been sporadic, at best, due to the civil unrest, a pattern has been set to ensure that People Living With AIDS are cared for by their Church.

• In Ghana, the Church is providing AIDS awareness education for the clergy, peer education for youth and counselling training for clergy. Additionally, AIDS prevention training is being offered to Sunday School teachers and class leaders to bring the message into the classroom. All Guild leaders are also being trained so that HIV/ADS can be discussed by all sectors of the congregation. Finally the state-sponsored HIV counselling manual has been sent to all dioceses in order to ensure continuity between the Churches and the government-sponsored AIDS prevention programmes.

• In Burundi, after years of domestic conflict and war, the clergy met for the first time in August. They talked about HIV/AIDS and the response across their Province. In the meantime, the Church has provided food and shelter and AIDS education as part of its activities in resettlement and stabilising a war-ravaged population.

• In the Province of the Indian Ocean, parents and youth are talking about AIDS together in round table discussions hosted by the Church. Members of the Mother's Union are also involved in sexuality and reproductive health train-the-trainers programmes in order to be in the community as AIDS educators.

• In Kenya, the church and government are collaborating to educate and make available information and education in schools and churches. Prevention is openly discussed and efforts are underway to provide resources for church-based care programmes.

• In Sudan, even ravaged by civil war and daily acts of violence, the church is providing education support for people living with AIDS.

• In Rwanda, the Church is offering direct assistance through support groups, which really support people where they are. Groups have assisted in the purchase of decent and clean homes for parishioners. Other groups are keeping their participants alive through the ending of stigma. Finally, the Church in Rwanda is developing Family-Focused Ministries, which work to support behavioural change for all ages.

• In Central Africa, HIV/AIDS is included in the theological curriculum for the preparation of pastors for ministry. However, the Province, which covers Botswana, Zimbabwe, Zambia, and Malawi, is also promoting voluntary Counselling and Testing (VCT). With regard to orphaned children, the Zambian Church has developed a school-based integration programme, which assists children and their recipient institution in returning to school. Additionally, the Church is providing nutritional and spiritual support to children. The new difficulty is the effects of the famine on the spread of HIV and survivability of those whose immune systems are already weakened.

• In Southern Africa, the Church has just completed strategic planning processes in 22 dioceses with more than 1,000 persons. Each diocese has a plan and direction, capitalising on work already underway. Additionally, there is a plan at the Provincial level as well, to ensure that dioceses are supported and programmes extended across the entire Province. Factors such as food shortages and the slowness of governments to respond are hampering efforts in this Province to move as quickly as it might.

• Across all of Africa, the thousands and thousands of volunteers in our men's and women's organisations, like Mothers Union, Anglican Women's Fellowship and Bernard Mizeki, are providing compassion and support for those who are sick and dying from the effects of AIDS.

What You Can Do

You have heard stories from Africa, but you may wonder, "What is your role in all this?" While Africa is being decimated by the pandemic, HIV/AIDS is not exclusively an African problem.

Over the next decade it's estimated that as many as 10 million members of our Communion, alone, may die from the effects of AIDS. How many families will be destroyed? How many churches will withstand this massive assault of death? Our Church has AIDS-what are we to do? Ask yourself: How does HIV/AIDS affect your community? What are you doing to help? And if you are standing back, you need to answer why.

Let's turn to the scriptures for direction for a way forward. I'll remind you of Luke 24. "Two of them were going to a village called Emmaus. They were talking with each other about everything that had happened. As they talked and discussed these things with each other, Jesus himself came up and walked along with them."

Jesus walked alongside those who were confounded by loss and confused about the way forward. To this end we turn to the Anglican Communion worldwide and we ask you to follow Jesus' lead and walk alongside the churches of the South and share our despair and sorrow.

If you abandon the South or throw up your hands in horror and say, "Clean up your own house," remember that it is your house too. And if we don't have churches doing what churches do best—knitting together communities and providing parishioners with core values and belief—then what are we left with?

We are faced with an enormous challenge to create a generation without HIV/AIDS. If we don't stand together, this hope will be but a distant dream. And the future won't just be lost to those in Africa, but it will be lost to us in the rest of the world.

What will our futures be when youth orphaned by AIDS are grown into angry young men and women, whose lives have been decimated by disease and poverty? I will tell you frankly: Banditry, gangs and chaotic violence will flourish. This is the reality of many African communities wrenched apart by the pandemic.

Ours is a global village—what happens in one country has an impact on another. You only have to look to 9/11 as a stark reminder of our comingled worlds. It would be naïve and inhuman to try to divorce yourself from the worldwide impact of this pandemic.

To guide us forward, let's turn, once more, to the Primates Statement and the six commissions, as these embody our vision and our imperative.

Prevention:

- We seek to guide and educate our people in prevention of the disease and encourage Christian teaching, which is frank and factual about abstinence and faithfulness.

Pastoral care:

- As pastors we are called to walk with those who are affected by the disease, to offer support and compassion and bring the Christian message of love, forgiveness and hope to the world.

Counselling:

- We are inspired and guided by the example of our Lord Jesus Christ who ministered to all without fear or discrimination.

Care:

- We affirm that safe and effective pharmaceutical treatment should be more widely available to alleviate suffering and extend life.

Death & Dying:

- We call upon our Churches to stand compassionately with those who are living with the disease, those who mourn and those who are dying.

Leadership:

- We wish to encourage collective action with government and non-governmental organisations. Such co-ordinated and joint action is the only way to address the enormity of the challenge.

In the words of the Primates Statement: "We raise our voices to call for an end to silence about this disease—the silence of stigma, the silence of denial, the silence of fear."

Let me share with you then a story from Africa.

Her name is Nesta. She is a woman in her late 30s, looking more like late 60s and dying from several AIDS-related cancers, among them, Kaposi's sarcoma. It has caused her legs to swell, making it very painful for her to walk the many kilometres for food and water. She lives in the Valley of a Thousand Hills, so named because there are dozens upon dozens of little hills up and down this rift valley outside of Durban. The hills are dotted small mud huts and whole villages.

As I drive Nesta home, she is in pain and weeping. I offer to carry her groceries down the embankment to her home. She replies, "I would appreciate that, but I am embarrassed for you to see where I stay. The roof leaks and the floor is wet. It is falling down as it is just mud." I insist on going promising not to judge her home.

She relented and seemed grateful for the help, as the walk to her home is steep. It took 10 minutes of steady descent to get to the little dwelling, precariously perched on the hillside. Upon arrival I found two adjoining buildings: one was the bedroom, and the other a padlocked kitchen.

Because praying is what I am supposed to do in this setting, I asked if we could pray a blessing on the house. She stopped, stared, and looking rather shocked she replied, "First I must let you see my family." I expected her 2 children, aged 10 and12, to appear from somewhere.

Instead she led me behind the house. There were 3-mounded earthen graves, covered by thorn branches to keep the goats and wild dogs away. The graves were of her recently deceased husband and two small children, aged 9 months and 21 months. Her family died of AIDS.

I gasped as tears formed in my eyes. Because the soil is so rocky, the graves are only about 3 feet deep. Thus it is imperative to pile earth high above a grave to keep the rot and stench at bay. She told how she had to bury them quickly under the cloak of darkness, since there was no money to pay for caskets. She went on to say that she was ashamed of how it looked in the community to be so poor.

She explained that her husband brought this killer home a few years ago from the Johannesburg mines. She didn't know he was infected until the death of her youngest child who was born infected. Then it took him, and now her. She's trying to earn enough with odd jobs to pay for her funeral so that her surviving children don't have to bury her under the cloak of darkness. But her time came way too soon for that.

But on this day we pray. We pray for her deceased children and for her husband. And as I walk touching each of those graves, I bless them as if the funeral had happened for the first time just now. As I finished the prayer, she leaned down to the earth, down to her husband's grave, and started pounding, crying out, "Where were you? Where were you? You should have been here to protect us. They came and took our food. You should have been paying attention. You should have protected us from our neighbours. Where were you?"

Then she explained through her sobs that her husband's ghost had the responsibility in death of protecting her family and had failed to do so. She asked again, "Is he angry with me? What have I done to him except to care for him and for our children? He should have been here to warn us or something. Where were you?" And then she fell into my arms weeping.

All I could do was stand there. I felt helpless to heal, helpless to comfort, helpless to give solace of any kind, helpless to answer. All I could do was stand there. For somehow I knew, deep inside, that she was asking something more, something of me, something of all of us in the developed world. Please, please, do not let the birthplace of humankind become the burial place of our humanity.

Somehow, in meeting or even capitulating to the challenges posed by this agony of AIDS, I find that I am becoming more human and more humane. Maybe it is the break from the lethargy of past achievements? Maybe it is the exhilaration of being congruent with the values and beliefs that have guided my life? Maybe it is that I am seeing Jesus again, as if for the first time, in Nesta and her millions of brothers and sisters and children!

I have also learned that following Jesus is not so much about doing something, as it is being a companion and standing there: standing there, and gazing into his eyes, much as I did with Nesta; and while there, feeling the gratitude and the awe that is life. The message is, "Don't just do something, stand there and be a companion: stand in the midst of muck and mire we call life."

Today you and I are invited again into relationship with God and with each other across the boundaries of nation, language, race and culture. We may even be comfortable and well enough to believe that we do not need the services of the Great Physician. Nevertheless, we are invited to act on Jesus' invitation to life. Jesus is passing through our lives, inviting us into companionship. All that we are asked to do is say, "Yes" to His, and "Yes" to our lives.

Millions of people just like Nesta invite you to join us on the road and companion us through the difficult times ahead.

Let me ask you, what have you heard about HIV/AIDS?

What have you seen about HIV/AIDS?

What do you feel about HIV/AIDS?

HIV/AIDS Resolves

Prevention

Workshops to help members of the Church and community in general
Teach people this issue
More information is needed for pastors as mediators for counselling
Research needs to take this issue seriously
By wearing a Red Ribbon to show solidarity
Incorporation about patterns of living and lifestyles that lead to risk of HIV
Teach Catechumens
Include AIDS prevention into Church School syllabus
Participate and initiate education programmes
Participate in practical care ventures even in countries far away
Speak and teach about values of abstinence and faithfulness
Educate clergy about AIDS
Hold on to each other in prayer
Teaching about sexual behaviour
Educate church community

Make prevention means available from the Church
Through education and consciousness awakening
Working in schools, workplaces and praying at daily masses
Reach out to high-risk sectors of the community
Develop curriculae for different sectors of society, including high tech
How can I be of service to Africa and her children?
AIDS should be part of our Christian education programmes
Educate the youth
Practices abstinence before marriage and faithfulness within
Doctors, nurses, teachers raise consciousness about the AIDS pandemic
Support Church of South Africa in steps they are taking
Create awareness of what causes AIDS
Use speakers from AIDS NGOs to educate church
AIDS education in Christian schools
Provide information on the use of the condom
Conferences/teaching all levels: young adults, children, teens
Be in touch with municipalities
Cooperate with secular institutions
Support grass roots efforts in fighting AIDS
Call upon the US to support efforts making HIV a chronic disease in the developing world
Educate about risks for transmission of HIV/corrective behaviours and prevention
Offer condoms free of charge to those who cannot control themselves
Offer regular medical check-ups for couples and adolescents
Offer medical exams for HIV for those intending to marry
We are not aware of an AIDS problem in our diocese—8 years ago we were told about it
Condoms
Education—ABC
Clinics
Begin early in life to educate children about HIV/AIDS
Educate about condoms
Abstinence and faithfulness must be realities and show how this is achieved
Support AIDS education programmes
Use Primates Statement
Need more information about AIDS—that it kills!
Facts and statistics help raise consciousness
Any links between sexuality stands and incidence of HIV
Church resources support government school education programmes
Support work in Africa on AIDS education
Strengthen partnerships between North and South
Informed prayer and education
Establish deeper ties with companion and link dioceses for support
Ask for help

Develop and implement programmes for all ages, especially under 25
Meet people where they are
Don't tell sexually active people to abstain, help them understand and avoid the risks
Distribute condoms
Constant awareness campaign: Youth MU Health Officials, pastoral visitors, Social Education
Eradication of poverty
Jobs for youth
Bible Study
Education on sex
Education to the youth
Practice Christian chastity and respect faithfulness to partners
Awareness
Training
Preaching on Sunday about AIDS
Use the media to get the message out
Educating
Meeting and Discussion on courses of Action which church can take
Maximize access to information
Maximum support from government sources
Maximum support for AIDS programmes at home
Encourage faithful relationships
Teach against promiscuity
Make condoms freely available
Ensure that migrant workers are accompanied by spouses
License prostitutes
Education about AIDS
Church teach about fidelity, abstinence until marriage
Prayer and practical help for projects and education
Be a source of non-judgement, information, advice, and support
Educate young people through the youth organisations
Educate about this horror and abstain from relations that are destructive
Target financial support to dioceses and provinces for AIDS work
Provide for orphans
Invest funds in school seminars, Sunday school training
Limit the spread of this disease
Joint efforts with government and NGOs
National Councils of Churches mobilized
Provide education and encourage morality
Speak the truth to young people not like churches that prohibit condoms, it is more effective to prevent than to repent
Church should encourage abstinence, however should provide support education and condoms for those who are cannot abstain, support is needed
Offer testing in church

Train dioceses and parishes
Bring facts to the public-tell the story
Covenant with churches doing AIDS ministry
Teach and evangelize vigorously
Educate about the dangers of casual sex

Pastoral Care

Put HIV/AIDS in General Church Programme
Church needs to know it role
Give care to allow people to feel part of the community
More money is needed to be raised for this purpose
Wear Red Ribbon
Take seriously the message of the Primates
Support local church and community AIDS support groups
Regular preaching about AIDS
Sex education in parochial and secular schools and youth organisations
Make People living with AIDS welcome in our Churches
Getting the message that AIDS is not a punishment from God
Informing unaffected people that they should not shun people with AIDS
Experience those who are affected by disease without condemnation
Walk with those in their journey to death
Provide material help to the infected
Prayer for infected and affected
Support, listen and respond
Financial and practical help where possible
People must be professionally trained
Be with those who are suffering
Support those with some by securing medicine and foods
Support families
Church needs should be where people are pastorally
Visiting and prayer with sick
Pastors need training to deal with AIDS-they must overcome prejudices
Clergy must tell how God loves people with AIDS
People with AIDS must be fully integrated into the life of the church
Church provide more information to its people
Training, support and information on how to be a caring community or individual
Feed and clothe
Small groups from churches should support people living with AIDS
Assist families
Spiritual counsel
Pastoral care includes challenging the systems
Make palliative treatments readily available
Teach and encourage local congregations to overcome prejudice and fear
De-stigmatise AIDS suffers

Help communities accept people with AIDS as part of the community
Educate caregivers
Make Primates Statement available
Train clergy and pastoral care workers to end stigma
Oppose discrimination
Support families and friends of those living with AIDS
Visiting and praying with those living with AIDS
Identify with the suffering
Stewardship is a lifestyle which includes AIDS prevention and support
Abandoning theologies of punishment that make God out to be a terrorist
Get AIDS message out—NOT a punishment from God
Must be preached in every pulpit in our Church
Training in lay pastoral care needs to be designed and funded
Trained ordained
Support lay who minister
Build AIDS work in the community
Preaching Sundays should include HIV/AIDS
It is my duty to save my people and the world from AIDS
Constant visits: clergy, MU, youth, parents for sacramental support
Pastoral care to all the affected
Encourage safer sexual practice and commitment of relationship
Practice Christian love toward all
Show love
Prayer and comfort
Provision of medicine and food
Develop diocesan partnerships and links
First engage in prevention
Challenge and train in skills
Non judgmental acceptance of people living with AIDS
Link patients and their families with persons and families in other countries who can help through prayer, solidarity, and finances
Being sympathetic is not enough; sympathy must go with practical help
Pay more attentions to others
Set upon an initiative creating guidelines for care and support
Pastors need special training
Overcome prejudices
Train clergy on how to say God loves them
Support programmes
Continue support for home-based care programmes
Training training training
Practical support and prayer
Organise special events, visit the sick and pray for and with those who suffering
Clear teaching on faithfulness in marriage
Sex education
Give examples of marital love

Encourage use of condoms
Learn—Educate and Pray
Action education and outreach
Work through dioceses
Communion and comfort should be offered for all who are suffering
Organise ministry teams to support parishioners and sufferers
Extend support through practical help-food cooking support
Do not discriminate
Help families
Make people aware that we are all affected
Educate our clergy about HIV/AIDS

Counselling

All the Church to be involved in counselling
Encourage Testing
Encourage acceptance
Encourage going for treatment
Identify qualified persons we can call upon to provide counselling on AIDS issues
Work in cooperation with institutions that are already attending this issue
Need to be close to those suffering from HIV/AIDS to give hope
Wear Red Ribbon
Identify with those living with AIDS
Education of congregation about the nature of the disease
Attend and educate about the needs of those suffering
Constant need for unconditional charity
Church challenged to put away old fears and prejudices so it a free to minister
Be hands heart and feet of Jesus
Implementing programme to prevent spread of AIDS
Provide spiritual guidance a comfort to those dying from HIV/AIDS
Establish counselling in churches
Educate pastors in counselling
Church should offer its resources—church hall office space available for consultation
Secure practitioners with state and organisations involved in the programme of support and nurture
Comfort the suffering
Advise on ways of preventing further spread of disease
Offer spiritual guidance
AIDS is not punishment
Support for uninfected
Be there with infected
People must be professionally trained
Give good guidance
Teach practical ways of living in the midst of AIDS

Train professional leadership in how to counsel and care
Visit in hospitals and clinics
Offer counselling services in the church
How to deal with sexual temptation
How to ask for help and assistance
Promote good sexual behaviour
Do more counselling
Provide peer-counselling training
Stress AIDS is not a punishment from God
See AIDS as horror and source that it is
Learn to respond with a level of human compassion
Training programmes for counselors
Church should talk with youth about sex
Church should refusing to use condoms in case there are people not abstaining
Patients should be cared for
Every teacher in the church should be commissioned and trained in AIDS education and how to talk to men and women
Learn to make referrals
Support AIDS hospices
Support people and programmes
Support Sex education in schools
Recruit volunteers
End discrimination against people with AIDS
Offer counselling services
Encourage fidelity and commitment among hetero and homosexual couples
Must see effective coordination between public authorities and Church
Clear teaching on chastity
Be with young people
Care for the dying
Hospices
Planning and delivery of services
Partner with community NGOs in offering support and services
Church should prompt public actions and advocacy, but not duplicate it
Our mission should be active counselling
Priest must do regular visits
Training is essential for counselling
Lead with an open heart
Move away from judgement
Give courage to the dying in order to die with dignity
Training of counselors
Promotion of groups for those living with AIDS
Appoint chaplains-lay and clergy-to look out for and care for people living with AIDS and their families
Listen and offer assistance

Educate clergy and leaders so their fears can be abated and they can educate and lessen fears of all
HIV patients must be given care to make them face life and courageously live
Do not stigmatize anyone
Share our care and concern for people living with AIDS
Work with those who stand in ignorance or judgement
Do not ignore
Listen
Non-judgmental care
Comfort the dying
Get alongside those in greatest need
Visitation by priests and counselors should be organised
Stigma reduction
Assist government and provide volunteers
Education is important, people must be informed

Care

Create an international fund from which others can be helped
Medicine
Food
Clothing
Educate the young children
Good Samaritan approach to caring and support
Follow Jesus' way in dealing with disease
Care and love people fearlessly
Share with others their burdens
Wear Red Ribbon
Targeted giving of money to appropriate funds
By pressuring pharmaceutical companies to care
Lobby through local government and agencies about care
Call for and support overseas mission and medical ventures
Support Africa with medical and financial commitment
Volunteers to work in areas of need
Demand readily available medicines
Loving people with AIDS
Lobbying for sound economic policy guiding nations
Establish care facilities
Expend resources on medicines and drugs for AIDS patients
To advocate and appeal for more affordable treatments
Lobby local government to facilitate the availability of drug treatment
Provide resources and medicines
Provide visitation that supports care to individuals and family
Pray for AIDS patients
Offer assistance and material support to the dying
People must be professionally trained

Develop pharmaceutical center in local parishes
Raise money to help with medications
Provide anti-Retrovirals
Provide Rehabilitation groups with funds and support
Church contribute regularly to ministry within HIV/AIDS
Practical support for medications, homes, and care
Provide medicine
People in church are helpful with care and support
Protest cutbacks in health care, particularly in palliative care
Find ways to support families living with AIDS
Provide clothing food and shelter-basic needs
Be available for dialogue
Political action to support international activities for drug availability
Advocate loosening of patent protections to make AIDS drugs available
Coordinated international campaign
Church and government should pay special attention
Train men and women to care
Special homes for those who suffer
Provide anti-Retrovirals and campaign for lowering pharmaceutical prices and making generics for treatment and care
Care for the sick and lonely
Providing medicines
Funds for income generation
Funds for AIDS awareness seminars
Funds for training of counselors
Provision of medicines and foods
Commitment is the key
Church must offer assistance in educating people
Offer help in treatment
Take to highest levels concerns to make drugs available and affordable
Provide care centers throughout the church
Develop Funds to support AIDS ministry
Regularly collect and distribute money to areas of need
Ensure support mechanism for those in their Provinces to feel supported, pastorally and financially
Ensure save environment and support services for those who go for testing
Church hospitals must be equipped to deal with the response to this crisis
Make treatment available to all who need it
Extend financial support
Challenge World Bank or developed nations to do more
Make life saving treatment available
Make preventive medicine available to people in need
Lobby South African through the British Commonwealth
Lobby for drug access in the Second and Third Worlds
Find ways of supporting hospitals in heavily affected area
Recruit physicians from around the world

Clergy should know parishes well enough to target healthcare and medical services
Teach weekly about AIDS in church school
Church supported hospitals must be equipped to deal with this
Church should care for widows and orphans
Provide assistance and support where needed
Open skills centers for assistance and survival
Change lifestyles and moral values to prevent HIV
This is the mission of the Church, to care

Leadership

Sensitize training the leadership
Training in Theological Colleges
Ensure AIDS is said during every service of the Church
Support our Church leaders to work in AIDS
Wear Red Ribbon
ACC promote AIDS ministry across Communion
Lobbying efforts
Arranging seminars and training
Consistent dripping on the stone—prayer, writing letters, educating friends/family
Partnering with local AIDS treatment groups
Form support and treatment groups
Offer leadership guidance
Give direction
Be a voice for those living with AIDS to government and community
Church must take leadership
Take some initiative
Be willing to cooperate offering the use of our churches to community
ACC and Anglican Communion supports practically and through budget AIDS ministry
Continuing advocacy for those living with HIV/AIDS
Educate the community and the church
Disseminate more information to more people about pandemic
Bishops and priests should take leadership
Expect and demand responsible action from government
This ACC should endorse international work being done and support reports
Request Bishops to be more publicly pro-active and vocal
Why didn't I know about Primates Statement?
Youth training is crucial
Take leadership in this pandemic seriously
Church must speak out on critical issues of prevention, care and treatment
Train special people to do this work
Church should lead where others cannot
Create awareness

Give support care and money
Training in skills
Capacity building
Enabling and empowering in resources
Support research into treatment and vaccines
This issue should be on the Communion's ecumenical dialogue so that the entire Church can respond in concert with the Communion
Ask for interfaith cooperation on this concern
Cooperative leadership
Special regard and concern for problems posed by drug abuse, prostitution and imprisonment
Church leaders and Christians must take responsibility
Challenge Governments and NGOs to be more effective in these areas
Lead by example
Let this issue never fall from the agenda of Government and NGOs
Preaching about pandemic
When I was hungry—you fed me is a model for the Church
We are all involved in some way . . . we must speak
Support Government and NGO programmes doing the work in these areas
Pressure SA government to support AB of CPSA and his efforts
Active role and interacting with the government and NGOs
Speak and act
Make a five-year plan
Work with government and NGOs to face the problem
Be unafraid to speak out
Avoid condemnation
Provide leadership education and training
Teach chastity and faithfulness
Goad government and politicians
Church leaders and clergy speak about AIDS more
Train leaders at Diocesan level
Preaching and encouraging all preach to talk about HIV/AIDS
Every congregation should provide volunteers to care
Take initiative in networking for support

Death and Dying

Visit and pray with the dying
Help those who remain
Develop a house for shelter and support
Comfort the dying
Mourn with mourners
Bury the dead
Structure teams to visit and provide moral support to persons affected and their families create fund to assist with funeral expenses for poor people

Church should provide decent burials
Support all people as children of God
Wear Red Ribbon
Bring messages of hope
Pray for the bereaved
Pay a visit to the dying
Care for the dependent
Provide financial support
By encouraging people with time and energy
Give time for hospital service and clinics at home and overseas
Forming support groups to be with persons dying from AIDS
Do more in education
Provide medicines to prolong life
Assist the dying
Pray with the dying and helpless
Offer consultation to the dying
End discrimination about those dying from AIDS
Help with funerals: personal support, food, expenses
Support the grieving families
Provide training in Spiritual aspect of death and dying
Teach that judgement is not punishment
Help plan funerals so that family can speak openly about cause of death
These are God's people in God's image
Bless the dying
Provision of pastoral care and counselling
Prayer
Assisting in funerals
Consoling the bereaved
Clergy and people must be available to care
Disperse information through the media
Church practice sensitivity with those who mourn and those who live
Feel dignity in death
Save people from Dying with Anti-Retrovirals
Church should support their people
Clear messages that support is in the church for those who suffer
Don't forget the caregivers
Share care and compassion so that no one feels alone
Set up homes for people to be cared for
Help each person receive a Christian funeral
Support grieving families

Report by the Anglican Observer at the United Nations

"Work and Mission of the Anglican Communion Office at the United Nations"

—ARCHDEACON TAIMALELAGI FAGAMALAMA TUATAGALOA-MATALAVEA

1. GREETINGS & PREAMBLE

1.1 May God be praised and I thank Him for the opportunity to serve you all as the Anglican Observer. Talofa and greetings in the mighty Name of Jesus Christ, our Risen Lord. In His name I also bring to you the greetings of those who attended the Global Anglican Congress on the Stewardship of Creation recently in South Africa.

1.2 It is certainly a privilege to address you for the first time as the Anglican Observer at the United Nations and therefore wish to briefly tell you a little about myself.

1.3 I'm from a very small country in the middle of the Pacific called Samoa (**Sa** meaning Taboo or Sacred and **Moa** being center—so my country's name literally translates to Sacred Center of the World maybe). Samoa is also known as the Heart of Polynesia. I served as Archdeacon of Samoa, in the Anglican Church of Aotearoa, New Zealand and Polynesia for 8 years.

After being a consultant to ACC6 in Nigeria I became a co-opted member for ACC7, 8 and 9 representing Gender Issues. I worked for the United Nations Development Programme for 25 years (first in Programming in Samoa, Philippines and Fiji and, later as Operations Manager in the Samoa Field Office). I have 9 children, 16 grandchildren and another is on the way.

1.4 I came to this position, therefore, with a deep sense of awareness about the connection between poverty, environmental destruction, economic development and gender issues. In order to help eradicate poverty; address the global HIV/AIDS pandemic; end the social and economic oppression of women; ensure the wellbeing of children the world over; and, support sustainable environmental practices in community development; I felt it essential that the ACC is fully involved in making sure that the global policies of UN member states include a strong gender perspective, and are based upon universal Human Rights.

2. BRIEF HISTORY OF THE OFFICE

2.1 Fifteen years ago, the Anglican Communion sought accreditation to the United Nations as a global multi-national organization. As such, the Anglican Consultative Council was voted into the UN family as an International Organization; Category II Standard of the Economic and Social Council (ECOSOC). Additional supporting documentation will be required to justify an up-grade to the first Category. This status will allow us to contribute directly to the decision-making process of ECOSOC.

2.2 The office of the Anglican Observer at the United Nations works to serve and satisfy the concerns of the Anglican Communion by advocating for solutions through the United Nations and its Agencies. These concerns are based on resolutions of the Primates and the Anglican Consultative Council.

2.3 The areas of the ACC accreditation to the UN ECOSOC and the United Nations Department of Public Information (DPI) are limited to only three areas. These areas of intervention are Development, Disarmament, and Freedom of Religion and Environment. We know that the Communion is fully involved in all areas of United Nations work and our churches are active partners in the areas of Poverty Eradication, Sustainable Development and Peace and Justice issues. In addition to working for Freedom of Religion and inter-faith initiatives, our churches are also involved in Health, HIV/AIDS and we also strive to safeguard the integrity of God's creation and sustain and renew the earth. The latter is the fifth mark of the Communion's Mission Statement adopted by ACC8 in Wales in 1990. We therefore hope that the churches of the Communion will assist us in the next two months in furnishing us with the details of their valuable work that can be included in our application for a higher status.

2.4 The first Observer was the Most Rev. Sir Paul Reeves, former Archbishop and Primate of Aotearoa, NZ and Polynesia. He was also the former Governor General of Aotearoa (New Zealand). The Rt. Rev. Jim Ottley, former Bishop of Panama held the post from1994 until early 1999. Both Observers were active in promoting human rights issues, including the special needs of the Indigenous Peoples, and in interventions for cancellation of Third World Debt, which is a major factor crippling the economies of Developing Countries.

2.5 Bishop Paul Moore maintained the office for a short while and was followed by the Interim Observer, Bishop Herbert Donovan also from ECUSA.

2.6 As Archdeacon Emeritus and as a lay person, it has been challenging to follow in the footsteps of those highly qualified and dedicated bishops. Nevertheless, upon hearing of my appointment, someone commented that it was great to belong to a Church that is Gender inclusive, and that laity represented over 85% of its membership.

2.7 My ministry in the post began a few days before September 11th, 2001. The memorable experience due to that event is documented in the Easter Message I wrote for *Anglican World* and is attached as ANNEX I.

2.8 The office has accomplished a great deal during the past year. Our small staff consists of Mrs. Yasmeen Granville-Anderson, Administrative Assistant, Revd. Canon Jeffery Golliher of the Cathedral of St. John the Divine, part-time consultant for Sustainable Ecology and Community Development and myself. In order to be able to cover all the important areas of concern, especially Human Rights, I have worked closely with several key staff members of the Episcopal Church Office. This cooperative effort has served us both well, enabling the office to have a presence at a wider range of UN meetings and ensuring advocacy and visibility while providing ECUSA colleagues with access to UN. Thom Chu, Director of the Ministries to the Young, was one such person. I also worked very closely with other colleagues of the ECUSA Church Center, especially the Peace & Justice Ministries and the Anglican & Global Relations Division.

2.9 The office was greatly assisted mainly for fund-raising activities by the Advisory Council (comprising mainly of US members) and five international representatives of ACC. It should be noted that the US population that generously donated towards the office in the past now needs to direct their attention to the victims of September 11th. Plans were also made for specific task forces of the Council, to further assist the office. Hopefully these will be activated in the near future.

2.10 With the assistance of Rev. Canon Samir Habiby in Europe, and with the blessings of the General-Secretary, the office has already established a small committee (about 5 members on volunteer basis) to cover issues there. Most of the UN Agencies are based in Europe, especially Geneva. The satellite committee will cover the activities of the UN High Commissioner on Human Rights; UN High Commissioner for Refugees; the World Health Organization; UNAIDS; the International Labour Organization; the World Trade Organization; as well as the World Council of Churches.

3. ACTIVITIES 1999 TO AUGUST 2001

3.1 The Office participated at the "World Summit for Social Development and Beyond" in Geneva (2000) which was the five-year review of the "Social Summit" held in Copenhagen which addressed issues of poverty and development;

3.2 The Office formed part of a team of experts who coordinated and contributed to the publication of the United Nations Environment Program's "Cultural and Spiritual Values of Biodiversity" (2000), a policymaking and educational manual mandated by the 1992 Earth Summit's Biodiversity Convention;

3.3 The Office co-sponsored and helped to coordinate a conference called "Genetic Engineering and Food for the World" at the Cathedral of Saint John the Divine (2001);

3.4 The Office was actively involved in efforts to organize better the religious community of NGOs, especially through the formation of the global Ecumenical Advocacy Alliance in Geneva (2001) whose primary objective is to address the root causes of poverty, conflict, and injustice.

4. ACTIVITIES FROM SEPTEMBER 2001 TO DATE

4.1 Similar to the UN Charter, the Anglican Communion has a Mission Statement for commitments: to spread the gospel; to baptize and nurture new believers; to respond to peoples needs through loving service; to break down unjust structures to maintain peace and justice; and, to safeguard the integrity of God's creation and to sustain and renew the earth.

4.2 Based on the above commitments, the office continued to be actively involved with other ecumenical partners in lobbying for monitoring the peace process in the Middle East, Madagascar, as well as West Africa, and to advocate for measures to research and remove obstacles hindering sustainable development including suffering from conflicts and poverty.

I also worked closely with Ecumenical partners in publicizing a study on "Iraq Sanctions: Humanitarian Implications and Options for the Future." This was published on 6 August 2002, the 12th anniversary of the date on which the Security Council first imposed comprehensive sanctions on Iraq. The publication made in association with the "Save the Children UK" offered recommendations for the way forward instead of violence, including sanctions.

In response to the question "Why America?" following September 11th, 2001, the Ecumenical working group at the UN got me into a sub-committee that organized and hosted a whole-day workshop,

"Unpacking Religious Dimensions after September 11—Christian Perspectives." The report of the workshop is attached as ANNEX II. The reflections received from the Archbishop of Canterbury greatly assisted the committee in this task.

I also wrote to the President of Pakistan and personally visited the Pakistan Permanent Mission concerning the senseless killings of Christians there and to solicit protection for the Rt. Rev. Mano Rumalshah of USPG and the Rev. Patrick P. Augustine of ECUSA who visited the country on a Peace and Reconciliation mission last month.

4.3 Your UN office was also actively involved in the following:

4.3.1 Monitoring, with other NGO's, of the Monterrey Consensus adopted in March 2002 at the International Conference on Financing for Development (FFD) to confront challenges of financing for development around the world, particularly in developing countries for poverty eradication and to achieve sustainable development for a fully inclusive and equitable global economic system. The NGO's were not satisfied with the Consensus, as it offered no mechanism to mobilize new financial resources to achieve the Millennium Development Goals (please see ANNEX III) adopted by the United Nations in September 2000. Governments were held responsible to raise their own funds for development. The NGOs did not approve of the prevailing economic model as prescribed by the World Bank, the International Monetary Fund and the World Trade Organization particularly, because of its differentiated negative impacts on people. There was little evidence in the Monterrey Consensus of a will to change. I was fully involved as member of the WCC Ecumenical Team, at the Prep-Committee meetings as well as the Conference. I was also joined, as another member of the ACC delegation, by Mr. Fiu Mataese Elisara-Laulu Director of Le Siosiomaga (Environment) Society of Samoa. He was fully funded by the UN Non-Government Liaison Services as a candidate from a least-developed country but needed accreditation under an ECOSOC NGO. Mr. Elisara wrote for us a 13-page report on this important conference.

4.3.2 Coordination of the Global Anglican Congress on the Stewardship of Creation held in South Africa recently and is being reported hereunder. The activities for this Congress started several months before I became the UN Observer.

4.3.3 Involvement in the NGO-Committee on the Status of Women for gender issues and to ensure compliance with CEDAW (Convention for the Elimination of all forms of Discrimination Against Women). Recent events advocated for the inclusion of Afghan women in the peace process and forming of an interim government in Afghanistan.

Two women from the Episcopal Church represented the Anglican Communion (through passes arranged by the Anglican UN Office) at the UN meeting earlier this year. I was constantly called upon to support advocacy tasks as the Anglican UN Observer for issues affecting women all over the world as in the case of the USA withholding contributions to the UN Fund for Population Activities; Rape cases in PNG and Southern Africa; and Stoning to death in Nigeria to name a few.

4.3.4 Inter-faith initiatives to empower women's leadership in development projects; HIV/AIDS (through the Hunger Project) giving recognition to leaders in Africa who are promoting community awareness about the dangers of this pandemic.

4.3.5 Canon Golliher's contributions were found valuable by the Ecumenical Team of the World Council of Churches for the UN Prep-committee meetings for the World Summit on Sustainable Development (WSSD) or Rio + 10 in Johannesburg. Mr. Elisara-Laulu who was accredited under the Sisters of Mercy International attended the last Prep-com in Bali and his report on this meeting was good briefing material for the Anglican Congress Team.

The World Summit required the nations of the world to critically review progress made, as well as obstacles, in reaching the goals of Agenda 21, the 1992 Earth Summit's comprehensive blueprint for sustainable development. The office co-hosted a side event on February 5th, 2002, to highlight global warming resulting in the loss of islands in the Pacific and erosion in Manhattan. Our contribution was to get the Samoa Ambassador to speak at the event, as he is the Chairman of the Alliance of Small Island States (AOSIS). The film "Rising Waters" which was shown at the side event is our gift to this meeting for viewing by ACC members.

4.3.6 Promotion of the General Assembly Resolution in November last year declaring an International Decade for a Culture of Peace and Non-violence for the Children of the World, 2001–2010. This calls for the church's involvement in the implementation of strategies for this decade.

The Episcopal Church with the assistance of the UN Office was able to secure two persons to represent the Communion at the Special Session of the UN General Assembly on Children, May 8–10, 2002. Since the *Convention on the Rights of the Child* was produced by the World Summit for Children in 1989, there is much work to be done to promote the rights of children. The first-ever address to the General Assembly by children is summarized in the Children's Forum Message "A World Fit for Us," the most important feature of which is to include the voices of children in decision making. Churches participated in a Global March for Children, which was included in Cable News Network's coverage of the Session. For ways to participate in supporting the implementation work in your region, contact UNICEF or the Global Movement for Children (www.gmfc.org). Additional UN documentation maybe viewed at the display area. Please take time to look at these documents as well as the a statement from the "Save the Children UK."

4.3.7 To continue the support to the issues of the Indigenous People, the office pursued accreditation of representatives from the Anglican Indigenous Network to the Permanent Forum in May 2002. Limited funds received from my speaking engagements (and deposited into our account) enabled the office to co-sponsor a press conference for the group. The permanent forum resulted in formulating statements advocating for the rights of indigenous people, empowerment and environment issues impacting on the indigenous people whose gifts of culture and traditional knowledge as well as practices could really assist in conservation activities for the environment. Most of these were addressed during the WSSD in South Africa.

4.3.8 Briefing of several groups, visitors and church congregations on UN initiatives and work of the Anglican Observer in representing the Anglican Communion at the United Nations. Speaking engagements included briefing of Mennonites groups; student groups visiting the Episcopal Church Center; groups meeting in the center; the Church Women United Service; St. Bartholomew (New York); Christ Church (St. Simon's Island at 4 different occasions); St. James (New York); Women of the New Jersey Convention (on a Servant Church); addressed a class at the Episcopalian General Theological Seminary (New York) and at the First 10th Anniversary of the Anglican Global & Ecumenical Studies at the Episcopal Divinity School (EDS).

4.3.9 Overseas missions included participation at the Peace & Justice Network meeting in New Zealand (November 2002); a Joint meeting of ACC Staff and Lutherans (Geneva); the Advisory Council meeting (England); Joint Standing Committee meeting (Ireland); the Primates Meeting in Canterbury; the establishment of the Satellite European Committee (2.10 above): and, the ACC Staff meeting in England.

At their invitation, I attended and addressed the General Synod of the Anglican Church of Aotearoa, New Zealand and Polynesia which was also an opportunity to advocate for support for ACC, the UN initiatives, as well as the Global Anglican Congress in South

Africa. I was also invited and attended in July, the National Conference of the Anglican Church of Australia—an opportunity to make connections advocating for WSSD issues and to connect with government officials to work through the church for sustainability of Development in Africa as well as the Asia/Pacific Region.

4.3.10 Early this year I wrote to and introduced myself to the Permanent Missions to the United Nations. Most responded positively and offered me their assistance within their respective capabilities/ capacities. I also visited several Missions to solicit their intervention on some of the issues raised by the provinces and especially those mentioned earlier under this section.

The work and interventions of the churches is well recognized by the United Nations. The UN Secretary General when responding to my letter of introduction clearly stated that the commitment and good work of the faith community is critical to the success of UN efforts. At the time of writing I am looking forward to participating with him at the September 11th Inter-Faith Service of Commitment to the Work of the United Nations, *A Celebration of Remembrance and Hope Dedicated to Victims of Violence Everywhere*, at St. Bartholomew Episcopal Church (NY).

5. THE GLOBAL ANGLICAN CONGRESS FOR THE STEWARDSHIP OF CREATION

5.1 Organized by the Office of the Anglican Observer in collaboration with The Rt. Rev. Geoff Davies of the Diocese of Umzimvubu, South Africa, the first Global Anglican Congress was held from 18–23 August, the week immediately before the United Nations World Summit on Sustainable Development, at the Good Shepherd Retreat Center near Johannesburg. In any case, this Congress was a needed response to the urgency of the planetary crisis before us now.

5.2 The letter attached herewith as ANNEX IV acknowledges the kind support received for this important event in the Life of the Communion.

The Congress planning team included several people. In the Observer's office, The Rev. Canon Jeff Golliher, my assistant for the environment and sustainable development, coordinated the Congress with Mrs. Yasmeen Granville-Anderson providing the essential secretarial and administrative support. Bishop Davies made all the local arrangements, and he was assisted by Kate and Joe McGervey, two ECUSA missionaries who are helping him with environmental ministry. Claire Foster of the Church of England and David Shreeve of the Conservation Foundation, based in

London, provided planning and logistical support from the beginning. Likewise, The Rt. Rev. George Browning of Australia greatly assisted the planning team with the literature for the Congress especially the drafting of the Statements earlier in the year. The Rev. Canon Eric Beresford of the ACC staff, was also on the planning team and assisted greatly during the Congress. Asha Golliher and Kate Davies also helped in planning the event in many ways and they participated actively in it as well.

The Rt. Rev. Simon Chiwanga kindly joined the Congress with enthusiasm to represent the Anglican Consultative Council and provided valuable advice/guidance during the discussions.

5.3 The Anglican Congress had several purposes. Its greater purpose was to help in building a community of faith and action around the planetary crisis—the impoverishment of people and the impoverishment of the environment. We wanted to meet as a response to the United Nations Summit, which marked the ten-year anniversary of the original Earth Summit in Rio de Janeiro. Also, we wanted to use that occasion as a springboard toward organizing a community of faith within the Communion itself. The representation was excellent. About eighty of us gathered at the Anglican Congress for a lively week of worship, discussion, and learning.

5.4 The program schedule of the Congress gives only a partial description of what the week was like.

We began each day with morning meditations and gathered at midday for the Holy Eucharist with sermons addressing different aspects of the planetary crisis in relation to the gospels. In plenary sessions, we covered major topics like water, food and agriculture, health and ecology with a focus on HIV-AIDS, energy, gender empowerment, community empowerment, ecojustice, and biodiversity. These plenary sessions were led by people who had professional expertise in the university or the church, and many were themselves delegates to the Congress. We also went on fieldtrips to see first hand the extent of human and environmental impoverishment in South Africa, as well as the ecosystems and efforts to restore them.

The Congress was not planned on an academic model of a conference. As stated previously, we were there to build a community of faith which could better respond to the issues. Our discussions were lively and participatory and the week was planned to provide as much first-hand experience as possible with group processes for community empowerment that all participants could take back to their home Provinces.

5.5 I feel it is important here to share with you some basic facts about the urgency of the planetary crisis before us.

Poverty and Ecojustice—As you maybe aware, the gap between the rich and poor, globally, is increasing. Economic empowerment is based, ultimately, on environmental health and well being. People need the capacity to care for themselves and their environments. This should be the goal of "development," which is not the same as economic "growth," and it is the real meaning of the term "sustainability." Poverty is as much about a shortage of power and empowerment as it is a shortage of money. For that reason, many NGO's, including the World Council of Churches Ecumenical Team (which some of us joined at the UN Summit) focused heavily on corporate accountability. The recent problems in the Enron Corporation are an example we all know. Economic and political power is being concentrated in the hands of the few, and that is why there were protests in Johannesburg, which I'm glad to say were peaceful.

Food and Agriculture—The use of genetically engineered foods remains a controversial issue, but here again the issue may not be one of good science, but of corporate power and control. While food production is increasing worldwide, the expansion of agriculture is creating a real threat to the ecosystems on which it depends—forests, rivers, wetlands, and biodiversity are being lost as the need for farmland increases. If this trend continues, the web of life will lose the capacity to support agriculture and provide the food we need.

Water—In addition to agriculture, which accounts for 90% of all water use, the growth of industry (power, chemicals, and paper) places increasing demands on water supplies. About half of all wetlands worldwide have already been lost. The normal flow of rivers (not including floods which are another matter) is literally drying up in all parts of the world, while the water that does exist is often polluted and unavailable for human use. Nearly half of the world's people will have water shortages within 20 years. The 'solution' to this crisis that is being explored is the privatization of water supplies, which many feel is no solution, but simply greater concentration of power in a few transnational corporations. This is a huge problem that will, in all likelihood, get worse in the future.

Biodiversity—Much of the web of life's rich diversity is found in forests, and forests are continually declining. In Latin America and Africa, the rate of decline is the greatest—between 5% and 7% per year. Nearly 30% of the world's watersheds have already been lost. Life in the oceans, fisheries, coral reefs, are being seriously depleted everywhere. In a nutshell, our natural heritage, the glory of God's creation is being destroyed, and it is on this that our economic life depends. This is the heart of the crisis before us.

Energy and Climate Change—The consumption of energy based on fossil fuels is growing, despite scientific evidence that petroleum-based energy is severely damaging the atmosphere. Carbon dioxide emissions are increasing on a global scale. As a result, sea levels are rising by about 1 centimeter per year. Major glaciers are melting. The Arctic and Antarctic are melting. Climate change is a fact of life, but it can also be unpredictable—both droughts and floods are a threat in certain areas in ways that are unexpected and severely damaging.

5.6 As Bishop George Browning from Australia said in a sermon at the Congress, this is all "gospel business." The Psalms tell us that "the earth is the Lord's" and the Book of Genesis tells us that we are called to be stewards of God's Creation. Participants in the Anglican Congress all understood this and found that our coming together was a hopeful sign of the Communion's ability to respond to the Gospel at this turning point in history. It was also clear that a major issue before us, not just as Anglicans, but as members of the human family, is one of empowerment. People everywhere have some understanding of what the problems are, despite differences in perspectives about specific solutions. The major message of the Congress is that the Church can be an instrument for the empowerment of everyone—women and men, young and old—in local communities and institutions. The health and well being of God's Creation is something around which all Anglicans can unite, together with people of other faiths.

5.7 With that in mind, the Congress wrote two declarations - one to the United Nations World Summit and the other to the Anglican Communion. Both declarations include suggestions for actions the Communion can take on all levels.

5.8 In addition, the participants of the Congress requested, unanimously, that the ACC be asked, to consider and vote on the following four suggested resolutions as stated in the letter distributed to you already:

5.8.1 asking all provinces of the Anglican Communion to place environmental care on their agenda;

5.8.2 asking all Anglicans to make their own personal commitment to care for God's world, respecting all life, for "the Earth is the Lord's and all that is in it" (Psalm 24:1);

5.8.3 establishing the Anglican Environmental Network as an official network of the Anglican Communion; and,

5.8.4 endorsing the declarations of the Anglican Congress to the United Nations and to the Anglican Communion.

The Congress members were duly briefed by both Eric Beresford and the ACC chairman on the guidelines for establishing Networks, and they determined to lend the Environment Network their full support and cooperation. I must say that we all hope you will give the suggested resolutions your support.

5.9 Finally, I want to share with you another kind of message from the Anglican Congress. I have in mind everything that the Congress meant. In a very real sense, it was a small model of the whole Communion. There was a tremendous amount of goodwill shown by everyone there. It was hard work, and it was fun. Delegates at the Congress who also attended the UN Summit said the Congress was more important and much more educational to them personally.

I worked for the United Nations Development Program for many years and I am very much aware of what the UN is like, what it can do well, and its shortcomings. We need to support the work of the United Nations, because it is the only truly global organization we have, and we must meet the difficult challenges before us together. And yet, the Anglican Communion is a global body too, and we are not always united.

We learned at the Congress that caring for God's Creation is something that can bring us together as people of faith, despite our differences on other issues. The Congress represented not only people from different parts of the world, but also people from all parts of the Church—laity and clergy, people with scientific expertise and others with knowledge of communities and congregations and how they might be transformed. We have incredible human resources to draw upon within our own Church to help and to share our gifts and the real wealth within us.

Some delegates spoke of discouragement, and even worse, severe poverty and fear among their congregations. They felt that people in their churches really wanted to help, but did not know how or did not have the opportunity. We need to find new ways to support them. It does not always require money, but it does require caring, empowerment, and commitment.

Some delegates expressed the desire to convene another Congress in a few years, recognizing the potential for something transformative in their lives and in the life of the Church. The Congress showed us that the Spirit, at this moment in history, is calling us together as a community of faith and as people who are and who want to be faithful stewards of God's Creation. For the Anglican Communion, this is an opportunity for renewal and unity as we work together to renew the earth.

6. ACKNOWLEDGEMENTS

I owe my being with you at ACC-12 to His Grace the Archbishop of Canterbury and the Selection Committee for my appointment. I thank you very much for your confidence in my ability to serve in this position of many opportunities to face the equally many challenges for the well being of our Global Community and especially the Anglican Communion.

The General Secretary and colleagues in the Anglican Communion Office have greatly helped me especially during the initial period of my settling into the position. Many thanks to you all.

Those who unselfishly assisted me most before and during my first few months in the post were the Rt. Rev. Herbert Donovan and Mary Donovan, the Gollihers, members of the Advisory Council and Mrs. Yasmeen Anderson. I greatly appreciate your kindness.

To the Presiding Bishop of ECUSA, Mrs. Phoebe Griswold and all my colleagues in 815, thank you most sincerely for the advice, the fellowship and making me feel at home at the Church Center. Thank you also for providing not only the office for the Communion but also the supporting/operations services for the Anglican UN Office.

Lastly but not least I wish to record here my sincere gratitude to the Presiding Bishop; the Co-Presiding Bishops; the clergy and my people in Aotearoa, New Zealand and Polynesia, especially those in my home parish in Apia, Samoa who are constantly praying for me and for their support in many ways. The communion of our Spirits provides the Mana, the Courage and Strength to undertake the duties of representing the Anglican Communion at the United Nations.

Soifua and May God Bless you All.

ANNEX I: EASTER MESSAGE 2002

What will Easter be like in 2002?

I have been dwelling on this thought since I was asked to write this Easter message for *Anglican World* a few days ago in Dublin. Some people will not expect anything spectacular to happen during Easter. It will be the same as before—a lot of church services especially during Holy Week, then the celebration of the Resurrection of Christ on Easter Day followed by a holiday on Monday. The less fortunate of course will still have their struggles with poverty, HIV/AIDS, fear of war, unpredictable weather due to global warming and many other social/economic issues that are prevalent in most countries, including the United States. This is true especially in New York where I now live.

My present ministry started in New York a few days before September 11th. It was not a pleasant beginning and it was through the Grace of God that I managed to remain calm whilst comforting others, including the members of my own family that arrived that same morning for my installation on September 16th. People were devastated. Screams were heard everywhere and my secretary fainted as her husband works in the vicinity of the World Trade Towers. What was God's message for me there and then?

When the contingent from Fiji and New Zealand could not make it to my installation, the Bishop of Polynesia, the Rt. Rev. Jabez Bryce, wrote, "Man proposes, God disposes. Perhaps there is a message there that 'your call' has to start in a humble way." And it was evident in the behaviour of New Yorkers that they too needed to re-cast their lives/attitudes to be more loving/caring in sharing each other's pain—the signs of humility and compassion were demonstrated everywhere. Many more people turned up for church services. Many smiled and greeted others with care and concern. In the past when I visited New York, I was told not to smile as no one would smile back and most New Yorkers were too busy thinking of how to excel in life in what they own and wear. What a transformation! People became more friendly and caring, especially at my parish of St. Peter's at Chelsea.

Of course, our food bank, like those in many other churches, continued for the less fortunate who have increased in numbers. The churches also became the sanctuaries and hospices for the homeless. What a wonderful way of using those buildings. St. Paul's at Ground Zero is a classic example of the Church enacting the mission of Christ on earth. The church staff and volunteers became and are continuing to be seen as the compassionate face, hands and feet of the Servant Christ.

On the global scene, the lives of many are affected by so much violence, injustice, debt and many other problems most of which were inflicted on them by forces outside of their reach and power. What can we offer but to be enablers for those unable to speak out for themselves thus bringing Hope to the whole people of God? Let's prove to the less fortunate that the Resurrected Christ left us behind to continue His Work with the guidance of the Holy Spirit.

For me, although far from my family and home in Samoa, through the Grace of God, Easter 2002 will be a period of doing just that. This will mean knocking at the doors of the United Nations as well as the

Government Missions to seek the appropriate assistance for the needs of the Anglican Communion. It can be overpowering at times. My strength of course comes from the Easter message to the Women, "Do not be afraid. Jesus is Alive." Alleluia!

ANNEX II: Unpacking Religious Dimensions after September 11—Christian Perspectives—Feedback on a Seminar at the Church Center for the United Nations

Is justice achievable by force? When do religious people become violent? What can we as Christians do to promote peace?

The Ecumenical Working Group for the United Nations has put those questions on the table. Should Christians not offer a more profiled statement concerning the US policies in Afghanistan after September 11? How can we speak and act appropriately to our creed and our mandate in society? On the 4th of December the Ecumenical Working Group held a three-part panel on the issue.

I. Report

The first panel **Unpacking Religious Rhetoric: Christian Understandings of "Justice," "Evil," and "War"** dealt with theological and hermeneutic questions.

"Beware of idolatrous language!" said Donald Shriver, President Emeritus of Union Theological Seminary, who moderated the panel. He was referring to President Bush using terms like "infinite justice," "crusade" as well as the picture of "Good against Evil." Even if a war seemed justifiable it could never be completely just, Shriver said. A gun should be always carried with a "heavy heart and a sense of tragedy" rather than with an attitude of innocent heroism. In this respect churches should be more reluctant to decorate their walls with American flags, the symbol of national pride.

Concerning terrorism, Shriver pointed out: "It has been said: There is no terrorism, only violence that can be used for just or unjust causes."

Larry Rasmussen, Professor at Union Theological Seminary, elaborated on the term "crusade." He contrasted it with pacifism and the just war theory and stated: "Just war and pacifism share the assumption that violence should be the exception and non-violence the norm." Hence "crusade" was a word of absolutist thinking that divided the world into good and bad, into "for us" and "against us." "In this view the attack on the Twin Towers was perceived to be an attack on civilization and on humanity." Rasmussen concluded ironically: "Then 'we' and 'they' are engaged in a holy war." Concerning peace, Rasmussen stated that military means for safety and security were rather promoting mistrust than peace. "Self defense is necessary," he said, "but it is better to use the language of crime and law enforcement, best pursued within the UN and other global institutions." "Incremental justice" should be sought instead of "infinite justice." Rasmussen concluded that the US should act out of a sober sense of peacemaking rather than out of innocence. "Innocence is a loser. See Romans, Chapter 12."

The third speaker, Pamela Harvey, minister of education at Riverside Church, dealt with the problem of Biblical hermeneutics. "Just war, crusade and pacifism are all in the text," she said. "The voice of Jesus must be the judge, the prism through which we view the text," she added, offering her criteria for a Christian hermeneutic approach. Further, Harvey stressed that it was fear, not hate that was the driver of war, quoting Harry Emerson Fosdick's sermon "Shall the Fundamentalists Win" from 1934. Real security, Harvey concluded, was not to be found in the war system but in the Christian understanding of justice: "Love the Lord your God with all your heart and your neighbor as yourself."

John Rempel of the Mennonite Church Committee at the UN led us back to the actual US policy. Rempel pointed out that he was missing an attitude of "soul searching" in the US government and civil society after the attack, which had always been a constituent aspect in Israel's faith when experiencing violence and despair.

Was President Bush honest, asked John Rempel further, when he proclaimed that he merely sought to install democracy in Afghanistan? Were there not also less altruistic interests like oil? He criticized the fact that the US churches on the religious right vindicated US actions and supported the just war attitude without even considering alternatives. On the religious left Rempel saw the danger of deprivation of traditional Islam by contrasting it to liberal western values.

He warned not to "drape oneself in morality by waving American flags" but rather to develop self-criticism and ingenuity concerning peaceful alternatives to force and violence.

The second panel **Unpacking the Roots of Violence and Terrorism: Religious Extremism and Global Injustice** was meant to explore the scenery of the US foreign policy in Afghanistan and the Middle East as much as to elaborate on the question of how Muslims perceive America and what makes the US a target of some Muslims' hatred.

Jennifer Butler, Associate for Global Issues at the Presbyterian Office for the UN, introduced this panel offering an analysis of reactions to September 11. She mentioned articles in conservative magazines that portrayed Islam as innately violent and quoted Jerry Falwell and Pat Robertson who wrote: "The Middle Eastern monsters are committed to conquering the world," and went on to say that God was allowing America's enemies to do so because of the sins of the "pagans, the abortionists and the feminists, the gay and the lesbians."

On the political left voices were to be heard, said Butler, that suggested that America deserved the strike at 9/11 because of its militarism, colonialism, or its support for Israel—equally dangerous simplifying assumptions. Finally, Butler appealed for new paradigms to understand and digest the attack. She suggested that this was a special challenge for a country that "seldom pays attention to events outside its own borders."

The first speaker at this panel was Azza Karam, the Egyptian director of the gender department at the World Conference of Religion and Peace, the only Muslim speaker. Karam asked first: Who is the war between? She urged not to see this war as a proof for the "clash of civilizations" but as a struggle against a criminal group named "Al Qaeda."

She showed some understanding for Al Qaeda's 3 points:

80 years of Muslim suffering after the collapse of the Ottoman Empire, occupation of Palestine, and US troops in Saudi Arabia and expressed concern that Western foreign policy did nothing to heal those "wounds" but rather widened them.

The second item of Karam's statement was "Religion versus secular society."

"The more you try to suppress something, the more it will assert itself," she said, arguing that religion could not be suppressed as an active part of public life. "When governments try to de-link religion from public discourse, there is a backlash."

As a third item Azza Karam warned her hearers to consider the present conflict as a war between religion and capitalism. She pointed out that fundamentalist religious attitudes, which existed in all religions and had to be distinguished from extremist violent attitudes, had never necessarily collided with democratic political structures and a free market. As an example she named Iran as a fundamentalist religious country with at least free democratic elections and a free market.

Tony Lang from the Carnegie Council on International Affairs spoke about the relationship of religion and politics in Islam. He stressed that Mohammed had also been a political leader, who, contrary to Jesus, used force. From a resistance fighter he became a governor. Of course it has to be kept in mind that the same happened to Christianity when Emperor Constantine linked Christianity with political power.

Lang stated that the use of force might be necessary in the current crisis, but he also stressed the necessity for Christians to follow the pacifist example of Jesus as much as possible. From the Christian point of view he found it important to realize that all mankind is corrupted by sin and that therefore no distinction between "good" and "evil" could be drawn.

To undertake a "war against terrorism," Lang said, would lead into the trap of presuming that one group could govern the whole world, "an assumption, that lacks humility and misunderstands human nature and politics."

Lang sees pathways for peace in the democratic sharing and mutual control of power. The Christian aspect of forgiveness might be a challenging paradigm also in the political frame. "Perhaps it will mean forgiving those in the world whose justified anger at the US has turned into unjustified violence."

The third panel **Unpacking Challenges for Christians in a Multi-Faith World: Pathways to Peace** was supposed to give ideas of how the ecumenical community might contribute to the promotion of peace effectively.

Elias Mallon, Dean of Auburn Theological Seminary led us into the subject by showing the psychological ambivalence of religion. "Religion, like dogs, can be warm and fuzzy, but also can kill," he stated, referring to the regressive aspect of religious faith that tends to use religion for comfort, compensation and self-affirmation. Mallon gave Biblical examples of religious absolutist symbols like the exclusive idea of the covenant that had promoted intolerance against others.

He stressed that we are responsible for our symbols and for our way to make use of them.

"The real war," Mallon went on, "is the one against totalitarianism." He took the story of the Syro-Phoenician woman who reminds Jesus that she as a foreigner was also God's child to show that variety among God's children does not have to be established.

"We must take responsibility for our religious symbols within the context of the religious order," Mallon concluded.

Jay Rock, Interfaith Relations, National Council of Churches of Christ, started by bringing us back to the 11th of September. "We hear it is a wake-up call," he said. "But what are we waking up to? Is it a new enemy, 'them' versus 'us'? No, there is no 'them,' only 'us' and we are in terrible trouble."

Rock argued against dividing the world into good and bad, insiders and outsiders. The progressive step for churches should be, said Rock, to affirm the basic sacredness of human life as God's creation and to cultivate compassion and reconciliation in civil society.

Tony Kireopoulos, a Greek Orthodox member of the United States Conference of Religions for Peace, stressed the interfaith aspect of peace promotion again. "How can we encourage tolerance? Teach, preach, exchange youth groups, raise young people to do the same," he said and further pointed to the importance of church involvement in political processes.

Donna McKenzie, Catholic professor at Fordham University, opened her statement by quoting Bishop Tutu: "There is no future without forgiveness." Concerning the church, McKenzie's view was that there was more an eschatological perception of future than an immediate approach to political problems and social crisis. The goal of infinite peace would stay an eschatological one, she said. But still there was the need for churches to respond, be involved and stand up against unpeaceful actions more resolutely. She reported that Catholic bishops in her opinion had failed to speak up critically against the US policies in Afghanistan but rather vindicated it.

As concrete steps toward peace McKenzie listed:

- Scrutinize our practices, own our history. Be vigilant.
- Develop dialogue. Provide for respectful dissent.
- Engage with other religions and traditions.
- Study conflict resolution.
- Create hope and confidence in the future.

II. Evaluation

On the whole we considered this event a valuable encounter. Most guests had come from local congregations, clergy, and lay people. We think that we could provide our guests with enlightening thoughts and motivation to invent new pathways to peace within their institutional frame.

As the Ecumenical Working group in the Church Center at the UN we think that it is important for Christian congregations, NGO's and other Christian institutions to evaluate their own Christian roots again and again and to reflect one's creed in response to political and social conflicts. We might ask ourselves: How can we as Christians show our special profile of values and convictions to civil society more effectively? How can our voice be heard as a true alternative to civil values and understandings of "justice"?

Reconciled variety is our goal among cultures and religions. But as Christians we also have the mandate to criticize political and individual actions we consider sinful. We have the mandate to show our conviction and to resist in nonviolent ways actions that promote intolerance, discrimination, and violence.

Reconciliation is the crucial aspect, the center of our faith. The cross is actually not a "fluffy" or "cozy" symbol. It is a challenge and a nuisance to many. (1 Cor) The cross is the symbol of overcoming evil with good. Of trust in the enemies. Of the freedom to refrain from revenge.

Our task is to bring that message to the world again and again. The contexts might change. This message will stay the same. And we can trust that it will find new paths every day.

ANNEX III: Highlights: Steps on the Road from Rio to Monterrey & Millennium Development Goals

June 1992: UN Conference on Environment and Development, Rio de Janeiro—Earth Summit, Rio de Janeiro, where 108 heads of state adopted Agenda 21, a global blueprint for sustainable development that has become the basis for many national and local plans. This conference also approved global covenants dealing with climate change and biodiversity amongst other issues.

June 1993: World Conference on Human Rights, Vienna—which reaffirmed international commitment to all human rights and to strengthening the mechanisms for monitoring and promoting human rights worldwide and led to the appointment of the first UN Human Rights High Commissioner.

April/May 1994: Global Conference on the Sustainable Development of Small Islands Developing States, Bridgetown—Affirmed that the survival of small islands developing states is firmly rooted in their human resources and cultural heritage, which are their most significant assets. Those assets are under severe stress and all efforts must be taken to ensure the central position of people in the process of sustainable development.

September 1994: International Conference on Population and Development, Cairo—Emphasized the importance of empowering women, advancing gender equality and guaranteeing choice in family planning. Also stressed that ensuring women ability to control their own fertility is a cornerstone of program in population and development.

March 1995: World Summit for Social Development, Copenhagen—Brought together 117 heads of states who committed their governments to eradicating poverty as an ethical, social, political and economic imperative. It also focussed attention on the negative side of economic globalization with regards growing gaps between rich and poor, shrinking social safety nets and increasing insecurity about jobs and social services in both developed and developing countries.

September 1995: Fourth World Conference on Women, Beijing—which agreed on a five year action plan to enhance the social, political and economic empowerment of women, improve their health, advance their education and promote their marital and sexual rights. The action plan sets time-specific targets, committing nations to carry out concrete actions in such areas as health, education and legal reform.

April/May 1996: UN Conference on Trade and Development, Midrand South Africa—Adopted a declaration for increasing partnership between developed and developing countries. Held discussions for multilateral investment framework to liberalize cross-border investments. Also agreed on a major reform of UNCTAD, the Agency was now to focus more on providing technical assistance.

June 1996: Conference on Human Settlement (Habitat II), Istanbul—Set out policy guidelines and government commitments to improving living standards conditions in urban and rural settings and to the full and progressive realization of the right to adequate housing. Broke new ground by involving mayors and other local officials in the formal proceedings.

November 1996: World Food Summit, Rome—Called for reducing the number of undernourished people in the world—800 million—by half by the year 2015, stressing participation by all governmental organizations and the private sector. Adopted the Rome Declaration and the World Food Summit Plan of Action, giving governments the prime responsibility for achieving food security.

June 1997: Earth Summit +5, New York—A special session of the UN General Assembly to assess implementation of Agenda 21. It found that despite progress in many areas, the global environment continues to deteriorate. Government leaders, including more than 50 heads of states agreed to take further action notably on fresh water, energy and transport. Few Concrete commitments, however, were made.

September 2000: Millennium Summit, New York—Attended by 147 heads of states, the summit approved a declaration that puts development, anti-poverty efforts and protecting the environment at the centre of the United Nations priorities. It calls for reducing the number of people living in extreme poverty (on less than US$1 per day) by half by 2015.

June 2001: UN Special Session on HIV/AIDS—Ratified declaration calling for a coordinated global effort to fight the pandemic and protect vulnerable groups.

March 2002: UN International Conference on Financing for Development, Monterrey Mexico—Where some 58 heads of states, 300 Ministers, and 12,000 participants adopted the Monterrey Consensus aimed at addressing the challenges of financing for development around the world. Particularly in developing countries with the goal of eradicating poverty, achieve sustained economic growth, and promote sustainable development as contained in the UN Millennium Declaration, in a fully inclusive and equitable global economic system.

The Millennium Development Goals (1990–2015):

1. Eradicate extreme poverty and hunger:

    - Halve the proportion of people with less than one dollar a day

- Halve the proportion of people who suffer

2. Achieve universal primary education
   - Ensure that boys and girls alike complete primary schooling
3. Promote gender equality and empower women
   - Eliminate gender disparity at all levels of education
4. Reduce child mortality
   - Reduce by two thirds the under-five mortality rate
5. Improve maternal health
   - Reduce by three quarters the maternal mortality ratio
6. Combat HIV/AIDS, malaria and other diseases
   - Reverse the spread of HIV/AIDS
7. Ensure environmental sustainability
   - Integrate sustainable development into country policies and reverse loss of environmental resources
   - Halve the proportion of people without access to potable water
   - Significantly improve the lives of at least 100 million slum dwellers
8. Develop a global partnership for development
   - Raise official development assistance
   - Expand market access
   - Encourage debt sustainability

World Bank estimates that if countries improve their policies and institutions, the additional foreign aid required to reach the Millennium Development Goals by 2015 is between $40–$60 billion USD a year.

ANNEX IV:
The Global Anglican Congress on the Stewardship of Creation

Johannesburg, South Africa, 18–23 August 2002

Grace and Peace to you all and Greetings in the name of Christ.

Having just returned from the United Nations World Summit on Sustainable Development and our own Global Anglican Congress on the Stewardship of Creation in South Africa, I have so much to share with you.

You may be aware that the results of the UN Summit were mixed but exhausting for most of us who there. However, I am glad to report that 'For the Life of the World' (the central theme of ACC-12) the Anglican Congress was a very successful event. Our deepest purpose in convening the Congress was to raise awareness and build a community of faith around the difficult and pressing realities we now face—issues of poverty, human rights, the need for sustainable communities and real economic development, and environmental degradation. We are all standing at crossroads now, and the choices we make in the days and year ahead will be better choices if we make them together, pray together, and act together. The problems and challenges are great, yet there are many good things happening, and sources of hope within our Anglican Communion.

I am therefore writing on behalf of the participants of the Anglican Congress to offer you our gift for "The Life of the World," in the form of the attached declarations written and agreed upon by the Congress. One was prepared for the United Nations Summit and was duly widely distributed there. The second was prepared for members of the Anglican Communion on all levels of its life and ministry. In addition to these declarations, the Congress discussed a great many issues and made personal commitments which I will share with you during my presentation to the ACC meeting. For the moment, however, participants of the Congress unanimously recommended, that I request ACC-12 through all of you, to consider and vote on the following four resolutions:

1. **asking all provinces of the Anglican Communion to place environmental care on their agenda;**

2. **asking all Anglicans to make their own personal commitment to care for God's world, respecting all life, for "the Earth is the Lord's and all that is in it" (Psalm 24:1);**

3. **establishing the Anglican Environmental Network as an official network of the Anglican Communion; and**

4. **endorsing for immediate action, the declarations of the Anglican Congress to the United Nations and to the Anglican Communion.**

I should also emphasize that the Congress considered the above resolutions with the recognition that God has entrusted to us, through the holy scripture, the responsibility to care for the world, that caring for God's creation is central to the Christian faith, and acknowledging in penitence that we have failed in our God-given responsibility.

While the content of the Anglican Congress as a whole necessarily involved issues that are of concern to all our networks, it also addressed the urgent need for the Communion to focus more directly on environmental issues. For that reason, the Congress has requested that the resolution be made by the ACC concerning the official establishment of the Anglican Environmental Network. We also felt that an endorsement of the two declarations would be helpful in calling attention to the ACC's commitment and shared concern during this time of planetary crisis. Despite the fact that the UN Summit is now over, the issues negotiated there will still be debated in the future and an endorsement of our letter to the Summit would still be useful both for Anglicans and others who share our concerns.

Allow me also this opportunity on behalf of the Congress, to offer my most sincere thanks to the Primates and others in our Provinces who supported, financially and otherwise, delegates to attend the Congress. This is, in itself, a sign of commitment and deep concern about the problems before us today. I also wish to express with much gratitude my sincere thanks to His Grace, Archbishop George Carey both for his blessings and his gracious letter of encouragement to the Congress and its participants. To the Rev. Canon John Peterson, who gave his approval for the Office (before I even got there) to be responsible for the event and for his valuable assistance in many ways including essential fundraising, I also offer many thanks. I also want to give my thanks to The Rt. Rev. Simon Chiwanga, Chairman of the ACC, who attended the Anglican Congress with enthusiasm and support. His sermon, presence, and many contributions to our discussions there were greatly appreciated by all.

I wish to pay special tribute to Dr. Darrel Posey, whose persistent prompting in the past years inspired the Coordinator to plan this Congress. Dr. Posey, an anthropologist and devout Anglican, passed away a year ago. He worked for many years to protect the Amazon Rainforest in Brazil and was a very close friend of Canon Golliher. He organized the Earth Parliament, a gathering of indigenous leaders at the time of the Earth Summit in Rio, and he was the original inspiration for our Anglican Congress. May his soul rest in peace.

Lastly but not least, I wish to acknowledge those who contributed generously to the costs of the Congress. My very special thanks goes to the Presiding Bishop of the Episcopal Church of the United States, The Most Rev. Frank Griswold, who graciously agreed without hesitation, to provide the major funding for the Congress. I would also like to thank the Compass Rose Society, the Anglican Communion Fund of the Archbishop of Canterbury, The ECUSA Peace & Justice Ministries through Canon Brian Grieves (for contributions to the Congress costs as well as funding for the participant from Brazil), The ECUSA Anglican and Global Relations Division through The Rev. Patrick Mauney; the Bishop of New York—The Rt. Rev. Sisk, the Jessie Smith Noyes Foundation through the Rev. Canon Jeff Golliher, and Devout Episcopalian as well as a devoted friend of my office, Mrs. Nancy E. W. Colton (Secretary to many Commissions of the UN including disarmament). Without their valuable monetary assistance, the Global Anglican Congress would not have been possible.

19 SEPTEMBER 2002

Financial Report

—The Most Reverend R. H. A. Eames, Chairman, Inter-Anglican Finance and Administration Committee
—Andrew Franklin, Director of Finance and Administration

Annual Audited Accounts of the Council

Every year, following approval of the ACC Standing Committee, Council members are sent copies of the audited accounts. These include information about the income and expenditure related to the core budget as well as about the various designated and special funds held. The report for the year ended 30th September 2001 was circulated with the papers for this Council meeting.

The audited accounts for the year ended 31st December 1999, the period ended 30th September 2000 and the year ended 30th September 2001 are laid before this meeting. Extra copies can be made available if individual delegates need them.

Report to Council

This report summarises the actual results related to the core budget items for the years 1999 to 2001 and the budgets for the years 2002 to 2005.

Summary of Actual against Budget Figures 1999 to 2001

The actual results for the above years compared to the budgets presented at ACC11 are set out in summary form in Table 1 with highlight comments following.

Detail of member church contributions requests and receipts are shown in Table 3.

Core Budget Figures 2002 to 2005

The byelaws of the Council stipulate that the Inter-Anglican Finance Committee, in collaboration with the Standing Committee, shall keep members of the Council and member Churches informed about each year's budget and about the forecast for each of the succeeding three years.

The forecast for the years 2003 to 2005 (note September year end) is summarised in Table 2 with some accompanying notes following.

The expenditure is based on current commitments and takes account of likely cost increases in relation to these commitments. There are two main constituents of expenditure, employment costs (44% of total) and the cost of meetings (30%).

Employment Costs

The employment costs will be affected by the recent actuarial valuation of the Church of England Pension (Defined Benefits) Scheme to which most of the ACC staff belongs. The actuary calls for an increase in contributions (including the staff contributions of 2.5%) from a rate of 21.93% to 27.61% with effect from 1 January 2003. The Council follows the General Synod of the Church of England salary scales and annual increases have been factored in for forecast purposes at the rate of 3.5% per annum.

Meetings

The costs of meetings included in the budgets continue to reflect the wishes of Standing Committee to make provision in the form of annual budget allocations to a number of meetings. Additional provisions have been made in the last year for the following areas:

- Increased activity in Inter-Church Conversations
- The new Anglican/Roman Catholic Working Group
- The Theological and Doctrinal Commission
- The Inter-Anglican Standing Commission on Mission and Evangelism

Request for 4%

It will be recalled that the need to cover these additional demands was recognised by the Joint Standing Committee in 2001 through an additional 4% contributions request over the next two years.

There has been a disappointing response by the provinces to pay this additional 4% and this will result in a deficit for 2001/2. The Finance Committee is faced with a dilemma. We wish to meet all the demands for expenditure placed upon the finances by the desired objectives of Council. It is clear that the major source of income to finance these objectives must be the contributions of member provinces and that payment of the contribution requests in full would result in a surplus.

A detailed projection of member church contribution requests is shown in Table 7. The amounts for the calendar years 2003 and 2004 have been advised to churches. Figures for 2005 are recommendations at this stage.

Budget Deficit

The projected deficit for 2002/3 is shown as £ 32382. Unless there is a sharp improvement in the level of contributions, even this position will not be achieved.

Provinces cannot rely on fundraising to continually bridge the gap between the objectives and their desire to fund them.

The Finance Committee will encourage greater communication with the provinces both face to face and by letter to inform them of the desired objectives and the dependence of the Communion on their support to achieve these. It is hoped then that the provinces will give a higher priority to paying their dues.

The Finance Committee cannot support the submission of unbalanced budgets and will not hesitate to recommend measures to reduce expenditure if it becomes clear that a shortfall in income from contributions is likely. The Finance Committee has appointed a working group to undertake a thorough review of expenditure to examine whether greater efficiencies could be achieved.

Acknowledgements

We recognise with gratitude the strong commitment of many of the member churches to the support of the Inter Anglican budget.

We recognise with gratitude the generous support given by the Compass Rose Society membership to assist in the funding of the Inter Anglican budget and also to Trinity Church Wall Street and others in assisting in areas not reflected in the core budget of the Council.

Anglican Consultative Council
Financial Report for ACC-12
Table 1
Inter-Anglican Budget Outturn 1999 to 2001

	1999			2000 (9 months)			2001		
	Budget	Actual	Variation	Budget	Actual	Variation	Budget	Actual	Variation
INCOME	£	£	£	£	£	£	£	£	£
Interest on deposits	15,000	22,589	(7,589)	11,250	18,200	(6,950)	15,000	30,069	(15,069)
Publications income	5,000	6,132	(1,132)	3,750	1,708	2,042	5,000	1,062	3,938
Services to other bodies	500	500	-	375	375	-	500	1,000	(500)
Grants for equipment		71	(71)			-			-
Donations & miscellaneous income	500	563	(63)	375	152	223	500	1,421	(921)
	21,000	29,855	(8,855)	15,750	20,435	(4,685)	21,000	33,552	(12,552)
Contributions from member churches	977,636	979,934	(2,298)	763,190	763,424	(234)	1,052,000	1,060,946	(8,946)
Total normal income	998,636	1,009,789	(11,153)	778,940	783,859	(4,919)	1,073,000	1,094,498	(21,498)
Special Fund Raising	235,000	228,719	6,281	176,250	164,411	11,839		243,784	(243,784)
	1,233,636	1,238,508	(4,872)	955,190	948,270	6,920	1,073,000	1,338,282	(265,282)
EXPENDITURE									
Secretary General's office	196,750	182,119	14,631	154,837	153,681	1,156	215,100	141,666	73,434
Communications department	110,850	112,182	(1,332)	86,213	79,229	6,984	117,400	109,064	8,336
Telecommunications/database department	48,100	48,556	(456)	38,550	42,299	(3,749)	53,300	52,504	796
Anglican World magazine	110,000	109,630	370	82,500	27,830	54,670	110,000	83,291	26,709
Mission and Evangelism department			-			-	-	33,726	(33,726)
Liturgical co-ordinator	6,500	7,757	(1,257)	4,875	7,080	(2,205)	7,000	8,908	(1,908)
Ecumenical Relations department	86,180	84,857	1,323	70,335	70,193	142	95,300	99,250	(3,950)
Finance and Administration department	143,400	136,076	7,324	115,800	100,053	15,747	160,050	121,258	38,792
Overheads (rents, office expenses, etc)	161,500	146,726	14,774	116,198	124,341	(8,143)	162,180	160,882	1,298
	863,280	827,903	35,377	669,308	604,706	64,602	920,330	810,549	109,781
Provision for meetings etc:									
Inter-Church conversations	48,000	48,000	-	36,000	36,000	-	48,000	62,625	(14,625)
Missio	15,000	15,000	-	11,250	11,250	-	15,000	43,500	(28,500)
Council and Standing Committee	90,500	90,500	-	93,750	93,750	-	125,000	125,000	-
Primates	25,500	25,500	-	19,125	19,125	-	25,500	50,500	(25,000)
Lambeth Conference	140,000	140,000	-	105,000	105,000	-	140,000	140,000	-
UN Observer's Office	24,000	24,942	(942)	18,000	20,035	(2,035)	24,000	27,977	(3,977)
Inter-Anglican Doctrinal			-	-	-	-	-	15,750	(15,750)
Provincial Emergencies Provision	25,000	25,000	-	18,750	18,750	-	25,000		25,000
	1,231,280	1,196,845	34,435	971,183	908,616	62,567	1,322,830	1,275,901	46,929
Surplus/(Deficit)	2,356	41,663	(39,307)	(15,993)	39,654	(55,647)	(249,830)	62,381	(312,211)

Anglican Consultative Council

Financial Report for ACC-12

Inter-Anglican Budget Outturn 1999 to 2001
Notes on Annual Figures:

Presentation:

The audited accounts for the years 1999 to 2001 are set out in the format required by legislation.

This paper presents the core budget figures in an abbreviated and simplified form.

For the purpose of budget comparison, this presentation gives a different view from that shown in the annual accounts. This presentation gives the figures in departmental totals.

The accounting year end was changed to 30th September in Year 2000 making that accounting period one of nine months only.

General Reserve:

Resolution 49 of ACC-6 provided that the General Reserve should be maintained at a level equivalent to four months' expenditure of the Secretariat.

1999

Income:

Member church contributions were £2,298 over budget.

Expenditure:

Expenditure was lower than the budget by £34,435.

The bottom line shows a surplus of income over expenditure for the year of £41,663 .

The General Reserve stood at £146810 at the year end, £129,157 less than required.

2000

Income:

Member church contributions were £234 over budget.

In setting the budget, it was realised that substantial support would be needed in addition to the member church contributions. Compass Rose Society giving provided £164,411 mainly in support of Communications expenditure.

Expenditure:

Expenditure was lower than the budget by £62,567.

The bottom line shows a surplus of income over expenditure for the year of £39,654 .

The General Reserve stood at £186,464 at the year end, £82,294 less than required.

2001

Income:

Member church contributions were £8946 over budget.

It was necessary to supplement the contributions with support from Compass Rose Society giving. This provided £243,784 in support of Communications .

Expenditure:

Expenditure was lower than the budget by £46,929

The bottom line shows a surplus of income over expenditure for the year of £62,381.

The General Reserve stood at £248,845 at the year end, £21,338 less than required.

Anglican Consultative Council
Financial Report for ACC-12
Table 2
Inter-Anglican Budgets 2002 to 2005

	2002	**2003**	**2004**	**2005**
	£	**£**	**£**	**£**
Interest on deposits	27,500	20,000	20,000	25,000
Publications income				
Services to other bodies	1,000	1,000	1,000	1,000
Communications Endowment	5,800	4,500	4,500	4,500
Donations & miscellaneous income	21,300	500	500	500
	55,600	26,000	26,000	31,000
Contributions from member churches	1,078,157	1,163,313	1,183,113	1,206,688
Total normal income	1,133,757	1,189,313	1,209,113	1,237,688
Special Fund Raising	218,750	230,000	240,000	250,000
	1,352,507	1,419,313	1,449,113	1,487,688
EXPENDITURE				
Secretary General's office	198,900	213,700	220,900	228,649
Mission & Evangelism	34,200	38,300	39,600	41,000
Communications department	119,950	128,775	130,000	133,900
Telecommunications/database department	52,600	66,300	68,600	71,000
Anglican World magazine	84,000	84,000	84,000	84,000
Liturgical co-ordinator	9,375	7,685	7,700	7,700
Ecumenical Relations department	110,195	117,885	122,500	128,000
Finance and Administration department	143,300	157,600	162,900	168,500
Overheads (rents, office expenses, etc)	180,525	183,200	185,825	188,385
	933,045	997,445	1,022,025	1,051,134
Provision for meetings etc:				
Inter-Church Conversations	58,750	59,750	60,750	61,750
Joint Unity Commission	9,500	9,500	9,500	9,500
Doctrinal Commission	21,000	21,000	21,000	21,000
Missio	38,500	43,500	43,500	43,500
Ethics & Technology	5,750	6,000	6,500	6,500
Council and Standing Committee	125,000	125,000	125,000	125,000
Primates	25,500	25,500	25,500	25,500
Lambeth Conference	140,000	140,000	140,000	140,000
UN Observer's Office	24,000	24,000	24,000	24,000
	1,381,045	1,451,695	1,477,775	1,507,884
Surplus/(Deficit)	(28,538)	(32,382)	(28,662)	(20,196)

Anglican Consultative Council
Financial Report for ACC-12

Inter-Anglican Budgets 2002 to 2005

Commentary on Budget Figures

Income

A small amount of income is expected from interest on deposits, publications sales, etc. The primary income source is **Member Church Contributions** (80% in 2002). At present these contributions do not provide sufficient income to cover the expenditure commitments. It has therefore been necessary to seek additional help through **Special Fund Raising** efforts (16% in 2002). The **Compass Rose Society** provides most of these funds .

Expenditure

The projections for the years 2003 to 2005 are based on the programmes and commitments in place in 2002.

The figures are grouped by activities. The **Secretary General**'s figures includes Travel office with **Mission and Evangelism**, with one staff member dedicated to that aspect of the work is now shown separately. The **Communications and Telecommunications** sections deal with internal (through the computer network) and external communications issues including the maintenance of the Anglican Communion Office database. Communications department also produces **Anglican World** magazine which is widely distributed through the Communion, partly on a complimentary basis and partly to subscribers. **Ecumenical Relations** department services the Inter-Church Conversations and deals with other ecumenical matters. **Finance and Administration** department deals with the finance and accounting, office administration and much of the logistical work for meetings. The **Overheads** include the rent and other office premises costs as well as the general office expenses, audit fees, etc.

The section **Provision for Meetings, etc** includes the annual provisions for the various meetings which have to be held. Also included is a contribution to the **Office of the Anglican Observer at the United Nations**, the overall budget for which (in 2002) is about £150,000.

Anglican Consultative Council
Financial Report for ACC-12
Table 3
Member Church Contributions 1999 to 2001

INCOME	1999 Request £	1999 Actual £	1999 Variation £	2000 (9 Months) Request £	2000 (9 Months) Actual £	2000 (9 Months) Variation £	2001 Request £	2001 Actual £	2001 Variation £
Aotearoa, New Zealand and Polynesia	34,991	24,473	10,518	27,293	17,763	9,530	27,800	26,225	1,575
Australia	101,670	74,624	27,046	79,302	53,685	25,617	110,000	68,166	41,834
Brazil	4,867	2,450	2,417	3,796		3,796	5,300	3,020	2,280
Burundi	216	424	(208)	169	169	-	300	58	242
Canada	69,222	53,226	15,996	53,992	48,912	5,080	74,900	56,449	18,451
Central Africa	7,030	-	7,030	5,483	3,750	1,733	7,600	1,250	6,350
Central America	1,298	1,298		1,012	1,012		1,400	338	1,062
Ceylon	1,190	1,190	-	928	-	928	1,300	2,214	(914)
Congo Democratic Republic (formerly Zaire)	541	1,061	(520)	422		422	600	1,013	(413)
England [inc. Diocese in Europe]	319,721	319,700	21	249,382	249,000	382	345,800	342,350	3,450
Hong Kong Sheng Kung Hui	20,000	20,000	-	15,600	15,600	-	21,700	21,475	225
Indian Ocean	2,920	2,920	-	2,278	2,278	-	3,200	3,159	41
Ireland	25,678	25,678	-	20,029	20,029	-	27,800	27,526	274
Japan	14,191	14,191	-	11,069	11,069	-	15,400	15,240	160
Jerusalem & the Middle East	3,980	3,980	-	3,104	3,104	-	4,300	4,260	40
Kenya	8,653	8,653	-	6,749	6,000	749	9,400	2,500	6,900
Korea	3,786	3,786	-	2,953	-	2,953	4,100		4,100
Melanesia	1,190	1,190	-	928	928	-	1,300	1,285	15
Mexico	1,298	1,199	99	1,013	1,080	(67)	1,400	1,455	(55)
Myanmar	1,190		1,190	929		929	1,300	4,547	(3,247)
Nigeria	16,494	16,494	-	12,866	12,866	-	17,900	17,713	187
Papua New Guinea	1,190	1,190	-	929	929	-	1,300	1,238	62
Philippines	5,678	2,709	2,969	4,429	1,271	3,158	1,900	1,771	129
Rwanda	1,082		1,082	844	844	-	1,200	281	919
Scotland	17,306	16,765	541	13,499	13,076	423	18,200	18,009	191
South East Asia	21,632	5,852	15,780	16,873	3,212	13,661	4,400	4,370	30
Southern Cone of South America	2,844	2,988	(144)	2,219	2,409	(190)	3,100	3,132	(32)
Southern Africa	13,498	13,498	-	10,529	10,529	-	14,600	3,509	11,091
Sudan	2,844		2,844	2,219	-	2,219	3,100	-	3,100
Taiwan		1028	(1,028)	-	848	(848)	-	1,157	(1,157)
Tanzania	5,678	5,678	-	4,429	4,429	-	6,200	1,476	4,724
Uganda	5,678		5,678	4,429	-	4,429	6,200		6,200
United States of America (including Province IX)	309,499	306,495	3,004	241,409	252,701	(11,292)	334,800	368,322	(33,522)
Wales	25,678	25,678	-	20,029	19,800	229	27,800	27,450	350
West Africa	2,163	2,163	-	1,688	1,688	-	2,400	1,762	638
West Indies	11,357	12,182	(825)	8,858		8,858	12,300	21,036	(8,736)
United Churches:									
United Church of Bangladesh	568	568	-	443	443	-	600	598	2
United Church of North India	1,190	1,190	-	929		929	1,300	2,213	(913)
United Church of Pakistan	1,190		1,190	929		929	1,300	-	1,300
United Church of South India	1,731	1,731	-	1,350	1,350	-	1,900	1,875	25
Extra-Provincial Dioceses:									
Bermuda Diocese	1,622	3,182	(1,560)	1,265	1,265	-	1,800	1,772	28
The Lusitanian Church	541	500	41	422	422	-	600	591	9
The Spanish Ref'md Episcopal Church	541		541	422	963	(541)	600	141	459
	1,073,636	979,934	93,702	837,440	763,424	74,016	1,128,400	1,060,946	67,454

Anglican Consultative Council
Financial Report for ACC-12
Table 4
Member Church Contributions 2002 to 2005

	>>>>>>>>>>2002<<<<<<<<<<							
	Request £	**Paid by 09/06/02 £**	**Unpaid Balance £**	**2003 Request £**	**Supplementary Request**	**2004 Request £**	**2005 Request £**	
Aotearoa, New Zealand and Polynesia	29,450	21,400	8,050	30,100	1,100	31,300	32,600	
Australia	116,600	38,885	77,715	119,000	4,400	123,800	128,800	
Brazil	5,600		5,600	3,400	200	3,500	3,600	
Burundi	308		308	300	10	300	300	
Canada	79,400	42,656	36,744	81,000	3,000	84,200	87,600	
Central Africa	8,050	-	8,050	8,200	300	8,500	8,800	
Central America	1,512	1,500	12	1,600	50	1,700	1,800	
Ceylon	1,412	325	1,087	1,500	50	1,600	1,700	
Congo Democratic Republic	698	150	548	700	30	700	700	
England [inc Dio in Europe]	366,575	356,225	10,350	374,100	13,800	389,100	404,700	
Hong Kong Sheng Kung Hui	22,975	22,300	675	23,400	900	24,300	25,300	
Indian Ocean	3,350	3,275	75	3,400	100	3,500	3,600	
Ireland	29,450	28,625	825	30,100	1,100	31,300	32,600	
Japan	16,300	3,850	12,450	16,600	600	17,300	18,000	
Jerusalem & the Middle East	4,600	1,075	3,525	4,700	200	4,900	5,100	
Kenya	10,000		10,000	10,200	400	10,600	11,000	
Korea	4,400	1,025	3,375	4,500	200	4,700	4,900	
Melanesia	1,412	1,375	37	1,500	50	1,600	1,700	
Mexico	1,513	1,500	13	1,600	50	1,700	1,800	
Myanmar	1,412	325	1,087	1,500	50	1,600	1,700	
Nigeria	18,950	18,425	525	19,300	700	20,100	20,900	
Papua New Guinea	1,413	1,238	175	1,500	50	1,600	1,700	
Philippines	2,050	449	1,601	2,100	100	2,200	2,300	
Rwanda	1,312	1,275	37	1,400	50	1,500	1,600	
Scotland	19,700	19,175	525	20,300	700	21,100	21,900	
South East Asia	4,700	1,100	3,600	4,800	200	5,000	5,200	
Southern Africa	15,500	-	15,500	15,800	600	16,400	17,100	
Southern Cone of South America	3,250	3,040	210	3,300	100	3,400	3,500	
Sudan	3,250	-	3,250	3,300	100	3,400	3,500	
Taiwan		1,126	(1,126)			-	-	
Tanzania	6,500		6,500	6,700	200	7,000	7,300	
Uganda	6,500	-	6,500	6,700	200	7,000	7,300	
United States of America (including Province IX)	354,900	346,386	8,514	360,000	13,400	374,400	389,400	
Wales	29,450	28,625	825	30,100	1,100	31,300	32,600	
West Africa	2,550		2,550	2,600	100	2,700	2,800	
West Indies	13,050	3,446	9,604	13,300	500	13,800	14,400	
United Churches:			-					
United Church of Bangladesh	698	685	13	700	30	700	700	
United Church of North India	1,412	325	1,087	1,500	50	1,600	1,700	
United Church of Pakistan	1,413	-	1,413	1,500	50	1,600	1,700	
United Church of South India	2,050	475	1,575	2,100	100	2,200	2,300	
Extra-Provincial Dioceses:			-					
Bermuda	1,950	1,875	75	2,000	100	2,100	2,200	
Lusitanian Church	698	698	-	700	30	700	700	
Spanish Rfmd Episcopal Church	697	-	697	700	30	700	700	
	1,197,010	952,834	244,176	1,217,800	45,080	1,266,700	1,317,800	
Budget "2002/3	304,970			913,350	33,810			1,252,130
Budget "2003/4				304,450	11,270	950,025		1,265,745
Budget "2004/5						316,675	988,350	1,305,025

Anglican Consultative Council
Table 5
Member Church Contributions 1999 to 2002

	>>>>>>>>>>1999<<<<<<<<<< [Excluding paid for prior years]							
	Budget £	Paid by 11/16/99 £	Unpaid Balance £	2000 Budget £	2001 Budget £	2002 Budget £	Supplementary Request	Total
Aotearoa, New Zealand and Polynesia	34,991	24,474	10,517	36,391	27,800	28,900	1,100	30,000
Australia	101,670	49,020	52,650	105,737	110,000	114,400	4,400	118,800
Brazil	4,867	-	4,867	5,062	5,300	5,500	200	5,700
Burundi	216	216	-	225	300	300	10	310
Canada	69,222	23,842	45,380	71,991	74,900	77,900	3,000	80,900
Central Africa	7,030	-	7,030	7,311	7,600	7,900	300	8,200
Central America	1,298	1,298	-	1,350	1,400	1,500	50	1,550
Ceylon	1,190	1,190	-	1,238	1,300	1,400	50	1,450
Congo Democratic Republic	541	541	-	563	600	700	30	730
England [inc Dio in Europe]	319,721	319,700	21	332,510	345,800	359,700	13,800	373,500
Hong Kong Sheng Kung Hui	20,000	20,000	-	20,800	21,700	22,500	900	23,400
Indian Ocean	2,920	2,920	-	3,037	3,200	3,300	100	3,400
Ireland	25,678	25,678	-	26,705	27,800	28,900	1,100	30,000
Japan	14,191	14,191	-	14,759	15,400	16,000	600	16,600
Jerusalem & the Middle East	3,980	3,980	-	4,139	4,300	4,500	200	4,700
Kenya	8,653	8,653	-	8,999	9,400	9,800	400	10,200
Korea	3,786	-	3,786	3,937	4,100	4,300	200	4,500
Melanesia	1,190	1,190	-	1,238	1,300	1,400	50	1,450
Mexico	1,298	1,199	99	1,350	1,400	1,500	50	1,550
Myanmar	1,190	-	1,190	1,238	1,300	1,400	50	1,450
Nigeria	16,494	16,494	-	17,154	17,900	18,600	700	19,300
Papua New Guinea	1,190	1,190	-	1,238	1,300	1,400	50	1,450
Philippines	5,678	1,505	4,173	5,905	1,900	2,000	100	2,100
Rwanda	1,082	-	1,082	1,125	1,200	1,300	50	1,350
Scotland	17,306	16,765	541	17,998	18,200	19,500	700	20,200
South East Asia	21,632	4,229	17,403	22,497	4,400	4,600	200	4,800
Southern Africa	13,498	13,498	-	14,038	14,600	15,200	600	15,800
Southern Cone of South America	2,844	2,988	(144)	2,958	3,100	3,200	100	3,300
Sudan	2,844	-	2,844	2,958	3,100	3,200	100	3,300
Taiwan		1,028	(1,028)		-	-		-
Tanzania	5,678	5,678	-	5,905	6,200	6,400	200	6,600
Uganda	5,678	-	5,678	5,905	6,200	6,400	200	6,600
United States of America (including Province IX)	309,499	243,927	65,572	321,879	334,800	348,200	13,400	361,600
Wales	25,678	25,678	-	26,705	27,800	28,900	1,100	30,000
West Africa	2,163	2,163	-	2,250	2,400	2,500	100	2,600
West Indies	11,357	11,357	-	11,811	12,300	12,800	500	13,300
United Churches:			-					-
United Church of Bangladesh	568	568	-	591	600	700	30	730
United Church of North India	1,190	1,190	-	1,238	1,300	1,400	50	1,450
United Church of Pakistan	1,190	-	1,190	1,238	1,300	1,400	50	1,450
United Church of South India	1,731	-	1,731	1,800	1,900	2,000	100	2,100
Extra-Provincial Dioceses:			-					-
Bermuda	1,622	1,622	-	1,687	1,800	1,900	100	2,000
Lusitanian Church	541	500	41	563	600	700	30	730
Spanish Rfmd Episcopal Church	541	-	541	563	600	700	30	730
	1,073,636	848,472	225,164	1,116,586	1,128,400	1,174,800	45,080	1,219,880

Table 6
Anglican Consultative Council
Reforecast 2001/2002

	Actual 2000/0	Budget	Estimate	Shortfall
		£	£	£
Aotearoa, New Zealand and Polynesia	28,900	29,450	28,625	825
Australia	114,400	116,600	68,000	48,600
Brazil	5,500	5,600	2,800	2,800
Burundi	300	308	300	8
Canada	77,900	79,400	56,700	22,700
Central Africa	7,900	8,050	-	8,050
Central America	1,500	1,512	-	1,512
Ceylon	1,400	1,412	1,375	37
Congo Democratic Republic	700	698	675	23
England [inc Dio in Europe]	359,700	366,575	356,225	10,350
Hong Kong Sheng Kung Hui	22,500	22,975	22,300	675
Indian Ocean	3,300	3,350	3,275	75
Ireland	28,900	29,450	28,625	825
Japan	16,000	16,300	15,850	450
Jerusalem & the Middle East	4,500	4,600	4,450	150
Kenya	9,800	10,000	4,900	5,100
Korea	4,300	4,400	4,250	150
Melanesia	1,400	1,412	1,375	37
Mexico	1,500	1,513	1,500	13
Myanmar	1,400	1,412	1,375	37
Nigeria	18,600	18,950	18,425	525
Papua New Guinea	1,400	1,413	1,238	175
Philippines	2,000	2,050	1,949	101
Rwanda	1,300	1,312	1,275	37
Scotland	19,500	19,700	19,175	525
South East Asia	4,600	4,700	4,550	150
Southern Africa	15,200	15,500	15,200	300
Southern Cone of South America	3,200	3,250	3,040	210
Sudan	3,200	3,250	-	3,250
Taiwan	-		1,126	(1,126)
Tanzania	6,400	6,500	6,400	100
Uganda	6,400	6,500	-	6,500
United States of America (including Province	348,200	354,900	354,900	-
Wales	28,900	29,450	28,625	825
West Africa	2,500	2,550	-	2,550
West Indies	12,800	13,050	13,046	4
United Churches:				-
United Church of Bangladesh	700	698	685	13
United Church of North India	1,400	1,412	1,375	37
United Church of Pakistan	1,400	1,413	-	1,413
United Church of South India	2,000	2,050	1,975	75
Extra-Provincial Dioceses:				-
Bermuda	1,900	1,950	1,875	75
Lusitanian Church	700	698	698	-
Spanish Rfmd Episcopal Church	700	697	-	697
		1,197,010	1,078,157	118,853

Financial Report for ACC-12
Table 7
Member Church Contributions 2002 to 2005

	>>>>>>>>>>2002<<<<<<<<<<							
	2002 Request	Paid by 09/06/02	Unpaid Balance	2003 Request	Supplementary Request	2004 Request	2005 Request	
	£	£	£	£		£	£	
Aotearoa, New Zealand and Polynesia	30,000	21,675	8,325	30,100	1,100	31,300	32,600	
Australia	118,800	21,059	97,741	119,000	4,400	123,800	128,800	
Brazil	5,700		5,700	3,400	200	3,500	3,600	
Burundi	310		310	300	10	300	300	
Canada	80,900	28,492	52,408	81,000	3,000	84,200	87,600	
Central Africa	8,200		8,200	8,200	300	8,500	8,800	
Central America	1,550	1,500	50	1,600	50	1,700	1,800	
Ceylon	1,450		1,450	1,500	50	1,600	1,700	
Congo Democratic Republic	730		730	700	30	700	700	
England [inc Dio in Europe]	373,500	269,775	103,725	374,100	13,800	389,100	404,700	
Hong Kong Sheng Kung Hui	23,400	22,500	900	23,400	900	24,300	25,300	
Indian Ocean	3,400	3,300	100	3,400	100	3,500	3,600	
Ireland	30,000	28,900	1,100	30,100	1,100	31,300	32,600	
Japan	16,600	16,000	600	16,600	600	17,300	18,000	
Jerusalem & the Middle East	4,700	4,500	200	4,700	200	4,900	5,100	
Kenya	10,200		10,200	10,200	400	10,600	11,000	
Korea	4,500		4,500	4,500	200	4,700	4,900	
Melanesia	1,450	1,400	50	1,500	50	1,600	1,700	
Mexico	1,550	1,500	50	1,600	50	1,700	1,800	
Myanmar	1,450		1,450	1,500	50	1,600	1,700	
Nigeria	19,300	18,600	700	19,300	700	20,100	20,900	
Papua New Guinea	1,450	1,238	212	1,500	50	1,600	1,700	
Philippines	2,100		2,100	2,100	100	2,200	2,300	
Rwanda	1,350	1,300	50	1,400	50	1,500	1,600	
Scotland	20,200	14,625	5,575	20,300	700	21,100	21,900	
South East Asia	4,800		4,800	4,800	200	5,000	5,200	
Southern Africa	15,800		15,800	15,800	600	16,400	17,100	
Southern Cone of South America	3,300	3,020	280	3,300	100	3,400	3,500	
Sudan	3,300	1,500	1,800	3,300	100	3,400	3,500	
Taiwan	-	1,113	(1,113)			-	-	
Tanzania	6,600		6,600	6,700	200	7,000	7,300	
Uganda	6,600		6,600	6,700	200	7,000	7,300	
United States of America (including Province IX)	361,600	252,470	109,130	360,000	13,400	374,400	389,400	
Wales	30,000	28,900	1,100	30,100	1,100	31,300	32,600	
West Africa	2,600		2,600	2,600	100	2,700	2,800	
West Indies	13,300		13,300	13,300	500	13,800	14,400	
United Churches:	-		-					
United Church of Bangladesh	730	730	-	700	30	700	700	
United Church of North India	1,450		1,450	1,500	50	1,600	1,700	
United Church of Pakistan	1,450		1,450	1,500	50	1,600	1,700	
United Church of South India	2,100		2,100	2,100	100	2,200	2,300	
Extra-Provincial Dioceses:	-		-					
Bermuda	2,000	1,900	100	2,000	100	2,100	2,200	
Lusitanian Church	730	730	-	700	30	700	700	
Spanish Rfmd Episcopal Church	730	-	730	700	30	700	700	
	1,219,880	746,727	473,153	1,217,800	45,080	1,266,700	1,317,800	
Budget "2002/3	304,970			913,350	33,810			1,252,130
Budget "2003/4				304,450	11,270	950,025		1,265,745
Budget "2004/5						316,675	988,350	1,305,025

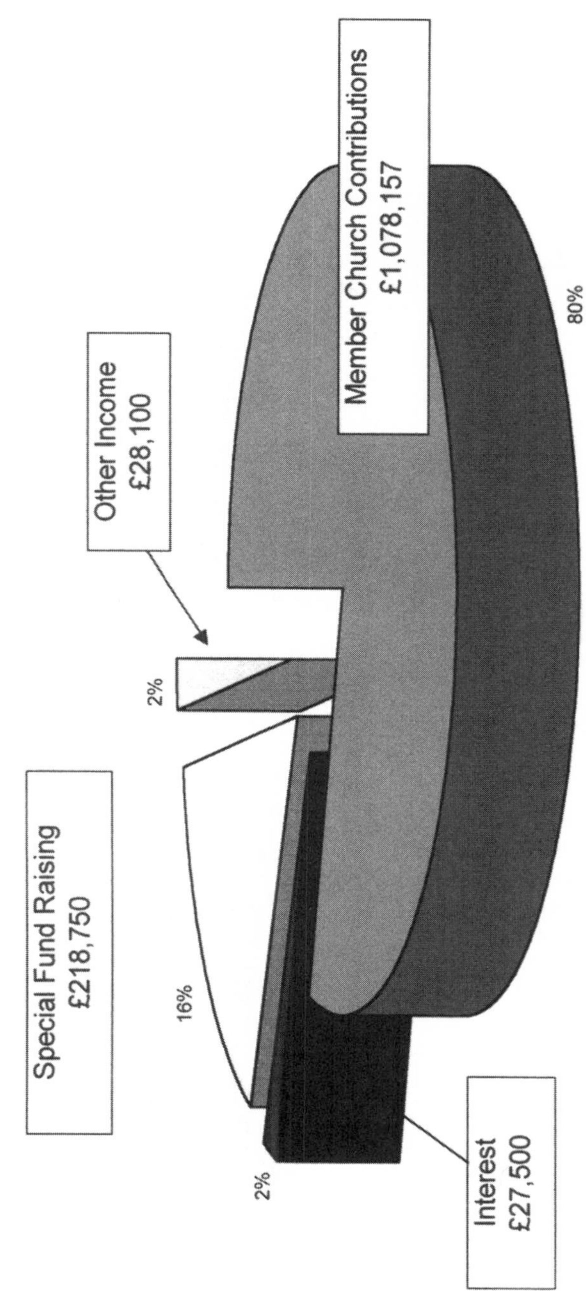
Inter-Anglican Budget Income 2002
Special Fund Raising
£218,750
16%
Other Income
£28,100
2%
Member Church Contributions
£1,078,157
80%
2%
Interest
£27,500
Total Income £1,352507

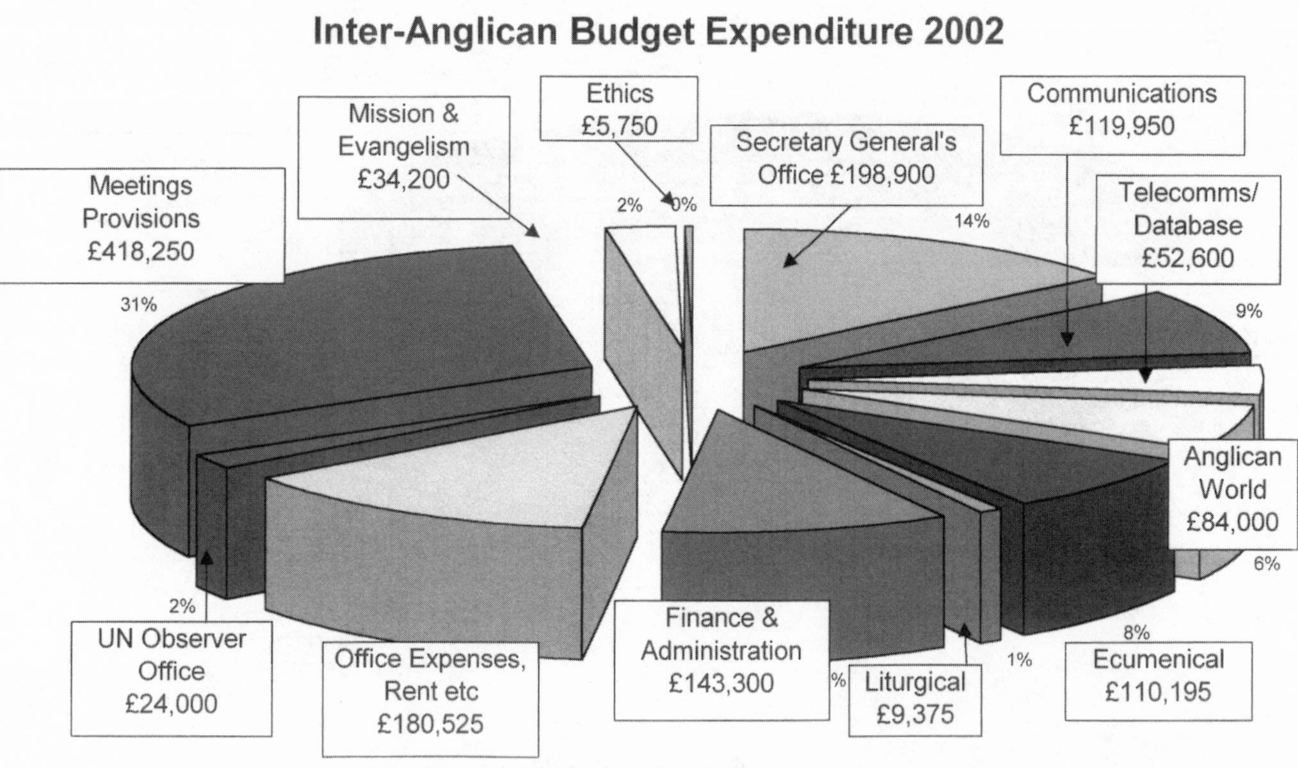
Inter-Anglican Budget Expenditure 2002
Meetings Provisions £418,250
31%
Mission & Evangelism £34,200
Ethics £5,750
2%
0%
Secretary General's Office £198,900
14%
Communications £119,950
Telecomms/ Database £52,600
9%
Anglican World £84,000
6%
2%
UN Observer Office £24,000
Office Expenses, Rent etc £180,525
Finance & Administration £143,300
Liturgical £9,375
1%
8%
Ecumenical £110,195
Total Expenditure £1,381,045

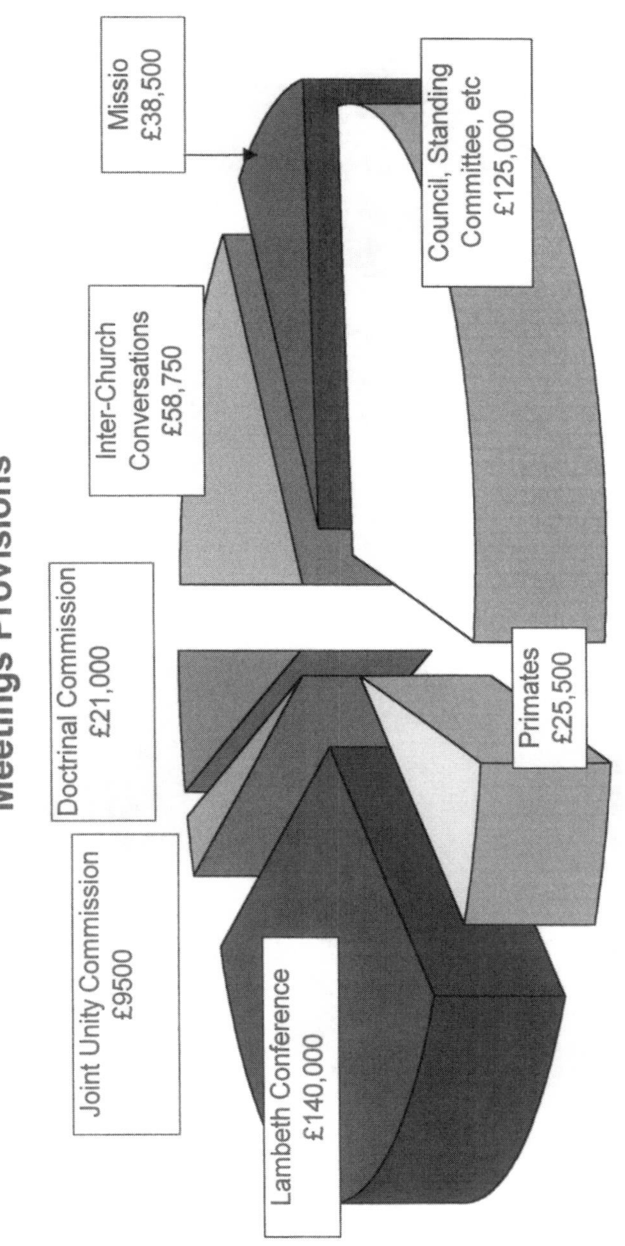
Inter-Anglican Budget 2002
Meetings Provisions
Joint Unity Commission
£9500
Doctrinal Commission
£21,000
Inter-Church
Conversations
£58,750
Missio
£38,500
Council, Standing
Committee, etc
£125,000
Primates
£25,500
Lambeth Conference
£140,000
Total Meetings Provisions

20 SEPTEMBER 2002

Address by Dr. Ishmael Noko, General Secretary, Lutheran World Federation

Introduction: On Returning to Hong Kong

Five years ago, a few days after the return of Hong Kong to Chinese rule, the Lutheran World Federation held its Ninth Assembly in this city. The Anglican Communion was ably represented at the Assembly by Bishop David Tustin and Canon David Hamid.

Since that time, Anglican-Lutheran relations have continued to progress. Important agreements of full communion have been entered into by churches of our communions. And the LWF President, Bishop Christian Krause, has upon invitation visited the Archbishop of Canterbury, Dr. George Carey.

Cooperation between our communions has developed and expanded at the global level in recent years. On this occasion I wish to extend my expression of appreciation to Canon John Peterson, the Secretary General of the Anglican Communion, with whom I have worked closely in recent years. Together we have instituted annual Joint Staff Meetings between ACC and the LWF, thereby implementing proactively one of the recommendations made by the Anglican-Lutheran International Working Group.

I am very grateful for the invitation to attend this 12th meeting of the Anglican Consultative Council, under the theme "For the Life of the World", in order to represent the Lutheran World Federation. I bring you greetings from the LWF Council, which has just concluded its meeting in Lutherstadt Wittenberg in Germany. One of the major items of business at this LWF Council meeting was preparation for our next Assembly, which will take place in Winnipeg, Canada in July 2003 under the similar theme "For the Healing of the World".

As the member churches of the Lutheran World Federation gathered in Hong Kong in July 1997, we stood on territory that had just passed from one of the last remaining colonial administrations, to political re-unification with mainland China. The colonial system under which Hong Kong had been administered represented an historical legacy which is now, fortunately, almost entirely extinct. But the government to which Hong Kong devolved represented a communist ideology that had already disappeared from much of the globe.

In 1997 we also stood on the verge of a new century and a new millennium, of which the great changes in Hong Kong seemed a herald. Meeting under the theme 'In Christ, Called to Witness', the member churches of the LWF were challenged to reflect upon their life and witness as churches in changing times, in which hope and apprehension combined in equal measure. Hong Kong provided a powerful symbol of these intermingled outlooks.

The 1997 Assembly was a further step in the journey of LWF member churches towards the fuller expression of our self-understanding as a communion of churches. The political transition in Hong Kong, with the uncertainties that it carried for churches as well as for the population at large, provided a context in which the notion of communion could be tested and experienced.

Like the LWF member churches, the Anglican family of churches describe their relationship as one of communion. The Anglican Communion therefore faces the same basic challenge as the LWF: to express communion in daily life and ministry. This common challenge, and our shared heritage in faith, are reflected in the growing strength of the Anglican-Lutheran relationship, as partners in the search for a greater visible unity of the body of Christ.

My presence here with you, in this city and this country, gives me a welcome opportunity to reflect with you on "Challenges facing the church today" as we seek to express more fully our unity in Christ, to carry out our Christian witness in the world. One important way for us to do this is to promote what I would call the 'Good Society'.

'The Good Society'

The vision of the 'Good Society' has been with us continuously since the beginning of human history. It is a vision and a quest common to all peoples, and reflects God's guiding hand in human history. The conflicts and injustices that have occurred among all these seekers of the 'good society' arise from the lack of a shared vision of what the 'good society' is or should be, and from confrontation between competing visions.

What is the 'Good Society'? How do we measure a society for 'goodness'? Is it possible to create a good society that is good for everyone? In the pursuit of the 'Good Society', does the end necessarily justify the means? How does the church participate in and help realize the vision of the Good Society?

It is essential in my view to avoid the temptation of defining the 'Good Society' by reference to existing evils in the world—as the sum of the opposites of those evils. Instead, we should proceed from the basis of fundamental ethical principles and faith values in order to discern the shape of a society based upon those principles and values. It is at this point that the consequences of the Gospel principles of reconciliation and communion must be identified.

The Social Witness of the Church as Koinonia (Communion)

The notion of koinonia has radical consequences for our social witness. In this presentation I would like to expound on that topic from a few different angles. But before I do so, let me give you some examples.

- *Globalization and fragmentation*

We live in an age in which globalization and fragmentation go hand in hand.

The world is certainly getting smaller. Incredible developments in communication technology, increased international travel, the growth of the global marketplace, and the establishment of transnational legal regimes in particular in the fields of human rights and international humanitarian law are increasingly bridging the divides of geography, distance, culture and political boundaries, and have brought the nations of the world much closer together. At the same time, and paradoxically through the same processes, fragmentation and alienation are on the rise—as indicated by the confrontations represented most vividly by the September 11 attacks just over one year ago and their sequel in the 'war against terrorism', by the increasing inequalities between rich and poor countries and people, by the growing tendency towards nationalism and xenophobia, and by the decline of multilateralism in international relations. In this paradox lies the moral ambiguity of globalization.

Churches are themselves fully implicated in the ambiguity of globalization. The very mission of the church is a 'globalizing' one. We are commissioned to bring the Good News to the whole earth, and to serve all the people of God. The body of Christ is a global body. A shared faith, contextualized in the many cultures of the people of God, is our prayer and desire. But the history of the mission of the churches, we must admit, does contain examples of the sort of cultural imperialism for which globalization is now criticized. And despite the many ecumenical advances that have been made, tensions remain among churches of the world along denominational, racial, political and cultural lines.

I believe that the answer to this globalization of fragmentation lies in the notion of communion, and that in this notion the churches have a great resource for their social witness in this context.

For instance, the member churches of the LWF in Argentina are living and ministering in the context of a collapsing economy and a social fabric which is under intolerable strain, in part due to the consequences of international economic policies in the area of sovereign debt and structural adjustment. Those churches are challenging the LWF to respond not only through emergency charitable means, but in our very life and ministry—as part of the body of Christ in which if one part of the body suffers, all are affected. This is the sort of challenge that a study document produced by the LWF Department for Theology and Studies, on 'Engaging Economic Globalization as a Communion', is intended to encourage member churches to reflect on.

- *Extreme poverty*

The persistence of extreme poverty in a world of unprecedented wealth cannot, from the perspective of communion, be tolerated. When the vast majority of the world's wealth is in the hands of a tiny minority, and one billion people must live—or die—on less than one dollar a day, our sinful state is painfully emphasized and the reality of our communion thrown into question. This issue does not only concern the need for an improved standard of living for millions of people. It concerns their inner life, indeed their very humanity. Poverty eats away at the self-esteem of human beings. We must remember that to a great degree, poverty is man-made. And we must recognize that this curse is not external to the life of the church. The church is itself poor. Its life is never outside the lives of those who suffer.

- *HIV/AIDS*

Similarly, in our response to the catastrophic dimensions of the HIV/AIDS pandemic, the perspective of communion provides fresh insight. It is already apparent that the extent of the pandemic (with infection rates of almost 40% in the most affected countries) will have fundamental social and ecclesial consequences. From the perspective of the church as the body of Christ, it is obvious that the churches' response to the HIV/AIDS crisis must not merely be compassion towards the 'victims' of HIV/AIDS, but a recognition that the church itself has HIV/AIDS. The true biblical calling of the church in the midst of this crisis is not to be a judgmental and excluding church but an accepting and consoling church; to internalize the challenge, rather than externalizing it; and not to obstruct and delay any efforts aimed at prevention, but to assist and strengthen them.

- *Gender equality*

The notion of communion also challenges the church and society with regard to the unfinished business of gender equality. Our communion is a communion of women and men, created equally by God and equally bearing God's image. Inequality is not just a question of existing differences in social status. It is a condition that, like poverty and illness, always threatens to deteriorate identity. It can be deeply detrimental to women's experience of self-worth, before God as well as in society. The implications of this truth is a matter that churches must resolve in terms of their internal relationships, and their ecumenical relationships, before any witness in the area of gender equality can be a faithful and credible witness.

- *Racial discrimination and other forms of discrimination*

Racial discrimination and other forms of discrimination are, by definition, denials of the God-given dignity of every human being. Though the institution of apartheid has been overturned, the prejudices it reflected remain strong in many different parts of the globe and are directed against many different groups. Discrimination against refugees and migrant workers, an issue that is very 'hot' here in Hong Kong as in many other parts of the world, is a particular challenge in our increasingly globalized yet fragmented world. The notion of communion transforms racial, ethnic and cultural identifications from points of antagonism and division, to a community of diversity and hospitality.

- *The caste system and similar systems of inherited social exclusion*

Even as an African who has experienced the effects of apartheid, I can say that one of the most entrenched and most severe forms of institutionalized denial of the common God-given dignity of every human being is the caste system of South Asia and the many similar systems of inherited social exclusion around the world. The discrimination suffered by the Dalits of South Asia, the Burakumin of Japan, the Osu of Nigeria and other affected communities, though varying in nature and degree, shares the common characteristic of excluding the members of these groups from the normal circles of society and ascribing to them a sub-human status. The church itself is not always free of these attitudes in the countries concerned, but the notion of communion calls us to be strong advocates against such discriminatory systems of inherited social exclusion.

- *Armed conflicts*

Armed conflicts, still so prevalent in many parts of the world, are one of the starkest, most extreme symptoms of lacking koinonia. It is almost not to be believed that at the start of the present third millennium after the birth of Christ, we experience investments in the arms industry increasing to dramatic proportions, and along with it an obvious trust in the use of armed force as an appropriate means to deal with various threats and provide solutions to difficult issues. Whereas billions and billions are spent on means to destroy, only fractions of those amounts are spent on nation building. The practice of koinonia calls us always to be in dialogue and constructive relationships with others. It calls us to invest more heavily than anything else in initiatives of reconciliation, reconstruction of areas damaged by war and programs to bridge the racial, ethnic, cultural and religious boundaries between us that so easily lead to conflict.

- *Environmental protection and conservation*

As Rev. Dr. Emmanuel Asante has recently written, a preservationist and conservationist approach to development is essential, from an ethical perspective. Drawing also upon African traditions, he argues that preservation and conservation of nature "lie at the heart of the African's general conception of human society, which involves the dead, the living and the unborn", and that "authentic development in Africa", and elsewhere in my view, "cannot be pursued in isolation of both the past and the future". Such an analysis reflects an inter-generational application of the notion of communion, which requires us to protect and conserve the natural environment as a heritage from the past and as a legacy to future generations.

The fundamental Gospel message of which the churches are the bearers is that of reconciliation. It is through reconciliation with God and each other that we are brought into communion—and into confrontation with the divisions and injustices of the world.

The message of reconciliation speaks also to the relationships between human beings and within all of creation, and has its necessary consequences in politics, the resolution of conflict, the management of economic relations, the protection of the environment, and the pursuit of justice in all the world's contexts.

I concur with the following statement: "If the churches have nothing to say about reconciliation, the churches have nothing to say."

The Search for Ethical Guidelines in a World of Failed Ideologies

The death of ideologies has been widely and perhaps prematurely proclaimed over the last two decades. The main competing ideologies of the past century provided certain frameworks for our social, cultural and spiritual lives. They defined territories and determined terms for interaction with each other. However, the inherent simplifications and distortions of human life and history are the great weakness of such doctrinaire certainties.

The ultimate collapse of the communist regime in the former Soviet Union demonstrated clearly the failure of an ideology which was designed to promote the *distribution* of common wealth and well being, but which proved incapable of *producing* wealth for distribution. The totalitarianism into which Soviet communism swiftly lapsed was an early sign of this failure.

Today, Western democratic capitalism, which ostensibly emerged triumphant from the long confrontation of the Cold War, has also begun to show its inherent fragility. Remarkably successful at producing wealth, neo-liberal capitalism has shown itself to be almost constitutionally incapable of distributing that wealth equitably and of providing a meaningful democratic franchise to the poor and vulnerable in a world ruled by market forces. The dramatically rising inequalities between rich and poor countries and people represents one of the greatest contemporary global challenges—politically, ethically and spiritually.

The failure of these ideologies to serve the common good has resulted in a kind of resignation and drift in the engagement, interest and even belief of people in a socially just form of governance.

In China, and especially in Hong Kong, an encounter is taking place between the two major competing ideologies of the last century. The 'one country, two systems' policy devised for the transfer of exuberantly capitalist Hong Kong to the rule of communist China presented what many of us considered the best available compromise for the resolution of an historical dilemma. As I see the situation in Hong Kong now, and in China as a whole, I still cannot discern what results this encounter between ideologies will produce. But on the whole I remain optimistic that transformation of systems—with a good outcome—is possible.

I also believe, in this very context, that it is essential for a "world ethic", as Hans Küng has called it, to be found. And I believe that the principles of communion and reconciliation must provide its essence. It is not only in the spiritual 'realm' that these principles should be given consequence, but also in the governance and community life of the people that God has created. Churches must not be reticent, in the midst of the void left by the failure of the competing ideologies of the twentieth century, to proclaim the political implications of the Gospel in its broad meaning. From the inspiration of the Gospel, contributions toward a global ethic may be made that unify and restore, rather than divide and fragment. It is my firm belief that we must be bold in this area at the present time. Our politicians are not providing what it takes to build better societies globally. Therefore, a heavy responsibility lies on us as churches and as faith communities to actively contribute to global ethical reflection and initiatives—without any form of triumphalism.

Towards a Truly Global Consensus of Human Ethics

At the present time in history, the language of good and evil, referring to individuals or nations, must be used with greatest care. Oversimplifications in this area are as dangerous for world peace as any ideology that history has seen before. Not only do they add dangerously inflammable religious overtones to political disputes; they also make it difficult, if not impossible, to discern where the lines between good and evil actually go in the complexity of human history.

As we struggle to achieve some measure of hope for the world and its future, we must not confine ourselves to self-asserting virtues over against our opponents. With all our appreciation for the values we wish to defend, we must also be aware that those values, or their implications, are not all necessarily good for others. The main way forward toward peace and reconciliation in today's tumultuous world is by way of recognizing the value of every human being in God's sight. It is essential that we strive for a global consensus of human ethics which corresponds to our understandings of communion and reconciliation.

Although I am keenly and painfully aware of the history of tribal conflicts that has ravaged many African nations through the century, I nevertheless wish to highlight a concept which is basic to my background, and that I believe can be a significant African contribution to a broad, cross-cutting communication on human values in the future. It is the concept of *ubuntu*.

This term, based upon the Xhosa word for 'people', carries an understanding of human life in community which is quite widespread in Africa. It is explained in the Zulu maxim *umuntu ngumuntu ngabandu*, or in the saying in my own langauge *motho ke motho ka batho*—both of which mean that a person is a person through other persons.

Of course, the widespread nature of this belief has not saved Africa from being repeatedly convulsed by conflict and violence. It is a promise that is yet to be fulfilled in many parts of the continent. But the concept of ubuntu nevertheless encompasses an understanding of the inseparability of the individual from the community without the loss or suppression of individuality that has not been reflected in either communist totalitarianism or in the neo-liberal capitalism dominant throughout the world today.

In the present period of history, tensions in the world have been increasing almost from day to day over the past months, and few global agents apart from the United Nations have been seriously contributing to increased building of trust and lowering of tensions. A truly global communication process on human ethics is called for. In such a process, different regions and different religions must be called to bring forth the best and the deepest levels of their heritage.

Ethics and values are not, however, static concepts. They are dynamic processes. The 'Good Society' itself cannot therefore be envisaged as a static and achievable point but only as a process, even if a consensus on ethics and values can be identified in any given society at any given time. Good processes towards the articulation and application of common values and ethics may themselves be the hallmark of a 'good society'. Such processes, involving a dynamic permanent dialogue among the members of the society, represent at the same time the 'seeding' of the 'good society' and its fruition.

Without good dialogical processes, the 'good society' cannot be conceived by external legislative structures or economic dogmas. Neither the imposed 'classless society' of the socialist dream nor the 'trickle down' fantasy of raw capitalism, nor any external structure or framework, can on its own bring about the 'good society' without a good process whereby the minds of both leaders and citizens are transformed.

The effort to impose an ideology on political opponents, by force, threat or intimidation, constitutes an essential part of the problem. The most important key to universal compassion is the ability to hold competing perspectives in our minds at the same time without feeling the need to reject or devalue the viewpoints of those with whom we do not agree. Individuals or groups will always have substantive differences in values. I do not propose that we should ignore the differences, but they must be held in a healthy dialogical posture.

To move forward in the search for the 'good society', we must find processes and relationships in which we can continuously identify shared values, recognizing the fact that such values may change over time, and work together for the application of those values.

Respect and compassion are the basic human needs in situations of deprivation. Human beings have the same basic needs, and the same basic feelings. Respect and compassion for pain and deprivation where they do occur is indispensable in the 'Good Society'. This may be a critical issue in relation to groups and individuals we have negative feeling about. Ability to relate empathetically to suffering in whatever context it exists is absolutely central to enlightened politics and a powerful antidote to group chauvinism.

Inter-faith Dialogue for Peace

All too many conflicts of the last decades have had religious aspects to them. It suffices to mention the Middle East, the Sudan, Indonesia, Kashmir, the Balkans and Northern Ireland. It is one of the great tragedies of contemporary history that religious faiths, instead of providing bridges, either have fueled conflicts or have been misused by political and military leaders to give deeper motivation to ethnic, social or economic conflicts.

At the same time we must recognize that in many armed conflicts with religious contexts, we are dealing with distorted, thwarted forms of religion, not representative of the relevant religions at large. In the Middle East, both Israeli and Palestinian acts of violence are being given religious motives. But we know very well that both Judaism and Islam are far deeper and broader than what comes through in the portraits we receive of extremist elements on both sides. They both have their own versions of ubuntu in them, which at the present time ought be a precious source of peace and mutual esteem, rather than an incitement to conflict and killing. This represents an enormous challenge to present-day and future religious leaders.

I am happy to recognize the important initiatives that have been taken in this area by the Archbishop of Canterbury.

I have had the privilege, myself, over the years to take part in several inter-faith consultations for peace organized by the Roman Catholic Society St. Egidio. I have great respect for the work carried out by this society which I follow with my prayers. Earlier this year, I also had the privilege, together with representatives of many Christian world communions and representatives of other faiths, to participate in the Day of Prayer for Peace in the World in Assisi, at the invitation of Pope John Paul II. As I wish to sincerely honour the tireless dedication of the pope to the cause of peace and interfaith reconciliation, let me share with you on this occasion the "Assisi Decalogue for Peace" which was proclaimed at the conclusion of that exceptional day. This Decalogue was subsequently sent to Heads of State and Government around the world.

In the Assisi Decalogue for Peace we committed ourselves, among other things,

- to proclaim our firm conviction that violence and terrorism are incompatible with the authentic Spirit of religion, and to doing everything possible to eliminate the root causes of terrorism,
- to frank and patient dialogue, refusing to consider our differences as an insurmountable barrier, but recognizing instead that to encounter the diversity of others can become an opportunity for greater reciprocal understanding,
- to support one another in a common effort both to overcome selfishness and arrogance, hatred and violence, and to learn from the past that peace without justice is no true peace,
- to take the side of the poor and the helpless, to speak out for those who have no voice and to work effectively to change these situations,
- to urge the leaders of nations to make every effort to create and consolidate, on the national and international levels, a world of solidarity and peace based on justice.

I believe we as churches are called to multiply events such as the Assisi Conference for Peace and to substantially strengthen our efforts at the level of ecumenical and inter-faith relations to establish firm ground for overcoming the many serious conflicts that have given such a tragic opening to the present millennium.

In a few weeks time, the LWF will be helping to facilitate a consultation among African religious leaders on the issue of interfaith dialogue and cooperation for peace in Africa. It will be the first time that a continent-wide conference on this issue will take place, bringing together representatives of churches, of Islam, Buddhism, Hinduism, Judaism, Baha'i and African traditional religions. I believe that it is essential—in this meeting and in all such initiatives-to move beyond declaratory and rhetorical commitments, to practical action against conflict and for a culture of peace.

Human Rights

The God-given dignity of every human being, the notion of communion, and the integrated combination of freedom and service, are closely mirrored in the provisions of the Universal Declaration of Human Rights and in the other instruments of modern international human rights law.

In these instruments, we find "recognition of the inherent dignity and of the equal and inalienable rights of all members of the human family", and the declarations that "All human beings are born free and equal in dignity and rights" and that everyone is entitled to these rights "without distinction of any kind, such as race, colour, sex, language, religion, political or other opinion, national or social origin, property, birth or other status."

These instruments provide us with a catalogue of rights to which the international community has accorded the status of binding international law, and that cover a comprehensive range of the elements of human dignity commonly threatened by both political oppression and economic injustice.

In emphasizing the obligation of recognizing and realizing these 'rights' for all people, human rights closely match church teachings on the principles of neighbour-love, and the God-given dignity of every human being. When political and economic regimes threaten the principles of human rights, it threatens these faith commitments, and vice versa.

As such, human rights help to provide a legal framework that reflects our most fundamental faith convictions, and which should guide policy in the direction of solidarity and community, rather than competition and domination. Churches, from the perspective of our faith convictions, must insist always that human dignity must take the highest priority in public policy, and that political and economic policies and structures serve no other purpose than that of the well being of the whole human family. Human rights law takes the same position, and provides the churches with tools and a framework of analysis for holding governments and other actors accountable. As churches, we minister locally and nationally and are at the same time part of a global communion. Together with all people of faith and good will, we have the responsibility to claim human rights and to use them on behalf of our own communities and on behalf of the whole human family.

Unity and Witness

Our ecumenical developments are important not only with regard to the real unity of the universal church of Christ in the world. They are also important for the way in which we as churches can be what Jesus called the "salt of the earth" together.

We know of developments in the world where the message of forgiveness of sins and reconciliation has extended far beyond the sanctuaries. The transition of power from white rule in South Africa is a major example. The values underlying the Truth and Reconciliation Commission in the same country is another example. Another prominent example is of course the importance of Christian values in the development of the Universal Declaration of Human Rights. We can also think of the broad effects of Christian-based diaconia in all regions of the world.

The effects of the faith and life of the church extend beyond all that we can observe, and certainly far beyond the reactions that we can analyze. The impact of the message and the values of our preaching and sacramental and diaconal life is only known to God. It is therefore a matter for our faith and our prayer.

If we have a concern for the impact in the world of our proclamation and our service, it is a concern that does not arise out of a wish for religious dominance. The main reason for this is the nature and meaning of the atonement and reconciliation in Christ. All that we represent as churches has the purpose of the salvation of humankind in its broadest sense.

We do not see the values that we represent as churches as uniquely Christian. Certainly, the way we proclaim God's forgiveness of sins is not universal among the world's religions. But it is our understanding that the will of God, as expressed, e.g., in the golden rule, which is a call to mutual love, is written in the hearts of all. Therefore, we do not address the world as strangers, needing to legitimize ourselves. The basic values of the church are not the exclusive property of the church. They are the property of all, for the good of all.

Progress towards the Visible Unity of the Church

Ecumenical developments around the world are first of all a result of our faith that unity is a divine gift. The many agreements that now exist between churches of our two traditions, and between churches of other traditions are a response to the prayer of Christ that his disciples may be one so that the world may believe. This prayer of Christ is not simply an exhortation to Christians to unite for the sake of the witness of the gospel. Christ's prayer for the unity of his disciples is inseparably connected to the gift of unity, at the core of which is the gift of the divine grace that is the nature of the Holy Trinity.

In Christ's prayer before his crucifixion that the gospel of John has conveyed to us, he prays to the Father saying,

> The glory that you have given me I have given them, so that they may be one, as we are one, I in them and you in me, that they may become completely one, so that the world may know that you have sent me and have loved them even as you have loved me.

It is in this light that we must see all our ecumenical agreements of church communion. They are much more than negotiated results among institutional churches. They belong to the different ways in which the unity given in Christ takes shape in the world. They are embodiments, at the level of our churches, of the real unity in faith we have with Christ and in Christ. This is of course the reason why in our dialogues we so strongly stress the areas having to do with the Word, the sacraments and the ministry. By focusing on these topics, we build up our mutual accountability in those areas that are constitutive in our relationship with Christ.

In Anglican-Lutheran relations ways have been found, particularly through the Niagara Consultation in 1987 and the various agreements of communion that have followed from this, to overcome hindrances for full participation in each other's sacramental life. The procedure followed here has been theological in the real sense of the word: It has allowed God and God's gifts in history to be the center of concern, above which no human institutions or traditions have authority. Our inherited church structures are always subject to the critical assessment that asks whether they appropriately serve the unity that is God's gift in Christ and the Holy Spirit.

In our dialogues, ways have been found to carry out such critique ecumenically, i.e., jointly, with a specific view to overcome hindrances that our different histories have resulted in. At the same time, we have found ways to enrich each other, by what Margaret O'Gara has called the "Ecumenical Gift Exchange".

The fact that we have found ways to achieve exchangeability of ministers at all levels is a clear reflection of the *theo*-logical approach of our dialogues. We have overcome tendencies that exist either to not deal sufficiently deeply with matters of sacraments and ministries or to uphold our own traditions as representing in themselves the full unity that Christ calls us to. In the ecumenical movement this may be our most important contribution for the years ahead. It represents a readiness both to share our gifts with each other and also to carry each other's burdens. In Christ, these two dimensions of common life are inseparable. Together, they represent ecclesial *ubuntu*!

The Anglican-Lutheran International Working Group

As we are gathered here, we have the privilege of having before us the report of the Anglican-Lutheran International Working Group, which was adopted in Porto Alegre, Brazil, in May and has since gone through its final editing. This week, in Wittenberg, Germany, the LWF Council received this report. We shall now send it to our member churches for study and response. The report has several recommendations in it, and we may wish to discuss them informally even here at this meeting.

Let me just inform you that one of the recommendations was already acted on affirmatively by our Council, as it approved the program plans in the area of ecumenical affairs.

The Working Group proposes that that a new Anglican-Lutheran International Commission (ALIC) should be set up, which should consist of church leaders and theologians. The proposed mandate of the commission is, among other things, to monitor and stimulate the continued development of Anglican-Lutheran relations around the world, to consider ways to promote the role and contribution of the Christian world communions in the wider ecumenical movement, and to facilitate the implementation of the various recommendations by the Working Group that our appropriate bodies will approve.

This proposal is the basis for a program that has now been approved by the LWF Council and formal information about this will be forward to the ACC appropriately. Obviously, the details of this proposal are still open for further discussion between us, after which we could also agree on an implementation process. As a proper instrument for such discussion we now have annual joint staff meetings between the Secretary General of the ACC and myself, together with staff persons related to the issues to be taken up.

As we proceed to receive this report, and to implement the recommendations we shall decide upon, let us do what we can to move steadily toward the goal of full, visible unity between our two world communions at the global level. This goal cannot be achieved en bloc. It can only be achieved step by step. But let us keep the goal clearly before us, and do all we can to move toward it, as a contribution to the unity of the universal church, the *una, sancta, catholica et apostolica ecclesiae.*

Current Developments in the World Council of Churches

Let me also inform you that our Council this week also discussed current developments in the WCC and notably the actions by the Central Committee of the WCC on Orthodox participation in the WCC in keeping with recommendations by the Special Commission that has worked in this area.

At our Council the question was asked whether, as a result of the decision of the Central Committee, controversial issues would now be excluded from the agenda of the WCC, whether the replacement of common worship by inter-confessional prayer represents an ecumenical setback, whether church relationships would become looser, whether the use of gender-inclusive language would become more difficult and whether the prophetic voice of the WCC would be inhibited.

In our Council it was emphasized at the same time that this new development in the WCC could be seen as a recognition of the value of different church traditions, as represented by the Christian world communions, in the ecumenical movement and in the life of the WCC. Giving space for the contributions of different traditions in the WCC is not a re-confessionalization of the ecumenical movement. It can strengthen the character of the WCC as a conciliar fellowship not only of individual churches, but also of Christian world communions. It can contribute to a more nuanced understanding and a higher appreciation of all the different church traditions that make up the membership of the WCC.

In this perspective, I strongly welcome the proposal presented by the WCC General Secretary for a *reconfiguration of the ecumenical movement.* This topic should rightly draw considerable attention from all ecumenical partners in the time ahead. The role of the WCC will and should remain a central one. We should clearly affirm this role. At the same time, we should now also draw on the best resources of all our traditions for Christian unity to develop further. And we should also clearly affirm the vision of a Universal Christian Council to be held one day.

Conclusion: There is Another Way!

When apartheid was abolished in Southern Africa, there were many who saw the dawn of a new day—not only for Africa, but for the world. A similar situation arose in 1989 with the fall of the iron curtain. The Christian churches played a significant role in both of these critical periods. We must make sure together that we do not fail to provide also today genuine reasons to hope for a just future for all.

What can we do?

We must listen to the prophetic voices of our time. And there are some who, like Jeremiah in his time, proclaim that there is a way forward. We are not destined to slavery and oppression. We must be ready for exodus, the alternative way. The cross of Christ itself shouts into the chaos of humanity that *there is another way!* Concretely:

1. We must proclaim the gospel of God's free grace loudly and clearly to all, for it represents a different value system than the ruthless competitiveness that has invaded our societies, and indeed our human lives. *There is another way!*

2. The overwhelming social and human tragedy, which is the HIV/AIDS pandemic, calls us as churches to continue and strengthen our commitment to serve and to help at all levels. In addition to giving firm support to all who are directly involved—in families, congregations and hospitals—we have a special responsibility to encourage and facilitate openness and direct communication. This is the only way in which this paralyzing plague can be faced and overcome. We must show that they belong fully to the fellowship of believers. In no way must we marginalize the victims in the life of our churches. *Yes, there is another way!*

3. We must achieve a better understanding of material equity. We must boldly proclaim God's ownership of the created world. The whole notion of personal and corporate property is a relative one if one believes in God. Economy is not a matter that must be left in the hands of the business community and financial institutions. Economy is—on all levels—also a question of justice, ethics and faith. *There must be another way!*

4. In the life of faith, it is not true that the ends justify the means, so that any option is open to us, as long as we see the goal we would like to reach. On the contrary, it is true to say that the means justify the ends. It is by the means that we make clear from the outset what we are after, what we seek to achieve. It is by practicing the golden rule and the love of our enemies that we can show as churches what life in Christian faith means. There is no other way. Or, I should rather say, as we are currently witnessing on the global scene politics and language of self-assertion and confrontation—rising to frightful levels: *There is, indeed, another way!*

5. Today the churches are shouting NO to violence against women and against children, of which human history has been deeply and tragically stained. Our deliberate commitment in this area must be broadened to include all those women, children and men that are victims of injustice and oppression. This must also include international criminal jurisdiction in respect of war crimes and crimes against humanity. *There are definitively other ways!*

6. The Anglican-Lutheran International Working Group has now submitted its report. It describes a wide network of communion relations around the world and provides some strong recommendations for the future. Let us grasp the opportunity that our growing together in communion gives us, to promote strongly and concretely the fellowship in

the human family that is God's gift, and is therefore our fundamental basis for hope for the world. *Let us together find the good ways!*

7. The ecumenical movement is currently moving into yet another of its many historical crises. We do not quite see how full and visible communion relations can be reached among the Christian world communions. We also do not see clearly what role the World Council of Churches will play in the future. In this situation we must not only proclaim the faith. We must ourselves live by the same faith. Faith that is open to the voice of the Holy Spirit. No renewal in church life has come as result of neglecting social and human needs. But much renewal has come from faithful attention and loyal service to the needs of the sick, the hungry and the oppressed—inspired not least by the Sermon on the Mount. It may well be that once again, this is the way that Christ calls us to walk.

With these remarks, I wish to thank you for the opportunity to address you, the Anglican Consultative Council. As families of churches we are very close to each other, in terms of faith, practices and polity. Let us continue to move forward in our communion relations at all levels, in our processes of mutual consultation, and in our various forms of co-operation. May God, whose wisdom surpasses all understanding, bless the life of your communion and its service in the world, to the glory of God, Father, Son and Holy Spirit. Amen.

21 SEPTEMBER 2002

The International Anglican Women's Network Report

—The Reverend Canon Alice Medcof, Coordinator,
Anglican Women's Network-Canada

The International Anglican Women's Network (IAWN) is pleased to submit this report to the Anglican Consultative Council.

IAWN continues to work toward its goal of linking Anglican women worldwide using regular postal services, including fax and internet technology.

The IAWN International Coordinator is compiling a list of link people from each Province. A newsletter, published by the IAWN link in Canada, will be sent annually. News from each Province will be requested and will be included in subsequent newsletters.

Linking is also available through the IAWN web site. On the web site is found previous newsletters and reports, and notices of upcoming events. A separate page for each Province will be set up as information is sent to the Web Master.

The web site www.iawn.org exists through the generosity of Anglican Internet Services. Our most grateful thanks go to the IAS Web Designer for his time and talent so unstintingly given. We are grateful, too, to the Archbishop of Canterbury, the Most Reverend and Right Honorable George Carey, and the Secretary General, the Reverend Canon John Peterson, for their kind words of support.

These means of communication lack one important factor: personal, face to face conversation. Whenever link people are together, enthusiasm for the network rises, organizational details can be worked through, and plans for the future proposed. We thank the Episcopal Church Women of ECUSA (www.episcopalchurch.org/ecw) for inviting international guests to their Triennial Meetings and waiving some of the costs.

As with all members of the Anglican Communion, the Anglican woman works locally and globally. She labours in her own vineyard, meeting her unique challenges with courage and vision, confident in the efficacy of prayer and committed to peace and justice. Her story, when added to those of others, defines our agenda: poverty, threat of HIV/AIDS, devastation of environmental disaster, and the horror of war. Women, for whom the global view is an all-encompassing passion, carry these stories to world leaders. Dr. Sally Thompson of the International Anglican Family Network often features women's stories in the IAFN Newsletter.

We congratulate Archdeacon Taimelalagi Fagamalama Tuatagaloa-Matalavea on her appointment to the Office of UN Observer for the Anglican Communion and thank her for listening to our proposals and supporting them. As finances permit, the IAWN is represented at the United Nations Commission on the Status of Women meetings. Several were present in 2000 at the Beijing + 5 Prepcom and the UN Special Assembly (see report to ACC Standing Committee, Kanuga, 2001). In 2002 two representatives attended the Status of women meeting: Marge Christie's report follows. At these meetings IAWN worked with ecumenical coalitions and with women of faith coalitions because the concerns of women often transcend religious boundaries.

Working ecumenically, and indeed, with all women of faith, is common throughout the world. We welcome the World Council of Churches Decade to Overcome Violence (www.wcc-coe.org) and pledge ourselves to work locally and globally to bring to light cultural and structural roots of violence. We are proud of, and support with prayer, Hanan Ashrawi. She is the Commissioner of Information and Public Policy for the League of Arab States and the Secretary General of Miftah, the Palestinian Initiative for the Promotion of Global Dialogue and Democracy. She is also a member of the Palestinian legislative council.

Anglican women and Lutheran women have a long history of working together ecumenically. Now those in the USA and Canada are embracing shared communion with joy as a consequence of conversations between ECUSA and the Evangelical Lutheran Church (www.elca.org/wo/) in America, 2000, and between the Anglican Church of Canada and the Evangelical Lutheran Church in Canada (www.elcic.ca/women), 2001.

Some Anglican women's conferences of note:

2000 ECW Triennial, Denver, Colorado, USA

2001 25th Anniversary of the Ordination of Women, Canada

2002 Mothers' Union Presidents' Conference, South Africa (www.themothersunion.org) Anglican Women's Congress for the Southern Province of Africa 10th Anniversary of the Ordination of Women, South Africa

The first woman ordained a priest in the Anglican Communion, Li Tim-Oi, is remembered by many. The Li Tim-Oi Foundation, Bristol, England, distributes bursaries to women of the Two-Third World who wish to train for leadership positions in the Church. One initiative being pursued in Canada, with the support of the USA and England, is the inclusion of her name in the Church Calendar. As well, her memory will be kept alive in Renison College, the Anglican College of the University of Waterloo in Canada, with the establishment of the Reverend Dr. Florence Li Tim-Oi Reading Room and Archives (www.renison.uwaterloo.ca)

The information in this report comes primarily from England, South Africa and North America. It is crucial that a pattern of reporting from IAWN links to the International Coordinator be formulated so that a fuller report be made to the ACC in the future.

The IAWN thanks the Anglican Consultative Council for including it in the roster of networks.

Anglican Urban Network Report

—The Reverend Isamu Koshiishi, Network ACC Contact
—The Reverend Dr. Andrew Daley, Network Coordinator

This report was accompanied by the Network's first Newsletter that carried reports, news, and stories of the Network and its members.

Background

Proposals for an Anglican Communion Urban Programme were developed following the 1998 Lambeth Conference of bishops, and considered at the 11th meeting of the Anglican Consultative Council (ACC-11) in 1999. ACC asked for the team developing the proposals to report to the Standing Committee the following year and the next full meeting of the ACC. Approval for the formation of the Network was given at the ACC/Primates Standing Committee in 2000.

In August 2000 the team developing the Network visited New York, at the invitation of the Bishop, to meet with interested parties including a number of key UN personnel. It was apparent that the concerns of group connected with both church, NGO and UN officers, particularly those responsible for the UN Human Settlements programme (Habitat), and its *Cities Without Slums* initiative.

Early in 2001 a letter was sent by the Secretary General inviting three nominations from each province for the core Network. About half the primates have so far responded. The core Network is complimented by a mailing list of a wider community of interest who support the Network through promoting its activities, in prayer and by voluntary contributions. (Mailing list members will receive Network publications and news.)

To trail some of the thinking behind the project the Network has published and circulated widely the booklet by Bishop Laurie Green *The Impact of the Global: An Urban Theology*. This was distributed with *Anglican World* at Easter 2001 and has received much attention. The booklet has been used in seminaries and parishes, and has also been used by ecumenical partners. Translations are being prepared in Spanish, Portuguese and Japanese.

Steering Group

In 2001 a steering group was established, which met in New York to look at initial plans for the Network and take part in the United Nations

Special Sessions on Human Settlements. Again the group found that the Network's concerns of human flourishing in a globalizing, urbanizing world were essential to the programmes of other groups. The special assembly was part of the preparation for the UN World Summit on Sustainable Development and a representative was sent to the recent Anglican Congress on the Stewardship of Creation in South Africa.

Members of the Steering Group are: The Revd Isamu Koshiishi, Japan; Canon Carmen Guerrero, USA; The Revd Chad Gandiya, Zimbabwe and The Revd Dr Andrew Davey, England, who acts as co-ordinator for the Network. Archdeacon Mike Kendall of New York acts as a consultant to the group.

Members of the Steering Group have met subsequently as pairs or threes on the fringes of other gatherings to monitor progress. It is proposed that an enlarged steering group should meet in early 2003 to develop a strategic plan for the Network and consider the appointment of a development officer.

Purpose

The Steering Group has identified that the purpose of the Network is to develop a structure of information and resources on urban mission and ministry within the Anglican Communion. Through nominated link people in each diocese the Network aims to share news, information and research among urban practitioners, ministers, theologians and bishops. It is hoped that a structure will be developed that will support and inform subsequent action research and a develop material for the next Lambeth Conference.

Focus for Future Work

The Steering Group have identified four foci for future work:

1. **Training for urban ministry**

   Understanding the challenges of the urban context

   - seminary, post-ordination, Bishops, lay leadership
   - exposure to prophetic theologians from all communities
   - tools for social analysis and training on using them

2. **Empowerment of the poor**

   Enabling the Church to be renewed by the urban poor

   - strategies for the empowerment of the urban poor in church and society

- enabling the voice of the poor to be heard
- celebrating the gifts/presence of the poor in the whole church, particularly in evangelism
- enabling exchange between those experiencing poverty

3. Interchange and communication between regions/provinces/networks

Sharing and encouraging

- sharing information, examples of good praxis, training materials, etc., supporting and encouraging emergent regional/provincial networks

4. Theological reflection and social analysis across boundaries

Learning together

- underpinning the above with a commitment to reflection and analysis
- informing and challenging the theological mainstream
- developing a critique of movements in urban analysis (and exposing those that demean or demonize the poor)

Finance

The Network's activities so far have been made possible through the generosity of a number of individuals and dioceses. Particularly important has been the support given by the Diocese of New York through its former bishop, The Rt. Revd. Richard Grein. The Steering Group recognises the need to develop a sound financial plan for the Network and this will be a key part of its agenda when it meets in 2003.

Finally

City-to-City Cooperation is the theme for this year's UN World Habitat Day (WHD) which is to be celebrated on 7 October 2002. We hope that the work of the Network will contribute to the dynamic relationships that are possible between urban Anglicans as we seek the peace and welfare of our cities across our planet.

Anglican Peace and Justice Network (APJN) Report from the Meeting, 23–30 November 2001

Table of Contents

Introduction

A Beginning

The 2001 APJN meeting in Aotearoa/New Zealand was memorable for two reasons: for the depth and seriousness of our agenda and discussions, but also for the atmosphere in which we met. Our brothers and sisters in Aotearoa/New Zealand have the great gift of an indigenous people, the Maoris, whose unique culture and spirituality have contributed enormously to the life of the church in the Province. The APJN participants from many Provinces of the Anglican Communion had the special grace of sharing this experience. And it was a sharing that helped us all understand and hear the issues before us in new ways.

The reports and discussions addressed major issues with worldwide resonance, ranging from the economic, social, and moral issues raised by Globalization and Poverty to worldwide peace and justice issues to the potential impact of Theological Education on the resolution of these problems. The APJN also heard frank reports on issues of Justice for Women and the plight of the worlds children, especially in societies disrupted by civil strife and war. And there were issues raised once more about the spread of the HIV/AIDS pandemic and the church's role in fighting it. The APJN was also reminded of the church's ongoing crusade against the use of the death penalty and the continuing concern for environmental issues as they impact our shared world.

APJN also heard specific reports and updates about the role of the Church in Areas of Civil/Regional Conflict. Unfortunately, some of these problems were familiar to APJN participants because of their long-term resonance in the world. Bishop Kumara of Sri Lanka reported in depth about the long civil conflict in his country, the church's place in his country's struggle for peace and reconciliation, and the steps being taken to finally resolve these complex issues.

The APJN was also brought up to date on Africa's most troubled regions, especially Rwanda, Burundi, the Democratic Republic of Congo, Zimbabwe, Sudan, and Angola and the church's role in these areas.

Interwoven with discussions of the world's conflicts and problems were practical discussions of how the Anglican Communion and the APJN might organize their resources to help resolve or alleviate them. The issue of Interfaith Understanding was raised as a tool in dealing with problems in Africa, the Middle East, and Asia.

Frankness was center stage here. As often is the case at APJN gatherings, the level of trust was great enough for participants to deal bluntly with issues across the board.

Section I: The Local Context: Report of the Indigenous Hosts from Aotearoa/New Zealand to the Anglican Peace and Justice Network (APJN)

The November 2001 Anglican Peace and Justice Network (APJN) meeting was held in Auckland, New Zealand. The gathering was organized and hosted primarily by New Zealand's indigenous Anglican Maori community. Dr. Jenny Te Paa, who served as convener for the APJN, is Dean or Principal of Te Rau Kahikatea, one of three distinctive and equal partner colleges that together comprise the College of St. John the Evangelist, the key theological college for the church in New Zealand. Working with a small team of colleagues from Te Rau Kahikatea, together with the national Anglican Social Justice Commissioner, and with the strong support of the Presiding Bishop of Aotearoa/New Zealand, the Rt. Rev. John Paterson, the host group, led by Dr. Te Paa, planned intentionally for the APJN agenda to pivot around a focused exposure to the specific historic struggles endured by the indigenous Maori Anglicans. The purpose was not only to highlight issues of historic injustice and subsequent conflict (which inevitably occurred wherever in the world the early colonial church imposed itself) but it was also intended by the host group to honor the extraordinary contemporary response of the dominant colonial or settler church in Aotearoa/New Zealand and Polynesia. The host group believes that the Anglican Church in New Zealand itself provides a classic case study of a globally unique and commendable initiative.

Background

In the years 1984–1992, the Anglican Church in New Zealand undertook the revision of its constitution. In undertaking the revision, the church was recognizing a need for powerfully symbolic, transforming action to be taken.

The church needed to express remorse for past injustices inflicted upon indigenous Anglicans, and it needed also to transform itself structurally so that these injustices might never be repeated. The result has been an irrefutably honorable attempt to practice redemptive justice. The three tikanga or partnership model which is at the heart of the New Zealand church's constitutional revision repositions Maori and Pakeha Anglicans within the church as equal partners. It is a relationship based on the historically established Treaty of Waitangi.

The Treaty of Waitangi was, and remains, the only officially recognized document that enables the original covenantal understandings for peaceful coexistence that were negotiated for historically, between the *people of the land* and the *newcomers*. The treaty allowed for British settlement and for the continuation and protection of quite specific indigenous rights. It was signed in 1840 between indigenous Maori and representatives of the British Crown.

Anglican church interests were writ large during that earliest period. Maoris had introduced Church Missionary Society (CMS) missionaries to Aotearoa in 1814. By 1840 the relationship between missionaries and the Maori people was one of mutuality and interdependence, and so, not surprisingly, it was CMS missionaries who worked with Maori people on the tasks of drafting, translating, and promoting the Treaty of Waitangi. Both parties were acting in good faith, a faith that was to be very quickly dishonored by those whose interests lay beyond the control of either one of them.

During this early period of Anglican Church history in Aotearoa/New Zealand, CMS missionary interests were soon overtaken by *colonial* Anglicans who were more interested in establishing a conventional ecclesial framework intended to serve the interests of the settlers. By 1857 the colonial church was ready to sign its first constitution, formally establishing the Anglican Church by voluntary compact in Aotearoa/New Zealand. This first constitution totally ignored Maori interests and ensured exclusion of Maori people from any of the key decision-making bodies and positions of leadership that were a necessary part of the infrastructure of the new church. It might well have been argued that in our *uncivilized* state, we Maori were unprepared for the demands of both ecclesial and political office.

The facts are that by 1840 Maori people were already *converted* in significant numbers, were literate and numerate, and were fast becoming adept at speculating on likely future developments in terms of colonial settlement. The facts are that the Treaty of Waitangi was entered into in good faith by two sovereign parties, one of whom was to almost immediately dishonor the agreement and, in the process, enact war and not peace, and to act unjustly rather than with justice.

The resultant long-term effect of continuously unjust and often brutal colonial imperialism upon indigenous Maori people was disastrous. Land and language, cultural traditions and knowledge, were all intentionally eroded through the imposition of unjust legislation. Revisionist history now shows clearly how intertwined Anglican interests were in the settlement of Aotearoa/New Zealand. Much of the legislation affecting land, education, justice, health, economic development, and housing, among many other concerns, were underpinned by what are now understood as extraordinarily racist ideologies.

In spite of the injustice of the Crown, the majority of Maori people remained faithful to the Anglican Church even as the very institution that owed its existence in New Zealand to Maori generosity, consistently marginalized its so-called Treaty partner. It is only through the very recent publication of revisionist histories that so much of the tragic truth of the experience of colonial imperialism is now being revealed. As with numerous other indigenous peoples throughout the colonized world, the Maori people have always maintained a high level of political consciousness and have resisted consistently and courageously against an often-overwhelming legacy of colonial cruelty. The stories of so many of these acts of resistance against overwhelming odds, both collective and individual, are only now emerging.

And so it was that during the mid-20th century, as indigenous struggle became a pervasive feature of the political social, and economic landscape of Aotearoa/New Zealand, the Anglican Church was among the first of the major public institutions to recognize and to admit to certain levels of complicity with the original colonial imperialists. The contemporary church sought first to acknowledge that complicity; to recognize the extreme devastation experienced by the Maori people; to express remorse for the suffering experienced by the Maori at the hands of the church; and finally the church agreed to develop and implement a Gospel-based model for future relationships which would reclaim the spiritual and political integrity of the original Treaty of Waitangi. It was this extraordinary redemptive commitment that saw the 1992 General Synod *bless* into existence a revised constitution. The new constitution provides for a treaty-based partnership relationship between Maori and Pakeha, while at the same time ensuring inclusion of the Diocese of Polynesia also as a partner by virtue of the church's historic legal obligation to that diocese.

The transforming challenge to the church has been and continues to be enormous. How does a previously monolingual and mono-cultural ecclesial institution reconfigure its decision-making structures, rewrite many of its regulations, and alter its power to more justly reflect the moral and practical demands of ethnically defined partnership? The contemporary church in Aotearoa/New Zealand and Polynesia is a dynamic and complex milieu, multiracial in composition, apologetically bicultural in overarching ideo/theology, and still overwhelmingly patriarchal in leadership.

And yet there are also many well-known examples of radical disruptions to the extant structural injustices: the first autonomous indigenous episcopacy; the first female diocesan bishop in the Anglican Communion; the first lay indigenous woman as dean of an Anglican theological college in the Communion; the first lay indigenous woman appointed as an Anglican Observer at the United Nations. All of these examples serve to make the Church in Aotearoa/New Zealand and Polynesia a key and unique site within the Anglican Communion for a network concerned with embracing peace and justice issues. It was the recognition of the uniqueness of the constitution of the Church in Aotearoa/New Zealand and Polynesia that led to the decision to hold the meeting of the APJN in this Province from November 23 to November 30, 2001.

While members of APJN were enabled to schedule a regular meeting agenda, and the reports from that agenda are contained elsewhere in this APJN report, each day of the meeting also provided opportunities for exposure to local context. The exposure included a two-day journey into rural tribal Maori communities to see at first hand just how small, isolated groups of indigenous Anglicans are organizing in order to overcome the residual burden of a not so distant colonial past. At the conclusion of the exposure, all members of APJN were invited to offer a brief reflection on the experience they had undertaken. The extempore prayer that follows encapsulates the sentiments of thanksgiving, of critical reflection, of sheer gratitude for what had transpired as the APJN adventurers went into the heartland of indigenous Maori Anglicans!

God of Peace and Justice, we give you thanks for the privileged experience of being one with the indigenous peoples of Aotearoa/New Zealand;

We give thanks for the wisdom of the elders we were blessed to listen to and to speak with;

We pray for humility as we are confronted with the reality of how complicated and individualized the lives of those who are not indigenous have become. We recognize the critical importance of human *connectedness* without which we can never truly become te whanau a Te Ariki (the family of Christ);

We give thanks for the graciousness of our indigenous hosts and abundance of food we were blessed with. We pray for forgiveness as we recognize the complicity of some among us with the historic injustices inflicted upon indigenous communities;

We pray always for solidarity with those people in God's world who have and who continue to experience loss and unnecessary suffering (the people of Palestine, Sudan, Sri Lanka, Congo, Burundi);

We offer gratitude to God for the opportunity to recognize similarities between our peoples' struggles (South Africa and Aotearoa). We give thanks for our common cultural understandings of the Communion of Saints and our common respect for the wisdom of elders;

We pray for wise discernment about the link between poverty and globalization. We pray also for the ability to critically assess the way in which *context* is used as a key determinant in defining poverty. We see poverty as a term relative to context but infinitely variable in its manifestations; We pray for the emergence of strong indigenous leadership in the years ahead;

We pray for relief from those globally dominant cultural values that powerfully, negatively affect young indigenous people. We pray for understanding of how legal deception operates at a global level, and we pray for the courage to resist this insidious form of institutionalized injustice;

We give thanks for the special blessing of contextual theology and for those theological educators who remain committed to ensuring that this form of theology is widely available to all those who would seek to serve the church in any form of ministry;

We praise God for the ongoing commitment of both Maori and Pakeha people to the Treaty of Waitangi, and in particular we acknowledge the special significance accorded to the Treaty of Waitangi by the Anglican Church in Aotearoa/New Zealand and Polynesia;

We give thanks to God for the people of Waimamaku for the unspoiled environment and utter peacefulness of the Waimamaku Valley;

We express regret for the way in which critically important culturally determined issues of land and identity have been displaced by the pursuit of more materialistic concerns;

Loving God we give thanks for the timely reminder of just how precious cultural survival is to all future generations. We recognize the gift of hospitality which always requires a measure of personal sacrifice and we note especially the extent of sacrifice made by the people of Waimamaku, who gave so generously of themselves to APJN, even though they are among the most economically deprived communities in Aotearoa/New Zealand;

We celebrate the capacity for God's people to transcend language and cultural differences and to overcome weariness after long journeys, in order to be fully present to one another;

We thank God for the recognition among APJN members of the enduring dignity of traditional cultures, for recognition of the enduring tragedy of colonial oppression, and for the hope we maintain in the strength and example of those New Testament communities that envisaged mutuality and interdependence among all people, in all things, at all times;

We give thanks for those who are willing to welcome strangers into their homes;

We recognize with urgency the critical importance for our church to support the work of documenting histories, particularly those of previously colonized or oppressed peoples;

We thank God for international meetings that allow quality time and space for building right relationships between participants, and especially give thanks to God for pilgrimages which call us all into new relationship with Christ;

We recognize with humility the inner strength of indigenous peoples that comes from faith and from the God-given capacity to overcome even the most challenging of political struggles;

We celebrate our witness of children who know so naturally what it is to share and to be unselfconsciously generous with one another;

We thank God for those people who are intimately attuned to all of God's creation, and we especially thank God for precious moments in isolated places where it is more readily possible to *be still and to know God;*

We thank God for sensitivity from friends and colleagues who recognize how to respond appropriately when the pastoral needs of one disrupt the group solidarity;

We give praise to God of all creation for our renewed appreciation of the inherent goodness of the rural lifestyle, for our renewed appreciation of the deep and inextricable connectedness between land and God's people;

We thank God for *'gracia'*, for the God given blessing of friendships among women;

We give thanks in abundance for the organic magic of the marae, especially for the capacity of the marae to stop people from hurrying and fussing unnecessarily!

We thank God for the hopes and dreams of the elders who, in spite of the legacy of injustice they have struggled mightily to overcome, still hold to a powerful vision of a better future for their children and grandchildren;

Finally, Loving God, God of Peace and Justice, the members of the Anglican Peace and Justice Network give thanks for the incredible experience of being able to meet in Aotearoa/New Zealand, to have been welcomed so warmly, and cared for so generously by the indigenous communities whose hospitality we have so deeply appreciated. We thank you for the opportunity you have provided the Anglican Peace and Justice Network to recognize anew the awesome responsibilities we all carry, as members of APJN throughout the world, to recommit ourselves with renewed passion and courage to doing the work of Peace and Justice in God's name. AMEN

Section II: Far-Reaching Concerns
Globalization and Poverty

[An APJN Committee Report]

To begin with, we acknowledge the complexity and contentiousness of this issue. We therefore propose in this report work to be undertaken in several ways and in various settings over the next year or so.

The APJN heard in its meetings reports from most of our participants of disturbing and negative trends that are directly related to the impacts of the unrestricted global movement of capital and the policies of specific trade instruments. Such impacts include:

- The displacement of subsistence and small-scale agriculture the world over by export crops being produced in many cases by international agri-businesses. The result is rural depopulation and swelling ranks of the homeless, unemployed, and precariously employed in cities.
- Deteriorating health, education, and social services, as a result of the imposition of structural adjustment programs based upon privatization and deregulation.
- Further loss of indigenous culture and, in some cases, land.
- A widening gap between an increasing number of poor people and a wealthy minority.
- Environmental degradation and destruction of habitat and species.

Women and children, and our natural world, are being disproportionately affected by these policies. The impacts are being experienced worldwide. Although the negative effects are doing the greatest damage in already vulnerable and debt-burdened southern countries, northern countries also reported serious increases in poverty, precarious employment, and unemployment.

The issue of water was cited for particular concern. In a context of growing water scarcity (by the year 2020, approximately two-thirds of the world will be facing serious water shortages), corporate interests are pushing with alarming success for the making water, this God-given gift essential to life, a tradable commodity. The experience of Bolivia, for example, shows that when water is privatized, costs escalate dramatically, jeopardizing the very existence of thousands.

The relatively new field of bio-prospecting was also cited as raising issues of concern for study and action. This term refers to the practice in which potentially beneficial genetic resources, many of which are the basis of traditional medicines, are identified and patent applications filed on the basis of discovery. This matter is of particular importance to developing nations where biotechnology corporations with corporate headquarters in the developed world have begun to engage in bio-prospecting. Pressure is currently being exerted through the World Trade Organizations Trade Related Intellectual Property Rights (TRIPS) agreement to extend the range of materials that can be patented, including higher life forms.

The APJN recommends the following responses:

1. Develop a theological framework for understanding the effects of the unrestricted flow of capital, the increased liberalization of trade in goods and services, and the new international agreements on intellectual property rights; policies commonly identified as the process of globalization.

2. Use such a theological framework to: (a) analyze these policies and instruments, and (b) develop recommendations for fair trade and a just economy.

3. Engage and educate on these issues at the levels of Communion, Primates, Provinces, dioceses, and parishes.

4. Engage and advocate on these issues with the bodies that initiate and implement these policies (e.g., the WTO, World Bank, and International Monetary Fund) and, where appropriate, national governments.

5. Work in solidarity on these issues with civil society, where appropriate.

The following resources will be needed for this work:

1. A solid policy base within the church

2. Development of appropriate campaigns for action (from parish to international levels)

3. Campaign materials (e.g., a short handbook, pamphlets, petitions)

4. Spokespersons

5. Allies (ecumenical, interfaith, secular)

Critical to the efficacy of this work will be:

1. An application of lessons learned in the Communion-wide cancellation of the debt campaign, especially successful debt reduction initiatives among the world's poorest countries led by ECUSA's Office of Government Relations.

2. The identification of resources already available and work in progress.

3. The application of the Lund Principle.

4. An offering of just alternatives along with a critique of the current situation.

Those who are going to serve in the Communion's working party on globalization should conduct research on the following issues:

1. The effects of drugs and the drug addiction trade on education and on family structure, especially in Africa.
2. The widening gap between the rich and the poor at the expense of Bretton Institutions funding conditionalities.
3. Consider whether globalization to some extent means the support of western nations in the fight against terrorism by dictatorial regimes in Africa that, in effect, terrorize their own citizens.

HIV/AIDS

[An APJN Committee Report]

The APJN 2001 meeting in New Zealand spent time addressing issues related to HIV/AIDS and the symptoms of the disease. The meeting spent time focusing on the report of the All Africa Consultation on HIV/AIDS which was held in South Africa during August 2001. Discussion by the group emphasized the following:

1. We are encouraged by the concerted efforts of the leadership of the Anglican Communion to devote time, people, and other resources in an attempt to address the challenges of HIV/AIDS, especially the devastating effects of the pandemic on the African continent. We also commend ECUSA's Office of Government Relations for its work to procure U.S. government funding to fight the pandemic.
2. The group expressed a concern around the issue of the way sex and sexuality was dealt with at the Consultation. It was noted that African culture mystifies the issues of sex and sexuality, which are not openly talked about. It is sad that the Consultation's Vision Statement, which articulates the need to break the silence, does not mention anything about responsible sexual behavior.
3. Individuals in the meeting shared experiences from their own contexts, which were perspectives from both developed and developing nations. We expressed the urgency to provide capacity to those who are responsible for this ministry in the areas of prevention, care, and counseling, as well as affordable medication. The meeting affirmed the World Council of Churches (WCC) document, which emphasized the need for the church to focus on the areas of theology and ethics, pastoral care, and justice and human rights.
4. The group expressed concerns about the allocation of resources among the donors and organizations within the Communion. We commend those partners who are making resources available to local initiatives, especially in Africa. We do not need large meetings of church leaders that just produce theologically and politically correct vision statements, but institute no concrete action. We need to strengthen the capacity of local initiatives, designed by the community,

to make a difference in a community coming to grips with the scourge of HIV/AIDS.

The APJN recommends that:

A. The APJN will pay particular attention to the justice issues related to the challenges of HIV/AIDS. We should seek ways for the APJN to use its position to influence policies and practices as a body within the Communion.

B. The APJN will seek to identify and affirm individuals and organizations that are already ministering to people living with HIV/AIDS and their families, and to encourage resource allocation towards locally developed community initiatives, and to discourage centralized donor programs that sometimes produce effects that are, overall, negative.

C. Each diocese should be encouraged to engage an HIV/AIDS worker who will get in touch with the relevant people in their community.

Justice and Peace Issues in the World

[An APJN Committee Report]

What happened in the United States on September 11, 2001, is indeed a tragedy to that country and cannot be justified. Our hearts go out to the people there in this time of disaster and sorrow. However, this is also a time in which we believe God is calling all of us, and especially the leaders of the United States, both political and religious, to wake up and listen.

We must listen to the difference between an act that cannot be justified and an act that has root causes based on previous attitudes and actions. Within recent decades, the world has suffered many such tragedies as the direct result of some of those attitudes and actions on the part of the United States. As the APJN, our hearts must go out to those victims as well.

As members of the Anglican Peace and Justice Network, meeting in New Zealand in November 2001, we believe we have a responsibility to call the church to respond. We are concerned that many people in North America and Britain remain unaware of the views of other peoples in the world and this will not only be unhelpful but also dangerous to the world order in the aftermath of the tragedy.

The church must take a more pro-active role in facilitating communication and better mutual understanding because it is imperative that the church take the initiative to make itself more aware of alternative perspectives if it is to make a difference among all people of the world.

There are many cases in point that we could present; however, in this response we present a perspective from Africa and the Middle East.

Governments and states use political language and jargon to justify their actions and policies toward certain groups. For instance, the use of the word "terrorism" differs from place to place and from time to time. Those who were branded "terrorists" by former colonial regimes are today the legitimate rulers of their countries. Nelson Mandela is an example of this abuse of terminology. The church must, therefore, be circumspect and very careful in the use of language and not be subject to the whims of any government or powerful group of the day in its use of such words as "terrorist" or "terrorism."

In analyzing the policies of the United States of America during the Cold War, one finds complete disregard for the future welfare of the people living in the areas affected by American intervention. The only requirement was that the intervention thwarted the hegemony and influence of the Soviet Union in the region in question. The United States, through the CIA, embarked on a policy of destabilizing what it considered to be Marxist governments. The coup against Kwame Nkrumah in Ghana, the assassination of Patrice Lumumba in the Congo, and the Angolan Civil War, which has been going on for twenty-six years, are but a few examples of the fallout from US Cold War policy in Africa, and are regarded as acts of "terrorism" by those affected peoples.

The invasion of Afghanistan by the Soviet Union resulted in the US funding and training the Mukajadeen, from which came the Taliban, both militarily and ideologically, in Pakistan. Osama bin Laden is the product of this policy. Today the US is working with the military dictatorship in Pakistan as it bombs the Taliban to extinction. This is a de facto recognition of military dictatorship, which is by definition anti-democratic.

We call attention to the way Israel has exploited the September 2001 events by increasing its oppressive measures against the Palestinians, for example:

- the occupation and siege of towns
- the assassination of people
- the destruction of homes
- economic strangulation
- human rights violations
- humiliation
- and the general dehumanization of Palestinians.

The APJN welcomes the declarations from both President George W. Bush and Prime Minister Tony Blair of the United Kingdom on the importance of the establishment of a viable Palestinian state, and calls for immediate steps toward an implementation of this goal on the basis of UN resolutions 242 and 338 and the withdrawal of Israel from all the territories it occupied in the 1967 war so that an independent and sovereign state of Palestine might be established on all of that land. It is only then that acceptable justice will be done and peace and stability achieved for both Palestine and Israel and throughout the region and the world.

We wish to convey the following key issues that were addressed at the November 2001 APJN meeting:

- The United States, British, and Canadian governments have quickly passed pieces of legislation after September 11 which could have an important and negative impact on the civil liberties of some people in those countries.
- A review is necessary of the dominating involvement by the US in the work of the United Nations, which often becomes a useless tool to peace resolution and reconciliation.
- We realize that all of this is a difficult truth to have to accept; nevertheless, as the church, God calls us to the truth and to seek God's justice as we attempt to walk with each other and with God in an effort to be God's prophetic voice at times like this.
- There can be no peace of God that truly surpasses understanding until there is recognition of root causes, repentance of attitudes and actions, justice, and genuine acts of reconciliation.

Young People in the Anglican Church

[An APJN Committee Report]

Young people are sadly underrepresented within networks and bodies in the Anglican Communion. The APJN realizes that the future of our church, and especially this network, is dependent on how we invest in our ministry to young people. It is crucial to integrate the participation of young people in all networks and other decision-making bodies of the Communion.

We acknowledge the plight of young people in developing countries who have limited access to information and opportunities. Young people do not have the resources to sustain a network within the Communion.

The APJN will strive to include more young people as participants in future APJN steering committee and network meetings.

We will propose to the Anglican Consultative Council meeting that resources be made available to revive the International Anglican Youth Network by allowing, as a first step, a meeting of young people in the Global South, which can be followed by a broad consultation of young people in the Communion.

Environment

[An APJN Committee Report]

Our exposure to the Canadian context has focused on the impact of colonialism on this country and on its indigenous peoples, the Maori. It is also evident in its ecology. For around 80 million years New Zealand was geologically and ecologically isolated from other landmasses. In that time a unique flora and fauna developed in this place with quite distinctive characteristics. They are exemplified in the national symbol of New Zealand, the Kiwi. Kiwis are flightless birds, able to survive, at least in part, because, prior to contact, New Zealand had relatively few predators. With the arrival of the European settlers who began to arrive in large numbers in the 19th century, all of this changed. Along with the settlers came new species of birds and plants and animals. The ecosystems of New Zealand were radically changed and indigenous species displaced. Now, the most commonly seen birds such as sparrows, blackbirds, starlings, song thrush, and chaffinch, are all imports from Europe, and the myna, an import from the tropics. Amongst the animals, the possum has exploded so that it now outnumbers sheep (another import) on these islands, and is rapidly destroying New Zealand's natural forests.

In these changes we see the experience of colonization inscribed on the land in the life of its plants, animals, and birds, and in the ecosystems they shape. All of this reminds us that exploitation and power leave their mark both on the human sphere, in our political, economic, and cultural relationships, and also on the land we inhabit and on the capacity of that land to regenerate and renew itself and to support future human societies and cultures. Environmental justice is not simply an add-on to the concerns of this network, but the all pervasive background and context within which peace and justice must be sought if it is to be sustainable.

In the modern context, the impact of colonialism continues not through political colonization, but through the economic pressures that lead to the unsustainable exploitation of land through the methods of agribusiness. The use of intensive farming in many contexts can leave the land unproductive and its people landless.

It is all the more disappointing to discover in the archives of the Anglican Communion Office that environmental concerns dropped off the agenda of this network early, and have not returned. Environmental concerns have been addressed in a number of Provinces. Still, even this work has been ad hoc and sporadic. The Lambeth bishops have also given attention to environmental issues. In 1998 they asked that a commission be established to engage these issues. In the absence of funding for a commission a network is being established, but this network will need to work closely with the existing networks whose work overlaps with environmental concerns. This inevitably includes the APJN.

Justice for Women

[An APJN Committee Report]

We have noted and are thankful that the Anglican Consultative Council appears to have in place an International Anglican Women's Network.

Unfortunately, we noted with much disappointment that the report of the Network (found on page 312 of Anglican Consultative Council XI, Scotland) entitled "The Communion We Share" did not address issues of justice in relation to women in a world that continues to violate the rights of women.

We have a model of respect for women in the very Scriptures that we use as a foundation for our faith as Christians in the actions of Jesus, for example:

1) John 8:1–11
A woman who is charged with adultery is brought to Jesus. He responds with the words, *Let anyone among you who is without sin be the first to throw a stone at her.* And he concludes by telling the woman, *Neither do I condemn you; go and sin no more.*

2) Luke 8:43–48
A woman who dared to touch the garment of Jesus and in so doing dared to challenge a religious system that had deemed her untouchable. And to which Jesus responded by saying, *Daughter, your faith has made you well; go in peace.*

3) Matthew 28:1–10
The women are the first to see the resurrected Christ and the first to go and tell others. We see here the first people to accept the very foundation of our theological understanding of the risen Lord and of the call to share that reality with others. Jesus said to the women, *Do not be afraid; go and tell.*

Therefore, the APJN recommends to the ACC that it must take seriously its actions and responses to peace and justice issues as they are directly related to women by establishing a Women's Justice task force as part of APJN. The task force would monitor all justice issues such as abortion, prostitution, slave trade of women, labor and commerce, domestic violence, rape/sexual abuse of girls and women, and HIV/AIDS from women's perspectives.

Children in Especially Difficult Circumstances (CEDC)

[An APJN Committee Report]

Who is greatest in the kingdom of heaven? Assuredly, I say to you, unless you become as little children, you will by no means enter the kingdom of heaven. Whoever humbles himself as this little child is the greatest in the kingdom of heaven; whoever receives one little child like this in my name receives Me. But whoever causes one of these little ones who believe in me to sin, it would be better for him if a millstone were hung around his neck and were drowned in the depth of the sea [Matthew 18:1–6].

Let the little children come to Me, and do not prevent them; for of such is the kingdom of God [Mark 10:14].

Much has been said and written about children living, suffering, or dying in especially difficult situations. Meeting in New Zealand, the members of the APJN shared stories and experiences on the many heart-rending and soul-wrenching instances of inhumanity perpetrated on children the world over. The numbers and the images are all too appalling. The scale of the problem is enormous. Much needs to be done.

We could only scratch the surface to show the human faces behind the numbers and to describe the dire situations in which the vulnerable children are found. Nevertheless, we identified the children in especially difficult circumstances (note: albeit euphemistic, this phrase has been used to describe the dehumanizing situations in which millions of vulnerable children find themselves) under four broad groups to include:

Child Soldiers and Children in Situations of War or Armed Conflict: Children who are physically involved in wars as soldiers and children who are at risk and are affected or traumatized physically, psychologically, or socially by such wars;

Child Laborers: Children who are exploited or commodified as part of the labor force;

Children Prostituted or Abused: Children who are trapped in situations of sexual prostitution or exploitation, paedophilia, drug abuse, and similar adversities that are forced on them by the global illicit sex trade and illegal drug trade;

Children Alone or Abandoned: The homeless, the street children, orphans, child refugees, child heads-of-households, children in hunger and survival situations, children in detention, disabled children, children affected by or living with HIV/AIDS.

Recognizing that the issues on children and the number of children involved differ greatly from country to country, we focused our attention and discussions on two examples in particular, namely:

The girl-child in African countries: We listened to stories of female children, as young as 8 months old, being abused sexually by men who practice a cult-inspired depravity that [assumes that in] penetrating a virgin's vagina with one's penis one can be cured of HIV/AIDS.

The child soldiers: We learned that there are more than 300,000 child soldiers, as young as 9 years old, fighting adult wars in forty countries worldwide. The Asia Pacific Conference on Child Soldiers held in Kathmandu, Nepal, in April, 2001, reported this estimate that excludes tens of thousands of children from areas of armed conflict in smaller countries, such as the Philippines, Aceh, East and West Timor.

From the papers shared, we were informed that armed violence and ethnic conflicts explode almost every month somewhere on earth and that the number of children devastated by these wars continues to increase. Add to these the children who are being used as human sweepers to detonate live land mines with their limbs, and we could only cry: God have mercy.

On child soldiers, a Filipino journalist wrote: "Child soldiers fight and die for causes or reasons they may know little or nothing about but with no fancy belief of dying as heroes other than they believe in what they are told: that fighting is essential for their own existence and dying is a necessity for the survival of others for a cause or a dream like justice, freedom and homeland." (Michael Bengwayan, Invisible Soldiers © Earth Times News Service)

Likewise, the Kathmandu Declaration Against the Use of Children as Soldiers noted that the roots of the problem of child soldiers include poverty, injustice, displacement, environmental degradation, arms proliferation, economic globalization, growing disparity among the rich and the poor, militarization of governments, World Bank/IMF policies, and the fast-growing population.

In addition, UNICEF has cited poverty, war, organized crime, discrimination against girls, globalization, traditions and beliefs, dysfunctional families, and the drug trade as among the causes of child exploitation.

Without doubt, children are God's gifts. From birth, they are entrusted to their elders for nurture, protection, and sustenance. Born with a trusting nature and an innate vulnerability, they possess innocence about what goes on in life. All too soon they pass from the age of innocence—many by force of circumstances, a few by choice. Sooner than later, they are confronted with the stark reality that good and evil are continuously battling to dominate life on this earth.

We recognize the role of the Primates as leaders of churches and faith-based communities. Together, they are vital vanguards, catalysts, and change agents in initiating and sustaining appropriate responses to the multifarious problems besetting God's children. The churches are well established at the grassroots and usually exist in places where disadvantaged peoples are found in conflict-ridden communities, remote villages, and poverty-stricken areas. Churches and faith-based communities serve as advocates for the poor, the refugees, the outcasts, widows and orphans, and the oppressed serve as sanctuaries and havens for acceptance, forgiveness, healing, and transformation.

Well linked internationally with partners-in-mission in mutual support and resource mobilization, the Anglican Communion and its Provinces can offer and provide concrete opportunities to share resources, experiences, programs, and ministries to respond to the needs of God's children.

Arguably, it has been said that the voice of the church might be ambivalent in dealing with the vital issues of children and that traditionally, the church has maintained a charitable approach in addressing the problems of children. Given such propositions, perhaps it is time for the churches to transform this traditional charity approach and start engaging in more relevant missions to respond to the cries of millions of children.

Listening to these cries and voices, the APJN calls on churches and all concerned to work together in a more responsive way to protect and promote the dignity and the right to life abundant of our children. The APJN urges the Anglican Communion and its Provinces to advocate and work actively on issues affecting children and to provide the means to initiate and sustain programs and ministries as we journey to a New Jerusalem where:

- all people live in peace with justice and with dignity and can function with their God-given gifts as human beings created in the image of God;
- all children are born wanted, needed, and loved by their families, able to grow and lead full and healthy lives, with their rights and dignity respected, secured and protected; and
- all children journey through life, enjoying life abundant, free from poverty, wars, violence, abuse, exploitation, sickness, pestilence, suffering, and other adversities that make the fullness of life less than what it ought to be.

In solidarity with kindred church organizations, institutions, congregations, communities, and partners-in-mission within and outside the Anglican Communion, APJN will continue to focus attention and awaken and sustain awareness on the issues of children living in especially difficult circumstances.

To every thing there is a season and a time to every purpose under the heavens [Eccl. 3:1]

It is time for our deeds to bring to life the thoughts and words expressed in this report.

Death Penalty

[An APJN Committee Report]

The Anglican Peace and Justice Network meeting at the Vaughan Park Retreat Center in Auckland, New Zealand, 23–30 November, 2001, after hearing reports of death penalty and torture in countries like Kenya which still enforce the archaic law of the death penalty as a means of curbing crimes such as robbery accompanied by violence or violent murder, makes the following statement on the death penalty:

- The APJN respects the sanctity of human life and believes that humans are created in the image of God. Theologically, we believe that the death penalty is immoral and outside of God's chosen realm.

- Countries that use the death penalty are failing to comply with the UN Convention on Human Rights. We challenge the practice of the death penalty for disproportionately targeting racial/ethnic minority groups within communities around the world.

- We request that the Primates of the Anglican Communion in countries where the death penalty is still being practiced, particularly in those led by dictatorial governments, to set up commissions to pressure their governments to abolish the death penalty. These commissions, when established, should challenge their governments to opt for life imprisonment instead of the termination of life.

Abolition of the death penalty should be a major priority in all countries under dictatorial regimes. Churches should demand the incorporation of clauses in their national constitutions respecting the sanctity of human life and the abolition of the death penalty, and of any form of torture that causes death to the victims of injustice and oppression.

Section III: The Church in Areas of Civil/Regional Conflict Overview: Areas of Concern

[An APJN Committee Report]

Participants in the November 2001 Anglican Peace & Justice Network meeting heard what has been happening in regional areas of civil conflict since the last APJN meeting in Seoul, Korea, in 1999. In particular, disturbing stories were heard from Rwanda, Burundi, Sudan, and Zimbabwe; and from the Middle East, where serious conflict and war exist between Israel and Palestine, and Sri Lanka. Cases of massacre, genocide, ethnic conflicts, and slavery were high on the agenda. After hearing these stories, the Network makes the following statement:

- There is a need for a comprehensive set of criteria in order to disburse development funds fairly, to uphold human rights and dignity, and to promote good governance and democracy in regions of civil conflict.

- Provinces and dioceses of the Anglican Communion should establish mechanisms for early warning systems and rapid response to civil conflicts.

- The church should challenge foreign countries not to fuel civil conflicts by generative revenue that is being used to better equip their armies rather than being directed toward development, peace, and reconciliation.

- The church and religious organizations and media should engage in advocacy and education efforts toward peace and conflict resolution.

- The churches should demand compensation from their governments for the victims of regional or ethnic conflicts.

- The church should influence the human rights bodies and organizations to act for the setting up of international tribunals/courts of justice to try the instigators of civil/regional conflict of the kind now taking place in Rwanda/Burundi.
- Truth and Reconciliation commissions, headed by church leaders of integrity, should be formed to investigate cases of genocide, murder, rape and other serious crimes and to establish the identity of the perpetrators of these crimes in the countries where they have been committed, namely: the Democratic Republic of Congo, Sudan, Angola, Israel/Palestine, and any other countries involved in similar activities.
- Empowerment for reconciliation and peace with justice should be part of the mission of the church in areas of conflict and the church should be prepared to engage in peace initiatives at all levels.
- The church should promote sincere dialogue between Muslims and Christians, and also between different tribes and peoples in regions torn apart by conflicts, bearing in mind that the causes of such conflicts range from racial, political, cultural, and religious issues to economic concerns in Southern Sudan, the Democratic Republic of Congo, Burundi, Rwanda, and other areas. (See section on interfaith understanding.)

Great Lakes Region

[An APJN Committee Report]

This region of Africa includes the Democratic Republic of Congo, Uganda, Tanzania, Burundi, and Rwanda, and it is an area of war and economic struggle. The conflict could also be identified as a great power struggle, and it is a struggle that has given rise to incidents of genocide. If you could generalize, you might say that this region has been caught up in a culture of war and genocide. These ills have been compounded, if possible, by poverty and the continuing spread of HIV/AIDS. Many people in this region are dying, some casualties of war and genocide, others of HIV/AIDS. And here, as in other trouble spots in the world, women and children, especially, are suffering oppression.

The church in the countries of the Great Lakes Region is caught up in these issues and needs to be empowered to make a difference. In 1999, Burundi, for instance, called upon the APJN to set up a pastoral visit by some of its members, which did take place with some impact on the government of Burundi showing international support for the church in Burundi and its people. Brian Grieves of ECUSA, Themba Vundla from Southern Africa, and Valerie Martin from Wales represented APJN in this pastoral visit. The APJN has a potential for being a presence in many countries of the Great Lakes Region.

The multiple problems of the region are ongoing. With conflicts, a refugee population has begun to move between the countries. There is a regional problem of caring for Congolese and Burundian refugees, among others. This is perhaps an area for APJN's concern.

An estimated million people were killed in Rwanda in a three-month period. In one way or another church leaders were involved in the genocide even if they did not take up arms. Religious leaders in Burundi managed to avoid becoming involved in genocidal conflicts because they have forged a unified religious front of Muslims, Roman Catholics, and Protestants who speak with one voice on these issues.

Burundi

[An APJN Committee Report]

Burundi in Transition

On November 1, 2001, a three-year transitional national government was inaugurated in Burundi, following eight years of civil war and a struggle for power sharing between the two ethnic groups : Hutu rebels and the predominantly Tutsi military. The war has taken the lives of an estimated 250,000 Burundians, most of them innocent civilians, and has resulted in more than 600,000 refugees and displaced persons. The transitional government, in which the majority Hutu political party, FRODEBU, shares power with the minority Tutsi party, UPRONA, is now headed by Buyoya for an 18-month interim period. During this period, Domicien Ndayizeye from FRODEBU will serve as vice president. A change in government is expected for the second 18-month period, after which elections are to take place.

Burundi's transition parliament was installed on January 5, 2001, according to the terms of the August 2000 Arusha agreement between 19 Burundian parties. FRODEBU has 65 seats, while the former single party UPRONA (pro-Tutsi) has 16. This corresponds with the seats they won in democratic elections in 1993, before the assassination of the country's first Hutu president and Burundi's descent into civil war.

On January 29th, 2002, Burundi's Constitutional Court approved 54 members for a transitional Senate, including two former presidents. The Senate will be a new, ethnically balanced institution, established under the August 2000 Arusha peace accord. Smaller political parties that signed the Arusha accord each hold three or four seats in the new transition parliament.

Cease-Fire But Not Yet

Dissident Hutu rebel groups CNDD-FDD (Force pour la Défence de la Démocracie) and FNL (Front National de Liberation) were not part of the Arusha process and have not laid down their arms. South African-led mediators continued their efforts to obtain a cease-fire. In January, Tanzania agreed to host the rebel groups with the aim of persuading them to join cease-fire negotiations in their country. The mediator of the Burundi conflict, former South African president, Nelson Mandela, conferred the task of the cease-fire negotiations on South African vice-president, Jacob Zuma. Zuma has been assisted in this work by the Gabonese president, Omar Bongo. Tanzania had previously hosted the Burundi political negotiations, which lasted more than two years and resulted in the signing of the Arusha Peace Accord. As this report is being prepared for APJN, innocent people are still dying from the continuing conflict between rebel forces and the national army.

Is Burundi Heading Toward Genocide?

The Burundi peace agreement is seen by some observers in the context of the 1994 genocide in Rwanda. The two countries have the same ethnically sensitive mix of Hutus and Tutsis. In the case of Rwanda, just after the Arusha Accord, there was an impasse that international opinion and the UN seemed to ignore. The political dilemma and fear of the future that the people of Burundi are facing at present is also being ignored by international opinion. Politicians in Burundi seem to be more interested in the transitional government and its power sharing arrangement. Supporters of this attitude insist that it is this transitional period that will determine who will lead the country in the future. However, as the war escalates in Burundi, and the prospect of real peace is declining on a daily basis, the world seems to be ignoring Burundi's cry for help. The longer this conflict continues, the more likely an out-and-out explosion of genocide becomes like that of 1994 in Rwanda.

Will Congo And Tanzania Help Burundi Find Peace?

Everyone knows that the Democratic Republic of Congo and Tanzania are, in one way or another, involved in what is happening in Burundi. The International Crisis Group has recently warned the international community that some 4,000 Burundian rebels who have been fighting in DRC alongside the Kinshasa regime of Laurent Kabala are now leaving Congo and returning to Burundi, where widespread civil war is looming. Other groups of rebels are attacking Burundi from the borders of Tanzania, behind an estimated 350,000 Burundi refugees. This point was emphasized in a recent report on the threat to the Burundi peace process. Unless the international community can persuade Tanzania to do something soon about the destabilizing situation in these camps, situated within 5 km. of the Burundi border, the report said, then nobody should be surprised if sooner rather than later they [the Burundians] will be provoked into resorting to military action against those refugee camps which are being used by the armed movements.

Pray for Burundi that:

- Those involved in fighting stop killing and a cease-fire is negotiated as soon as possible.
- The political leaders work towards a consensus and succeed in the three-year transition that was inaugurated on November 1, 2001.
- Nearby countries, particularly Tanzania and the Democratic Republic of Congo, assist Burundi by stopping the rebels attacking Burundi from their territories.
- The international community will break its silence and show more interest and focus on the political impasse in Burundi; that they will help prevent genocide from happening in Burundi by deciding immediately to discourage the proliferation of arms in this region.
- The church in Burundi, as a good example of unity, would be a real facilitator and channel for peace, an advocate for justice and security for all.
- Church partners and friends would give a hand in the prophetic mission of peace and reconciliation assigned to the church in Burundi, keeping in mind that other negative issues such as HIV/AIDS, International Debt, ignorance, and poverty, which are harming our society, are not small evils.
- The position of the church in Burundi is clear and simple. We are pleading with those fighting to stop killing people and opt for a cease-fire and negotiation. That the peace accord agreed upon in Arusha should be respected and implemented. The church is ready to act as one of the facilitators alongside Mandela and other NGOs working for peace in and outside of Burundi.
- That the Congolese refugees gathered in nearby Bujumbura and suffering from lack of shelter, food and medication may be helped, and that the Burundi refugees returning from Tanzania may arrive safely and be cared for.

By faith we can surely believe that Burundi will find peace.

The Zimbabwean Situation

[An APJN Committee Report]

The current problems of Zimbabwe seem to have started with the rejection of the referendum on a new constitution by the Zimbabwean populace. This new constitution was drafted by the government appointed Constitution Review Commission. Hitherto the ruling Zimbabwe National Union Patriotic Front (ZANU PF) had been in power since 1980 and had won all the parliamentary elections since then. These were held regularly in 1985, 1990 and 1995. ZANU PF had become so arrogant and complacent that they concluded that whatever they presented to the people of Zimbabwe would be accepted without question—hence the referendum on the new constitution. This referendum was held in February 2000. As a build- up to the plebiscite, ZANU PF expressed surprise that the whites were registering in great numbers and were preparing themselves to vote, as if that were not their democratic right as citizens of the country. They also encouraged their domestic workers and farm workers to do so. Come voting day and the new draft constitution was rejected. So ZANU PF blamed the white sector of the population for this slap in the face. For the first time in the history of Zimbabwe it became clear that ZANU PF could be beaten in an election poll, and one was due in June 2000 and the writing was on the wall for the ruling party.

The "war veterans" were unleashed, and invaded the white commercial farms. Amongst these "war vets" were youths aged 18, 20, 21 and so on. The invasion of the farms were accompanied by unprecedented violence. The commercial farmers took the government to court, and the courts ordered the government to remove the invaders from the farms. The police were also accomplices in this act, and did not lift a finger to control the lawlessness that had become the order of the day in Zimbabwe. The courts ordered them to act and maintain law and order. All the court orders were ignored. Not only that, but the government granted amnesty to all those who were found guilty of kidnapping, public violence, arson, malicious damage to property and murder. If it were not for this violence ZANU PF would have lost the elections. The opposition Movement for Democracy (MDC) won 58 seats to ZANU PF's 63.

The judges who ruled in favour of the commercial farmers were forced to resign. Failing which, things were made so difficult for them that they found it impossible to function. President Mugabe then appointed his own lackeys to the bench. The judiciary is packed with Mugabe's men. The lawlessness is then given a semblance of legality. The invasion of the farms meant that farming was seriously disrupted, hence the shortage of maize meal (the staple food), sugar, cooking oil, salt, and bread.

The unemployment rate is 76%, inflation is at 116%, there is a serious shortage of foreign currency, violence and lawlessness are still the order of the day. If one uses violence to grab power, then one will use violence to maintain that power.

The presidential elections were flawed and accompanied with violence. There is a concerted effort to criminalise the MDC. Most of the leaders, including Morgan Tsvangirai the President and Welshman Ncube the Secretary-General, are facing treason charges.

Legislation that is similar to the abhorrent apartheid laws has gone through parliament. The most notorious of these are the Public Order and Security Act and the Access to Information and Protection of Privacy Act. Journalists have to be licensed by government appointed bureaucrats and private media have to be approved of by the Ministry of Information.

Famine is crippling the country, the economy is completely destroyed. The farmers' houses, cattle and crops and property will become state property 45 days hence. They are being forcefully evicted. The future of Zimbabwe is very ghastly to contemplate.

Role of the Church in the Sri Lankan Conflict

[A Report to the APJN by the Rt. Rev. Kumara B. S. Illanasinghe, Bishop of Kurunagala]

[The conflict in Sri Lanka has long been of concern to the APJN. An APJN delegation visited Sri Lanka in 1998. Little attention has been paid by much of the world media to this conflict. Hence, the APJN asked Bishop Kumara to provide this report so that the whole Communion might better understand the situation.]

The Nation

The island nation of Sri Lanka has been referred to as the Pearl of the Indian Ocean and The Cradle of the Universe. There is no distinguishing set of features that mark Sri Lankans. The races have blended from East and West, since the island is strategically placed along the sea routes, and traders and visitors have left their mark from ancient times.

Sri Lanka is a pluralistic country of people belonging to many races, following many religious traditions, speaking different languages, and traditionally living in specific geographical areas, even though a large sector of the population is living as mixed populations in the urban areas.

Ceylon, as Sri Lanka was once known, was colonized first by the Portuguese, then by the Dutch, and finally the British. The entire island came under British domination in 1815. Western dress, manners, and names are still popular in Sri Lanka, although movements for an indigenous cultural identity began even before independence from the British in 1948.

Political Trends in Post-Independence Sri Lanka

Sri Lanka has been fortunate to have achieved independence without a bloody struggle, due to the political maturity, the statesmanship and the genuine commitment of the then leaders who belonged to all the communities, but struggled together with a shared vision. However, it was only a nominal political independence that was won. The political power that was wielded by the British was handed over to an elite leadership in Sri Lanka, a group that was Western oriented due to their upbringing and Western education. This reality led to a continuation of the same style and structure of administration that had been used in colonial times. The only difference was that the personnel involved were Sri Lankans.

The above pattern of things continued until 1956, when, under the charismatic leadership of the Hon. S.W.R.D. Bandaranaike, changes were introduced in the political arena, and the status of the common people was lifted, recognizing the Pancha Maha Balawegaya (Sangha, Veda, Guru, Govi and Kamkaru), the five leading powers in traditional Sri Lankan society. These powers were the Buddhist monks, the native physicians, the teachers, the peasants, and the labor force. Bandaranaike also introduced Sinhala as the official language and gave special recognition to the vernacular languages the Swabhasha. Even though in retrospect we can now understand some of the sad repercussions of this historical move, no one can deny that it had lasting progressive effects in the areas of education, social development, employment opportunities, and many other important aspects of life in Sri Lanka.

The next important change took place in 1972 when Sri Lanka was made a Democratic Socialist Republic, still continuing to remain within the Commonwealth of Nations. The period up to 1972, a difficult one for all Sri Lankans, was marked by many labor disputes, and unrest among peasantry and students, culminating in a youth uprising in 1971. A high rate of unemployment, lack of educational facilities, and similar problems, faced by the rural youth, compelled them to take up arms.

The year 1977 saw the unprecedented landslide victory given by the people to the United National Party. The United National Party government was led by Hon. J.R. Jayawardena, who later became Sri Lanka's Executive President. Jayawardena introduced radical changes in the economic sphere. A free and open market economy saw the light of day in Sri Lanka. His was a total and final shift from the socialist policies of the earlier independence government.

The constitution of 1978 established the office of Executive President, with very broad powers, and Parliament headed by a Prime Minister. The country has experienced, since 1978, the wide-ranging ill effects of concentrating executive power in one person, and making the Parliament subservient. The office of President is hardly accountable to anyone, except in certain less important areas. Over 17 long years, people had not benefited much from these reforms and they eagerly awaited a change from a repressive rule. At this time there began to be a strong movement on the part of many to change this situation and to once again strengthen the role of the House of Representatives, and to make the Executive President accountable to the Parliament.

Frustrations have also surfaced in the area of race relations. The long patience of the Tamil people in the face of repeated and almost regular riots, killings, and looting had to end. The troubles broke out and were the worst in the history of the country. The happenings of Black July led to the militant groups among the Tamil community deciding to take up arms and fight for a separate state to be called Elaam.

In 1994 the opposition alliance, the Peoples Alliance led by Mrs. Chandrika Bandaranaike Kumaranatunge, came to power with many promises, as usual, of restoring democracy, abolishing the Executive Presidency, etc. The main concern for the people was the promise that the national conflict that had lasted over a decade was to be resolved and peace brought to the country. There was a lot of hope and the president herself showed much courage in offering a package of political reforms to solve the problems faced by the Tamil people in the country, to alleviate the fears of the majority Sinhala community, and to establish peace and justice among all communities of the country. But it was sad that the whole process ran into many difficulties, caused by extremist, fundamentalist factions. War erupted again in 1995.

Thus, we see that there have been clear phases in the post-independence history of Sri Lanka, where specific socioeconomic and political changes have impacted the lives of the people. The church on the whole has attempted to respond positively and creatively over the years, guided by the values of the Gospel. However, we cannot ignore the fact that the church in this country is basically a middle-class community that to a great extent has been unable to disconnect itself from the colonial heritage and the continuing domination experienced in contemporary times from a variety of power blocks all over the world. There is no doubt that this situation has, to some extent, hampered the mission of the church in modern Sri Lanka.

Present Cross-section of Sri Lankan Society

The very fabric of Sri Lankan society has deteriorated and been demoralized over the last few decades, mirroring similar crises in other parts of the world. The war in the North-East has continued without an end in sight. This very clearly illuminates the brokenness both of the world and especially that of our country. For the sake of their own future, all political parties have put off the search for a solution that would establish equality, right of self-determination and identity for the Tamil people. Violence has crept into all areas of Sri Lankan society. Violence seems to have become the order of the day for many people in our society seeking to achieve their ends. Our national suicide rate has increased.

In the face of the current emergency, the democratic rights of the people are held hostage, while the current constitution has critically affected the role of Parliament. It appears that the people of our country are fast losing the trust and confidence in practical democracy and democratic institutions elections, for instance. Hence the crying demand for independent commissions like the Police Commission, the Elections Commission, the Public Service Commission etc., however fragile the functioning of such commissions might be.

Sri Lanka has already experienced the dangerous trends that can result in an unstable political situation. Unfortunately, the political leadership has succumbed to the desire for power either by holding on to it or by making use of every opportunity to gain it, at any cost to the nation and the people. There is sufficient evidence for us to believe that the country at large has been saddened by the lack of statesmanship shown in solving our national problems. There is a great need to continue to uphold in our prayers the leaders and others who create opinion in the country.

Amidst recent events, prominent people in public life have been forced to admit corruption in their own dealings. Dishonesty and injustice are rampant in the society, and ordinary people have become the victims. The criminal underworld has been active quite openly with definite political support and nurture. The numerous detected cases of abuse of children and women and the prevalent abuse of drugs and the results of such practices speaks volumes for the moral and spiritual degradation of the society. Religious and social disharmony has resulted from the actions of those persons and groups that have destroyed the social institutions of the people.

In our fast-moving world, we find that information is available easily and freely, but the desire to gain wisdom is lacking. Therefore, true wisdom is hard to come by. The media play a dominant role in creating opinion in any country. But the performance of the media in Sri Lanka has been rather pathetic. Freedom of the media is a fundamental right of the people, and all media are expected to function with utmost responsibility. However, a good majority of the media in Sri Lanka have opted to serve either their own commercial or political interests. It is certainly incumbent on all media in a democratic society to serve the interests of the people, not their own special or partisan interests.

It is in the midst of such sad and seemingly hopeless realities that the Christian community is called upon to be truly obedient to the challenges of the Gospel. We need to reflect on our role, bearing in mind the challenges and the opportunities available.

The Christian Community

The instability within the country has created a state of shock among many religious people, and they are at a loss about how to proceed. There is confusion among the progressive sections of the Christian community as regards their social responsibilities and roles in the context of the society we live in, a society in which social abuses are on the rise, where social values are being eroded, and the cost of living is rising, Christians are being called upon to be a truly witnessing community.

The progressive Christians, who in the past had rendered much service amidst social problems and pressures, are today in a crisis situation themselves, facing many dilemmas. Lack of accountability and transparency in managing funds and the shifts in visions of international Christian funding organizations have caused a fall in obtainable funds. On the other hand, aid obtainable by fundamentalist Christian groups is on the increase. This has discouraged some dedicated and committed mainstream Christians who have worked hard for social transformation in past decades.

It is in this environment that the church in Sri Lanka is struggling to be faithful to the demands of the Gospel, and has continued the ministry of reconciliation and peace making.

Ministry in the Plantations and the Peasantry

As much as the church has committed to work for national reconciliation, the area of the plantations remains a major concern. The Tamil population in the central hills is mainly from the plantation sector, and of Indian origin. The difficult realities of working and living conditions in these areas have not improved over the years. The national conflict has taken precedence over the problems of the plantations. The lack of facilities in the areas of education, health, and housing continues. A policy of suitable wages for work performed still seems a remote goal. The women and children are facing enormous social and moral difficulties in their homes. Domestic violence is widespread. The feeling and the experience of being discarded and marginalized is very real in many families.

The problems of the upcountry peasantry, too, are a matter needing immediate attention. Together with plantation workers, they face the non-availability of land to work or to own themselves.

Ministry in these areas has gone on and has maintained these communities and congregations. However, more concerted efforts are needed, because of the changing character of these communities. Some of them are increasingly becoming bilingual. The church has to consciously give sufficient attention to these areas to develop a meaningful and a relevant ministry there.

A majority of the areas in Sri Lanka are rural. It is true that the rural society is very much intermingled with the urban culture, and continuous interaction is a reality because of the movement of people. However, our rural society must be preserved, for it has much that can be shared with the people of the towns and cities. One of our most important tasks is to prepare and strengthen the rural community to withstand and resist the pressures of globalization. The simplicity of the rural life needs to be protected at any cost. The mission of the church in the rural areas is struggling to take into account the ethos and the life style of rural Sri Lanka. The challenges and the problems faced by rural people need to be identified. The desires and the aspirations of the people at the grass roots level should have a determining effect. While recognizing the challenges and the limitations in the rural sector, the opportunities must be channeled for the welfare of the community. Guided by the ministry of Jesus Christ in the rural areas of Palestine, the priorities in mission have to be identified. A clear study and a deeper understanding of how Jesus related to the community and was sensitive to the feelings of people will be useful to be undertaken by the church.

The church has realized that an organized implementation of a teaching ministry to equip the people of God is an urgent necessity. Specific areas like prayer groups, bible study groups, and social responsibility groups are being encouraged and facilitated. Music and song are integral parts of a witnessing Christian community. Equipping of the people of God involves specialized training. It is necessary to identify the leaders and those talented in other areas and arrange programs for their training. More and more innovation and creativity is a pressing need in working with our brothers and sisters.

One of the effective ways of making the faith our own is to bring it closer to the life situations of the faithful. Indigenization assisted in fulfilling this goal in the early days. There is a need now to identify the path for indigenization in today's world.

Indigenization Today

We have already seen the determined approach of the pioneers in this direction. The church has to admit that over the years this emphasis has faced set backs for many reasons, throughout the whole church. It appears that our indigenization is increasingly becoming limited to ceremonies and the like. This is not the most popular and the most advantageous path for us to take. Technology and media have diverted the attention of the people to the so-called prosperous world. There have been many attempts to justify such shifts, even theologically. It may also be that we have lacked the spiritual will to continue the pioneering work in this area. However, the need for a more in depth and inclusive approach to indigenization is the call of the day when we continue to live and witness among people who follow three other major religious traditions. We have been culturally enriched and nurtured by these living religious traditions. The Gospel has to be communicated in the language and the idiom of this vast majority among us. Therefore, it is necessary to identify the contemporary trends and approaches to indigenization.

The media of song, music, architecture, dance, drama and other art forms of both Sinhala and Tamil cultures have already been engaged in this field. The challenge today is to use and engage the cultural resources of the island, which are traditionally not Christian, to communicate the Good News. This calls for new and innovative ways of doing Christian theology in our world. Sri Lankan folk literature, the religious traditions, the cultures, the peoples movements, stories of the Spirits movements, religious festivals and rituals, peoples symbols and images are some of the resources that can be identified to do Christian theology and to facilitate the communication of the Gospel in Sri Lanka. The church has to prayerfully allow the Holy Spirit to generate that spiritual will and the courage in us to be obedient to Jesus, who incarnated amidst the history and the culture of the Jewish people.

National Reconciliation: The Church's Prime Task

Amidst many such challenges the national conflict remains the prime concern for the church in Sri Lanka today. But there have been many other priorities of concern for mission in recent times in addition to what has already been mentioned. The problem of the deteriorating state of human rights in the country, the large-scale threats to democracy, the plunder of the environment, and matters pertaining to medical ethics, the abuse of children, the challenges posed by the fundamentalist approaches to the faith, threats to ecumenism and the rise of denominationalism are some of these concerns. While taking serious note of such issues, it is now important to concentrate on the main issue that is disturbing us all, the need for national reconciliation and establishing peace with justice and fair play.

Have we been adequately sensitive to the challenges posed by the national conflict and the resulting war, as a community comprising both Sinhala and Tamil ethnic groups? To what extent have we been able to raise this as an issue of dialogue within the church? It is true that we do not experience the direct impact of the war in southern Sri Lanka. But the devastating impact of destruction elsewhere in the country is felt in all spheres of life. The task of the church should be to facilitate an authentic and clear understanding of the conflict among our people. It is necessary for all of us to have firsthand information about the agonies of those Sri Lankans who have been caught up in the war and whose lives have been changed or destroyed by it.

Stand of the Church

In addition to this, I believe it is necessary for us to know what we believe as a church on the issue. Here are some of the positions already evolved during the long struggle of the church in this connection. The church has always believed that Sri Lanka should remain a united country and that no forms of division will be acceptable. In this context, the welfare of all communities will have to be taken care of, ensuring the dignity and the rights of all. We believe that the solution lies in constitutionally entrenched devolution of power to ensure wide participation in the governing process. For this process the church supports a negotiated settlement. A military solution has never been an option for the church, and it rejects all forms of violence to resolve any form of conflict among human beings. The war should be stopped immediately, and the church believes that justice and good will should be maintained and every effort should be taken to alleviate fear, suspicion, and hatred. This can only be done through repentance, forgiveness, and our total commitment to the ministry of reconciliation. We also believe that it is important for those committed to peace to work together for a lasting solution.

The Response of the Church

The church in Sri Lanka has always believed that God has placed the church in such a time and place as this. At this time of crisis the church has been given the opportunity to fulfill the purpose of God and to face the challenges inherent in God's purpose. The community of faith also believes that they have been called by God to reject all forms of violence, which are essentially a manifestation of human sin. This sinfulness has been manifested in the war in the cruelest form for over two decades. Every citizen of Sri Lanka has been affected, either directly or indirectly, by the misery and continuous suffering brought to our country by war. It is said that human beings who have been made in the image of God are distorted and disfigured as the ultimate result of any war. Therefore the church has condemned and rejected war and all forms of violence. The basic principle of the Gospel of Jesus Christ is to affirm life in all its fullness.

The human person needs forgiveness for the cruelest form of violence perpetrated by humankind, in crucifying Jesus on the cross. Christ endured violence, to the extent of dying on the cross so that sin might be defeated completely. Jesus essentially endured violence on the cross in order to reject violence as a means to resolve human conflicts and to redeem humanity from all consequences of violence.

It is against such backdrop that the church in Sri Lanka has resolved to be an agent of reconciliation and peacemaking. The church is placed in a very strategic position to do this, being the only religious group that claims to include faithful from both of the nation's major ethnic communities. Therefore it is not only a responsibility but a right. The church is mindful that the ministry of reconciliation is not an easy one but a costly and a risky one. The consequences of misunderstanding can be disastrous for individuals and communities.

We observed that the war has brought about untold sufferings to the people, a good majority of them being innocent victims without much voice. The church has realized that it is necessary to be identified with the thousands of such victims and to be their voice. The church has taken on the responsibility of ensuring the welfare of all communities irrespective of caste, creed, or ethnicity, and to be mindful of the needs of smaller, powerless minority communities. The church has also learnt to work together with all well-meaning people crossing the boundaries of religion and language and within the Christian community to transcend denominational barriers. The church has, over the years, kept vigilant watch over the values of the Reign of God and the genuine rights of people. This has empowered us to speak out for the truth, believing that truth alone will make us free. Seeking peace and pursuing it has become the challenge to face and we must be ready to do it at any cost.

With such commitment, the church in Sri Lanka has been genuinely involved in practical terms in enhancing and strengthening the peace building capacity of the various denominations. It is appropriate at this juncture to examine the practical ways by which the church is struggling to make an effective response.

The Community of Faith as Peace Makers

The Vision

While the Protestant denominations have been working together for some time, there is also a desire and a commitment to work together with the Roman Catholic Church in Sri Lanka. With the leadership and the guidance shown by the National Christian Council of Sri Lanka (note: I am grateful to the National Christian Council of Sri Lanka for the recent documentation), the church's vision entails that all communities religious, ethnic, political and secular pursue a relationship of reconciliation so that the dignity and equality of opportunity and justice leading to a unified Sri Lanka may be realized. In order to achieve this, the war must come to an end and all forms of violence, visible and institutional, must be overcome and social trust and reconciliation deepened. The Christian community already engaged in this process has a continuing prophetic and a pastoral role to play ecumenically in this task.

It has been proposed as joint action for delegations from the church to meet the President and the Prime Minister from time to time to express whatever concerns that may arise and to urge them to work together in the peace process. Joint statements are being planned to encourage all parties concerned to stay in the peace process, no matter what the consequences of such a commitment might be. It is also important to pursue matters of concern and facilitate understanding on emerging issues, with visits to the Vanni (LTTE controlled area of the country).

The Memorandum of Understanding

The church has welcomed the Memorandum of Understanding signed by the government and the LTTE as an opportunity to give more space for a new orientation towards national reconstruction. This can only be a first step in the long and difficult journey that we need to embark on in order to achieve lasting peace and prosperity, and to reconcile all the communities of our country. The church has already made a request through a signature campaign to ensure that all issues in the MOU be fulfilled as quickly as possible. The church further reiterates this by facilitating education and awareness programs among all Sri Lankans.

Education and Awareness

The church believes that education and awareness is necessary for all Sri Lankans and has committed to assist in this area by organizing activities to strengthen the peace process, both within society and the church. Peace education and activities related to conflict resolution are uppermost among our priorities. This is planned through the educational institutions, the churches, and with the public at large. This will also include issue-based activities like sharing information on campaigns, detainees, war, arms dealers, protest and boycott of racist or warmongering media, the cost of war etc. This will also involve monitoring media reports, using media to promote peace, and creating awareness among journalists for responsible reporting. While giving due consideration to such issues, the responsibility of the church in alleviating suffering and other activities relating to relief and rehabilitation are not forgotten.

The church considers that this area needs wider participation of persons and groups. At this very opportune time in the history of Sri Lanka, it is important to work together with people of other faiths recognizing the multi-faith reality of Sri Lankan society. While organizing and participating in peace marches and interfaith vigils, there is a necessity for interfaith seminars and consultations for dialogue and reflection, which in turn can lead to formulating principals for harmony among ethnic and religious groups.

Relief and Rehabilitation

This has involved continuous assistance to those affected by the war and the conflict in general. The speedy resettlement of the displaced communities and individuals, the rehabilitation of combatants, and sharing the cost of such activities are urgent priorities. Peace building by way of relief and rehabilitation will also include strengthening interaction between communities separated by war in given geographical locations, trauma counseling with a focus on peace building, peace building among children, and responding to related issues such as widespread crime and an active criminal underworld. This will automatically involve initiating study and reflection on the linkages between crime and the ethnic conflict, raising awareness about crime and the underworld and joining in activities connected with them. This will lead to many issues also linked to the state of human rights, for which all parties involved in the conflict are separately and jointly responsible.

Human Rights

It has become necessary to motivate people in the churches to carry out relief and rehabilitation programs. Representations are to be made to the

LTTE on the pass system, the conscription of children, and tax collection. A campaign for uniform identity cards for all citizens of Sri Lanka, the issues connected with detainees and deserters. These issues, all matters if high priority, include seeking assistance for those who find themselves in this situation from lawyers dealing with human rights concerns, identifying and promoting potential training and linking up of support, and dealing with the whole issue of demilitarization of all combatants.

Conclusion—The Task of Stewardship

The church has inherited the stewardship of the ministry of Jesus Christ. We have the calling to continue with the risen Christ the work of reconciliation of Jesus during his earthly pilgrimage and on the cross. We have the task of being the stewards of the mission of Jesus Christ of proclaiming the Good News as very clearly depicted in the Gospels. This demands affirmation of life in every sense.

In addition we have been entrusted with the stewardship of the resources of God's church. The scriptures have shown that, creative skills of management and administration are marks of a good steward. It is important to be mindful of the responsibilities that have been entrusted to us of being good stewards of God's resources in the church, invested in God's people and in all other material investments.

Section IV: Principles Shaping Work in the Communion Overview

(An APJN Committee Report]

All peace and justice work needs to be shaped by two principles that ought to govern all work at the Communion level: the principle of subsidiarity and the Lund Principle.

The principle of subsidiarity states that decisions should be taken at the most local level appropriate to the decision. In our context, this would mean that decisions that are essentially within the jurisdiction of nation states within a Province, and which do not materially impact other Provinces should be made within the Province. Strategies for the development of sustainable agriculture might be an example of this, although if it involved extensive deforestation it would have long-term impacts well beyond national boundaries. In fact many environmental questions cross Provincial boundaries and are regional or even global in scale. The most obvious examples of this would include questions of access to water around watersheds that cross international boundaries, the commercialization of water, acid rain, and global climate change issues. In all of these areas there is a need for consultation that will extend beyond the boundaries of ecclesiastical Provinces. Again, the relevance to the work of this network is clear where environmental degradation becomes a source of conflict and reason for large numbers of refugees, as in a number of examples from the African context.

The Lund Principle states that we should always act ecumenically where possible and only act alone where issues of conscience prevent us from acting together. We are going to want to encourage participation in ecumenical initiatives where Anglicans are able to participate. This is going to include the World Council of Churches' initiatives in this area. They include work on climate change and participation in UN summits on environmental matters. While our participation in these initiatives is crucial, it is also important that we act ecumenically out of some sense of what it is that we, as Anglicans, would want to contribute. Thus ecumenical initiatives do not obviate the need for effective work within the Anglican Communion.

Theological Education

[An APJN Committee Report]

The APJN is aware that one of the most important tools for embedding a peace and justice consciousness in the life of the church is theological education. By this we mean not simply the training of clergy, but theological education of the whole people of God for the ministry of God in the world.

This education, whether carried out in traditional theological college settings, through theological education by extension, through adult education programs, or education for ministry programs, or through the educational programs of local churches, needs to be aimed at the formation of Christians for their vocation and ministry. At present, the church's systems of theological education are largely inadequate to this task. Theological maturity is not simply a product of increased understanding but is reflected in the transformation of the life of the church and its members to reflect the life of Christ. This is not possible unless peace and justice perspectives are embedded in all aspects of theological education.

In saying this we are not simply saying that peace and justice issues need to be on the curriculum although they certainly do. Even here it is not enough to add courses on peace and justice issues as if they were discreet areas of concern to be dealt with separately. All aspects of the curriculum need to be scrutinized in terms of the ideological commitments that shape what is taught and how it is taught. Biblical studies, historical and systematic theology, church history, and all the disciplinary areas that have characterized the theological curriculum are practiced in ways that reveal assumptions about the type of community we have been, and aspire to be. Yet changes to the curriculum also need to be accompanied by changes in the practice of theological education. Peace and justice issues are at stake in pedagogical practice, in assessment of students and of the outcomes of theological education, in teacher-student relationships, in admissions and appointment policies of our institutions. We cannot hope to bring about the sort of transformation we seek unless the context for theological education, as well as its content, reflects the vocation of the church to peace and justice. In particular we need to encourage the presence of more young people, more women, and more persons of color in theological education. We also need to reject the assumption that theological education is only, or even primarily, about preparation for ordination. To encourage a learned ministry in the absence of a learned laity sets up a power differential that leads to a dependency at odds with the existence of communities of peace and justice.

Theological education of the type we would hope for needs to be contextual and responsive to the needs of the church in its particular, social, cultural, and economic settings. Often such contextual theology is encouraged by the experience of other contexts, which allows us to see our own through new eyes. We would, therefore, recommend and encourage the establishment of intentional exchange programs for faculty and students as well as cooperative ventures between all centers for theological education throughout the Communion with a view to sensitizing all colleges to the impact of peace and justice issues both within their own context and within the wider Communion.

Towards Interfaith Understanding

[An APJN Committee Report]

A number of the themes and key issues raised in the APJN meeting are directly connected to concerns about interfaith understanding. The ongoing regional conflicts in the Middle East, Sri Lanka, and parts of Africa; the response to the events of 11th September 2001 in the United States; the exclusion experienced by many ethnic groups in our cities; and aspects of the impact of globalization all have inter-religious dimensions.

We propose that representatives of the Anglican Peace and Justice Network meet with representatives of the Anglican Interfaith Network to explore the following:

- the promotion of dialogue and interfaith understanding in areas of conflict
- the role of religion in peacemaking and reconciliation, mediation, and overcoming cultures of violence
- assessing the impact of dialogue in the prevention of conflict

We recognize the need for ongoing work to build interfaith understanding with an emphasis on understanding real and perceived injustices; promotion of reconciliation. This is as necessary in local communities among immediate neighbors as it is among the leaders of faith communities. We also need to understand better the relationship between local conflicts and the stereotypes played out by global powers.

Anglican Congress/Gathering

—Feasibility Group Report

This Report is a revision of the preliminary Report, presented to the Archbishop of Canterbury, after a four day meeting of the Feasibility Group in December 2000. It was revised by the Feasibility Group at a two day meeting in November 2001 in the light of comments made by the Joint Standing Committee of the Primates and the ACC and the Meeting of Primates in March 2001 during their meetings at Kanuga Conference Center. The Report consists of a brief summary of the Terms of Reference and the process of our meeting. The central section is devoted to the proposal. We conclude by recommending that this event take place. Although the material in the discussions of the various councils of the Anglican Communion have referred to an Anglican Congress, in our meeting we have come clearly to the conclusion that the event with which we are concerned should not be called a "Congress" but a "Gathering". This term more adequately expresses the character of the event and throughout this Report "Gathering" is the term which is used. We believe that this event can, under God, be a fulcrum point in the life and renewal of faith in our Communion.

1. The Brief

The Meeting of the Anglican Consultative Council in Dundee, Scotland, in 1999, passed Resolution 14 in the following terms:

Resolution 14: Anglican Congress:

This ACC

(a) Receives the report on the proposed Anglican Congress;

(b) Welcomes the positive suggestion of the Archbishop of Canterbury during the ACC discussion that an Anglican Congress should be held in association with the next Lambeth Conference;

(c) Notes

i. the discussions which date back to ACC-9,

ii. various expressions of support for such a Congress,

iii. the comment in *The Virginia Report* which acknowledges "the creative opportunity an Anglican Congress might, from time to time, offer the Communion for the renewal of its life, witness and mission," and

iv. the estimated cost structures and advice of the Inter Anglican Finance Committee;

(d) Recommends

i. That there should be an Anglican Congress in association with the next Lambeth Conference;

ii. That such an event should be held in the first decade of the 21st Century at a place to be determined by the Archbishop of Canterbury in consultation with the Joint Standing Committee;

iii. That for the Congress the Archbishop of Canterbury invites the diocesan bishop, and on behalf of the Primates and the ACC invites 4 other persons of whom 3 should be lay, at least one person a woman and one under the age of 28; and

(e) Requests the Archbishop of Canterbury, the Secretary General and the Joint Standing Committee to put in hand such planning and financial provision as would make this Congress a reality.

The Feasibility Group was established upon the invitation of the Archbishop of Canterbury and consisted of the following persons:

Co-Chairs:

Canon Maureen Sithole	Southern Africa
The Revd Dr. Bruce Kaye	Australia
Mr. Albert Gooch	U.S.A.
The Most Revd Peter Kwong	Hong Kong
The Rt Revd Harold Miller	Ireland

The Group met on the understanding that its task was, in the first instance, to prepare a report which would be presented to the Archbishop of Canterbury, then to the Joint Standing Committee of the Primates of the Anglican Communion and the Anglican Consultative Council for a Final Report to be presented to ACC-12 in Hong Kong, September 2002. At this meeting the Executive decision would be taken to proceed with the Gathering according to terms which would be finalised at that meeting. The Report that follows has been modified and adapted in the light of comments made by the Joint Standing Committee and the Primates.

2. The Process of Our Meeting

The Feasibility Group met for four days, 12–15 December, at Partnership House, Waterloo Road. Our meeting was facilitated by the Secretary General, Canon John L. Peterson, and Mrs. Deirdre Martin and had the assistance of the staff of the Anglican Communion Office. We express our very great appreciation to these people for their support and encouragement. We met at 8:45 each morning for Morning Prayer and our meetings went throughout the whole of every day concluding before dinner. In this week we have had the opportunity to eat together, worship, pray, discuss, walk and talk together. We have got to know each other, to appreciate each other's gifts and our shared commitment to the renewal of the life of faith in our Communion to which the Gathering looks.

The Group met again in November 2001. The absence of Dr. Bruce Kaye was much regretted. It was agreed the Group would meet again at the time of the meeting of the Joint Standing Committee of the Primates and the Anglican Consultative Council in February 2002 to finalise the Report for ACC-12. In light of the lack of adequate information about possible venues, the Group is considering another meeting when information has been received.

3. The Proposal

In this Report we make one single proposal about the Anglican Gathering in 2008. The proposal which is contained in this report was in many respects not the first choice of the members of the Feasibility Group. The first choice for most of us was that there should be an Anglican Congress which stood on its own as an element in the life and renewal of the faith of Anglicans throughout the world. We recognised the strategic importance of the Congresses held in Minneapolis and Toronto and the initiatives which produced those events. The fact that they stood separate from any of the decision-making instruments which were in existence then gave them a certain integrity and independence of contribution to the life of the Anglican Communion. A similar independence would have marked out very clearly for a Congress in the new Millennium the particular contribution that such an event would make. The value of a separate event was seen by us to reside in its capacity to stand as an alternative to activities which sometimes are marked by political tendencies and special interest interventions in a way which often eclipses the common grass roots commitments and concerns of Anglican Christians around the world.

However, in our discussions it became clear that such a stand alone event was not a practical possibility in terms of resource availability (not only of money but of energy and time) given the kinds of time horizons and time tables that are involved. It would not be possible to think of a Congress being organised in less than five years but the presence of a tradition of a Lambeth Conference in 2008 produced an environment in which the interpretation of the phrase "in association with the Lambeth Conference" inevitably came to mean in close proximity to such a Lambeth Conference. This Report does not comment on what particular form the next Lambeth Conference might take and in that sense does not make any assumption that it would be like the previous Lambeth Conference in terms of its formal structure or programme content. Those are really matters for the Archbishop of Canterbury.

In drafting the proposal for an Anglican Gathering in 2008 in association with the Lambeth Conference in that year, we have been careful to structure these proposals in such a way as to protect and enhance the particular contribution that this kind of event in the life of Anglicans throughout the world can make.

Our proposal therefore is embodied in the following ten points which at this stage are expressed in relatively summary form but we trust are indicative of the essential character and direction of the Gathering which we are proposing.

1. The Context of the Gathering

1. The Third Millennium has begun with much celebration and rejoicing but, at the same time, it has been launched with political conflict, violence, suffering, poverty, environmental degradation and the possibility of misdirected biotechnology. Anglicans live out their Christian vocation in the midst of these forces which diminish the value and possibilities of human life.

2. And yet we are called to testify to the fullness of life which we have in Christ Jesus. A life which both points beyond the immediate to the new heaven and the new earth and is also expressed most powerfully in the midst of these challenges.

2. The Vision

We will

- gather Anglicans from every part of the Communion to celebrate the presence and activity of God in our lives *and in the world,*

- call people to unite under the guidance of the Holy Spirit, sustained by Word, Sacrament, common prayer and thanksgiving,

- give people time and opportunity to know each other and to hear stories of Anglicans living in different cultures and traditions,

- assist participants to confront those forces which diminish the quality and value of life,

- empower Anglicans to renew their commitment to a clear Gospel mission and a vision of justice, peace and fullness of life in Jesus Christ,
- return from the gathering inspired by a richer vision of the global Anglican community of faith and the challenge to engage with their own local community.

3. Participants

Resolution 14 of ACC-11 suggested that the Archbishop of Canterbury invite the diocesan bishop and on behalf of the Primates and the ACC invites four other persons of whom three would be lay, at least one person a woman and one under the age of 28.

We have reviewed this formula carefully in the light of the concern that such a Gathering should have a strong lay element and that the participants who bring their stories to this Gathering should represent the struggles of Anglicans to pursue their Christian vocation in the volatile social and political circumstances which mark the beginning of the Second Millennium. If the representation is cast in the terms of dioceses then the very wide range of sizes of diocese would potentially leave some imbalance in the proportions present at the Gathering in terms of actual numbers of Anglicans around the world. While accepting the formula from ACC-11, we recommend that invitations to the Gathering should allow for more participants from dioceses which have more active Anglican members. We have not been able to develop a precise formula for this purpose but something along the lines of an extra person for dioceses with over twenty thousand attendees and an extra three (at least one clergy and one lay) for dioceses with over fifty thousand might suffice. We imagine that Provinces might be asked to make "best guess" judgements on these figures.

We envisage that there will be ecumenical guests at the Gathering.

4. The Programme Structure

In our discussions it became clear that such a Gathering needed to be able to address the questions that confront Anglicans where they are but not simply in the particularities which belong to their local circumstances. Rather there should be an over-arching mission theme to the Gathering which is then set within the perspective of challenges which are global. Such global challenges would be found in everyone's local circumstance to some degree or another. The sorts of global challenges which we have in mind as being the framework within which contributions which are made to the over arching mission theme of the Gathering include political instability, violence, environmental degradation, poverty, inter-faith conflict, violation of human rights and persecution.

We also believe that it is very important that the Gathering should be marked by a celebration of the presence and activity of God in the lives of Anglicans around the world. In that sense therefore the programme should contain a good deal of story telling, of worship and rejoicing in the graciousness and the grace of God and in attending to the Scriptures in the form of Bible Study.

The thrust of this structure of the programme is that it is outward looking towards the mission commitment of each and every Anglican.

A more detailed programme will of course need to be developed once a final commitment is made by the ACC, but we believe that the programme should have the following elements:

- A combination of plenary sessions and small listening groups
- Occasions for diocese/provincial groups to meet and touch base with each other
- Sections in the programme which provide a choice of activities
- "Breathing spaces" in the programme
- Worship which represents the different styles in the Communion
- Visits to local churches
- Opportunities for excursions
- The opportunity for people to bring the challenges they face at home.

The key emphatic elements in the programme should be:

- Sharing and story telling
- Public Bible expositions
- Focal point plenary worship

In all of this the preparation process and the programme must provide encouragement and opportunity for participants to dream dreams and be able to share them.

5. The Outcomes

We envisage that there will be different kinds of outcomes from this Gathering but what we certainly do not imagine is that there will be any resolutions or declarations which are the result of sectional or plenary voting. We believe that such a process would be a contradiction of the character of the Gathering which we envisage and would diminish significantly the sort of contribution which we believe this Gathering can make to the life of the Anglican Communion.

The outcomes therefore that we envisage are conceived of in terms of the individuals who attend and the groups to which they belong, namely their dioceses and provinces. We have in mind that everyone who participates in this Gathering will go home with a wider awareness of the activity of God in the lives of their fellow Christians in other parts of the world. They would therefore have a more vivid sense of their connectedness within the Body of Christ and the commonalities which exist between themselves and other Anglicans around the world.

6. Location

We have reviewed the question of location both in terms of cost and of the symbolic significance that would be envisaged. We are aware that there is a great deal of transition taking place in the growth in church numbers around the globe in the Anglican Communion. We are also aware that as the first decade of the new millennium proceeds changes are likely to emerge in that pattern and indeed in social and political circumstances within which Anglicans are called to live out their Christian vocation. Costs are important questions and while it is envisaged that these should be kept minimal, we envisage that it is important that those who can least afford to pay their travel costs should be asked to pay less and therefore the Gathering should be located in a place which facilitates that principle.

It is very difficult to be absolutely precise about travel costs at this time but having examined the present pattern of costs and also the availability of appropriate facilities, the Church of the Province of Southern Africa has agreed to undertake a Feasibility Study. A back-up site elsewhere in Africa is also being investigated as well as other venues in the Anglican Communion.

7. Timing

We envisage that this Gathering should take place during the months of July. Since we expect that the Gathering will be held on a university campus this means that it would be held in the university vacation. It is for that reason that the months of July or November/early December were suggested. However, when looking at alternatives we realised it would not be practical to hold the event too close to Christmas. We recommend that the Gathering should last for ten days, not including travel time. Lay people especially find it difficult to secure extended periods of time to attend these kinds of events and when travel time is taken into account ten days seems to us to be not only feasible but an adequate length of time for the development of the sort of experience which we envisage in the programme.

8. Relation to the Lambeth Conference Tradition

The resolution of the ACC referred to this event being held "in association with the Lambeth Conference". The Feasibility Group have developed a conception which has a clear vision and purpose and which enables the association with the Lambeth Conference of bishops to be given effect.

In formulating this proposal we have been conscious that the Archbishop of Canterbury is the one who invites bishops to the Lambeth Conference.

The Gathering proposed in this report is shaped by the emerging mission situation, a situation which confronts the lives of all the people of God and which calls for a response from them. We are driven by the demands of this challenge to say that the Lambeth Conference of bishops thus could most appropriately take place following the Gathering. We believe it would be impossible for it to take place in parallel with the Gathering since there could be no rationale which would justify separating the bishops from the rest of the church in such a programme. It would also be inappropriate for it to precede the Gathering.

In saying that this plan locates the Lambeth Conference after the Gathering we do not imply anything about the character of that conference of bishops though we believe that the particular ministry of bishops for the church could be greatly enhanced by the experience of the Gathering which is proposed in this report.

Clearly different options for the Lambeth Conference can and should be considered before a final decision is made. The Lambeth Conference of 1998 drew together all bishops and spouses together for prayer, Bible Study and fellowship. The financial implications of including all bishops and spouses in a Lambeth Conference following the Gathering would have to be taken into account. Excluding spouses and suffragan/assistant bishops could disappoint expectations.

One option which we believe could work well would be a retreat for the Primates before the Gathering and then the Lambeth Conference following the Gathering.

9. Finances

By resolution 14 of ACC-11 (1999), the Anglican Consultative Council recommended that there should be an Anglican Congress in association with the next Lambeth Conference and requested the Archbishop of Canterbury, the Secretary General and the Joint Standing Committee to put in hand such planning and financial provision as would make the Congress a reality.

The Feasibility Group has considered the need for financial provision to facilitate the initial planning process of the Gathering. The Feasibility Group suggests that authority be given to allow the annual budget provision currently designated for the Lambeth Conference to be available for the event as a whole. The size of the event might mean an increase in the provision.

Noting:

1. that the constitution of the Anglican Consultative Council gives responsibility for the Inter-Anglican Budget, including the costs of the Lambeth Conference, to the Inter-Anglican Finance Committee in collaboration with the ACC Standing Committee and in consultation with the member churches, and

2. that Resolution 7 of ACC-11 gives ultimate authority for the establishment of priorities for the Anglican Communion to the Council or the Joint Standing Committee,

the Feasibility Group requested the Inter-Anglican Finance Committee to consider this suggestion at its meeting at Kanuga at the end of February, 2001 and make an appropriate recommendation for consideration at the subsequent meeting of the Joint Standing Committee.

The Inter-Anglican Finance Committee at its meeting in March 2001 recommended to the Joint Standing Committee that the expenses of the Feasibility Group for the Gathering could be underwritten from the funds set aside for the Lambeth Conference until the meeting of ACC-12 in 2002.

The Feasibility Group wished to express the principle that each participant in the Gathering should be responsible for the cost of their transportation and Conference Fee. However, having expressed that principle, they also wished to ensure that people should not be disadvantaged because of their inability to find the necessary funding. It was envisaged it would be necessary to raise a Bursary Fund to support those who would need financial assistance.

10. Organisation

The Feasibility Group recommends the Archbishop of Canterbury as President of the Lambeth Conference and the Anglican Consultative Council, in consultation with the Secretary General, create a Design and Management Group for the Organisation of the Gathering and suggests the following structure:

Design and Management Group

FINANCE	All aspects of finance, including budget, Fund raising, financial management, Bursary administration.
WORSHIP	All aspects of Worship and Pastoral Care during the Gathering
BIBLE STUDY	All aspects of Bible Study during the Gathering.
PROGRAMME	All aspects of the Programme, including speakers, plenary and small group activities.
PROMOTION	All aspects of promoting the Gathering in the Communion and the wider public, which would commend participation, including preparation of all necessary materials for this purpose.
LOCAL ARRANGEMENTS	To secure all local arrangements including lodging, meeting halls, hospitality and local transportation, including necessary trans portation on Campus.
TRANSPORTATION	Provision of adequate assistance to participants to travel to and from the Gathering, including reservations and fare negotiations.
COMMUNICATIONS	The provision of communication services including communication within the Gathering and with the Church and public media, including print and electronic services and any services required for the follow through operation of the Gathering.
FOLLOW THROUGH	To secure effective follow through for the Gathering, planned in advance and part of the Gathering's role in facilitating the renewal of the life of faith of the Communion, including publications, video, and study guides.

We believe that such an Organising Group would need a lead time of at least six years.

4. Recommendation

The Feasibility Group respectfully recommends that the Joint Standing Committees reaffirm that an Anglican Gathering should be held in a suitable venue in 2008 in association with the Lambeth Conference and that it should be held according to the terms outlined in this report.

January 2001
[Revisions made by Revd Dr Bruce Kaye 27 November 2001]
[Further Revised by Feasibility Group 29 November 2001 and 1 February 2002]

International Anglican Family Network (IAFN) Background Paper and Report

—Dr. Sally Thompson, Network Coordinator

Background Note

The year 2002 marks the fifteenth anniversary of the Family Network (IAFN).

Originally based in Australia, the Network commissioned research and produced resource papers on important family issues for the 1988 Lambeth Conference. The headquarters of IAFN then moved to UK and the project was placed under the management of The Children's Society, a major voluntary society of the Church of England and the Church in Wales. Pilot-funding for two years from the Scottish Episcopal Church, together with continued funding from The Children's Society, enabled the appointment of a part-time co-ordinator in 1992.

The aim of the Network is to provide information about family projects and work being done to support families throughout the Anglican Communion. Regular newsletters highlight particular issues affecting the family and the ministry of the church and others in that situation.

1993–1998

Newsletters were produced on Refugees and Their Families (Spring 1993); HIV and AIDS and the Family (October 1993); Elderly People and the Family (March 1994); Cohabitation—A Challenge for the Church? (October 1994); Street Children (February 1995); Tackling Poverty in Families (October 1995); Women and Violence (Lent 1996); Strengthening Marriage (Michaelmas 1996); HIV and AIDS and Young People (Advent 1996); Moving Families: Migration Immigration and Asylum (Easter 1997); The Challenge of Parenthood (Michaelmas 1997); Young People: Risk, Exploitation and Abuse (Advent 1997); Families and Disability (Easter 1998).

A major development since 1996 was the publication of the newsletter as an integral part of *Anglican World*. This has greatly increased its circulation and strengthened links with the ACC.

1998–2001

The Network produced resource material on family issues for the 1998 Lambeth Conference, (Families—The Challenge to the Church) and funding from United Thank Offering, USA, enabled the production of a special publication (Women's Voices: Lambeth 1998) following the Spouses' Programme. Newsletters on the themes of Prostitution and Single Parent Families were published in the Trinity and Michaelmas (1999) *Anglican World*. For the Advent 1999 publication, the theme of the newsletter was Water and the Needs of Families. Fathers and Families was published in Easter 2000, Prison and Families in Michaelmas 2000 and Faith in the Family in Advent. In 2001, the issues printed were Education and the Family (Trinity 2001), Children and War (Michaelmas 2001), Family Breakdown (Christmas 2001).

The newsletters are sent to subscribers to *Anglican World* and members of the Network, a wide range of people working in projects concerned with supporting families. They are generally sent free to the Two Thirds' world. Articles are being received from an increasing range of countries, setting out some of the problems and providing encouragement by telling of the (often unknown) work being done. They constantly explore and educate about the chasm between the developed and the developing world. Some separately printed copies are available, and some of the most recent newsletters are published on our web site.

Funding and Current Programme

During 1994–1999, funding was obtained from additional UK sources, and the work for 1999–2001 was made possible by a grant from USA. The link to *Anglican World* reduced postage and publication costs. further international funding has enabled IAFN to continue its work in 2002. A newsletter on Women and the Family was published in the Trinity *Anglican World* and a newsletter on The Burden of Care will be published at Michaelmas. Work has now started on the issue Food and the Family.

A further expansion of IAFN's work is being planned with a pilot consultation, on the theme of Violence and the Family, to be held in Africa early in 2003.

Some administrative support for IAFN is currently provided by the Anglican Communion Office.

International Anglican Family Network (IAFN) Report For ACC-12

I. General

The International Anglican Family Network has continued to produce regular newsletters on family issues which are published in *Anglican World*. After consultation, the themes are selected by the Management Committee. Every effort is made to obtain articles from a wide range of countries and authors, those with practical experience of working with families, within the Anglican Communion. Having been in existence for 15 years, IAFN is becoming known to an increasing number of people, and the problem with each newsletter is how to fit the material sent into the space available. Although based in UK, we have been successful in building up interest and support in the developing world. There is regularly a sizeable and vivid input from different countries in Africa, many of the articles written by women and others working in "grass roots" projects. In an effort to further build up international contacts, IAFN wrote in December 2000 to all the Provincial Secretaries about the possibility of suggesting "consultants" for their Province who could help with identifying projects and people to write about the particular problems affecting families in their area and the work being done. Helpful responses were received from Sri Lanka, Papua New Guinea, Australia and New Zealand. But more work needs to be done on this. The Mothers' Union is represented on the IAFN Management Committee and provides many world wide contacts. Links are also being forged with the USPG and CMS and Christian Aid.

2. Newsletters published

Since the Report to ACC-11, newsletters have been produced on the following topics:

Prostitution (Trinity 1999)
Single Parent Families (Michaelmas 1999)
Water and the Needs of Families (Advent 1999)
Fathers and Families (Easter 2000)
Prison and Families (Michaelmas 2000)
Faith in the Family (Advent 2000)
Education and the Family (Trinity 2001)
Children and War (Michaelmas 2001)
Family Breakdown (Christmas 2001)
Women and the Family (Trinity 2002)

The topics are wide ranging, difficult, and yet not without hope. In the **Single Parent** newsletter, for example, some of the articles reflect growing understanding of the difficulties of single parents and the realisation that they are often victims and the Church cannot, if it follows our Lord, dismiss them as sinful and do nothing to ease their plight.

Many of the themes are also relevant to the Women's Network, and IAFN looks forward to continued and increased co operation with this developing Network. Apart from the **Women and Family** newsletter, several articles in **Education and the Family** underlined the particular difficulties for girls and women in obtaining even basic education in many parts of the world and the often terrible results for the family of this lack of education. But the Family Network does not forget the importance of men and the **Fathers and Families** issue was a very significant one and underlined this. Similarly, the two newsletters on HIV and AIDS made clear the importance of men in taking personal responsibility in combating the spread of the pandemic.

3. Funding and Administrative Support

As for all the Networks, funding has been a struggle. In 1999, funding was obtained largely through a range of UK sources, including support from many UK Bishops, and with help from The Children's Society of the Church of England and at that time of the Church in Wales, which since 1988 has acted as "host organisation" for IAFN. Through the help of the Secretary General, additional funding was obtained from a private source in USA for the year 2000–2001. Work in 2002 has been made possible by a further grant, again obtained with the help of the Secretary General, from another private international foundation. After fifteen years of invaluable financial and administrative support, which made possible the development of the Family Network, The Children's Society has had to cease to act as "host organisation" due to cut backs made necessary by its large funding deficit.

The Network is very grateful for the IT and administrative support now provided when necessary by the ACC office. Email enables rapid contact with some contributors and makes it possible for cuts and queries about articles to be speedily checked back with some authors. Communication still remains a problem for those without e mail or faxes which work. But it is very important that we do not exclude people without these facilities and that is why the printed version of the newsletters is paramount.

4. Change of Office

Since 1992, the IAFN office has been based in Co-ordinator Sally Thompson's home. With the retirement of her husband as Bishop of Bath and Wells in December 2001, she and the office have moved from the Palace to a much smaller establishment with a PO Box number address. This and the e mail address is given on the background note. One of the consequences of the move was the need to sort out filing cabinets and replace reams of paper with a database of IAFN contacts. These now number over 1,200 and the list is still growing.

5. Planned Developments—Pilot Consultation

As mentioned in the report to ACC-11, it has long been the hope of IAFN to hold a conference of practitioners on family issues. The newsletters have built up a wide range of contacts, but clearly face-to-face meetings and group work have a particular value. The funding obtained for 2002 has been sufficient to enable the appointment of a second part-time worker for the Network who is in the process of organising a pilot consultation in Africa. The theme is to be **Violence and the Family** and it is hoped that the meeting will be held early in 2003. The issue of violence has arisen in several of the newsletters and meetings of different organisations, and consultation with the WCC consultant for the **Decade to Overcome Violence** has provided many useful contacts. It is very much hoped that, if funding can be found, this meeting in Africa will be the first of a series, with subsequent ones being held in other regions of the Communion.

6. Assessment of IAFN's work

The newsletters continue to arouse considerable interest and widespread appreciation. 500 copies of each issue are printed as a separate print-run, in addition to those published in *Anglican World*, and extra copies are regularly asked for by organisations and individuals. For example, 200 copies of **Fathers and Families** were requested for a secular international conference held on this issue in USA. Since late 1999, the text of the newsletters is available on the IAFN web-site which is linked to that of the ACC. We are also currently exploring the possibility of having the text translated into French and Spanish on the web.

By concentrating on a particular issue the newsletters underline both the vast differences between parts of the Anglican Communion and many underlying similarities within this one great family. We hope that they increase understanding between parts of the Communion and help to educate both the developed and the developing world. Huge divisions can be caused by different perceptions which often derive from cultural history. And we are often very ignorant of each others' perceptions and culture. Many people in UK believed, and probably still believe, that AIDS is caused by homosexuality; some in Africa did not know that we had AIDS in UK and the Western world.

7. Network needs support

The value of the newsletters depends on the material we are sent. The Management Committee is based in UK. This means meetings can be reasonably frequent and cost little. We have a most helpful international addition with Bishop John Paterson becoming our President and he is kind enough to attend meetings whenever possible. But to have a true and increasing international perspective we need an ever-widening circle of contacts, of people who write about their own experience, both the problems and the progress. And to achieve this we need the help of members of the ACC to identify people and projects and topics for future newsletters. As I have said, we plan a regional meeting in Africa early in 2003 and have drafted a resolution asking for your support.

The ACC affirms the developing work of the International Anglican Family Network and urges all African Provinces and members to support the pilot consultation on Violence in the Family to be held in Africa early in 2003.

The current newsletter we are working on is **Food and the Family**. We are looking for articles (300–500 words long) which cover one or more aspects of the following issues: famine and difficulties in obtaining food; the impact of globalisation, agricultural problems; family and community self-sufficiency; local experience of "fair trade;" malnutrition and other health issues; pollution and unsafe food; junk food; family meals as a focus of relationships and celebration; eating disorders. The latest date to receive material for this newsletter is October 14th. As always in IAFN publications, we want to hear both of the problems faced by families in as wide a range of countries within the Anglican Communion as possible, and also of practical projects, generally linked with Churches, which work to help.

The consultation on violence and the family will provide material for a newsletter and It is also planned to produce a future issue on **Child Labour**. Please let me know of contacts for this. Finally, we welcome ideas of topics for newsletters.

As our Bible studies have suggested, networking is at the heart of the life of Christian communities and we hope that the Family Network will further develop as a result of this meeting and your participation.

Report of the International Anglican Youth Network (IAYN)

—A. Candace Payne, Network Coordinator

The IAYN continues to face many challenges in relation to youth ministry across the Anglican Communion. Since ACC-11 in 1999, numerous attempts have been made to contact the youth officers named by the Provinces through telephone calls and electronic and regular mail. In most cases, these attempts have proven futile. The reality is that there has been a rapid turnover in youth workers which has not been communicated by the Provinces to the ACC office. Contact has therefore been limited or absent in most cases.

In the past the IAYN functioned as a coordinating body for a meeting or gathering which sprung up and died. The vision for the Network is "to be a source of guidance and support to all youth across the Anglican Communion". For this vision to be realized there is a need for continuous communication and dialogue. A Church without youth is a dying Church. The influence of the Church can make the difference in the lives of many young persons. There are many vibrant youth movements across the Communion which can be strengthened and further empowered with the support from fellow brothers and sisters from across the Communion.

With the challenges of increasing violence and crime, drug abuse and HIV/AIDS, which is wiping out many of our youth, we have the responsibility as Christians to educate, support and minister to youth across the Communion. This Network can be a rich resourceful base for a church which, in some provinces, struggles to attract and retain its youth. The IAYN must be enabled to facilitate the sharing of ideas and resources to guide and support the youth workers and leaders in our churches. This can be achieved through an intentional and active approach to youth ministry. Through the media of a prayer diary, on-line communication, newsletters, meetings, gatherings and exchanges, the Network can realize its vision. The Communications Department of the Anglican Communion Office has indicated that a web link on the Anglican Communion web site can be developed.

For the Network to be revitalized and be effective, the following are imperative:

- **Information on Youth Officers**
  Effective communication is a vital component in the success of any organization. We need up-to-date information of the Provincial Youth Officers or key contact Youth Representative in order to compile a database from which correspondence can be sent.

- **Funding**
  The Network requires dedicated administrative support, communication materials and resources for other activities. We are currently pursuing funding for the next meeting of provincial youth officers. It is hoped that continuous financial support can be obtained, but this hinges on an ongoing youth programme.

- **Commitment**
  Commitment from the leadership of the Church is vital to support and enable active participation from the youth of their provinces in the IAYN. It is through intentional planning and facilitation of effective youth ministry that the Church can be assured of continual growth.

The Way Forward

Continuous efforts will be made to gather information from the Provincial Offices in order to facilitate communication. This information is critical to the convening of a meeting of provincial youth officers, which is proposed to take place in late 2003. We therefore urge the Provinces to be committed and supportive of youth ministry in their respective provinces and the across the Anglican Communion and the work of the IAYN.

International Anglican Youth Network (IAYN)
Provincial Youth Contact Questionnaire

The information gathered in this questionnaire will be used to compile a database of provincial youth leaders, which will be used to carry out the work of the IAYN.

Name of Province:

Is there a Provincial Youth Officer/Contact Person? Yes No

Please provide the following details:

Name:

Title:

Address:

Tel. No. (office)

Tel. No. (home)

Fax No.

E-mail Address:

Submitted by:

Date:

Thank you for your time and information.

Anglican Communion Refugee and Migrant Network Report

—The Most Reverend Ian George, Network Chairman

The Anglican Communion Refugee and Migrant Network (ACRMN) was revived on Archbishop Carey's initiative after the Lambeth Conference of 1998. Its Chair is the Archbishop of Adelaide, South Australia, Archbishop Ian George.

Provincial Contact Persons

The Network has built up gradually, with the appointment by local primates of contact people for their Province. Not every primate has appointed a contact person, and we have received varying amounts of information from the nominated people. For some the issue of refugee people is not a pressing one; for others it is so pressing that reporting on activities has a low priority compared with attending to the needs of refugees in their midst.

Refugee Sunday

With the encouragement of the Archbishop of Canterbury we have asked the Provinces to nominate a date for Refugee Sunday to be observed in Anglican churches. Suitable dates vary between different countries, depending on the season of the year and other commitments. England has designated the Feast of the Epiphany. New Zealand is encouraging observance on the Sunday closest to World Refugee Day, 20 June. Australia's Anglican churches align themselves with other mainstream denominations in observing the last Sunday in August. In Papua New Guinea it is the fourth Sunday in September and in the Congo the second Sunday in November. The Episcopal Church in Jerusalem and the Middle East replied poignantly: "In our part of the world refugee day is observed daily."

Information Sharing

In reply to my request for information from which to compile this report I have received a variety of responses. There is a striking difference in attitude between Western countries to which refugee and displaced people are trying to get entry and those, particularly in Africa, where there are people congregating unwillingly because they have been displaced from their homes and cannot return.

From Canada: (Elsa Tesfay Musa)

"In Canada, we are faced with tough times for refugees and immigrants, particularly immigrants and refugees of colour. In the aftermath of the September 11 tragedy in the US, the Canadian government has pushed through "anti-terrorism" legislation giving it wide powers which civil rights groups fear may be used to curtail the rights and freedoms enjoyed by all Canadians not just those that the government suspects of being terrorists. And, unfortunately, the government, the right wing, media, etc., are exploiting the public's fear of terrorism to lash against refugees. There is an incorrect perception that Canada is "too welcoming of refugees" and the public is calling for even stricter refugee and immigration laws.

Given the anti-refugee climate we currently find ourselves in, church based refugee advocates are wanting to refocus our energy towards educating the public to change the anti-refugee climate and have more of our constituency become more vocal in their support of refugees and the rights they are entitled to as human beings. We feel that all our past efforts aimed at government to bring about a fair and just refugee/immigration policy will be for nothing if the public is not with us. And, given the public's reaction to September 11 and the xenophobia and racism against the "foreigner" that that has brought to the open, we definitely need to do more to challenge ourselves and our constituency to "risk accompanying the uprooted", as the WCC year of the uprooted statement put it.

The Primate's Fund gave a total of $C183,015 during 2001 in refugee grants to countries in Africa, the Middle East and India as well as to projects in Canada."

The Sudan: (Archbishop Joseph Marona)

"Among the devastating effects of the civil war in the Sudan is the displacement of our clergy, church works and the entire rural people into the towns of Juba, Wau, Malakal and Khartoum. They have been forced to abandon their areas and homes and now live in displaced camps under inhuman conditions. . . . The total number of people displaced to Khartoum is about 4,500,000, Juba about 600,000, Wau about 300,000 and Malakal about 250,000, leave alone those who are overseas. Not forgetting the others displaced to neighbouring countries in East Africa, Uganda, Kenya, Ethiopia and Central African Republic, Democratic Republic of Congo and countries of North Africa, Egypt and Libya. There are also Southerners displaced to the Middle East, Syria and Lebanon.

With the good news of the current peace talks in Nairobi, Kenya, definitely the Episcopal Church of the Sudan (ECS) is faced with massive problems of settlement, rehabilitation, reconstruction and repatriation of the above-mentioned numbers of people. . . . The ECS really requires the resources for the church to commit on behalf of its people and the Anglican communion should be prepared to stand alongside us to fight the good fight as we prepare to lead our people across to their own birth place."

From the United States: (Richard Parkins)

"The US Refugee Program is now in a crisis stage given the significant slowdown in the movement of refugees from overseas camps since September 11, 2001. Whereas the President signed a determination in November of 2001 obligating the United States to admit 70,000 refugees this year, to date only 13,000 have arrived. The prospect of the US achieving its admissions ceiling of 70,000 prior to the end of the US federal fiscal year (September 30, 2002) is remote. It would be remarkable if even 35,000 refugees were to be admitted to the US this year. The most serious impact of this situation is the small number of African refugees who are likely to reach US communities this year. Of the 70,000 persons, 22,000 refugees were to have come from Africa. Probably less than 10% of the African ceiling will enter the US this year.

The concern of the US Government with enhanced security has been the major stumbling block to a more normal flow of refugees. While reiterating to the Government, the absence of any evidence that refugees are perpetrators of terror and the reality that refugees are among the most scrutinized of any immigrant group coming to the US, the Government has targeted refugees for special security attention. This difficulty has been compounded by the security requirements surrounding the interviewing/processing requirements of the overseas US program.

Episcopal Migration Ministries along with eight other national resettlement agencies has been at the forefront of an advocacy effort to highlight the adverse consequences of a substantially diminished US program. The concerned Congressional oversight committee of the US Congress conducted a hearing to confront with Immigration and Naturalization Service and the Department of State with the possible failure of the US to reach its 70,000 refugee admissions ceiling. Church based and non-sectarian agencies and their networks of local resettlement providers have been engaging in community efforts to mobilize support for the resettlement program, focusing much of their attention on the Administration and Congress in an effort to redress the downturn in the US resettlement program. On June 20th, affiliates nationwide will as a part of World Refugee Day lift up the plight of refugees—themselves victims of terror—as a way of bringing pressure to end the stalemate that continues to leave thousands of refugees stranded in squalid refugee camps overseas.

The church agencies increasingly promote churches as essential partners in the resettlement of refugees. As more refugees arrive with large families and often with their experience of upheaval and torture quite recent, the nurturing influence of congregations is seen as an important ingredient of good resettlement. EMM has participated in meetings with churches nationwide to underscore the need for a larger pool of churches to support its resettlement work. EMM is producing a video for release in a few months which will lift up church sponsorship."

In Ireland: (The Very Rev'd Peter Barrett)

The background to the Irish situation

Before 1993 there were never more than fifty applications in any one year from asylum-seekers wishing to come to Ireland. The new regulations governing asylum cases applies to Ireland as much as anywhere else in the EU.

Latest available statistical information
Inward migration to Ireland, 1995–2000 (Central Statistics Office, Dublin)*

Origin	Percentage	Number
Returned Irish	50%	123,100
UK	18%	45,600
Rest of EU	13%	33,400
USA	7%	16,600
Rest of World	12%	29,400

'The number of asylum-seekers to Ireland has increased in recent years and has levelled out at approximately 11,000 per year. This is slightly higher than the EU average per head of population, but it is also the case that the total number of asylum-seekers and refugees in Ireland is much less than many other EU countries per head of population as there were virtually no asylum-seekers coming to Ireland before 1996.'

The main countries of origin for asylum-seekers in Ireland in 2000 were:

Nigeria	3,404 asylum seekers
Romania	2,384 asylum seekers
Czech Republic	403 asylum seekers
Moldova	388 asylum seekers
Congo DR	358 asylum seekers

***Towards a National Action Plan against Racism in Ireland" Dept. of Justice and Law Reform, March 2002**

Total cases finalised by Office of the Refugee Applications Commissioner, 20.11.2000–31.12.2001*

Recommendations to grant asylum	467
Recommendations to refuse asylum	
Substantive, after interview	4,056
Manifestly unfounded, after interview	600
Failure to appear at interview	1,975
Unprocessable	372
Total	12,577

***Office of the Refugee Applications Commissioner, Annual Report 2001**

Applications for asylum from unaccompanied minors
During 2001, over 600 applications for refugee status were received from unaccompanied minors which marked a very considerable increase in the number of applications from this group. Concern was also expressed at some applicants who claimed to be minors but whose ages could not be verified. Indications are that the concerns are justified. The majority of those tested were found to be over 18 years old.

What are the feelings of refugees coming to Ireland?
Lack of understanding of why refugees come here generates a lot of heated debate, much of which is ill-informed. There is almost no Irish research on the needs and patterns of settlement of immigrants. A detailed survey, limited to Vietnamese and Bosnian programme refugees, was conducted by five government departments in 1997.

"The experience in Ireland has shown that policies aimed at assimilating refugees into Irish society do not work." (*Cultivating Pluralism*, ed. by Malcolm MacLachlan and Michael O'Connell)

Bosnian refugees, when asked, stated:

- They had suffered considerable personal loss;
- Many had experienced the trauma of war, injury, death of loved ones;
- They were seeking security and peace in Ireland;
- They were very fearful.

Vietnamese refugees stated, in addition to the above:

- They were seeking to reunite their families.

Most refugees were negative about having to flee their homes and all:

- experienced sadness, depression, grief;
- were fearful and suffered panic attacks;
- felt lost, confused and insecure. Also felt they had no control over their lives;
- 43% of Bosnians said they were worse off by coming to Ireland.

What challenges face newly arrived immigrants in Ireland?
Refugees confront numerous challenges upon their arrival in Ireland and need support in dealing with them.

- **Housing** in hostels is provided initially, but as soon as they are registered refugees they must seek their own accommodation in the private sector. This has proved very expensive and often (especially refugees of colour) are discriminated against.
- **Employment** is usually non-skilled and for many refugees who are highly-educated, this adds to their loss of self-worth.
- **English language skills** are not available in any systematised manner and this prevents many refugees from finding work or integrating into Irish society.
- **Dealing with Irish bureaucracy** can be extremely frustrating and slow and many refugees do not have adequate assistance in establishing their entitlements.
- **Many refugees suffer severe depression and/or psychological trauma** which are not helped by being incarcerated in overcrowded and often very noisy hostel accommodation. Privacy and security of belongings are also concerns for many refugees.
- **Asylum seekers may not officially work or study** in Ireland until they have had their status as refugees confirmed and that can take a very lengthy time.
- **"The policy of putting asylum seekers into a limbo of several years' duration, where they are prohibited from working, and they and their families discouraged from learning English, is souring the whole induction process for immigrants,"** says Fr. Bill Toner, director of the Jesuit Centre for Faith and Justice in Dublin.

Safeguards for the future

Every state has the right to control the numbers of people who may wish to enter and settle within its borders and the fact that Ireland is such a small country with only 4 million inhabitants, makes it even more important that the host community does not feel threatened by immigrant numbers.

Irish government policy is increasingly based on the premise that increased numbers of migrants into Ireland are necessary for the continued expansion of the economy. Ms Mary Harney, the Tanaiste, stated: **"It is in our own economic self-interest that we adopt a more open attitude to immigration."**

Most of those invited to take up the vacant jobs are, however, from within the EU or the Eastern European states awaiting membership of the EU. None of them may stay in Ireland when their work permits expire unless invited to do so.

Positive efforts needed to help refugees integrate
Few workers are invited from beyond Europe and so, most Irish people's experiences of non-Europeans are as asylum-seekers who may be granted refugee status. This may tend to suggest that asylum-seekers—many of whom are black—are not here for genuine reasons and that some of the scare-mongering evident in the tabloid press is true. We all, and especially the churches, need to make serious efforts to help refugees integrate into Irish society.

- English language classes are especially helpful as a way to reach refugees;
- Help with understanding the language of official documentation is usually needed;
- Discussion after service with refugees who come to church makes them feel welcome;
- Listening to those who express racist comments and trying to respond with the facts is an important way to defuse it;
- There is a considerable body of information on refugee law and social service assistance available from refugee organisations. Those who wish to, can obtain this information and pass it on to those who need it.

In England: (Charles Reed)

The Church of England Board for Social Responsibility wrote a Submission as a response to the Government's White Paper called "Secure Borders, Safe Haven—Integration with Diversity in Modern Britain." This response pointed out inconsistencies in government policies relating to migrants and asylum seekers and queries the assumptions relating to "citizenship" which is a key point of discussion at the moment.

It canvasses social issues relating to location of migrant groups, employment opportunities and Accommodation Centres. In the context of community attitudes and support mechanisms the report says, in part: "In building these partnerships it is hoped the Government will bear in mind extensive networks belonging to Churches and other faith communities which could be effectively deployed to help develop integration schemes."

In Australia: (Archbishop Ian George)

The Anglican Church has been one of those providing settlement assistance for offshore refugees coming in under the Humanitarian Program. Reorganisation of the mechanisms of resettlement two years ago required church groups to reassess their involvement and modify it in different ways. This work continues, but an increasing amount of energy has been taken up in adding our voices to those of others who are protesting against the government's policy of indefinite mandatory detention for asylum seekers who come by boat, the "Pacific solution", which deflects all asylum people who come by boat (by no means all the asylum seekers in the country) to poorer Pacific neighbours, and the continuing hostile statements about people who come here in irregular ways. A government which funds a multicultural program called "Living in Harmony" is also consciously fomenting hostility towards one small group of people (the 'boat people') which is spreading throughout the nation and inciting hostility towards anyone who looks different, no matter why they have come to Australia. Church groups are actively involved with resettlement and support assistance in most states and, at least in South Australia and Western Australia, in encouraging and participating in activities which improve understanding and relationships between Christian and Muslim communities.

General Synod set up recently a Working Group on Refugees.

Anglican welfare agencies throughout the country are providing a wide variety of assistance from housing to basic domestic requirements, English language classes to assistance in finding employment, coaching of children, coordination of volunteer helpers and assistance with government welfare programs.

The Anglican Board of Mission, the Archbishop of Sydney's Overseas Fund and Anglicord (based in Melbourne) are all sponsoring funding programs in various overseas places. Anglicans are very active with the National Council of Churches in Australia in funding programs for refugees and development (in 37 countries), especially in Thailand and the Middle East.

I notice a marked difference in the priority activities of the Provinces in Africa.

From the Joint Refugee Service In Cairo: (Mark Bennett)

The Joint Relief Ministry (JRM) works with displaced people from the Horn of Africa. The JRM offers spiritual support, medical clinics, limited material relief in the form of food and emergency funding, income generating projects, skills training, education and advocacy. It is estimated that there are approximately 30,000 displaced people in Cairo and the numbers are growing.

In 1998 there was an attempted suicide at All Saints' Cathedral. This was a catalyst to a workshop being held at All Saints' Cathedral, Cairo, "Towards Better Mental Health", to ascertain the mental health needs of the displaced community. The workshop was widely advertised and IOM, psychiatrists and other interested bodies were invited. Two major needs were identified:

1. Emotional support in times of crises.
2. Help with applications and appeals to UNHCR who are responsibility for determining refugee status in Egypt.

As a result:

1. A therapeutic listening centre "Sadaka" was developed.
2. An advocacy organization , subsequently named "Musa'adeen", was planned.

Musa'adeen

A committee was formed with representatives from both branches of the Joint Relief Ministry and representatives from the displaced community.

A handbook was developed to guide individuals in how to apply to UNHCR for status determination and to be used to train members of the displaced community to help those who could not help themselves. The group worked closely with the UNHCR. A video was made to help to allay fears and prepare applicants to present their cases well.

The handbook and video were completed by April, 1999. A training course was planned. Trainers, facilitators and a location were identified. The duration of the course was to be 6 sessions of 3 hours each. The aim was to train 35 displaced people who represented different nationalities and ethnic groups and who were from different locations in Cairo, so that they could help members of their communities to apply for refugee status to UNHCR. The training was advertised and 35 people were registered. In the event 60 people were trained because it was difficult to turn people away.

The effectiveness of the services was carefully evaluated and they were modified according to what had been learnt.

From Tanzania: (The Bishop of Western Tanganyika, The Rt Rev'd Gerard Mpango)

"In October 2000 we founded a non-government organisation to act as our professional and legal arm to handle the refugee activities especially those related to working with UNHCR. It is called SAMARITAN ENTERPRISE KEEPERS ORGANISATION (SEKO). Although SEKO is legally autonomous, it works closely in partnership with my Diocese and I am SEKO's Executive Chairman. . . . In addition to SEKO's activities, our churches are involved in Ministry with uprooted people at the local level. I can sum up our on-going activities in three priority areas:

1. Solidarity with Burundi Refugees through exchange of visits. Our local churches have been paying visits to the camps in order to be with and learn from refugees. This enables local people to learn about uprootedness and to pray for one another. Invitations to meals and to church festivals are a part of this work.

2. Advocacy to influence the Tanzanian Government to continue with open door policy to refugees and immigrants. "Refugee fatigue" is affecting the long time spirit of hospitality to refugees and affecting government policy. Bishop Mpango met the President of Tanzania and received his assurance that no refugee will be repatriated against his or her will.

3. The Youth formation and change initiative. This is a program designed to focus on change in the attitude and behaviour of youth as it relates to creating a non-violent culture among them. We encourage interaction between our youth in local churches and those in the camps. We hold workshops and seminars on non-violent culture when we have funds to do so.

Bishop Mpango was recently elected to be the Moderator of Southern African Churches in Ministry with Uprooted People. This is a Ministry of churches in 14 countries in Eastern and Southern Africa.

There are over 500,000 refugees in Western Tanzania and a range of agencies implements necessary services to them. The Diocese has a long history of involvement in refugee issues and is involved in development work as well as relief. SEKO's on-going activities are:

1. Child Care and Tracing

2. Youth and Adolescents Activities—care for vulnerable individuals (providing second-hand clothes, plastic sheeting, buckets and soap—one piece per person)

3. Community based rehabilitation
4. Gender Activities—women's rights, improved participation of women in educational and life skill activities, training in basic business operations, saving and credit schemes; protection from violence (male and female participants); HIV/AIDS education and services.
5. Formal education—enrolment and provision of classrooms, desks, stationery. There is a shortfall of more than 50 classrooms and more than half the children do not have a desk to sit at. Post-Primary Education includes Secondary education and income generating projects.
6. Non-formal education. Micro-projects to train in management skills, material support, skills development, vocational and life-skills training, literacy and language training, nursing training. Involvement of girls in education is increasing but most teachers at any level are volunteers and request some sort of payment as an incentive to continue, rather than seek paid work elsewhere.
7. Agriculture/crop production.

The pressing needs of refugees are a lack of plastic sheeting for shelter, the need for firewood for cooking and soap—"this item has not been distributed for nearly three years now due to financial constraints both from UNHCR and other related donors."

From the Congo: (The Rev'd Beni Bataaga)

The 50,000 People of the Territories of Djugu and Irumu are cared for by the Anglican Church:

- Physically by the Archdeacon of Buni and his group who supply food and medicine when financial support allows them to do so.
- Spiritually by the Provincial Evangelist who organises seminars, preaches, visits and supplies sermon leaflets.
- Administratively by The Rev'd Beni Bataaga, who collates reports from the six Dioceses of the Congo, forwards these to appropriate agencies, seeks funds for refugees and displaced people and acts as a spokesman for them. Travel between the dioceses is limited and dangerous and so visiting has been very difficult.

There is Still Hope

In the Diocese of Boga, in the Democratic Republic of the Congo, there have been violent clashes between the Bale and Hema tribes. Many people have fled to Bunia to escape these conflicts. In Bunia it has become evident that the need to live together has overridden the previous enmity: "They use the same shops, in the same market, live in the same areas, worship God in the same church, receive the same Holy Communion and receive the same humanitarian aid offered by the Churches or by the NGOs. Thus we often ask the question: what is the point of killing each other when circumstances oblige us to live together?"

The Federation of Women of Bunia encourages education and specifically teaches that the family is the foundation of society, and when the family is destroyed the whole of society is destroyed. The teaching and principles are put into practice, for example, when a woman has a baby and the other women, regardless of their tribe, visit and support her. When one is in hospital the same occurs, and they help each other in work in the fields. It is a step on the way to justice and a durable peace.

In June this year Mr Bataaga wrote: "We are tired of this war. It doesn't want to end. . . . The situation is beyond control."

From the Diocese of Natal: (Frank Kantor, Refugee Co-ordinator)

The influx of refugees and asylum seekers to South Africa has continued unabated over the past year. The official number of asylum seekers and refugees in South Africa is approximately 50,000 people, but the number is closer to 80,000, excluding others who come from neighbouring countries and do not qualify for refugee status. Most come from the Great Lakes Region—Democratic Republic of Congo, Burundi and Rwanda. There are also growing numbers from Ethiopia and Somalia. Of these approximately 20,000 refugees live in KwaZulu-Natal, mostly in Durban or Pietermaritzburg.

Once the status of refugees has been confirmed South Africa's official policy focuses on integration. This can take up to two years, during which people are not permitted to work or study. They thus have no official support system. This is where the Church and other social agencies have a critical role to play in provision of food, shelter and clothing for newly arrived refugees, as well as advocacy and lobbying on their behalf.

The Anglican refugee co-ordinator is a founder member of the KZN Refugee Network, which brings together interested and affected parties, including government departments. He has been involved in conflict resolution within refugee communities and between the refugee community and some South African nationals. He has facilitated advocacy and lobbying activities within the network and a workshop for refugees to assist them to be their own advocates.

The Co-ordinator is working with Hutu and Tutsi refugees from Rwanda and Burundi to increase trust between them and has facilitated a Business Opportunity Workshop for refugees. He is one of the spokespersons for refugees at the bi-monthly meetings of the KZN Church Leaders

Group, which aims to solicit appropriate responses from senior church leaders. World Refugee Day and Refugee Sunday are observed and encouraged with presentations by visiting speakers and information.

He continues: "The needs of refugees and other uprooted people in South Africa remain critical at a time when the xenophobia is also increasing due to the perceived job threat posed by *'foreigners'*. In such an environment, which is mirrored in many of the developed countries, the Church has a critical role to play in educating people about the needs of refugees and immigrants and in mobilizing resources to meet these needs. In addition, refugees have rights which are recognized in our Bill of Rights as well as UN Protocols, and it is the duty of the Church and other agents of civil society to ensure that these rights and the human dignity of refugees is upheld at all times.

"To do this funds need to be raised as the UNHCR considers South Africa a low priority area. . . . Should the Anglican Church be in a position to contribute to the work of responding to the growing number of uprooted people in South Africa, and KwaZulu-Natal in particular, this would be most appreciated."

The Future of the Network

1. Communication: This is extraordinarily difficult with some provinces from whom we never hear any response to e-mail, fax or letters.

2. Advocacy: We asked all provinces to tell us of some successful exercises in advocacy (especially with government) so that others might benefit from the experience. Only a few replied.

3. Education: It is clear that most provinces desperately need a great "stirring up" of awareness and concern amongst leadership and worshippers, especially in "first-world" countries. This indicates a need for leadership from the diocesan bishops and commitment of energy to the one "who is my neighbour".

4. The current and imminent refugee situation: A delegation from the Refugee Council USA to West Africa and Egypt (The Ivory Coast, Guinea, Ghana, Sierra Leone) in late 2001 reported that "refugees face a bleak future". Not only is "compassion fatigue" seriously affecting European, North American and Australian governments and communities, but as the numbers of refugees and asylum-seekers increase, fewer seem to find an opportunity of resettlement in a host country. The impact of September 11th, 2001, has been felt around the globe, making governments both suspicious of the stranger and excessively cautious about "security". The "war against terror" is working against many of those who are already victims of terror in its many different forms. The UN has reduced its work in this area by 20% due to reduced financial support from donor countries.

5. The Anglican Communion: We may be one of the continuing global organisations which could make a difference in this area. If it is to do so substantial resources will need to be found to enable that to be guaranteed.

6. A Future Gathering: The Network does not seem to be able to develop on electronic communication. No gathering of key people has taken place since 1992 in Amman, Jordan. There is a need to bring together up to 15–20 key people in 2003 but at present the Network has not the funds to do so.

On a Personal Note

I receive correspondence from people in refugee camps and with other Anglican connections asking for help. It can be help to get a Bible, to continue education, to get medical help, to be resettled in Australia. It is distressing to say how little I can do. We each have to ask of ourselves and our local churches how we can best respond to the needs which are in our communities, in our country, in our world.

Beijing + 5 Report to Standing Committee: Kanuga 2001

—ANGLICAN NGO DELEGATION

Report to the Anglican Consultative Council on the participation of Anglicans at the Forty-fourth Session of the Commission on the Status of Women, 28 February to 17 March, 2000, New York NY, USA.

The Commission on the Status of Women is acting as the preparatory committee for Women 2000: Beijing + 5 known officially as The United Nations Special Session of the General Assembly: Women 2000: Gender Equality, Development and Peace for the 21st Century.

The UN Special Session will be held 5 to 9 June 2000 in New York, five years after the Fourth UN world Conference on Women, Beijing. It will appraise and assess the progress achieved in the implementation of the Nairobi Forward-Looking Strategies for the Advancement of women (NFLS) and the Beijing Platform for Action (PFA), and to consider further actions and initiatives toward that end. The General Assembly designated the Commission on the Status of Women as the preparatory committee (PrepCom) for the review.

The Anglican Communion has Observer status at the United Nations. The interim Anglican Observer is the Right Reverend Herbert A. Donovan Jr.; Office: Episcopal Church Center, 815 2nd Avenue, New York NY 10017 USA, Telephone 212-867-8400, FAX 212-867-7767.

Anglican Participants:
The Anglican Consultative Council is an NGO (non-governmental organization) in consultative status with ECOSOC (the UN Economic and social Council). As such, it was entitled to send 5 participants to the CSW. The Anglican delegation was coordinated by Ann Smith, Director of Women's Ministries for ECUSA; and, as schedules permitted, was made up of: Sarah Anderson (New York), Sally Bucklee (Washington), Marjorie Burke (Maryland), Mable Katahirwe EDS (Uganda), Alice Medcof (Canada), Pauline Muchina UTS (Kenya), Julia Mulaha (Kenya, Ann Smith (New York). They were registered under the auspices of the ACC. Many other Anglican women were present, representing a variety of NGO's.

Ways in which women could engage in the process:

(1) Voting members of the CSW

The Commission on the Status of Women has 45 members who each have four-year terms. Belgium, Benin, Bolivia, Brazil, Burundi, Chile, China, Cote d'Ivoire, Croatia, Cuba, Democratic Republic of Korea, Denmark, Dominican Republic, Egypt, Ethiopia, France, Germany, Ghana, Indian, Iran, Italy, Japan, Kyrgyzstan, Lesotho, Lithuania, Malawi, Malaysia, Mexico, Mongolia, Morocco, Norway, Paraguay, Peru, Poland, Republic of Korea, Russian Federation, Rwanda, Saint Lucia, Senegal, Sri Lanka, Sudan, Thailand, Turkey, Uganda, United Kingdom.

(2) Delegations from each UN member state

All member states of the UN are engaged in refining the two draft working papers: The Official Declaration and the Outcome Document. They could submit their comments on the papers in advance of the 44th session of the CSW and could send delegations to the UN to engage in the ongoing dialogue throughout the session. Most of the people comprising the country delegations were women. The countries grouped themselves into: EU (European Union), JUSCANZ (Japan, USA, Canada, New Zealand, Norway, Switzerland, Liechtenstein, Australia, Iceland), G77 + China (mainly developing nations), and The Holy See.

(3) Many, many NGO's

There are hundreds of organizations which have consultative status with ECOSOC, Economic and Social Council. Those who could, sent women to speak on their behalf. Organizations with similar interests formed caucuses, for example: Health, Violence Against Women, Youth, Religion. The caucuses met as needed, formulated new wording for the Outcome Document, strategized how to lobby those with voting privileges, organized educational programs such as panel discussions and distributed informational materials.

(4) Sitting in and listening

As much as possible, the UN allowed everyone to attend the working sessions. Daily, the NGO's would meet at 9:00 am for a briefing. Individual member nations, such as the USA and Canada, held regular meetings for their NGO's. WomenAction published a daily newspaper. It was easy to be in constant information overload.

Women of Faith at the UN

Included in the United Nations Charter is the recognition that spirituality is an integral part of human nature. The Beijing Platform for Action (PFA) was the first major UN document to say so explicitly. This was the result of so very many women of faith going to Beijing and making the point that their spirituality was the driving force behind their concern for humankind. Anglicans were amongst them. Indeed, at noon, every day, Anglicans gathered in the Peace Tent to pray. The "Noonday Prayer for Beijing" and the document "Religion in the Platform for Action" are appended.

At the 44th Session of the CSW, there were a variety of religious views represented. Very broadly, they can be divided into three groups: (1) The Holy See; (2) those who oppose the PFA; (3) those who support the PFA.

Group 2, those who oppose the PFA, numbered up to 50 persons at a time. They could be easily distinguished by blue buttons on which was printed FAMILY. This extreme right-wing group, sponsored by a recently authorized NGO, REAL Women, Canada, believes that if everyone lived a faithful monogamous (mother and father) family, or lived a celibate life, all women would be happy, hence there is no need for the PFA. They were visible, vocal, and disruptive and caused distress to the women whom they confronted, threatened or stalked. The women's caucus of the EU sent a strongly worded letter to the UN authorities. It is hoped that the presence of this right-wing group and their tactics will not result in all religious groups being barred from the UN.

The Holy See signed the PFA in 1995. They seemed to be quite conservative in their approach to making the PFA a stronger document for women's rights and safety.

Women who identified themselves as Anglican were a part of group 3. They met on their own for spiritual nurture and to set an agenda for the future of Anglican women. They allied themselves with others in group 3 as opportunity permitted: "Ecumenical Women 2000 Plus" numbered over 30 women from Episcopal UN Office, Church Women United, General Board of global Ministries, Lutheran World Federation, Presbyterian UN Office, National Council of Churches of Christ, and the UWCA. "Religion Counts," an interfaith caucus, chaired by Marion Stevens, an Anglican from South Africa, met daily to support one another, discuss how to make women of faith visible, and to plan programs. Visibility was achieved by the distribution of small pink stickers which read: "Women of Faith believe in the PFA".

Programs included:
"Religion: Women's Liberation, Women's Bondage: Religion and the Platform for Action" Jean Hardisty, Riffat Hassan (Muslim), Teresa Hinga (Roman Catholic), the Rev. Rose Abby (Presbyterian, Ghana).

"Religions for the PFA" Marion Stevens (Anglican), Frances Kissling (Catholics for a Free Choice), Ani Choying Drolma (Buddhist nun), Karen Manz (Lutheran).

The speakers on these panels supported the view that religion can be a liberating force in women's lives, or it can be a tool for their oppression. Religious teachings from different faith traditions have often sanctioned violence against women, including domestic violence, rape and female genital mutilation. Despite such religiously sanctioned violence, women of faith from various traditions have worked within their traditions to offer new interpretations of religious teachings and to advocate that their institutions help end violence against women. Women are transforming their religious traditions, denouncing patriarchal teachings and offering new interpretations that liberate women from oppression.

A petition in support of Tibetan Buddhist nuns was prepared and circulated.

Work on the document is not finished. Intersessional meetings will be held. Submissions deadline is April 15th.

Next steps for women of faith:

- Keep Bishop Donovan up to date so that he can confer with his counterparts from as informed a stance as possible.
- Determine what the Anglican Communion's position is on the PFA. Were steps taken based on the PFA in 1995? How have we attended to promises made? Should further steps be taken?
- The International Anglican Women's Network had as one of its principles that PFA. Has an assessment been done on our performance since our founding in 1996?
- Poverty is one of the most disempowering aspects of women's lives. Are there gender specific guidelines for assigning relief and development money in budgets in all provinces of the Anglican Communion? (For example, the Canadian Primate's Relief and Development Fund has gender guidelines biased towards projects which benefit women.)
- Education is crucial for women in developing nations. Taking the ECUSA Women of Vision training programs worldwide is money well spent. Holding global conferences also results in new learnings that "spin off" to many women "back home".
- It is women who are most aware of women's human rights, and how these rights are being limited. It is beneficial to have directors in the national Church Houses that are sensitized to create a list of email addresses of the Anglican women who were at the CSW meeting, and circulate this list to everyone on the list. Continue to link ecumenically.
- Support the World March of Women 2000.

Web Sites/Email Addresses:

The UN Development Fund for Women (UNIFEM) 304 East 45th Street, 15th floor, www.unifem.undp.org

International Women's Tribune Centre, 777 UN Plaza, 3rd floor
email: iwtc@igc.org

Conference of NGO's (CONGO)
NGO Status of Women Committee
777 UN Plaza, 8th floor
email: congongo@aol.com

UN Division of the Advancement of Women
UN Plaza, 12th floor
www.un.org/daw
Email: daw@un.org

WomenWatch UN
www.un.org/womenwatch/daw

WomenAction 2000 (NGO) www.womenaction.org
Email: info@womenaction.org

The United Nations Special Section of the General Assembly: Women 2000: Gender Equality, Development and Peace for the 21st Century, 5 to 9 June 2000, New York NY USA

The United Nations General Assembly Special Session (UNGASS) was held to appraise and assess the progress achieved in the implementation of the Nairobi Forward-Looking Strategies for the Advancement of Women (NFLS) and the Beijing Platform for Action (PFA), and to set targets for the future. Each member nation was asked to report on the actions taken since 1995 on upholding and promoting the status of women. These were summarized in an outcome document (prior to 5 June) which the UN delegates discussed in detail during the Special Session.

In many of the nations women studied the report of their country and wrote a critique. These, too, were summarized and published as the "NGO Alternative Global Report." This data was used by NGO's to lobby delegates, delegations, and the caucuses in an attempt to strengthen the final document.

Anglican Presence at the UN

The Anglican Communion has Observer status at the United Nations and is in consultative status with ECOSOC (the UN Economic and Social Council). The interim Anglican Observer is the Right Reverend Herbert A. Donovan Jr., Episcopal Church Center, 815 2nd Avenue, New York NY 10017, telephone 212-867-8400, FAX 212-867-7767.

The Anglican NGO delegation had three members: Ann Smith (USA), Dr. Pauline Muchina (Kenya), and The Rev. Canon Alice Medcof (Canada). Many other Anglican women were present as delegates, as members of delegations and as members of a variety of NGO's Each had her own responsibility and focus. Smith, Muchina and Medcof went specifically as women of faith. They linked with other women in two caucuses: *Ecumenical Women 2000* Plus (Church Women United, General Board of Global Ministries, Lutheran World Federation, Presbyterian UN Office, National Council of Churches of Christ, World Young Women's Christian Association, Episcopal UN Office) and *Religion Counts* (an international inter-faith group) with members from Ecumenical Women 2000 Plus, Roman Catholic, Jewish, Muslim, Hindu, Buddhist. The two caucuses co-sponsored an event each day from 1:15 to 2:30 pm in the Chapel of the UN Church Center, attracting many women.

At the United Nations itself, the ACC was given two passes which were shared by Smith, Muchina and Medcof who were able, thereby, to observe the Special Session at work and attend NGO briefings.

There will be much to be said once the work is completed and analysis made by the various NGO caucuses. As of Thursday 8 June, some highlights are:

As a result of pressure from many sources, the subject of domestic violence is commonly known. When domestic violence was named in various paragraphs there was very little resistance compared to 1995. With satisfaction, it is noted the "honor killings" was specifically names in 130b, together with the call for national legislation and other measures.

One paragraph on the environment, number 106b, was deleted. The original wording was: "Reorient environmental and agricultural policies and mechanisms to incorporate a gender perspective so that all governments in cooperation with civil society begin monitoring and informing women on water quality, and support women farmers with education and training in sustainable food production, particularly organic." The Environment Caucus sees the loss of wording regarding water quality and sustainable food production as very grave.

Paragraph 132c generated a lot of discussion and was referred to a small group for negotiation. It states (all suggested phrases included), "Encourage a greater appreciation for the central role that religion, spirituality and belief play in the lives of women and men, in the way they live and in the aspirations they have for the future. Respect and promote the right of women and men to freedom of thought, conscience and religion. Protect and promote women's rights to freedom of thought, conscience and religion as inalienable rights which must be universally enjoyed." That women be able to worship God, freely, is a contentious issue.

APPENDIX from the International Women's Tribune Center Brief History of UN Women's Conferences From 1975 to 2000

In 1995 nearly 6,000 official delegates from 189 countries and over 30,000 women gathered in Beijing united in their desire to achieve equality, development and peace for all women. The Fourth World Conference on Women resulted in the Beijing Declaration and the Platform for Action (PFA) which were adopted unanimously by government representatives. The Declaration and the PFA built on the agreements reached at the previous World Conferences for Women (World Plan of Action, Mexico City, 1975; A Programme for Action, Copenhagen, 1980; Forward Looking Strategies, Nairobi, 1985).

The PFA constituted a powerful plan for empowering women and achieving gender equality. It defined a set of strategic objectives and spelled out actions to be taken by national governments, the international community, non-governmental organizations, and the private sector to remove obstacles to the advancement of women in twelve critical areas. In addition, Beijing was the first global conference in which women's issues were explicitly linked to human rights. The PFA mentions "rights" approximately 500 times and includes human rights as one of the twelve Critical Areas of Concern. With this new legal authority, women activists left Beijing full of optimism, re-energized and determined to lobby their governments and the international community to make sure the Platform for Action would be implemented quickly and effectively.

Assessing Progress Five Years after Beijing

Beijing + 5 gives us a chance to assess the work of the last 5 years and has begun an important discussion about the need for targets and indicators to measure what progress has been made. Targets make progress visible and measurable and they allow activists to monitor change, or lack thereof. The majority of existing targets for women's progress relate only to health and education, hardly sufficient to examine all areas of women's lives. Using the few measures that we have available to us, what progress have we made?

What do the indicators show? So far, the results are in from more than 100 countries which have responded to a questionnaire requesting information about the implementation of national action plans. Despite a few isolated examples where women's lives have improved, in most cases progress has been slow and in some cases, governments have even moved backwards.

Women in only six countries have achieved "equality" using the three composite indicators of gender equality and women's empowerment selected by the UN indicator framework:

- Approximate gender quality in secondary school enrollment;
- At least a 30% share of seats for women in parliaments or legislatures;
- An approximate share of nearly 50% of paid employment for women in the non-agricultural sector.

The national reports, supplemented by other studies, also reveal: Women constitute 70% of the world's poor—a situation often referred to as the feminization of poverty.

Globalization and Poverty

Structural adjustment policies required for World Bank loans and economic globalization affect women more than men. Removing local banks from the decision-making process for the allocation of credit gives big corporations easier access to loans and impedes small businesses (microenterprises) from getting loans. These small businesses are often the sites for women's economic participation

Donor nations have been unable to meet commitments to increase development assistance.

Further structural adjustment policies have forced governments to reduce spending on social welfare eliminating an important source of support for single mothers with young families and the disabled of elderly. Government cuts have also decreased the level of state-provided health care affecting the availability of reproductive health care and education and maternity care.

Women's Participation in Power and Decision Making

In Beijing, governments endorsed the goal that 30% of decision-making positions should be held by women by the year 2000. While 22 countries have adopted laws and policies to advance equal participation of women in decision making, this goal has not been attained.

Only in the Nordic countries, where women constitute 50% or more of elected officials, have women achieved any real results. Meanwhile, women's presence in parliaments in the former Soviet Union and Eastern European countries, which averaged 30% under communism, have fallen drastically during political transition and is down to 3% in many of the newly independent states. Worldwide, women are just 11.7% of parliamentarians and at the United Nations itself, only 8 of 180 Ambassadors to the UN are women.

Violence Against Women

Despite the widespread adoption of laws against domestic violence, women continue to fear violence in their homes, in their communities and in conflict zones.

The foregoing facts and figures are from UNIFEM and WEDO (www.wedo.org/monitor/findings.htm)

22 SEPTEMBER 2002

Archbishop of Canterbury's Sermon at a Eucharist Service

Holy Trinity Church, Kowloon

On behalf of all ACC-12 members we are delighted to be with you this morning and to share in your worship. The hospitality of the Province of the Hong Kong Church has been quite unforgettable and we are all so very grateful to your Archbishop and bishops, clergy and people for your care and support.

Although we come from different parts of the world we have one important thing in common I suspect. We all have a home and therefore we all have a place which we call home. I don't know if you have noticed it but in the letters of St Paul, Paul often begins his letters by referring to the two homes that every Christian has. Consider the letter to the Philippians: 'Paul and Timothy to all the saints in Christ Jesus who are at Philippi.'

The first address was a shared spiritual home—in Christ Jesus. Wherever we come from, we belong to him: to Jesus Christ. The second address is the church family where we belong geographically. In the case of Paul's readers it was Philippi. In our case you may belong to a church family here in Kowloon or Hong Kong or back home in Kampala or Kingston, Jamaica.

In the epistle read to us just a moment ago Paul brings the two homes together and what he says comes as a challenge to us all.

In verse 21, he says very movingly: 'For me to live is Christ and to die is gain.' But how could St Paul be so sure of that hope? And, for that matter, how may we?

I believe St Paul's strong conviction of eternal life arose from a relationship he enjoyed with his Lord. We know that Paul was a very able and wise man. He was very unlikely to be a Christian follower simply because of emotion or because he clung to a vain hope. No. He was convinced of the truth of the resurrection. He had met the risen Lord and through prayer and a daily walk with God he knew he was embraced by God's love. So Paul was absolutely sure of this—to die is gain. However, he gave up the greater glory of martyrdom for the lesser joy of belonging with the saints at Philippi. Why? Because of Paul's desire to assist the Church in Philippi to proclaim the gospel fearlessly.

Just this week in our Conference we have been helped in our understanding of HIV/AIDS through Canon Ted Karpf who assists the Archbishop of Capetown in his ministry. Ted only came into this ministry through a remarkable experience that happened twenty years ago.

Ted was a priest in the diocese of Dallas in Texas. One night in 1983 a knock at the door revealed a man standing there who had a terribly disfigured face. His face and entire body were covered by the cancerous lesions and sores that one sees in people in the advanced stages of the HIV/AIDS virus. The man explained that he had been to six churches before and each had rejected him. He said simply: 'Will you allow me to come to your church and die here?'

Ted did not know what to do. There were many rumours about this terrible disease and it was said that if you drank from a communion cup that someone with this disease had shared you too would contract the virus. But Ted thought about the gospel and its welcome to all. After that initial hesitation he said: 'My church is open to you. I will stand by you.'

The trouble was, that his Church didn't agree. There was uproar when the man came among them. The people left in droves until within a few months there were only 21 people left. On one occasion only three people turned up to a main Eucharist. But Ted battled on; he realised that the Church must not reject this sad man, already rejected by six other churches. As he got to know the man he found out that when the man had said originally that he wanted to die in the church he meant that he wanted to commit suicide. But as the sick man realised that he was actually loved by Ted he responded to the care and love. He realised that he had found a real home of love and support. And he had his wish—when he did pass away, he died upheld by the love of Ted and a few of those who stood by him.

That is an illustration of a caring church in action which became a real home to a very needy man. Because of who we are—in Christ—we are called to make, wherever we live, bear the marks of our heavenly home where the love of God reigns and Christ is glorified.

But I believe the modern church needs to recover some of St Paul's conviction of the glorious hope of life with God.

Many people, including Christians, are afraid of death. Woody Allen, the great Jewish film producer, once said: 'Death? I'm not afraid to die! I simply don't want to be around when it happens.' But we will be around. And it will happen to us all one day. Let us as Christians start to see death as St Paul saw it: 'For me to live is Christ and to die is gain.' And that conviction is strengthened as we spend time in God's presence; as we deepen out prayer life and as we spend time with other Christians in serving our needy world.

And that takes me into my second point.

Verse 27 is one of the few times when Paul is keen for his audience not to miss the seriousness of the point he is about to make. So, he says, 'Now, the important thing is that your way of life should be as the gospel of Christ requires, so that whether or not I am able to be with you, I will hear that you are standing firm with one common purpose, and that with only one desire you are fighting together for the faith of the gospel.'

Listen to the strong words again: 'Stand fast in ONE spirit, with ONE mind . . . striving together for the faith of the gospel.' Paul is drawing on the image of the Roman army—which was noted for its discipline and unity. One spirit; one mind; in the proclamation of the gospel.

And we members of ACC need to embrace this great ideal. We must stand together as a disciplined body and defend the precious unity of the Church. I believe that if we want ACC-12 to stand for something very important it must be our interdependence. Not our independence where we say: 'I have no need of you.' But our interdependence where we say: 'I need you and we are committed to stay and stand together' confident and alert to the needs of our world.

One spirit—that might mean that we are one in our concern for one another. That we be One mind—that might mean that we belong together and try to share the same outlook; adopt a common language in our response to the needy.

Let us note that Paul is keen to encourage the Philippians to fight for the faith of the Gospel side by side with one another. He longs for the unity of the Church. He desires that we fight together for the faith of the Church. After all, that's what armies do, they co-ordinate amongst themselves a common strategy for dealing with the common problems they face.

Notice he says twice in that verse—your focus must be on the gospel. It must show in your behaviour, your conduct and it must show in your overriding concern for the gospel.

Just as the soldiers in the Roman army of Caesar Augustus had to focus on one thing only. serving their Lord, so we belong to the army of Jesus Christ. His gospel, his good news, must be our over-riding concern.

So in our Eucharist today we are being reminded of the two homes to which we belong to. We are being welcomed to fellowship with Christ at his table and also directed to the world in which we live and carry out our ministries. In the early Church, the Eucharist was often seen as the 'medicine of immortality.' It gives us life. The Father says to us—you belong to me.

But the Eucharist also says: 'We belong together; we are members of one family. We are embraced by God's love.'

So people of the Province of Hong Kong, members of this congregation, members of ACC—deepen your love and concern for one another. Be like that man Ted in reaching out to all in need. And may all of us know the assurance that was expressed so magnificently by St Paul: 'For me to live is Christ and to die is gain.' That will keep us going when all else fails.

23 SEPTEMBER 2002

Report on Interfaith Initiatives: "Al-Azhar Al-Sharif" and "The Alexandria Declaration"

The Archbishop of Canterbury has been involved in a number of interfaith initiatives, two of which have culminated in important agreements, Al-Azhar Al-Sharif, and the Alexandria Declaration.

Al-Azhar Al-Sharif

At the time of the terrorist attacks in New York and Washington on September 11th 2001, representatives of the Archbishop of Canterbury were in Cairo working with distinguished Muslim leaders on an agreement for a programme of Christian-Muslim dialogue. For several years Al-Azhar, the 1,000 year-old university and international centre for Sunni Muslim scholars, has had an official committee for interfaith dialogue, with its office close to that of the Grand Imam, the most senior person in the Azhar and acknowledged as the principal religious figure in Egypt. The Archbishop has twice lectured at the Azhar (in 1995 and 1999), and Dr Tantawi, the Grand Imam, was his guest at Lambeth Palace in 1997. It is from these meetings, friendship, and serious discussion that a deepening dialogue between Al-Azhar and the Anglican Communion has evolved.

The Al-Azhar Agreement, on which the two sides worked last year, was formally signed by the Grand Imam and the Archbishop at Lambeth Palace on 30 January 2002.

The Alexandria Declaration

This initiative was launched last autumn when the Archbishop was asked by both Jews and Muslims to help bring together the religious leadership of the Holy Land. The aim was to find a way for Muslims, Jews, and Christians to hold a conversation that might in time contribute towards a political settlement. In January, more than twenty religious leaders met in Alexandria in Egypt, where they heard accounts of violence and destruction, persecution and fear, exclusion and rejection. Yet there was still hope, and a desire to co-exist in peace with neighbours. It was sobering to discover that several of the distinguished Rabbis and Sheikhs live within ten miles of one another but had never met.

To the joy, and not a little surprise, of the assembled leaders, they were able to conclude an unprecedented agreement, the First Alexandria Declaration of the Religious Leaders of the Holy Land. The Holy Land, the Declaration reminds us, is Holy to all three of our faiths.

Communiqué From the Anglican/Al-Azhar Dialogue Commission

The Joint Commission, which is composed of a delegation from the Anglican (Episcopal) Church and the Permanent Committee of Al-Azhar for Dialogue between the Monotheistic Religions, held its second meeting at the Office of the Sheikh Al-Azhar on Tuesday and Wednesday, the 3rd and 4th of Rajab 1423, which corresponds to the 10th and 11th September 2002, in accord with the text of the Agreement signed by both sides at Lambeth Palace on January 30th, 2002.

At the beginning, the Joint Commission expressed its feelings of deep gratitude for the opportunity to renew and deepen the friendship between both parties through engaging in frank and encouraging dialogue and co-operation. The dialogue was noted for its openness and constructive spirit.

The Commission discussed the topics that were on its agenda:

1. Peace is inseparable from justice

The Commission noted after discussing the papers on this topic presented by both sides that Al-Azhar Al-Sharif and the Anglican Communion agree on the importance of not separating peace from justice, and that the sacred texts of both religions clearly affirm peace and the realisation of justice among people, and reject oppression and partiality.

2. Acceptance of the other from theological, historical and practical perspectives

The Commission noted that the Agreement on dialogue signed by both sides states that one of its goals is: 'To encourage Anglicans to understand Islam and to encourage Muslims to understand the Christian faith.'

After listening to the statements of the members from both sides, and the scriptural texts cited in the two religions, the Commission affirmed that both faiths believe in the acceptance of the other and in living together in brotherhood, co-operation, love and peace, rejecting aggression from one group towards the other.

The Joint Commission called on religious leaders, both Muslim and Christian, to strive to provide accurate and respectful teaching about the other faith, and to correct misrepresentation about it. It also stressed the importance of accurate information about both faiths in the curricula of schools and colleges; the portrayal of each faith should be without distortion and acceptable to its own adherents. The Commission also encouraged the exchange of visits among religious leaders.

3. The Stance of the Commission concerning current events in the world, especially in the Middle East

The Commission discussed crisis situations in various parts of the world such as Iraq, Sudan, Nigeria, Pakistan, Kashmir, Indonesia, Chechnya and the Philippines. The Commission called for the implementation of the principle of peace which is inseparable from justice for the benefit of all.

The Commission affirmed that the current crisis in the Holy Land is creating an inhuman situation for all concerned, is undermining international efforts and resolutions for reconciliation, and presents a threat to world peace. The Commission expressed its support for all efforts to bring about security and a just peace for all. It also supported the ongoing work of the Permanent Committee which resulted from the Alexandria Conference of January 2002. This Conference encouraged representatives of the three religions in Palestine and Israel to resolve the Arab-Israeli conflict through peaceful means.

As to the possibility of war in Iraq the Commission affirmed its concern that the authority of the United Nations should not be by-passed, and that further efforts should be made to seek peaceful solutions.

On the first anniversary of the events of September 11th 2001, members of the Commission committed themselves afresh to working together for a world in which all human beings can live side by side in peace, justice and mutual respect.

Religious Leaders Reach Unprecedented Joint Accord on the Holy Land [Press Release]

More than a dozen senior Christian, Jewish and Muslim leaders from the Holy Land have concluded an unprecedented joint declaration pledging themselves to work together for a just and lasting peace.

The agreement, to be know as the First Alexandria Declaration of the Religious Leaders of the Holy Land, was approved today (Monday 21 January) at a landmark conference of religious leaders in the Egyptian port, chaired by the Archbishop of Canterbury, Dr. George Carey.

The seven-point declaration pledges the faith leaders to use their religious and moral authority to work for an end to violence and the resumption of the peace process. It also envisages the establishment of a permanent committee of leaders from the three religions in the Holy Land, to pursue the implementation of the declaration. The accord also calls on Israeli and Palestinian political leaders to implement the Mitchell and Tenet recommendations.

Dr. Carey said: "The Holy Land is holy to us all-Christian, Muslim and Jew. We have a shared duty therefore to do all we can to make it a land of peace and harmony. I hope too it will come to be seen as an historic moment for the co-operation of our three faiths in the region."

The conference received support in advance from both the Israeli Prime Minister, Ariel Sharon, and the President of the Palestinian Authority, Yasser Arafat. Dr. Carey said he hoped its outcomes would also receive the clear backing of political leaders. He said: "Of course no declaration by religious leaders or anyone else can act as a magic wand—a panacea for all the ills and injustices, the savagery and inhumanity that have scarred and continue to scar the Holy Land. We are not so naïve. But it is our duty and our desire to do what we can to bring forth good from evil—hope from despair."

The conference, which began on Sunday, is the first occasion on which such senior figures from the three religions have held focussed discussions in this way. It is being co-hosted by the Grand Imam of al-Azhar al-Sharif—Dr. Mohamed Sayed Tantawy, the most senior Islamic figure in Egypt and holder of one of the most prestigious positions among Sunni Muslims worldwide.

The First Alexandria Declaration of the Religious Leaders of the Holy Land

In the Name of God who is Almighty, Merciful and Compassionate, we, who have gathered as religious leaders from the Muslim, Christian and Jewish communities, pray for true peace in Jerusalem and the Holy Land, and declare our commitment to ending the violence and bloodshed that denies the right to life and dignity.

According to our faith traditions, killing innocents in the name of God is a desecration of his Holy Name, and defames religion in the world. The violence in the Holy Land is an evil which must be opposed by all people of good faith. We seek to live together as neighbours, respecting the integrity of each other's historical and religious inheritance. We call upon all to oppose incitement, hatred and the misrepresentation of the other.

1. The Holy Land is Holy to all three of our faiths. Therefore, followers of the divine religions must respect its sanctity, and bloodshed must not be allowed to pollute it. The sanctity and integrity of the Holy Places must be preserved, and freedom of religious worship must be ensured for all.

2. Palestinians and Israelis must respect the divinely ordained purposes of the Creator by whose grace they live in the same land that is called Holy.

3. We call on the political leaders of both parties to work for a just, secure and durable solution in the spirit of the words of the Almighty and the Prophets.

4. As a first step now, we call for a religiously sanctioned cease-fire, respected and observed on all sides, and for the implementation of the Mitchell and Tenet recommendations, including the lifting of restrictions and a return to negotiations.

5. We seek to help create an atmosphere where present and future generations will co-exist with mutual respect and trust in the other. We call on all to refrain from incitement and demonization, and to educate our future generations accordingly.

6. As religious leaders, we pledge ourselves to continue a joint quest for a just peace that leads to reconciliation in Jerusalem and the Holy Land, for the common good of all our peoples.

7. We announce the establishment of a permanent joint committee to carry out the recommendations of this declaration, and to engage with our respective political leadership accordingly.

Delegates:

His Grace the Archbishop of Canterbury, Dr. George Carey
His Eminence Sheikh Mohamed Sayed Tantawy
The Sephardi Chief Rabbi Bakshi-Doron
The Deputy Foreign Minister, Rabbi Michael Melchior
The Rabbi of Tekoa, Rabbi Menachem Fromen
Rabbi David Rosen, President of the WCRP
The Rabbi of Savyon, Rabbi David Brodman
Rabbi Yitzak Ralbag, Rabbi of Maalot Dafna
Chief Justice of the Sharia Counts, Sheikh Taisir Tamimi
Minister of State for the PA, Sheikh Tal El Sider
Mufti of the Armed Forces, Sheikh Abdulsalam Abu Schkedem
The Mufti of Bethlehem, Sheikh Taweel
Representative of the Greek Patriarch, Archbishop Aristichos
The Latin Patriarch, His Beatitude Michel Sabbah
The Melkite Archbishop, Archbishop Boutrous Mu'alem
Representative of the Armenian Patriarch, Archbishop Chinchinian
The Bishop of Jerusalem, the Rt Revd Riah Abu El Assal

Anglican Principles Towards Better Inter-Faith Relations in Our World

—THE RIGHT REVEREND KENNETH FERNANDO

Prepared for the Network of Interfaith Concerns of the Anglican Communion

1. We confess our failures and lack of love, respect and sensitivity to people of other faiths in the past. We intend to forgive one another, seek the forgiveness of others and commit ourselves to a new beginning.
2. We affirm that good inter-faith relations can open the way to better inter ethnic relations and peace throughout the world.
3. We recognize building true community [koinonia], both among persons and various ethnic and religious communities as our primary objective. We need to develop a global theology that will be appropriate for the unfolding sense of a globalized world.
4. We affirm the importance of promoting a culture of dialogue within and among all religious communities, and indigenous traditions.
5. We condemn violence and terrorism as being against the spirit of all true religion and we pledge ourselves to removing their causes.
6. We shall respect the integrity of all religions and ensure that they have the freedom to follow their own beliefs and practices.
7. We believe that the different religions are enriched by identifying agendas in which they can collaborate such as making peace, protecting the environment, eradicating poverty, and ensuring the human dignity of all.
8. We affirm that it is important for us all to listen to and learn from other religions so that we can value religious plurality as a factor that enriches our communities.
9. We endeavor to live out and explain the truths of our own religion in a manner that is intelligible and friendly to people of other faiths.
10. Cultural diversity as well as religious diversity in our communities will be affirmed as a source of enrichment and challenge.

Report of Network for Inter Faith Concerns of the Anglican Communion (NIFCON)

—Clare Amos, Network Convenor/Coordinator

In this report I will attempt to summarize the activities and development of NIFCON during the 3 years since the last meeting of the ACC, although inevitably the report will concentrate on the period since August 2001 when I myself have been most directly involved in the Network.

NIFCON's mandate was renewed at the Lambeth Conference 1998, and a specific reference to monitoring Christian-Muslim relationships was inserted. Since then the Network, effectively the UK Support Group, has been seeking and developing ways to give 'flesh' to the aims of NIFCON stated below:

- The sharing of information, stories and resources across the nearly 40 provinces of the world-wide communion
- Appropriate dialogue and friendship with people of other faiths
- Sensitive witness and evangelism where appropriate
- Mutual solidarity and prayer where there are places of difficulty and conflict
- Local contextual, and wider theological issues.

Up till August 2001 Revd John Sargant acted as Convenor of the Network, giving one day a week to this work. Some important steps were taken which laid the groundwork for the developments in NIFCON that have taken place during the last year. A five year plan for the development of the work of NIFCON was drawn up and began to be activated at a residential meeting of NIFCON held at Launde Abbey Leicestershire in autumn 2000 which drew in participants from the USA and Jordan. A brief history of NIFCON and inter faith relationships in the Anglican Communion was written by Andrew Wingate, a member of the Network. Discussion took place about a possible inter faith consultation in the Pacific Rim—and funding was given to Revd Fergus Capie who was on a sabbatical visiting the region to enable him to make initial sounding regarding this. The group also did some preliminary work to seek to fulfil its mandate to monitor Christian-Muslim relationships.

With the resignation of Revd John Sargant in August 2001, Clare Amos took over as Convenor/Coordinator, initially on an ad hoc and temporary basis. However funding was obtained in autumn 2001 from the Parthenon Trust as a result of the efforts of John Peterson which has allowed Clare to be formally seconded by USPG to NIFCON for one day a week (with her time paid for) and in addition for a half-time Administrator, Susanne Mitchell to be appointed. These new arrangements formally came into effect in April 2002. During the last few months therefore NIFCON has had the benefit of more staffing than ever before in its existence and this has facilitated a number of key developments:

- A website has been developed (www.anglicannifcon.org) which carries news about NIFCON and inter faith events and resources, particularly relating to the Anglican Communion.

- The network of NIFCON correspondents, which had effectively been in abeyance over the last few years is gradually being re-established and developed. Much of the correspondence relating to this dates back as far as 1994, so clearly there is a considerable amount of work to do to find up to date personnel around the Anglican Communion who are willing to keep us informed about inter faith issues in their province and region. Our work is considerably facilitated by the development of the use of email in recent years, and the correspondents network also ties in with the establishment of our website, which provides a useful and obvious platform for news and views to be shared.

- Work is progressing on the setting up of a quarterly Christian-Muslim digest, in association with the Department of Christian-Muslim studies at the university of Birmingham. It is hoped that this will eventually be funded ecumenically-and our intention is to have this up and running by the start of the academic year 2003.

- A key publicity visit took place to the United States in May 2002 by one of our Bishops President, Rt Revd Kenneth Fernando. This has both raised the profile of NIFCON in America and resulted in a reasonable amount of additional funds being raised. We are very grateful to Bishop Fernando for the enthusiasm and effort he put into this visit.

- NIFCON is involved in supporting the publication, both financially and via the input of work from David Thomas, Susanne Mitchell and Clare Amos, of a celebration volume for the 90th birthday of Bishop Kenneth Cragg in March 2003.

- Discussion and work is afoot to ensure that there is an international consultation at some point in 2003. This may in fact be held in India rather than in the Pacific Rim. A decision will be taken on this at the NIFCON Support Group meeting on October 7.

- As a result of a regular NIFCON 'presence' in Partnership House, both in the Anglican Communion Office where Susanne Mitchell is based and at USPG where Clare Amos works most of the time, the profile of NIFCON has been increased. Visitors to the Anglican Communion Office now often meet representatives of NIFCON, Lambeth Palace staff increasingly consult NIFCON in relation to inter faith matters, NIFCON staff receive invitations to inter faith events etc. There is regular contact between the NIFCON Coordinator and Canon David Marshall, the Archbishop of Canterbury's Chaplain dealing with inter faith issues. There is also a considerable amount of 'cross over' between Clare Amos' work as Theological Officer of USPG and the work she does for NIFCON. We are grateful for the way in which the establishment of a base for NIFCON in the Anglican Communion Office has also facilitated administrative support (accounts, cheque handling etc.).
- A task that needs attention shortly is the clarification of the NIFCON structures. A paper will be presented on this to the October Support Group meeting.

Clearly the profile of inter faith issues has been raised considerably during the last year, and its importance to the life of the Anglican Communion has been highlighted. The work that NIFCON does is not a 'luxury' but a key part of the Christian witness of the Communion.

We would urge delegates to respond please by ensuring that NIFCON has correctly identified those who are willing to keep us informed about inter faith issues in their province and region. Details can be emailed to clarea@uspg.org.uk or susanne.mitchell@anglicancommunion.org

Ethics and Technology Report

—The Reverend Canon Eric B. Beresford, Consultant for Ethics

Introduction

The position of Consultant for Ethics, with a particular focus on environmental issues, and issues related to the ethical significance of the new technologies that are so dramatically reshaping our lives, was created at ACC-11 in Dundee, Scotland. At that time the ACC Standing Committee acted in response to the call of Lambeth to strengthen the capacity of the communion to act on these issues in Motions 1.8 (On Creation), 1.9 (On Ecology), and 1.12 (Calling for a Commission on Technology and Ethics). The attached documents represent the written part of the report that will be submitted by the Consultant for Ethics. They consist of:

Proposal Re: Anglican Communion Environmental Network Prepared by The Rev. Canon Eric B. Beresford, Consultant for Ethics, Anglican Consultative Council "To Strive to Safeguard the Integrity of Creation and Sustain and Renew the Earth" (from Five Marks of Mission, Adopted at ACC-6)

Rationale

Anglicans are committed to environmental stewardship. Church leaders have placed environmental issues high on the religious agenda over recent years. Addressing the recent Anglican meetings that preceded the World Summit on Sustainable Development in Johannesburg, South Africa, the Archbishop of Canterbury said, "We have an inescapable obligation to cherish the living planet that has been entrusted to us by our creator." He also commended the joint declaration signed by Pope John Paul II and the Ecumenical Patriarch, Bartholomew I. This stated that "Christians and all other believers have a specific role to play in proclaiming moral values and in educating people in *ecological awareness*, which is none other than responsibility towards self, towards others, towards creation." On this basis they called for "an act of repentance on our part and a renewed attempt to view ourselves, one another, and the world around us within the perspective of the divine design for creation."

The 1998 Lambeth conference reflected this urgency. According to the report of section 1, "The whole creation is an act of Divine love." The bishops went on to observe that despite the promise of such an insight, and despite the vocation which it would seem to set forth for Christians around the world, "the social and political resolve to create a more ecologically sustainable way of life has not materialized." In order to give concrete content to our vocation, as Anglicans, to care for creation they called for the establishment of a commission on the environment with staff support. This proposal that the nascent and unofficial Anglican Environmental Network receive official status is an attempt to respond to these concerns in a manner consistent with the structural and financial capacity of the ACC.

Current approaches within the Communion are not adequate. Environmental issues have been actively pursued in several provinces of the Anglican Communion, and clearly a lot can and should be done at the local and provincial levels. Anglicans have acted as advocates for environmental stewardship. They have provided support and leadership to local initiatives to protect the environment. They have sought to educate individual Anglicans and local church communities to become better stewards of creation. As an example of this, they have developed resources to help Anglicans monitor the environmental impact of the lives of their own church communities. However, this alone is not enough.

We have to face the fact that often those Provinces where issues are most urgent are least equipped to deal with them. Such Provinces need the help and support of the wider communion. They need access to information about the best strategies for environmental action and advocacy. They need information about the sorts of issues that are being addressed in other parts of the communion. Most of all, they need a means by which to communicate their stories and seek the support and assistance of the wider church.

In addition to this, many environmental issues cannot be dealt with on a province-by-province basis. For example:

- Resource extraction in the developing world is often conducted by companies whose corporate headquarters are in the industrial north. Effective intervention to ensure that such activities are carried out in a sustainable way is best achieved where there is cooperation between the partner churches to engage in advocacy, both in the countries affected, and in the countries where the relevant companies are based.

- Biodiversity and species extinction need to be addressed at the global level. Species are most obviously affected by habitat loss, but this loss of habitat is not simply a local or regional problem. It is often linked to economic pressures that reach beyond national boundaries. An example of this would be the loss of rain forest to make room for the growth of cash crops. Other factors affecting biodiversity at this time include the ongoing trade in materials derived from endangered species and the use of intellectual property rights to gain control over the biological and genetic resources, particularly of countries in the developing world. Both of these issues need to be addressed globally.

- One of the most urgent issues at the present time is the access to fresh water. The river systems and great lakes that are an essential element in securing such access often cross international boundaries and the use of these resources becomes a source of potential conflict. Cooperation between partner churches can be an important resource in overcoming this conflict and bringing about just and sustainable solutions.

- Global warming is an issue that most severely affects nations in the developing world. Many of the island nations of the Pacific face catastrophic loss of land as a result of the predicted rise in sea levels. Meanwhile the greatest contributors to greenhouse gas emissions are the developed nations of the north. The World Council of Churches has developed some excellent resources here. Nonetheless, whilst it is important that we draw on such ecumenical work effective action will still involve coordination and communication at the level of the communion.

All of this supports the implied position of Lambeth that the Communion must have adequate structures through which the Church might strengthen its response to the serious environmental challenges that the world is currently facing. Further, it is clear that none of the existing networks has been able to fulfill this function. The most likely location amongst current networks would be the Anglican Peace and Justice Network. However, while it reflected briefly on environmental issues at its first meeting, the range of issues pressing for the attention of this network is vast and the environment quickly, and predictably, fell from the agenda. The evidence is that if we are to give the environmental crisis the attention it needs we will need a structure that focuses intentionally on our Anglican responsibility to just and sustainable environmental practices. This does not mean that such a network could or should act in isolation. Indeed, this proposal pays careful attention to the need for networks to interact when particular issues need to be addressed from multiple perspectives. An environmental network would be well placed to initiate such interaction since its concerns overlap with those of several other networks. These include the Anglican Peace and Justice Network, the Anglican Urban Network, the Anglican Indigenous Network, the Anglican Women's Network, and the Family Network. We have already begun to undertake steps to foster effective interaction.

Activities to Date

Following the appointment of the Consultant for Ethics after ACC-11 we began to gather names of contact persons on environmental issues from each of the provinces. One of the things that became immediately clear is that many provinces have a limited awareness of the environmental initiatives being undertaken within the province. This meant that even at this preliminary stage it was sometimes possible to help provincial offices to identify environmental work being undertaken within their jurisdictions.

The Consultant for Ethics began to design a web site that could be used for communication of news about environmental initiatives and for the sharing of resources. The intention is that this web site will be placed under the Anglican Communion web site although at present it is set up to make it clear that the web site is not that of an official network of the communion.

A project to model cooperation between provinces around contentious environmental issues was proposed and is currently being negotiated. The particular proposal relates to a joint conversation between ECUSA and the Anglican Church of Canada on water resources. Water is the subject of some friction between the governments of Canada and the USA at present. It is hoped that these conversations might help the two churches to identify areas where they might work together in coordinated advocacy strategies within their respective jurisdictions. It is hoped that this project will provide models for similar conversations elsewhere.

The Consultant for Ethics has met with the Anglican Peace and Justice Network, and with members of the Anglican Urban Network to discuss strategies for cooperation. This was reflected in their presence at the meetings held in Johannesburg. Letters have been written to the conveners of the Anglican Indigenous Network and the Anglican Women's Network.

A gathering of Anglicans from around the world was organized to coincide with the UN World Summit on Sustainable Development, which met in Johannesburg in August of this year. It was called the Global Anglican Congress on the Stewardship of Creation. The organization of the conference was housed in the Office of the Anglican Observer to the UN. The provinces nominated delegates to the congress and they were responsible for their travel expenses. The UN Observer raised funds with the assistance of the Secretary General to pay for operating expenses and for the reimbursement of invited speakers. Delegates were present from 21 provinces, and a number of Anglican Environmental Initiatives from around the world. The Right Rev. Simon Chiwanga was present on behalf of the ACC, and representatives of the Anglican Peace and Justice Network, and the Anglican Urban Network were also present. The congress issued two statements, which are appended to this document. They also passed a motion asking the ACC to commend these statements and also asking the ACC to make the emerging Anglican Environmental Network an official network of the Anglican Communion. It was clear that those present at the congress understood the event as a formative event in the development of such a network. They clearly expressed the view that the meeting had been fruitful and that there should be future meetings. The Right Rev. George Browning has offered to provide logistical support and hospitality for a meeting in Canberra, Australia approximately three years from the date of the Congress. It was also suggested that the meeting focus more on networking and less on invited speakers. This would greatly reduce the need to raise any additional funds.

Structuring the Network

From the above it is clear that the aims of the Anglican Environmental Network are not only consistent with and supportive of the initiatives of the member churches of the Anglican Communion, but are a response to a repeated request to take environmental issues more seriously. In order to fulfill its mandate it is recommended that:

- The network shall consist of nominated members from each of the province who shall be invited to attend network meetings and will be those consulted on proposed projects and initiatives.
- The network shall encourage wider networking through the use of web based and "chat room" communication.

- The Network shall be responsible for establishing and maintaining an up to date web site that will enable Anglicans to keep abreast of environmental work around the communion. The web site will be the primary means of communication around the network. Letters on issues of critical importance will be circulated from time to time through the office of the Consultant for Ethics.

  - The web site will include official resolutions and statements on environmental issues by the ACC, the Lambeth Conference, the Primates, and the Provincial Synods of the Anglican Communion. These resolutions will provide the policy basis for the activities of the network.

  - The web site will provide information about environmental initiatives by member churches.

  - The web site will provide contact information for provincial representatives and those working on environmental issues on behalf of their churches provided both the province and the individual consent to this information being made available.

  - The web site will provide access to and information about resources developed by member churches where these can be made available.

  - The web site will include a chat facility to enable Anglicans to share their concerns and insights about the environmental issues that they are dealing with. This facility will also provide a forum for discussion and debate of more contentious environmental issues. This will be a separate function from a closed email list for official provincial representatives. It will be made clear that statements on this facility will be the responsibility of those making them and do not necessarily reflect the views of any part of the Anglican Communion. The chat page will be moderated by the consultant for ethics who will consult with the Secretary General and provincial representatives when appropriate.

  - The web site will link to other relevant environmental web sites.

- The network will report on all meetings to the ACC and its standing committee. The general activities of the network will be reported through the office of the Consultant for Ethics.

- Initiatives of the network will be undertaken in consultation with the Consultant for Ethics and the Secretary General and, where appropriate, the Anglican Observer's office at the UN.

- Meetings of the network will be organized in consultation with the Consultant for Ethics, the Secretary General and the UN Observer's office.
- The costs of travel to network meetings will be borne by participants and/or their provinces.
- Additional funding will be sought only when necessary and on the advice of the Secretary General.
- The UN Observer's office, and those networks with mandates that overlap with the environmental network, will be invited to all network meetings and informed of other network initiatives and activities where appropriate.

Motions Passed by The Global Anglican Congress on the Stewardship of Creation

1. Motion endorsing the work of the Congress.
Moved that this congress request the Anglican Consultative Council to endorse the statements produced by the congress (The Declaration to the United Nations World Summit on Sustainable Development and the Declaration to the Anglican Communion), and that the ACC, in keeping with its support for environmental stewardship, make the Anglican Environmental Network an official network of the Anglican Communion.

2. Motion asking the ACC to request provinces to monitor their environmental practices.
[The text of this motion will be provided by Office of the Anglican Observer to the UN.]

The Global Anglican Congress on the Stewardship of Creation: Declaration to the United Nations World Summit on Sustainable Development

We desperately need a change of spirit. The environmental debate is as much about religion and morality as it is about science. Sustainable development is one of the most urgent moral issues of our time. It begins in sustainable values that recognize the interrelatedness of all life. Sustainable development cannot be defined in economic terms alone, but must begin in a commitment to care for the poor, the marginalized, and the voiceless. Therefore it is sustainable community that we seek. The ecological systems that support life, the qualities that sustain local communities, and the voices of women, indigenous peoples and all who are marginalized and disempowered must be approached from this perspective.

As we move into the third millennium, it becomes increasingly obvious that human beings are set on a path of unprecedented environmental destruction and unsustainable development. A profound moral and spiritual change is needed. Human exploitation of the environment has yielded not only benefit, but also appalling poverty, pollution, land degradation, habitat loss, and species extinction. Despite political and scientific debates in some quarters, it is clear that human behaviour has overwhelmingly contributed to ozone depletion and global warming. We desperately need to change.

We write as representatives of the Anglican Communion. Our 70 million members are present in 165 countries across the globe. They speak from their experience of the problems of development in both urban and rural communities. At all levels of the life of the communion the environment has repeatedly been identified as one of the key moral and religious challenges before us.

Religious faith properly understood can and should be a major force for change towards sustainable development, sustainable communities, and a healthy environment. Anglicans accept the need to oppose all forms of exploitation. Specifically, we believe that a better, more holistic, and religiously informed understanding of Creation, which recognizes that human beings are part of the created order not separate from it, will make a major contribution to the transforming change of spirit that is essential in the third millennium. We are committed to putting our faith into action.

Many different religious traditions start from the belief that the world primarily belongs to God and not to human beings. Land, sea and air belong first and foremost to God. At most they are entrusted to human beings who are expected, in turn, to respond with gratitude and to hand them on faithfully and intact to generations to come. As stewards of the environment human beings are required by God to act faithfully and responsibly. Other theological perspectives within the Christian faith also support a renewed ethics of caring for the whole creation.

All religious traditions call their believers to disciplines of life that show respect for the environment that we inhabit. We value life more than possessions. We value people more than profits. Based on this shared commitment this Anglican Congress calls on people of all faiths to act together by:

- seeing creation as good, beautiful and sacred;
- understanding that humanity is a part of the created order, not separate from it;
- evolving a new relationship with the created order founded on stewardship and service, with production and consumption restrained by genuine need and not simply governed by desire;
- locating our unity in the Spirit that breathes life into all things;
- celebrating the glorious God-given diversity that is everywhere.

We therefore call upon Governments of all nations to support sustainable communities, by:

- working together for peace, justice and economic prosperity within a context of ecological stability;
- refusing to subordinate the good of all for the good of some;
- recognizing the intrinsic worth of non-human forms of life, and committing ourselves to strengthen and enforce the protection of endangered species;
- recognizing the intrinsic worth of the diversity of life, as well as the inextricable link between biodiversity and cultural diversity on which the survival of indigenous peoples, indeed all humankind, depends;
- rejecting the destructiveness of the culture of militarism, that spends disproportionate amounts of money on armaments when so many people in the world are still hungry, and stockpiles nuclear weapons and materials at great cost to the environment and to human well being;
- recognizing that environmental degradation constitutes a violation of the universal declaration of human rights. Poverty and environmental degradation are interwoven and it is the poor, and the exploited, often on the basis of race and gender, who suffer most from this degradation;
- recognizing that development is not sustainable if it steals from present and future generations. The security of future generations can only be attained by addressing the urgent questions posed by the intolerable burden of unpayable debt, the challenges of unsustainable agricultural practices, and by the reduction of greenhouse gas emissions to ecologically stable levels. To this end we recommend serious consideration of the principle of contraction and convergence;
- affirming that the rivers and the land, the sea and the air are a global commons, entrusted to human beings to be handed on faithfully and intact to generations to come.
- defining the rules of international trade in ways that demand greater corporate responsibility in promoting greater inclusion of the marginalized and more sustainable environmental practices.
- recognizing that current rates of HIV/AIDS present a profound challenge to sustainable community, which must be met by adequate and equitable access to education and treatment.

The Global Anglican Congress on the Stewardship of Creation: Declaration to the Anglican Communion

Brothers and Sisters in Christ, we greet you and speak to you in the name of our Trinitarian God, Father, Son, and Holy Spirit: Creator, Redeemer, and Life Giver.

We write as representatives of the provinces of the Anglican Communion gathered in response to the planetary crisis and immediately prior to the World Summit on Sustainable Development. With the blessing of the Archbishop of Canterbury, the General Secretary of the Anglican Consultative Council, and the chair of the Anglican Consultative Council, our purpose is to consider the Communion's responsibilities to God and God's creation at this critical time. At the last Lambeth Conference in 1998 our Bishops again identified the environment as one of the key moral and religious issues of our time and their principles have been part of our reflection.

We have come together as a community of faith. Creation calls us, our vocation as God's redeemed drives us, the Spirit in our midst enlivens us, scripture compels us.

> *Where were you when I laid the foundations of the earth? Tell me if you have understanding.* Job 38:4

> *All things came into being through him, and without him not one thing came into being.* John 1:3

> *We know the whole creation has been groaning in labour pains until now.* Romans 8:22

Our planetary crisis is environmental, but it is more than that. It is a crisis of the Spirit and the Body, which runs to the core of all that we hold sacred. It is characterized by deep poverty: impoverished people, an impoverished Earth. As people of faith, Christ draws us together to share responsibility for this crisis with all humanity.

In the twentieth century, the human impact on the earth increased enormously. In the last thirty years alone, human activity has destroyed many of the planet's natural resources. Climate change, flooding, habitat destruction, desertification, pollution, urban expansion, and famine have all played their part. A third of all fish species and a quarter of all mammal species are in danger of extinction. One billion people now suffer from a shortage of fresh water. Scientists have said the web of life is unraveling.

People must be willing to face change and participate actively in the decisions before us all. Unjust economic structures have taken from people and the land without giving in return, putting at risk all life that is sustained by the planet. Greed and over-consumption, which have dictated so much of economic development in the past, must be transformed into generosity and compassion. Transformation is, at its heart, a spiritual matter; it includes every aspect of our lives. As members of the Anglican

Communion, at all levels of its life, we must play our part in bringing about this transformation toward a just, sustainable future. Now is the time for prayerful action based on the foundation of our faith.

In 1998, the Bishops of the Anglican Communion resolved to face these challenges and provided the scriptural and theological justification for the involvement of the Church in caring for creation. We recognize this and other ongoing work of people in the communion. Such work needs our support. However, it is not enough.

We urge you to acknowledge the gravity of our call to prayer and action. Both individuals and decision-making bodies of the Church at all levels need to be actively involved in addressing these problems. As brothers and sisters in Christ's Body and as fellow Anglicans seeking to fulfill our baptismal covenant and witness to the power of the Holy Spirit in Christ, we ask you, in your parishes, dioceses, or provinces, acting at the most appropriate level, and in cooperation with ecumenical and interfaith partners wherever possible to undertake the following:

- To acknowledge that the Church's mission must now take place in the context of a life and death planetary crisis whose impact affects all aspects of the Church's life and mission.
- To bring prayers and actions concerning ecology, environmental justice, human rights, and sustainable development to the forefront of public worship as well as private and corporate reflections on the Holy Scriptures.
- To support the struggle of indigenous peoples to maintain their cultural heritage, natural heritage, and human rights.
- To encourage all members of our congregations to understand that God calls us to care for the creation by making our communities and environments better places for the next generation than they were in our lifetime.
- To actively support initiatives in all Churches and communities that are concerned with the planetary crisis.
- To help publicize and network information, developments, events, publications and all sources of knowledge among our friends, neighbours, congregation members, Church leaders, and government officials.
- To encourage links among our provinces, dioceses, and parishes worldwide to increase understanding of the many issues involved and how they are interrelated.
- To support opportunities for younger people to experience first-hand how people in their own and other congregations and communities

are affected by the planetary crisis and how they can work to change the world in which they live.

- To promote training and educational programs in all aspects of the planetary crisis even as they relate to our worship and community life.
- To encourage diligently our secular and Church leaders, lay and ordained, in all parts of the Anglican Communion to place the planetary crisis at the highest level of their concerns.
- To encourage and support public policies that reflect the principles of sustainable community.
- To request all bodies within the communion to undertake an environmental audit and take appropriate action on the basis of the results. To commit ourselves both to energy conservation and the use of sustainable energy sources.
- To demonstrate simplicity of lifestyle in our patterns of consumption to counteract greed and over-consumption. Such greed dictates so much of our economic past that it must be transformed into generosity and compassion.

Christ has no hands but ours, and he calls us to offer ourselves to share in his work of healing and reconciliation so that all creation may know that, "The truth shall set you free."

Motion Commended to the ACC by the Joint Standing Committee, Belinter House, Dublin, February 2002

This council views with concern the increased levels of exclusion and marginalization of the world's most vulnerable peoples as a result of the changes in the application of international patent law.

- Patents on medications, particularly those related to HIV/AIDS are making antiviral agents inaccessible in parts of the world where their availability is critical.
    - This practice is particularly unjust where populations in the developing world have been used for clinical research on medications they will not be able to afford once trials are completed and drugs approved for use.
- The practice of applying for patents on genetic and biological materials means that the developing nations are finding it increasingly difficult to maintain control over their own genetic and biological resources.
    - This practice represents an extension of patent law into areas for which it was not designed.

- It threatens to further commodify our relationships to the natural world at a time when the commodification of the natural world is already putting immense strains on global ecosystems.

- The practice threatens to transfer the ownership of, and access to, the biological and genetic resources of developing nations to patent holders who for the most part are for-profit biotechnology companies with their corporate headquarters in the developed world.

- While the new biotechnologies are promoted, in part, in order to increase food production and quality, patenting practices seem more likely to promote increasing inequalities in access to the food supply.

While we recognize that patent rights are intended to protect legitimate commercial needs and interests, this council invites member churches of the Anglican Communion:

- To engage in advocacy within their jurisdictions and cooperation with each other to ensure that ongoing changes to patent law both at national levels, and at the level of international trade agreements (GATT—General Agreement on Tariffs and Trade/TRIPS—Trade Related Intellectual Property Rights Agreement) to protect the needs and interests of vulnerable populations and of developing nations.

- To avail themselves of the resources of the consultant for Ethics at the Anglican Communion Office to support this work.

- To communicate their activities to the ACC through the office of the consultant for Ethics.

Report of the Coordinator for Liturgy

—The Reverend Dr. Paul Gibson

1. The International Anglican Liturgical Consultation

More than 70 Anglican liturgists representing 30 provinces of the Anglican Communion gathered in Berkeley, California as the International Anglican Liturgical Consultation in August 2001. The principal subject of the Consultation was ministry and the theology and liturgies of ordination.

Members of the Consultation had been working for some years on baptism, eucharist, and ministry, the agenda of the 1982 Lima Conference of the Faith and Order Commission of the World Council of Churches. The subject of ministry had already been explored by two informal meetings of Anglican liturgists and the adoption of a statement by the Berkeley Consultation brings this particular task to a conclusion.

The Consultation based both the theology and practice of ordination firmly on the baptismal nature of the church, emphasizing that the people of God are revealed in baptism to be a holy people ministering to the world in the name and manner of Christ. God bestows a variety of gifts to build up the body of Christ and enable its mission. Ordained ministers are integral members of the body, called by God and discerned by the body to be signs and animators of Christ's self-giving life and ministry to which all are called.

The Consultation described the role of the bishop in terms of pastor and teacher and suggested that the rites of ordination and seating of a bishop should affirm and celebrate the bishop's ministry in and among the people.

Presbyters are called to share with bishops in the oversight of the church especially in identifying and nurturing the gifts of the Spirit given to the community for the work of ministry. The Consultation noted that the terms "presbyter" and "priest" are both used among Anglicans and both are appropriate. However, the ordination rite should affirm the priesthood of the whole baptized community and the sacramental, pastoral, and teaching relationship of the presbyter to the community.

The Consultation noted that historically deacons were the managers of the local church, responsible for charitable and social work. The calling of the deacon is consequently to embody and activate the Christ-like service of the whole people of God in the world.

The Consultation noted that there is movement in some parts of the Communion towards direct ordination to the presbyterate and even the episcopate. While recognizing that there is precedent for both direct and sequential ordination and that both have merit, the Consultation suggested that Provinces should be free to consider direct ordination.

The Consultation stressed that the act of ordination belongs to the community as a whole, with the bishop presiding as the focus of the church's unity. Because an ordination is an ecclesial event in which the church's life and ministry are ordered, it should take place in the context of a eucharist celebrated at a place and time when all the church's ministries may be most fully represented.

The Consultation developed a significant list of practical reflections and suggestions to help local communities realize its theological ideals.

The Consultation engaged in a lively discussion of the possibility of using elements other than bread and wine at the eucharist and agreed to recommend to the Standing Committee of the Anglican Consultative Council that a survey be conducted to discover current practice in the Communion. The recommendation also suggested that the ACC form a small working group, including members of the Consultation, to study the data and draft a report with guidelines for further consideration by the Consultation and the ACC Standing Committee. (See item 2 below.)

Sue Parks, Director of SPCK Worldwide, visited the Consultation to tell members that the SPCK is unable to provide financial assistance for liturgical publishing to a level that would meet both demand and need. Noting that one of the defining characteristics of Anglicanism is mother-tongue worship, she asked who would support Anglican liturgical publishing if Anglicans themselves don't provide the resources? She said she brought to the problem to the Consultation because she felt that a liturgical conference is the forum in which the liturgical publishing needs of two-thirds world churches should be taken seriously.

The Consultation elected Paul Bradshaw, Joyce Kurari, and Tomas Maddela to be new members of the steering committee. The steering committee elected Paul Bradshaw to be chair of the Consultation.

A meeting of members of the Consultation is now being planned for 2003, to be held at Cuddesdon Theological College, near Oxford. (Meetings of members more or less coincide with congresses of the international and ecumenical academy Societas Liturgica; in order to secure the broadest possible representation of the Communion, full Consultations are held only every four years with meetings at the two-year interval between them.) The principal subject of the meeting will be liturgical formation and the need to equip church leaders, both ordained and lay, to provide liturgical direction which is creative and builds the church as God's people.

2. Elements at the Eucharist

On the recommendation of the International Anglican Liturgical Consultation the Joint Standing Committee recommend

1. that the Anglican Consultative Council commission a survey of practice in relation to the elements of Holy Communion in the provinces of the Anglican Communion, and of the ground given for any departure from traditional usage; and
2. that in the light of such a survey, the Joint Standing Committee establish a working group including members of IALC, IASCER, and IATDC which will study the data and present a report with suggested guidelines to the Joint Standing Committee.

In anticipation of some discussion before action is taken on 2.1, I have conducted a brief preliminary survey of the Provinces, united churches, and extra-provincial dioceses asking (1) if the use of elements other than wheat bread and fermented grape wine has been suggested seriously in their context, (2) if elements other than wheat bread and fermented grape wine are actually used and, if so, what they are and how often they are used, (3) if canons or other resolutions provide for the use of elements other than bread and fermented grape wine, and (4) for any other relevant information. Eighteen replies have been received to date, some of them very detailed. This is a large and helpful response.

A major problem in processing the data is the distinction between de jure and de facto practice. As one respondent put it, "The answers to questions 1 and 2 in your questionnaire are 'No', but they leave no room for relevant or anecdotal and hearsay experience. Although the answer to question 2 must be 'No', we do know that there are some places which do depart from the norm."

- Eight respondents answered the first two questions with an unqualified "No."
- Eight respondents qualified their answer to question 2 in one way or another, indicating that deviations were, in fact, known to exist. Most of these deviations involved the use of rice bread or other gluten-free bread suitable for communicants allergic to gluten, and the use of grape juice or de-alcoholized wine by individuals or communities where alcohol was a problem. One province uses a liquid produced by boiling raisins in water and adding sugar. One province uses "flour bread, biscuit, round cake, Coca, Fanta, etc."

- Only one province has legislated for deviations from the bread/wine norm.

If the Council decides to ask a working group to study the data and present a report with suggested guidelines, there are a number of point for their consideration.

(a) **ecumenical**. Concern has already been expressed that deviation from the ancient bread and wine tradition could affect seriously our conversations with churches who consider it to be an unquestionable norm. The Lambeth Quadrilateral, which was adopted by the 1888 Lambeth Conference as the basis of Anglican involvement in ecumenical conversations, includes the following article: "The two sacraments ordained by Christ himself—Baptism and the Supper of the Lord—ministered with unfailing use of Christ's words of institution, and of the elements ordained by him." Anglicans have treated the bread and wine tradition as one of the four planks in an ecumenical platform. Abandonment of that tradition could be seen as the adoption of an anomalous position.

(b) **theological**. Although I am not attempting to promote the substitution of other substances for bread and wine, I have already suggested in a preparatory paper prepared for the International Anglican Liturgical Consultation that I believe a case might be made for such practice because the act of sharing food as the actualization of the kingdom announced by and in Jesus is the primary focus of the eucharist, to which all else is secondary. What is at stake is not mere convenience or even prejudice but the integrity of the eucharistic celebration. Whatever food is used at the eucharist should carry symbolic freight as profound as bread and wine in middle-eastern and Mediterranean cultures. It should come to the table of the Lord with the same intimations of nurture, fellowship, generosity, dignity, and solemnity. It is noteworthy that when one of the members of the International Anglican Liturgical Consultation reported that his province (which did not respond to the questionnaire) commonly used a particular soft drink instead of wine it was the ecumenical partner at the Consultation (himself a member of a denomination that commonly uses grape juice) who questioned whether the substance in question could bear the theological weight of the blood of Christ If deviations are to be made, we must ask what is their symbolic significance and consequently their theological significance?

3. New Liturgical Texts

New liturgical texts continue to appear in the various provinces of the Communion. The Church of England continues to work at its *Common Worship* series, which has already provided valuable models for the consideration of other provinces. The Church of the Province of Kenya is in the publication process even as I write. I had hoped to have a copy of their new Prayer Book at this meeting of the Council, but expect to have one soon. It is important that copies of all the material we produce be sent to me for location with our permanent collection.

Launch of the Anglican Web Portal

—The Reverend Canon Ogé Beauvoir

Dr. Carey, Bishop Chiwanga, Members of the Anglican Consultative Council, Canon Peterson and Canon Rosenthal. Thank you for this opportunity to celebrate with you the expansion of a very significant communications initiative.

I bring you greetings from Trinity Wall Street, especially from the Rector of the Parish The Reverend Dr. Daniel Paul Matthews, the members of the Trinity Grants Board, and the Deputy for Grants, The Reverend James G. Callaway, Jr.

Today we are celebrating the launch—the start—of an expanded telecommunications ministry by the Anglican Consultative Council and the Anglican Communion Office.

The centerpiece of this initiative is the development of an "Anglican Web Portal," a special web site with web pages that will serve the communication and program functions of the ACC and will also be the focal point for every official Anglican web site across the entire Anglican Communion.

This builds on more than a decade of commitment to and successful use of the Internet and the Inter-Anglican Information Network for email intercommunication and electronic publishing.

And it also builds on the experience of the growing number of Anglican web sites that have been launched in recent years, especially those in the global south where we have a large number of new Anglicans.

Many Provinces, dioceses, and missionary organizations are developing their own information networks.

In consultations conducted by Trinity Grants with telecommunication leaders in various parts of the Communion, it became clear that there is a need to create a more comprehensive web site that would help web visitors identify and find and make use of information and resources on all of the official web pages in the Anglican Communion.

At this point, allow me to tell you how Trinity Wall Street got involved in strengthening telecommunications in the Anglican Communion.

In 1984, Dr. Bruce Merrifield, then Chairman of the Trinity Grants Board, suggested that Trinity should develop a special focus on telecommunications as a means of empowering the Anglican Communion in the Southern hemisphere, the third-world countries. Dr. Merrifield was concerned that the exponential development in computing and electronic communication would leave those Anglican churches even further behind the developed world than they already were.

The challenge from Dr. Merrifield was to "level the playing field". The Trinity Grants Program adopted it, and since, Trinity has made dozens of grants as part of our telecommunications emphasis. They have ranged from Provinces and dioceses in Africa, Latin America & the Caribbean, and South East Asia to Ecumenical organization like All Africa Conference of Churches, and Communion-wide bodies such as the Anglican Communion Office. Funding everything from network development to training and database creation, we have worked and are still working with partners throughout the Communion to help bridge the digital divide that Dr. Merrifield and others identified as early as 1984.

You will agree with me that the great digital divide has not been yet overcome. However, over the past eighteen years or so, it has been deeply satisfying to see how the sharing of our material resources has enabled our Church partners around the world to access electronic communication. Today, many churches of our worldwide Anglican Communion can tell their stories to the world in a way not possible for most institutions in their societies. Partnership being a two-way street, the capacity-building that our grants have enabled has brought us blessings in return by communicating to us news of their activities, which inspires us so much as we try to be true to the Gospel in our own time and context.

And that is the background of how the pioneering ACO web site is now becoming the official Anglican Web Portal.

The people behind the scenes planning and producing the portal include Canon James Rosenthal, Father Kris Lee of ECUSA, Father Peter Moore of Australia, Mr. Christopher Took of the Anglican Communion Office and a group of telecommunication specialists who have been providing ideas and advice. They include Rev. Dr. Joan Ford, Mr. Thomas Lopez, Mr. Dennis Johnson, and Rev. Canon Emmanuel Adekola. That group will soon include a number of others from around the Anglican Communion. Fr. Lee of ECUSA, who is also adjunct staff to the Anglican Communion Office, has been instrumental to the launch we are celebrating today. He has been, and continues to be, a great asset to the Trinity Grants Program over the years.

The work of the group, under the leadership of Fr. Lee, will become part of the new Inter-Anglican Commission on Telecommunications when that is inaugurated next February.

The Compass Rose Society is the new partner in making the Anglican Web Portal dream becomes true. Through its Executive Director, Bishop Herbert Donovan, the Compass Rose Society has already made a significant contribution toward that project, and will continue to do so in the years to come.

The Trinity Grants Program is pleased to provide funding to the ACO for web portal development, and for the hiring of a full-time web manager, Christopher Took, and also for the work of the new Inter-Anglican Commission on Telecommunications.

There is one who must be acknowledged for setting the tone and providing the leadership through the years for the exploration and use of these emerging communication technologies for the work and witness of the Church. The web portal planners and countless others in the Church have been greatly motivated by the frequent and tireless encouragement they have received from Archbishop Carey to consider the use of computer tools for mission and ministry.

He has been a model by his avid and enthusiastic and even experimental use of the Internet as a tool for research and intercommunication in his own ministry. Thank you, Archbishop Carey.

The official web portal for the Anglican Communion can be thought of as a "window on the web." The portal will lead people to and point to all official Anglican web sites. The portal will soon point to every official web site published around the world by Anglicans.

And as a special service, the web portal will publish official news and information in co-operation with provinces and dioceses that want to get the attention of the rest of the world but are not vet able on their own to prepare and publish web pages.

The new web portal will also develop a vast library of educational resources that can be viewed, copied or downloaded and used by Christian education leaders or researchers.

The portal will publish material in at least *five of the major world languages* used across the Anglican Communion. We would be grateful to hear from you about the best way to do it.

An intercommunication service of the portal will be email discussion groups that will facilitate business planning or topical discussions by participants in scattered parts of the world. New email groups that have recently started are discussing Mission and Evangelism strategies.

The portal is also planning to offer web pages for the Companion Dioceses program. That will allow companions in different parts of the world not only to learn about each other but to publish greetings, prayers and visitation plans and photographs.

For the first time, private web pages will be offered for official committees and other groups whose members are in different parts of the world. It will allow them to work online collaboratively on drafts of reports and documents before they are published. They will use web pages that are password protected so that only them can see and work with those special pages.

The web portal will offer databases of names and statistics available to the general readership on the Internet, and also selected data for sharing only by those who are given access by a password.

These new databases will also include calendars of conferences and events around the Anglican Communion or listings of Distance Learning such as Theological Education by Extension courses.

We are very mindful of those many regions of the world without high technology or access to the Internet.

For those parts of the Anglican Communion that are in those regions the web portal will be helpful in sensitizing and mobilizing Anglicans in other parts of the world to increase their partnerships in hands-on mission and ministry and to increase their outreach contributions.

As more Anglicans learn about the needs of their sisters and brothers in the Sudan or Congo, or Sierra Leone, for example, the more likely will they find creative ways to provide support and personnel to serve there.

While Anglicans in the Sudan or Congo, or Sierra Leone may not have Internet, millions of Anglicans worldwide do and they can become meaningful partners in prayer and mission with them.

Much of the support for people in these dire circumstances has come because modem communication has made their needs known and real in cities and towns and parishes thousands of miles away from the sights and sounds of daily suffering.

Now let's look at the Home Page of the new Anglican Web Portal. Here is what is called the "Home Page," the "Front Page," the "First Page" of the new and official Anglican Web Portal. It is the starting point for finding and using the information and services that the portal will offer. When you visit www.anglicancommunion.org in the next few weeks you will be greeted by this new page.

Here is where the *top news story* of the Anglican Communion News Service will be published. Some stories will include still photos and audio reports. In the future there may also be video stories from ACNS. And here is the *complete web site of Anglican Communion News Service* where you can find all of the current and past news stories and official photos published by ACNS. The latest edition of *Anglican World* magazine will be highlighted in this part of the portal's Home Page. Here is where the *Archbishop of Canterbury* welcomes readers to the Anglican Web Portal and to the Anglican Communion. A very large section of the web portal will offer scholarly essays and stories of *Anglican Spirituality*. Here is an article that gives the reader background on what is meant by Anglican Spirituality. The Anglican Communion Office has developed a very good set of web pages that provide an "online tour" of all Anglican Provinces. Let's have a look at the Anglican Church of Canada. And the Church of Nigeria. And The Anglican Church in Aotearoa, New Zealand and Polynesia. Those are some examples.

The web portal will soon include links to official news releases and photos published by the news and communication offices of the Provinces.

The work done by the Anglican Consultative Council programs and networks will have their own web pages. Here, for example, is where you can select pages of about "Mission and Evangelism" or about "Ecumenical and Doctrinal Studies" or about "Ministry Networks."

Anglican agencies and organizations, too, can be found on the Anglican Web Portal. Here is the link to "The Compass Rose Society," and here is the link to "Anglican Internet Services".

In the Anglican Cycle of Prayer, yesterday, Sunday (September 22), Anglicans around the world prayed for the Church of Nigeria, its ministries and its primate, Archbishop Peter Akinola. And to learn more about the Church of Nigeria that they prayed for, church members and leaders across the Anglican Communion can use the Internet to have a look at the web pages published online by our colleagues in Nigeria. And if you want to find out what the web address is for the Church of Nigeria web pages, you would need only to check the Anglican Web Portal and you will find the web address there, as well as statistics and information and highlights about mission and ministry in Nigeria.

The Anglican Web Portal will take you instantly across the miles to the places where we have brothers and sisters in the Anglican Communion. And we will pray not only for them but also with them and *we will be able more effectively than ever before to work with each other as Christ's presence in the world.*

Joining me is The Reverend Canon Emmanuel Adekola, Director of Communications for the Church of Nigeria. He is a member of Task Force working with the ACO Communications department toward the development of the Anglican Web Portal. The Primate of Nigeria,

Archbishop Akinola, is an experienced user of electronic communication. And he is now building in the Church of Nigeria, our fastest growing Anglican Province, a huge and private telecommunications network to interconnect all of his dioceses. With the network, the leadership will be able to stay in close and frequent contact even though their offices are great distances from each other. The network is also publishing an official web site for Nigeria and is part of the new Anglican Web Portal.

24 SEPTEMBER 2002

Report of the Colleges and Universities of the Anglican Communion (CUAC)

Application for "Network" Status

The Colleges and Universities of the Anglican Communion (CUAC), The Episcopal Church Center, 815 Second Avenue, #315, New York, NY 10017

Background

The Colleges and Universities of the Anglican Communion (CUAC) was formed as a world-wide association of Anglican colleges and universities of higher education as a result of an International Conference of representatives assembled at Canterbury in 1993 (Christ Church College, UK), to be:

> a continuing association in the spirit of mutual respect, reciprocity and support

in order to:

- enhance international/intercultural understanding through education
- examine issues of values within the context of church-related higher education
- examine further the potential within the Anglican Communion to serve God and the world more effectively, imaginatively and creatively

through:

- development of visits and exchanges for students, faculty and administrators
- engagement in volunteer service to people in need
- scheduled meetings and conferences on topics related to higher education
- regular communication by bulletins and newsletters
- joint curricular development

- sharing of institutional and educational resources
- scholarly journals, research, and joint degrees

Activity

Since its inception in 1993, CUAC has established Internet, FAX, and mail communication with between 140–150 member institutions in some 16 countries. It has created yearly two to three Service Learning programs for students of its member institutions variously in the United Kingdom, the Philippines, India, Canada, Ecuador, United States, and Japan. Student scholarships have been made available for those whose institutions have limited resources or negative exchange rates.

CUAC has facilitated student and faculty exchanges and cultural visits between different member institutions across the world. It provides some financial support for institutions participating in these endeavors.

It has established a M.A. program in affiliation with the International Partnership for Service Learning and the University of Surrey Roehampton, UK. which provides opportunities to reflect on the nature of Service Learning for post-graduate students. CUAC maintains a regular international Newsletter *Compass Points* published at least once a year, and it established the international journal *Prologue* in 1999 to circulate research and literature of interest and resource to Anglican institutions of higher education. It has published three volumes to date.

CUAC arranges for its membership to meet every three years in different representative areas of the Anglican Communion, those being Canterbury (1993), New Delhi (1996), Toronto (1999), and Tokyo (2002). Most delegates are supported by their home institutions to attend such a conference, but CUAC provides Travel Scholarships to enable an equitable cross section of representation world-wide.

In the past five years, regional and national "Chapters" of CUAC have been formed or recognized (UK, USA, Canada, India, Japan, Australia) to further the national and provincial work of the Communion in higher education generally.

Finance and Organization

In 1999, one of the founders of CUAC, the US Association of Episcopal Colleges (AEC), a voluntary association of colleges and universities of ECUSA, contributed its organizational structure and a small endowment to enable the furthering of both CUAC as an international association, and the AEC as an American "Chapter" of CUAC. The two organizations are currently being provided rent free offices in the Episcopal Church Center (at a value of $25,000. USD) as the contribution of the Episcopal Church to their ministry. The CUAC-AEC endowment makes possible the operation of a central office at the Episcopal Church Center in New York and provides oversight, networking and support for both organizations through the services of a General Secretary and support staff (60% CUAC, 40% AEC) on an operating budget of about $175,000. USD.

Limitations and Opportunities

There is no doubt that an association such as CUAC could not survive without the inexpensive communication resources of the Internet, and the collaboration it enables in terms of international programs. As this technology of communication expands in both reach and capability, so too can the programs and services of CUAC expand to be an effective instrument of communion in the field of higher education.

CUAC's field of operation to date has simply been those institutions of higher education which are a "college or university associated by history and tradition with the Anglican Communion or an association of such institutions". Its membership follows those nations and cultures which saw the establishment of Anglican colleges and universities within the colonial era, and whose subsequent history did not involves loss of the ecclesiastical tie of these institutions. This produces discrepancies in the "mirror" of CUAC to the Anglican Communion, the most obvious one being the absence of Anglican colleges and universities in South Africa, as a result of the Anglican opposition to apartheid.

However, it has been clear from CUAC's initiation in 1993, that there are many nationalities and cultures where the presence of the church in higher education is held by theological colleges and seminaries. Many such institutions have shown interest in CUAC to provide an instrument of communion for them in the world arena, just as CUAC has begun to fulfill that need for Anglican colleges and universities within higher education.

To this end, the 2002 Triennial Conference of CUAC mandated its association to:

- form a Task Force of representatives of both theological college and higher education colleges and universities to explore and research the creation of a second "current" within CUAC of theological colleges and seminaries.
- identify and collect addresses of Anglican theological colleges and seminaries world wide.
- solicit financial support to help CUAC contact and research the interests and needs of such institutions
- invite such institutions, if they are interested, to form an international association of theological colleges and seminaries as an autonomous "current" of theological colleges within CUAC, and

possibly to share with higher education colleges and universities those administrative and communicative functions which may easily and efficiently be maintained jointly.

There is no doubt that CUAC can function as one of the instruments of unity of the Anglican Communion.

Conclusion

The Colleges and Universities of the Anglican Communion (CUAC) therefore requests the Anglican Consultative Council to recognize CUAC as a Network of the Anglican Communion in the general area of colleges and universities of higher education (including theological colleges and seminaries if, after consultation, they so wish).

In this respect, at its recent Triennial Meeting in Tokyo (March 18, 2002) CUAC approved the following:

4) Application to the Anglican Consultative Council for Network status.

The following guidelines for Networks adopted by the Anglican Consultative Council were presented to the meeting:

The Anglican Consultative Council may recognize Networks addressing particular themes and concerns throughout the Anglican Communion on application, in accordance with the following guidelines. The Networks shall be identified in the published edition of the minutes of the meeting of the Council.

1. *(a) The subject matter of the Network shall be consistent with and supportive of the initiatives of the Provinces and member Churches of the Communion.*

   (b) The Network shall identify an acceptable process of accountability to the Anglican Consultative Council.

   (c) Through the Secretary General the Network may propose subjects for consideration by the Anglican Consultative Council and shall be available whenever possible to consult on subjects on which its members hold expertise.

   (d) The Secretary General of the Anglican Consultative Council shall call meetings of representatives of the Networks for mutual consultation from time to time and may on occasion invite representatives of the Networks to meet with the Joint Standing Committees.

2. *(a) Networks are encouraged to seek funding for their budgets from any appropriate source, in consultation with the Secretary General.*

(b) Networks receiving funds from the budget of the Anglican Consultative Council shall account for their use, as required by the Standing Committee of the Council.

(c) Networks seeking all or part of their budget by general appeals to the Provinces and member Churches of the Anglican Communion should obtain permission of the Secretary General of the Anglican Consultative Council.

Motion: That CUAC apply to the Anglican Consultative Council to be recognized as an official "Network" of the Anglican Communion.

Carried Unanimously.

Anglican Communion Legal Advisers' Consultation Report

—THE REVEREND CANON JOHN REES, LEGAL ADVISER

Primates' Terms of Reference

At the Primates' Meeting in Kanuga, USA, March 2001, it was agreed that:

> *A conference of Legal Advisers of the Provinces will be held to give follow up to Professor Norman Doe's paper, looking at the parameters of an identifiable Anglican common law and how an understanding of such common law can enhance our global Communion.Cross-linking to the relevant ongoing ecclesiological studies under way by IASCER is desirable.(Action Plan)*

A Consultation of Legal Advisers took place at the new International Study Centre in Canterbury (UK) between 6–13 March 2002.

Legal Advisers

Provincial Representation

Seventeen Provinces and Churches were represented at the Consultation. This was a good representation but we were aware that it was under half of the Provinces. You will find the individual Legal Advisers' brief biographies in Appendix I to this report. Each addressed the consultation, giving details of:

- his or her own Province or Church,
- its canonical and legal structure, and
- current legal issues facing it.

Expert Resources

The Legal Advisers were addressed by Professor Norman Doe of the University of Wales, Professor Richard Helmholz of the University of Chicago, and the Reverend Canon David Hamid of the Anglican Consultative Council. Copies of their addresses and notes are available on request, or may be downloaded from www.anglicancommunion.org.

The themes which each speaker addressed were:

Professor Norman Doe

The core of Professor Doe's paper was the material provided to the Primates' Meeting at Kanuga in 2001. This paper had been further refined since that meeting and has been published in the *Ecclesiastical Law Journal.* In addition, Professor Doe gave an introductory talk on underlying jurisprudential issues and introduced the material for seminar discussion.

Professor Richard Helmholz

Professor Helmholz drew upon his expertise as an ecclesiastical legal historian of great distinction. He explained the background to the development of Anglican canon law from its pre-Reformation roots, through the Reformation period (where he emphasised particularly the continuities, rather than the discontinuities) and the formative role of Richard Hooker's *Laws of Ecclesiastical Polity*.

The Reverend Canon David Hamid

Canon Hamid gave a wide-ranging and provocative address in which he discussed the *koinonia* of Christianity worldwide, the essential structure of Churches, their relationships with one another, the nature of 'communion' as contrasted with federation or monolithic styles of organisation; and the 'provisionality' of Anglicanism.

Principles of Canon Law Common to the Anglican Communion

General Propositions

In the light of these presentations we examined (in groups and in plenary sessions) 'the parameters of an identifiable Anglican common law', and established the following propositions:

1. There are principles of canon law common to the Churches within the Anglican Communion.

2. Their existence can be factually established.

3. Each Anglican Province or Church contributes through its own legal system to the principles of canon law common within the Anglican Communion.

4. These principles have a strong persuasive authority and are fundamental to the self-understanding of each of the Churches in the Communion represented amongst us.

5. These principles have a living force, and contain in themselves the possibility for further development.

6. The existence of these principles both demonstrates unity and promotes unity within the Anglican Communion.

Evidence for the Propositions

We used a range of criteria to determine whether a principle is part of the canon law common within the Anglican Communion.

Professor Doe helpfully provided several examples of principle drawn from various laws he had examined. Working from these we found that there is a high degree of unity on various central aspects of the life of our Churches.

Applying the same approach to a selection of principles, we tested them against the laws of the Churches represented by the Legal Advisers attending the Consultation. Here again, we found a high degree of commonality of approach among the Churches of the Communion.

Examples

We examined shared principles, under six headings, namely:

- Order in the Church
- Ecclesiastical Government
- Ministry
- Doctrine, Liturgy and Rites
- Church Property
- Inter-Anglican Relations

These were offered not as an exhaustive statement but as a cluster of examples around which we were able to achieve broad consensus.

Shared Problems

As the result of the personal presentations from each of the legal advisers, we identified a number of current legal issues which are of concern to the Churches. We attach as Appendix II some examples of these. We considered them, and agreed that there is a pressing need for further work by the Churches, with the assistance of their Legal Advisers, on these issues.

Many of the issues raise questions of policy, but once more this exercise demonstrated the high degree of commonality among the Churches.

Recommended Action

The legal advisers recommended that the Primates' Meeting request ACC-12 to establish a Network of Legal Advisers, which will:

1. produce a statement of principles of Canon Law common within the Communion;

2. examine shared legal problems and possible solutions;

3. provide reports to the Joint Standing Committee of the Primates Meeting and the Anglican Consultative Council as the work progresses.

The Primates' Meeting in April 2002 endorsed this recommendation, and now make this request to ACC-12.

Appendix I
Brief Biographical Information About Participants

Anderson, Charles

Charles Anderson is the Head of the Legal Department of the Church in Wales Provincial Office with responsibility for legal advice to the Bench of Bishops, the Governing Body, the Representative Body and their respective committees. Prior to this position, he worked for 21 years in private practice both in London and the provinces.

Bleby, David

He has been Justice of the Supreme Court of South Australia since 1997. He is Chancellor of the Diocese of Adelaide and Member of the Appellate Tribunal of the Anglican Church of Australia (ACA). He is also the Chairman of the Church Law Commission of the ACA and Chair of the Committees of the General Synod of the ACA. He is, in addition, a Member of the Standing Committee of the General Synod and of the Diocesan Council of the Diocese of Adelaide.

Bracks, Raynold Paul

Admitted in 1986 as an Attorney and in 1999 was admitted as an Advocate of the High Court of South Africa. He specialises in Corporate Law. He serves on a voluntary and part-time basis as the Registrar of CPSA and the Vice-Chancellor of the Diocese of Johannesburg, one of the Dioceses of the CPSA. In his own church in the parish of Christ the King Coronationville, he is a Lay Minister and is also chair of his church's council.

He also serves as chair and Executive Member, Trustee and Director of more than 20 NGO's and Church organisations. As a result of his position as Registrar and Vice-Chancellor, he automatically serves as Trustee of various Church Trusts, including the Bishopscourt Trust.

Burrows, Brian

He has been Chancellor of the Ecclesiastical Province of Rupert's Land (one of the four provinces of the Anglican Church of Canada) since 1992, former Chancellor (1987 to 1997) and Vice-Chancellor (1983 to 1987) of the Diocese of Edmonton.

Currently, he is a Judge of the Court of Queens Bench of Alberta and parishioner at All Saints Cathedral, Edmonton.

Cameron, QC, Sheila

Sheila has recently retired from daily practice at the Bar, where she had had a distinguished practice in planning and parliamentary law. She served in a number of senior ecclesiastical appointments, as Chancellor of the Diocese of Chelmsford for 30 years, and of the London Diocese for 10 years. She has been Vicar-General for Archbishop Robert Runcie and George Carey. She was appointed Dean of the Arches and Auditor in 2001, and serves also as a member of the General Synod of the Church of England.

Cheng, Moses Mo-Chi

He is the Senior Partner of the law firm of Messrs P. C. Woo & Co and also serves as an independent non-executive director of a number of public companies. Between 1991 and 1995 he was appointed and served as a member of the Legislative Council of Hong Kong. Currently, he is serving as chairman and member of the various government advisory boards and committees as well as non-governmental organisations.

He is a member of the vestry of St. Paul's Church, Hong Kong where he has served in various capacities. And the moment, he is serving as the Chancellor of the Province as well as the Diocese of the Hong Kong Island. He also serves as a member of the Standing Commission of Education of the Province.

Davidson, Bruce N.

He is Chancellor of the Diocese of Auckland, New Zealand and member of the General Synod of the Anglican Church in Aotearoa, New Zealand and Polynesia. He has been a barrister and solicitor of the High Court of New Zealand since 1961. He is still in private practice as a lawyer and is a partner in Minter Ellison Rudd Watts, Auckland.

He serves on the boards of several public and private companies, charitable trusts and Southern Cross Healthcare. In addition, and he is a former Council Member and President of the Auckland Law Society and Vice President of the New Zealand Law Society.

Farlam, Ian

Ian Farlam is a Judge of Appeal of the Supreme Court of Appeal of South Africa and Provincial Chancellor of the Church of the Province of South

Africa. He has advised the Synod of Bishops on a number of legal issues including the ordination of female priests and the consecration of female bishops.

Fernando, Deveni Vidanelage Vyoa Sriyanganie

She is an Attorney-at-law holding a Bachelor of Laws degree and a Master of Laws degree. She is presently employed as a Deputy Legal Draftsman in the Legal Draftsman Department in Sri Lanka. She has been actively involved in the work of the Diocese of Colombo and in the local Parish and was appointed as the Registrar of the Diocese in 1999.

Georges, Bernard

Barrister (Gray's Inn 1978), Attorney of the Supreme Court of Seychelles (1981) and Notary (1980). He is a Member of the National Assembly of Seychelles (2001). He is also in private legal practice in the Seychelles as well as being the Diocesan Secretary and Chancellor of the Anglican Diocese of Seychelles.

He is Chancellor of the Church of the Province of the Indian Ocean and a member of the Anglican Consultative Council.

Giwa-Amu, Steven I. O.

He was called to the Bar at the Inner Temple, London in February 1958. Between 1966 and 1970, he was the Solicitor General of Midwestern Nigeria. He still remains a legal consultant to the firm of Giwa-Amu & Co., solicitors and advocates. He became a Knight of St Christopher in 1994 and was elected Provincial Registrar of the Church of Nigeria in 1997.

Hitt, Lawrence R.

He is the national president of the Association of Chancellors in the United States (the Episcopal Chancellors' Network). Mr Hitt has served as Chancellor of the Diocese of Colorado since 1990 and has been elected four times as a General Convention Deputy. He is also a judge on the Province VI appellate court of review and a member of the Province's Executive Council.

For fourteen years, he has served as a national officer and director of the charitable organisation, Big Brothers, Big Sisters of America. In addition, he works in private practice in Denver and serves on the boards of several governmental and non-profit organisations.

Hoskins, Richard

Richard is the Chancellor of the Episcopal Diocese of Chicago and is a senior lecturer at Northwestern University School of Law.

He is also a Member of the Standing Commission on Constitution and Canons of the Episcopal Church. He is the Senior Partner and Partner-in-charge of the Intellectual Property Group of Schiff Hardin & Waite, Chicago. He is a Fellow of the American College of Trial Lawyers and of the American Bar Foundation and also serves on the Visiting Committee of the University of Chicago Divinity School.

Kim, Chin Man

Professor Kim has studied medieval English literature at University College, London and then taught at Korea University, Seoul and other institutions until 1996. Since 1996 he has taught Anglicanism at Sunggonghoe (Anglican) University. He has also served as a delegate to three meetings of the Anglican Consultative Council.

Lalwet, Floyd P.

Mr Lawlet is presently the Associate Chancellor and in-house Legal Counsel of the Episcopal Church in the Philippines. He also lectures on Canon Law at the St Andrews Theological Seminary. Aside from engaging in private practice, he is presently Deputy Director for the National Legal Aid Committee of the Integrated Bar of the Philippines.

Majok, Majok Mading

Majok Marding Majok graduated in law from the University of Khartoum in 1981 and since then has been working as a Government Attorney. In addition, he holds a PostGraduate diploma in International Relations, having majored in international law. He has been a member of the Synod of the Diocese of Renk and since 1996, been Chancellor of that Diocese as well. In 2000, he was a member of the Electoral College that elected the new Archbishop and was consequently appointed as Chancellor of the Episcopal Church of the Sudan.

Newell, Lawrence Michael

He is the Chancellor of the Anglican Church of Papua New Guinea and was admitted as a barrister and solicitor in Papua New Guinea in 1975. He is admitted to practice in Australia and is a Fellow of the Institute of Legal Executives in the United Kingdom.

He has held various positions within the Papua New Guinea Law Department and then with the Department of Prime Minister before becoming Registrar the Supreme and National Court of Papua New Guinea (as well as Sheriff and Admiralty Marshall). He is also a member of various government committees, particularly in the field of law and order.

Phay, U Mya

He is currently the finance director of Myanma Petrochemical Enterprise, a member of the Yangon Diocesan Trust Association, former Chairman of the Planning in Finance Committee of the Church of the Province of Myanmar. In addition, he is Legal Advisor to the Myanmar Church and Treasurer of the Myanmar Council of Churches.

Ramadhani, Augustino

Justice Ramadhani is a Justice of Appeal of the Court of Appeal of Tanzania, Judge of the East African Court of Justice and Vice-Chairman of the National Electoral Commission of Tanzania. He is also Registrar of the Anglican Church of Tanzania.

Rees, John

John Rees is a solicitor and partner in the firm of Winkworth Sherwood, which has branches in both Oxford and Westminster. He is the Provincial Registrar for the Archbishop of Canterbury, and Legal Adviser to the Anglican Consultative Council. He has served on the General Synod, and is Vice-Chairman of the Legal Advisory Committee of the Church of England.

As a priest of the Church of England, his strong interest in Anglican Communion affairs derives from service as a volunteer hospital administrator before ordination, at Multan in Pakistan; and as a lecturer in Christian Ethics for several years in an ecumenical theological College in Freetown, Sierra Leone.

Stevenson, QC, Ronald

He was in general legal practice between 1953 and 1972 and was a Judge of the Court of Queens Bench of New Brunswick between 1972 and 1994. And roughly the same time, he was Chancellor of the Diocese of Fredericton (1977–1989). In 1989, he was installed as Chancellor of the Ecclesiastical Province of Canada and remained so until 2000.

He has also been heavily involved in the General Synod of the Anglican Church of Canada since 1986 and its Chancellor since 1999.

Appendix II
Shared Problems

Below is a list of current legal issues identified and considered by the Legal Advisers attending the Consultation:

1. Clergy and secular employment law.
2. Applicability of Civil Law standards to the Church.
3. Recourse by Church Members to the Courts of the State.
4. Child Protection.

5. Arbitrary action by Bishops.
6. Clergy Maintenance.
7. Financial Contributions to the Church.
8. Secret Societies.
9. Discrimination against people within the Church.
10. Marriage and Polygamy.
11. Clergy and Political Activity.
12. An understanding of Church Law by Church members (clergy etc).
13. Inter-Anglican Relations: Recognition of Ministry.
14. Inter-Anglican Relations: Territorial Jurisdiction.
15. Minority Dissent and Disagreement within the Church.

Report of The Executive Council for French-speaking Anglicans Throughout the World

—THE REVEREND CANON OGÉ BEAUVOIR
(PRESENTED IN FRENCH)

On behalf of the members of the Executive Council, I thank you very much for giving us these precious minutes of your time. Above all, we are grateful to you for your unconditional support to the work of our group.

Among the seventy-two million Anglicans reported throughout the world, many do not speak English as their first language. Apart from millions of Anglicans worshipping in Swahili and other local languages in Africa, in many other parts of the world nearly another four million speak, read, and worship in Portuguese (110,000), in Spanish (170,000), and nearly three million in French; and the non-English-speaking Church continues to grow. The French-speaking community is the oldest in the world of non-English Anglicanism. As early as the sixteenth century, French-speaking Anglicans were using a French translation of the Book of Common Prayer.

Creation of RENCONTRES

In 1985, a group of French-speaking Anglicans, under the leadership of The Reverend Canon Dr. Jacques Bossiere, founded the Asociation Rencontres at the American Cathedral of the Holy Trinity in Paris with the following objectives:

1. to identify the French-speaking Anglican Churches in the world;
2. to stimulate and encourage their activities;
3. to assist them with all possible means, especially in the area of the theological education of clergy and laity.

Very quickly, Rencontres reached out to:

- French-speaking Provinces of Africa: Burundi, Congo, Indian Ocean, Rwanda;
- The Anglican Church of Canada (dioceses of Montreal, Ottawa and Quebec);
- The Episcopal Church of USA (dioceses of Haiti, New York, and Southeast Florida, the Convocation of the American Churches in Europe);

- The Province of West Africa (diocese of Guinea, and the Missionary Area of Cameroon).

Fellow English-speaking Anglicans around the world welcomed the creation of Rencontres. In 1988, its founder, Dr. Jacques Bossiere, attended Lambeth Conference as observer. And the full recognition of the francophones presence within the Communion came when the Primate of the Anglican Church of Canada, Archbishop Michael Peers, presided, for the first time in French, over one of the sessions of Lambeth Conference.

French-speaking Gatherings

Limuru, Kenya, 1996
The first International Conference on French-speaking Anglicanism was held in Limuru, Kenya in March 1996. ANITEPAM, the African Network of Institutions of Theological Education Preparing Anglicans for Ministry, has been instrumental in organizing that meeting. Dedicated to the formation of English-speaking clergy, ANITEPAM recognized immediately the need for and the advantage of an organization focused on Francophone Anglican ministry.

The goal of that first meeting of French-speaking Anglicans was to provide an opportunity for the participants to share their experiences, and reflect together on the priorities regarding theological education in French throughout the Anglican Communion. Each member of the conference was fully aware of the sufferings engendered by war and political conflict in many areas of French-speaking Anglican world, and of the impact that might have on the training of the church leadership.

In addition to the important work of the conference, the participants were able to share a week of prayer, and Bible study, while discovering their diversity and the richness of so much held in common in their lives and ministries. They resolved to establish a partnership, which would promote effective communication between themselves and their churches, and other Anglican organizations, especially those which are English-speaking, in order to discover and utilize theological, human, spiritual, and material resources available throughout the Anglican Communion.

The participants affirmed that the Church cannot exist apart from the culture in which it lives, and that all aspects of the Church's life (theological, spiritual, pastoral, liturgical, and artistic) make up the work of evangelization which reaches out to all.

That first conference provided the opportunity to representatives from thirteen nations to meet and to enjoy an unparalleled fellowship, established a foundation for future collaboration among French-speaking Anglicans worldwide.

The Executive Council for French-speaking Anglican throughout the Anglican Communion was created at Limuru in 1996. Its purpose is to serve as liaison among the consultative and executive organizations of the Anglican Communion. The Executive Council has been approved as a Non-Governmental Organization (NGO) with consultative status at the United Nations. In the first two years of its existence, the Executive Council has established and deepened a network of collaborative relationships with ANITEPAM, the CLCF (or Center for Christian Literature in French), SPCK (the Society for the Promotion of Christian Knowledge), and the Anglican Communion Office. The Most Rev. Michael Peers, Primate of Canada, agreed to be named Honorary President of the Executive Council.

Canterbury, England, 1998
The second meeting of the Executive Council took place in July 1998 in Canterbury in the days preceding the Lambeth Conference. Because of the unique timing of the two conferences, the Executive Council was able to invite all of the French-speaking bishops as well as observers and theologians from the Reformed Church, the Roman Catholic Church, and a diverse representation from the nations of the Anglican Communion. During the Canterbury conference, many excellent papers were presented by our Anglican colleagues, and invited guests from other Churches. All of these contributed greatly to our understanding of the issues facing the non-English-speaking Anglican world. The papers presented addressed the key issue of inculturation in language and practice in Africa, France, Haiti, Canada, and the Indian Ocean.

At that second conference, the Executive Council established a Commission of French-speaking Theologians to be directed by the Rev. Isingoma K. Kahwa Henri, Director of the Theological Institute of Bunia. Shortly after his return to the Congo, the Rev. Isingoma was called to be the Bishop of the Diocese of Katanga, but has continued to serve as the Commission director. An important source of support for this commission will be the establishment of centers for the selection, translation, and distribution of theological texts in French.

The Rev. Dr. Jacques Bossière, President of the Executive Council, concluded the Canterbury conference with the following reflections:

1. French-speaking Anglicanism continues to grow with approximately forty bishops and the creation of new dioceses.

2. There has been an expansion in the number and depth of publications in French, including the Rencontres Newsletter in English and French, the *Cahiers de l'Anglicanisme, L'Episcopalien,* and the publication in French of the revues from CAPA and ANITEPAM.

3. The Executive Council continues to promote and support more extensive ecumenical relationships with French-speaking Churches both locally and internationally.

Paris, France, 2000
The third meeting of French-speaking Anglican bishops and theologians took place in Paris in May 2000. The theme of this important meeting was "Justice, Reconciliation, and Peace in Jesus Christ, Roots of a Living Faith." Bishop Jeffrey Rowthorn of the Convocation of American Churches in Europe gave his full support to the project.

The participants agreed that Anglicanism needs to be "de-anglicized" so as to allow the integration of all cultures into the work and worship of the Anglican Communion. Bishops, priests, lay delegates, and theologians from Africa, the Indian Ocean, Haiti, Seychelles, France, Canada, and the United States participated.

Île Maurice, Océan Indien, 2003
The fourth meeting of the French-speaking Anglicans will take place in Mauritius next year.

Future of the Executive Council

Our future within the Anglican Communion is really bound to yours. We are all part of that Anglican mosaic where unity in the diversity should be protected. The Executive Council intends to continue to work with you toward a better integration of the French-speaking Anglicans into the worldwide Anglican Communion. Our diversity and differences should be celebrated, but not be used as source of conflicts or division. Therefore, the Executive Council for French-speaking Anglicans throughout the world request to be granted the status of Network in the Anglican Communion. Such recognition will clearly express that spirit of acceptation and tolerance, which has been, over the centuries, a great characteristic of Anglicanism, and an important aspect of our ecclesiology.

Conclusion

As I conclude, let me thank publicly all of you who have been supporting our ministry morally and also financially. We are deeply grateful to the Anglican Church of Canada, especially the National Church and the Diocese of Montreal, and the Episcopal Church of the United States of America. Thanks to the Secretary General of the Anglican Communion, Canon John Peterson, for his ongoing support to the Executive Council. Special thanks to Canon David Hamid, of the Anglican communion Office, who never stops working toward the full integration of the francophones and other minorities into the life of the worldwide Anglican Communion.

25 SEPTEMBER 2002

Sermon at the Closing Eucharist

—The Right Reverend Dr. Simon E. Chiwanga

Performing With Care Our Ministry As Christ's Ambassadors (2 Corinthians 5:18–20)

In the name of the Father, the Son and the Holy Spirit, Amen.

> *All authority in heaven and on earth has been given to me. Therefore go and make disciples of all nations, baptizing them in the name of the Father and of the Son and of the Holy Spirit, and teaching them to obey everything I have commanded you. And surely I am with you always, to the very end of the age (Math. 28:18–20).*

At this Closing Eucharist, we are offering our praise and thanks to God for completing successfully the 12th Meeting of the Anglican Consultative Council, we are commissioning those who have been called to various positions of leadership in the ACC, and therefore, with them we are offering ourselves, as we will pray at the end of the Eucharist, to be sent "into the world in peace . . . to love and serve with gladness and singleness of heart." These two events, our rich experiences at the 12th ACC Meeting, the gospel and the other readings for today, all remind us of the Great Commission, our being sent to proclaim Christ to the world.

The Bible uses various images to describe those sent by God on mission. Today, in this short homily, I want to focus on an image that St. Paul uses—Ambassadors of Christ.

> *All this is from God, who reconciled us to himself through Christ and gave us the ministry of reconciliation; that God was reconciling the world to himself in Christ, not counting men's sins against them. And he has committed to us the message of reconciliation. We are therefore Christ's ambassadors, as though God was making his appeal through us (2 Cor. 5:18–20).*

The whole Church, not just individual Christians, is called to be an ambassador of Christ. In the Epistle we read today St. Paul says that God's intention "was that now, through the Church, the manifold wisdom of God should be made known to the rulers and authorities in the heavenly realms, according to his eternal purpose which he accomplished in Christ Jesus our Lord."

What does it require to be an ambassador? No doubt there are many answers, but I want to focus on one particular answer that is given in the question our President, the Archbishop of Canterbury, will ask those to be commissioned:

> *You have been called to this ministry.*
> *Will you perform it* ***with care***
> *to the honour of God and to the benefit of the Church?*

It is the idea of performing our calling *with care* so that God can be honoured and the Church can benefit that I want to lift before you today as I leave the Chair of ACC.

The Gospel reading we have just heard puts before us the great commission that our Lord has given to His church, and we take it with us—every one of us—as we leave ACC-12 and go back to our Provinces, to our Dioceses, to our Parishes.

Of course, we take many things with us—things we have seen and heard and done together. How are we going to present these to our constituencies **with care** so that God can be honoured and the Church can benefit, without transferring our personal frustrations and bitterness to the extent of obscuring the essential lessons and blessings we have experienced together. As it has been said in many occasions, there are many more things that unite us and worth telling than those which divide or hurt us. How are you going to tell the story of ACC-12 with care so that God can be honoured and your Church can benefit? I was particularly moved by the insightful contribution of Mrs. Elizabeth Braver, one of the delegates from England, when she drew our attention to the need to formulate our resolutions **with care**. She said, "We must not give any who would speak ill of us the ammunition to threaten the good work we have done." That to me is a good example of performing our ministry, as ambassadors, with care so that God can be honoured and the Church can benefit, instead of benefiting the devil.

Performing our ministry with care means also trying as much as possible not to hurt the conscience of others. The image of the body that we read in the Epistle to Ephesians demands that when one member hurts the whole body hurts. Often in our struggles for perfection the damage we do to others is almost unforgivable, especially when the hurt and abuse that we hurl at each other becomes our goal, becomes something we thrive on. While being honest about our convictions might we be also honest that we don't always understand the plight that someone next to us lives. How can there indeed be a sense of covenant that we were reminded of in the Old Testament lesson? It is so easy to engage in bashing of this person or that group for whatever reason it might be. It is often then very embarrassing or even awkward that the person we have just dismissed agrees with us on the next topic of the agenda.

The sense of building community and indeed communion has never been easy, but our Lord never had it easy either. His tiny band of men, twelve, even with only twelve there was the sense of competition, huge problems, ego and most devastating of all, betrayal. Betrayal, dishonesty is the complete antithesis, the complete reversal of what we claim as members of the Anglican family of Churches. The quote from John 8 verse 32 circles the cross of St George in the compass rose of the ACC: "The truth shall make you free." When we cloak the truth, when the truth is not in us, we die. We die a spiritual death, we die a death that is so hard to bear, that it becomes difficult for us to even look at ourselves in a mirror. Again, the Apostle Paul wrote, "Speak the truth in love," and that also means Love and speak the truth."

We shall also take with us the worship in which we have taken part in the various Churches of this vibrant, caring and evangelizing Hong Kong Sheng Kung Hui. There was the sharing of our faith and of our experiences in our Bible Study groups, the ecumenical greetings which have been given with such warmth, the presentation on HIV/AIDS, the reports of the Networks, and the resolutions.

But just below the surface of all our discussions has been the large question—What is the Anglican Communion? How does it order its affairs? How do we learn to trust each other? How do we wrestle together with the questions and the issues that can so easily divide us? In other words, how can we strengthen the bonds of our communion with care so that the mission of God in God's world can be carried out most effectively?

Of all the things I have heard over the last few days, I want to hold onto a word spoken by Bishop Joseph of the Mar Thoma Church in his greetings earlier this week. Do you remember what he said as he spoke about developments in our Communion with which his own church might not necessarily agree? He used these words, "We accept what we can accept; and we respect what we cannot accept."

I believe there is something there that is very important. What we *accept* will be determined for us by our understanding of scripture, of tradition, of reason, and of the mission in which we are all caught up. And though there will be important differences in opinion from time to time, *respect* is still possible if we are able to trust each other's integrity and commitment to the Gospel. That is performing our ministry as ambassadors of Christ with care.

And these things matter because of our belief that the Anglican Communion has an inheritance of faith of which we are rightly proud. We dare to believe that the Anglican Communion has an important contribution to make to that coming great Church for which we pray, that Church in which all who confess the name of Christ are one.

Today's reading from the Old Testament speaks so clearly of not only God's covenant with us but also our covenant with God and our covenant with each other. It is hard to imagine how anyone looking from my perspective today could think or even ponder that it might be possible for such a group to agree or disagree on anything in an unanimous way. Whether it be the reality of a very close vote or the reality that we all face different experiences. We still in our covenant relationship seek to be one with God and with each other.

To be in covenant implies a sense of mutual trust and indeed mutual acceptance. A covenant, whether between friends or with God grows, as we promise with St. Paul in his letter to the Ephesians to say with humble heart "although I am the very least of all the saints this grace was given to me to bring to the gentiles the news of the promises of the riches of Christ" and to make everyone, everyone see what is the plan of the mystery hidden for ages in God who created all things.

I can't help but think also of Isaiah's words we read, as I think about those gathered here who I have had the privilege of serving in my capacity as Chairman of the ACC over the years. The 49th chapter of Isaiah verse 12, the whole concept of covenant verse 8: "I have kept you and given you as a covenant to the people." Isaiah, Paul and the words of Jesus himself are indicative of and speak clearly to the need for us, the Communion, Anglicans around the world to truly be the Body of Christ. We say at the Eucharist "We break this bread to share in the Body of Christ." "We who are many are one. For we all share Christ's bread." Performing our ministry, as ambassadors of Christ, with care will promote the health of the Body of Christ.

And of course at the end of the day it is our unity in our Lord and Savior, Jesus Christ, which is the only thing that matters. It is His incarnation that was the starting point in our Bible Study. It is His ministry of compassion, of healing, of new life, that has shone through the reports of our Networks. It is His call to discipleship that we have tried to hear as we have brought forward our resolutions expressing our concern and our commitment to God's kingdom in God's world today. It is His death and resurrection that we proclaim as the beginning and the end of the faith and the hope and the life that we share in Him. And so we go back to our homes—confident in the God who has given us Himself in Jesus Christ, and who in giving us Himself has given all that we need and all that we have to offer to His world in love.

Whether we are from Africa or the United States, Canada or England it really does not matter from where we come. The struggles for human dignity, the struggle for justice and the struggle for acceptance are ever upon us and with us. How many of us can say that within our own covenants of marriage, in the covenant we have with our families and yes, in our covenant with God, that we are always faithful and caring?

As Anglicans we rejoice in our heritage of relying upon scripture, tradition and reason to guide us in our faith, order, our worship and our service in that tradition. Let us be true agents of those incredible words from the prophet Micah. As I prepare this sermon I realize that many times over the last years I have exalted you my brothers and sisters, while exalting myself and my own Church with the words that Micah so clearly tells us. I commend to you the whole book of Micah but of course nothing says it like the words we find in the eighth verse of the sixth chapter. "He has told you O mortal what is good and what does the Lord require of you but to do justice to love kindness, to walk humbly with your God." I am wondering if in our public displays of disunity how many people have been kept from the saving knowledge of Christ. I wonder how many people turn away from the Church when they see our priorities, our navel gazing and concerns for structures rather than human beings and our call to make disciples.

I salute you in the name of the Risen Christ for the good that we have done together over these years. The Lord is not finished with us yet. We proclaim, "Christ has died, Christ has risen, Christ will come again." And when Christ comes and calls each of us home may we all pray that in that calling he will say, "Well done good and faithful ambassadors. Come share with me the glory, the glory of the Trinity of the saints and light."

I wish you all, including the new leadership of ACC, God's rich blessings, and Goodbye!

Bible Studies and Study Groups

—The Right Reverend Kenneth Fernando, 16 and 17 September
—Dr. Sally Thompson, 18 and 19 September
—Dr. Jenny Plane Te Paa, 21 and 23 September
—The Most Reverend Ian George, 24 and 25 September

16 September 2002
The Rt. Rev. Kenneth Fernando
John 1:1–14

General Introduction

Religions have caused much conflict in our world but they also have the seeds of reconciliation. Better inter-faith relations hold the key to peace within and among nations. In our nations we have to find common ground among the religions on which to build true community. We Christians have a chequered record. We have caused conflict. Examples? We have also sown seeds of reconciliation and peace. Examples ? Will a re-reading of St. John's Gospel help us to establish better inter-faith relations?

Introduction to the Gospel

St. John seeks to communicate with all people and explain the significance of Jesus Christ to the Jewish/Greek/intellectual and rational world of his time and all time. St. John has affinities with St. Paul (Romans 2:14–29 and Acts 17:16–34) and seeks to evaluate other faiths positively. The Gospel is addressed to all people who are concerned about true Life and the way to it and may be ready to hear the Gospel in terms that are related to their religious beliefs and experience. Whatever a person's understanding of salvation may be that expectation is fulfilled and completed by the unique revelation of God in Jesus Christ.

Are there some people who deny absolutes ? And see no need for salvation?

St. John postulates the existence of a Logos—common ground among all (?) people who recognise absolutes. The prologue summarises the whole Gospel:

1. He uses signs that are universally recognised bread, vine, light, water, life.
2. He avoids Jewish thought forms and OT references are few.
3. He is not ecclesio-centric—no last supper—but includes feet washing.
4. There are no miracles only signs.

The Prologue

Verse 1
In the beginning of time? before time? In principle? Primally? At the heart of all things? The Gospel does not begin with Abraham or the nativity. It is set against the background of eternity.

Logos:

1. Jewish Torah—Word of the Lord by which the heavens were made, Prov 3:19 and 8:22-30. It has a substantive existence outside the human mind and existence.

2. Philo—student of Jewish and Greek thought medium of creation and divine government and of intercourse between God and humans.

3. Heraclitus.(fl. 500 BC) taught that Logos is source of order in the world.

4. Rational principle which gives meaning and significance to all existing things like Sanatana Dharma (Hindu) Eternal Natural Law or Tao (Chinese philosophy) the unseen underlying law of the universe from which all other principles and phenomena proceed. And concepts of reality in African, Native Indian and aboriginal myths.

Logos occurs only in the prologue, but the implications of the 14 verses are spelt out in the whole Gospel. (Rev. 19:13; 1 John 1:1–2; Col. 1:15–20). Logos is pre-existent creative, divine.

Verse 2
Logos is not an agent subject to God but God's very self. There is a gradual movement towards a theistic understanding, and here we part company with Greek philosophy and Buddhism.

Verse 4
What is the Life which is found in Logos and in Jesus? (Jn. 20: 31; 5:40; 10:10, 10:28 and 14:6).

Verse 5
Light and Darkness (Jn. 8:12; 9:5; 11:10; 12:35–36; 12:46; and 13:30).
John the Baptist is called in as a witness to point not to himself but to the Light.

Verse 9
True Light: new revelation that lightens every person. Voice of conscience, moral sense, desire to seek truth. "Every check on animal lust felt by the primitive savage, every stimulation to a nobler life in God revealed within his soul." (W. Temple)

All that is noble in all religions and secular ideologies is of God.

In every situation there is always a light piercing the darkness. John the Baptist points to that light.

- What of the post-modernist world ?
- What of Evangelism today ?

Verse 10
A pathetic statement. Why does the world not recognise the Logos ?

Verse 11
Now the reference is clearly to Jesus Christ. Israel like all other nations rejects Him.

Verse 12
Rejected by His own people but received by a few. We are children of light or darkness in so far as we receive Him or reject Him. (Jn. 7:40–43 and 10:19–21)

Verse 13
Plural is more likely than singular. It is a reference to the regeneration of us all which like the birth of Jesus Christ is the activity of God alone. He knew me when I was yet in my mother's womb.

Verse 14
Logos became flesh. Complete identity of word and flesh. God comes down to the human person and takes up the human person to God's self. Spirit and matter are brought together. He pitched His tent among us. For a moment ? His presence among us is an ever present reality. Full of grace and truth. All our strivings after truth now cease. We see him face to face.

His glory is His incarnation and humiliation. It is the glory of the Father (John 14:2).

Bible Study
17 September 2002
The Rt. Rev. Kenneth Fernando
John 4:5–26

Jesus participates in an inter-faith dialogue breaking gender and cultic barriers to present the truth as found in Him.

All cults including the cults of Jerusalem and Gerizim are replaced by worship in spirit and truth.

Earlier in the Gospel water is turned into wine, old temple worship in transformed into a house of prayer, and old life sees a new birth (Nicodemus). Law is replaced by grace and truth (Jn. 1:17).Water was literally life giving in a dry and parched land then as now. People would often have fainted or died in the heat of Palestine.

Wells were places of refreshment and meeting. Jews and Samaritans did not share vessels or wells like so many in the Indian sub-continent even today. Wells are often reserved for special castes and classes of people. A Buddhist story: Ananda says to a woman of the Candala caste, "Dear Sister, I ask not your caste or religion. I only ask for water. Give it to me if you will."

Human need makes brothers and sisters of us all when we feel such needs, express them to others and fulfil the needs of others. This provides a starting point for dialogue.

Women were treated with contempt in Jewish society; Jewish males were not permitted to greet women, not even their wives, in public. Synagogue worship day by day:

> V. Blessed art Thou O lord who hast not made me a woman.
>
> R. (Women) Blessed art Thou O lord who hast fashioned me according to Thy will.

"Samaritan" is a term of abuse in this Gospel. (Jn. 8:48)

The Text

Verse 2
Why did Jesus not baptise?

Verse 5
It was a spring not a well, so it already had flowing, living water provided by Jacob.

Verse 6
At two o'clock in the afternoon Jesus must have been really tired and thirsty. This provided him with an opportunity to start a dialogue.

Verse 8
The disciples had left him alone, providing the opportunity for a one-to-one real dialogue.

Verses 10 and 14
Living water—what does this signify? (Ezekiel and Psalm texts)

Verse 16
God's gifts must be shared. But we must also come to terms with the truth about ourselves before we can receive them.

Verse 18
Five husbands—perhaps there is no allegory here, but plain fact.

Verse 20
The woman is embarrassed by the disclosure of the fact of her many husbands, so she changes the subject.

Verse 22
Salvation is from the Jews. Transitionally. The Jewish faith shone out among the religions around the Mediterranean then.

Verse 23
In spirit and in truth. What does this mean? Can people of other faiths worship in spirit and in truth? The father seeks such persons to worship Him. Only worship in spirit and in truth is acceptable before God.

Verse 26
Yet I that am talking to you I AM.

Bible Study
18 September 2002
Dr. Sally Thompson
I Corinthians 12: 14–26
The Community of Hope

Indeed, the body does not consist of one member but of many. If the foot would say, "Because I am not a hand, I do not belong to the body," that would not make it any less a part of the body. And if the ear would say, "Because I am not an eye, I do not belong to the body," that would not make it any less a part of the body. If the whole body were an eye, where would the hearing be? If the whole body were hearing, where would the sense of smell be? But as it is, God arranged the members in the body, each one of them, as he chose. If all were a single member, where would the body be? As it is, there are many members, yet one body. The eye cannot say to the hand, "I have no need of you," nor again the head to the feet, "I have no need of you." On the contrary, the members of the body that seem to be weaker are indispensable, and those members of the body that we think less honourable we clothe with greater honour, and our less respectable members are treated with greater respect; whereas our more respectable members do not need this. But God has so arranged the body, giving the greater honour to the inferior member, that there may be no dissension within the body, but the members may have the same care for one another. If one member suffers, all suffer together with it; if one member is honoured, all rejoice together with it. (NRSV)

Discussion Questions

Consider as many, or as few, of these questions as you wish. In light of St. Paul's teaching on the body:

- How can we make the diversity of the Anglican Communion a resource rather than divisive?
- How can men and women, in their relationships with each other and their contributions to society, achieve the mutuality spoken of by St. Paul?

- How can the Anglican Communion achieve a greater degree of mutuality and understanding?

Bible Study
19 September 2002
Dr. Sally Thompson
Luke 24:13–35
The Community of Hope

Now on that same day two of them were going to a village called Emmaus, about seven miles from Jerusalem, and talking with each other about all these things that had happened. While they were talking and discussing, Jesus himself came near and went with them, but their eyes were kept from recognising him. And he said to them, "What are you discussing with each other while you walk along?" They stood still, looking sad. Then one of them, whose name was Cleopas, answered him, "Are you the only stranger in Jerusalem who does not know the things that have taken place there in these days?" He asked them, "What things?" They replied, "The things about Jesus of Nazareth, who was a prophet mighty in deed and word before God and all the people, and how our chief priests and leaders handed him over to be condemned to death and crucified him. But we had hoped that he was the one to redeem Israel. Yes, and besides all this, it is now the third day since these things took place. Moreover, some women of our group astounded us. They were at the tomb early this morning, and when they did not find his body there, they came back and told us that they had indeed seen a vision of angels who said that he was alive. Some of those who were with us went to the tomb and found it just as the women had said, but they did not see him. Then he said to them, "Oh, how foolish you are, and how slow of heart to believe all that the prophets have declared! Was it not necessary that the Messiah should suffer these things and then enter into his glory?" Then beginning with Moses and all the prophets, he interpreted to them the things about himself in all the scriptures.

As they came near the village to which they were going, he walked ahead as if he were going on. But they urged him strongly, saying, "Stay with us, because it is almost evening and the day is now nearly over." So he went in to stay with them. When he was at the table with them, he took bread, blessed and broke it, and gave it to them. Then their eyes were opened, and they recognised him; and he vanished from their sight. They said to each other, "Were not our hearts burning within us while he was talking to us on the road, while he was opening the scriptures to us?" That same hour they got up and returned to Jerusalem; and they found the eleven and their companions gathered together. They were saying, "The Lord has risen indeed, and he has appeared to Simon!" Then they told what had happened on the road, and how he had been made known to them in the breaking of the bread. (NRSV)

Discussion Questions

Consider as many, or as few, of these questions as you wish:

1. What do you make of the teaching that the Messiah must suffer and rise again and how should it affect the way we view suffering in the world?

2. Share some signs that suggest that the Anglican Communion is a community of hope.

In an age of mass migration and isolation, how can we do more to welcome and affirm strangers?

Bible Study
21 September 2002
Dr. Jennie Plane Te Paa

Micah: 6: 6–8

In preparing these Bible Studies I have been mindful of the need and thankfully the increasingly expressed recognition among many of us as members of the global Anglican Communion that it is important for us to transcend our parochialisms. So today I want us to endeavour to focus upon the issues which arise daily for those of God's people who live their lives on the very edge of 'decent' human existence rather than at the perceived centre of any universe.

I would like us to imagine ourselves to be as the authors of the Old Testament, particularly the prophets, all of whom were inspired by God and yet who were daily confronted by the pressing contemporary concerns of; race relations, personal survival and fulfillment, liberation, tyranny, famine, war, disease, poverty, matters of religion and state.

With this in mind we turn now to our text for today and let us pray that by the power of the Holy Spirit we might be opened to discerning the glorious mystery ever present, ever possible as we consider afresh the timeless words of Holy Scripture.

> *"With what shall I come before the Lord, and bow myself before God on high?*
>
> *Shall I come before him with burnt offerings, with calves a year old?*
>
> *Will the Lord be pleased with thousands of rams, with tens of thousands of rivers of oil?*
>
> *Shall I give my firstborn for my transgression, the fruit of my body for the sin of my soul?"*
>
> *He has told you, O mortal, what is good;*

> *and what does the Lord require of you but to do justice, and to love kindness, and to walk humbly with your God?*

Our reading this morning, at least the last verse, is of course a 'classic' text for the radical Christian activists for justice. How many paintings does this text adorn, how many posters, how many times is it used as an impassioned plea for action against injustice? I love these words and I confess I have them inscribed in my own private covenant commitment which guides all I do in my work for our Church.

We know the text is framed overall within a covenant lawsuit being set against an ungrateful people (Israel) with the prophet acting as attorney. The earlier witnesses to the action (v.1–6), the mountains and the hills, are subject to the Lord's charge, "How hard has it been for you to get what it is that I have been appealing to you to do." "No, I don't want curses, burnt offerings or human sacrifice—all I require of you is to do justice, to love kindness, to walk humbly with your God." Simple beyond belief one would think.

The text is one which we love to personalise, just as I have already done. It makes us feel good to know it, to quote it and most of us can without doubt justify our claim to live by it.

BUT! 'doing justice' is not easy. Speaking of it is relatively so, but 'doing it' is quite a different matter. The radical activist prophet is always a target for condemnation. "Don't make us feel guilty or uncomfortable. Don't raise issues unnecessarily, don't upset the status quo!" But unless and until we both name and act against injustice then what chance, kindness, let alone humility, let alone truly walking with God?

At this moment there is one group in our world for whom I wish to advocate—I did so for them in Washington last week and I want to do so again here in Hong Kong. You see I am concerned that so often as 'very important Anglicans'! as self-determining adults, we so easily forget those whom Jesus himself declared are key to the kingdom of heaven. Matthew 18: "Then Jesus called a small child and said unless you are transformed and become as little children you will by no means enter the kingdom. Therefore whoever humbles themselves as this little child, whoever receives this little one in my name, receives me" (paraphrased).

The catalyst for my Bible Study question today is a photograph which appeared just 2 or 3 weeks ago in our national newspaper—it is a photograph which continues to haunt me. It is the photograph of a beautiful young boy now convicted and imprisoned for murder. I think also of the two little girls recently brutally murdered in Soham in England and of little Milly Downer whose bones were found this morning—another innocent child intentionally murdered. I think of all the children of the Holy Land living lives of unspeakable terror amidst seemingly unending violence. I think of the small girl babies of South Africa being subjected to the most appallingly brutal experience of rape (by way of a perverse hope for a cure for male HIV/Aids), of the beautiful children of Afghanistan still tentatively emerging from the recent massive bombing of their land. The First Nations children of Canada, the Aboriginal children in Australia, so often born into situations of gross societal disadvantage as a result of historic colonial legacy. I think of the child laborers pressed into service throughout Asia and of the small girl children lured or sold into prostitution. I think of the children of Iraq where war may be imminent, the Congo where war remains intolerable. I think of the hundreds of orphan children who so suddenly and tragically lost parents in 9/11 in the United States. Yesterday we saw the desperate situation for children in Southern Colombia, in Zimbabwe and today in Abidjan on the Ivory Coast, all of these 'little lives' being lived on the very edge of decent human existence-powerless and utterly dependent—everywhere 'our' children, and surely all children are 'our' children who need us to advocate for their interests.

So as we reach that part of our ACC gathering where our own minds and hearts are with our families, our children and grandchildren, can we pause for just one moment to consider the plight of the millions of God's precious little ones who need us, who depend on us to 'do justice' for them, to 'love kindness' for them and to 'walk humbly with God' with and for them?

Question for Study Groups

What must we do as Church to ensure justice and kindness and humility characterise our ministries with, and for, all of God's precious 'little ones'?

Bible Study
23 September 2002
Dr. Jenny Plane Te Paa

Mark 12: 28–34

One of the scribes came near and heard them disputing with one another, and seeing that he answered them well, he asked him, "Which commandment is the first of all?" Jesus answered, "The first is, "Hear, O Israel: the Lord our God, the Lord is one; you shall love the Lord your God with all your heart, and with all your soul, and with all your mind, and with all your strength." The second is this, "You shall love your neighbour as yourself." There is no other commandment greater than these." Then the scribe said to him, "You are right. Teacher; you have truly said that 'he is one, and besides him there is no other'; and 'to love him with all the heart and with all the understanding, and with all the strength,' and 'to love one's neighbour as oneself,' this is much more important than all whole burnt offerings and sacrifices." When Jesus saw that he answered wisely, he said to him, "You are not far from the kingdom of God." After that no one dared to ask him any question.

Questions for Study Groups

1. What are the Gospel qualities of 'neighbourliness' which ACC should adopt and practice in the years ahead?

2. How can ACC reconcile the myriad temptations and distortions which contemporary identity politics pose to our ability to truly love God AND our neighbours as ourselves? (For example, identity politics arise when there are disagreements, misunderstandings and rejection over any one or all of the following differences between human beings: racial, gender, sexuality, economic, age, class, clerical, citizenship state, religious, political.)

Although I am now a thoroughly urbanised indigenous woman, there was a time when I was a young girl! Way back then, I was privileged by the experience of small rural tribal village life. Everyone knew everyone. My grandparents, aunties, uncles, cousins AND all those not related by blood, for example, the Priest, the teachers, the public servants, together with migrant families, were regarded as 'belonging' to one another. Everyone literally knew everyone else *and* everyone and *everything* moved quite interchangeably between everyone else's house! Everything was communally perceived and managed. While one or two households 'theoretically' owned the fishing boats, the catch was always distributed throughout the village with special consideration being given to the widows, the sick and the poor. While one or two families may have 'theoretically' owned the best sweet potato patches, everyone in the village would receive bags of sweet potato in exchange for watermelon, or fresh meat, or fresh bread or jam or whatever other specialities were regularly traded between all who lived in the village.

When my great-grandfather died in the worst-ever flu epidemic which ravaged Maori communities in the early part of the 20th century, all the relatives collected funds over a number of years to enable his widow to send one of his sons, my grandfather, to the College I now work at, St John's Theological College. In fact, during that historical period, by way of rebuilding those communities devastated by the epidemic, the elders would travel around each of the small villages identifying those who were considered as future leader prospects. Those chosen were supported by the communal funds, meager as they were, to become the teachers, the Priests, the doctors, the future professionals. Everyone sacrificed a little so that the whole community could flourish. Everyone without exception also supported the Church—my village was and remains strongly unequivocally Anglican, so much so that it is also strongly, unequivocally ecumenical! So it seemed to me as a child at least that my people certainly loved God and without doubt because of their actions, they certainly loved one another.

When I think about all of this social history today then I realise that my people were always traditionally and powerfully, 'as neighbours' with and for one another. No one ever stopped to count the cost of what they were giving or receiving or sharing. No one ever stopped to calculate the relative worth of anything—goods and services simply flowed when and where necessary. I have tried in every way possible to maintain as many aspects of that lifestyle, of that sense of neighbourliness and faithfulness as I possibly can but of course so much now gets in the way.

What has happened that the simple lifestyles many of us have been blessed with experiencing have been so eroded by our contemporary circumstances? What has happened to that pervasive sense of 'connectedness' where 'neighbours' once enjoyed such high levels of intimacy, of mutuality, of shared delight in all that was part of their daily lives? Why do we now actually need to ask ourselves, "OK, today how is it that I have demonstrated in some tangible way just how I love the Lord with all my heart and soul and mind, and how because of that I have also loved my neighbour as myself?" As I pray each day I sometimes find myself struggling to identify ways in which I have been truly loving or truly neighbourly—so what is the problem?

Well I have a theory—a totally untested one, but I think it has to do with the ways in which what I call 'identity polities' have corrupted and perverted our capacity for the sort of wholesome and unconditional 'neighbourly' relationships of which I spoke earlier. *I think that what we have done in our 'over-excitement' at finding and embracing the post-modern tools of critical theory, is that we have ended up essentialising all manner of human identity categories at the expense of focussing (as Mark's Gospel implores us to do), on simply cherishing each other's full humanity because we love God.* Remember, "There is no other commandment greater than these."

Archbishop Carey named many of the things to which I am referring in his Presidential address. For example, I was especially touched by his plea for those who have Pension Funds, to share them with those who do not. This seems like an entirely respectable, entirely reasonable 'neighbourly' thing to do. Unfortunately, for some reason, those who have economic advantage currently feel no sense of neighbourliness toward those who do not. In this case, economic difference is therefore corrupting our capacity for unconditional neighbourly relationships.

Archbishop Carey went on to name many of the factors he considers problematic to preserving and protecting the unity of our Communion. Identity politics are writ large in every instance of potential and actual schism. For example some among us do not consider women good enough to be our neighbours, gay folks definitely attract the worst kind of rejection—many of us definitely don't want any of 'them' in our neighbourhood. Some among us say migrants can't be trusted, Islamic folks are suspect, Saudis also. Some of us who are coloured are even saying white folks shouldn't be allowed in our neighbourhood and so it goes on. What about my little village where there was room for all and all were mutually interdependent and mutually accountable, wholly on the basis of their common humanity—their human 'connectedness' as 'neighbours'? *It is absolutely true that all of the human 'differences' between everyone in the village were actually merely incidental.*

Returning to our text, we recall that this Gospel teaching of Jesus comes at a very crucial time—the disciples are with Jesus in Jerusalem. We now know as Jesus himself knew then, that the final drama was imminent. Jesus was in real confrontation with the religious leaders over issues of prayer and piety, life after death, tributes to Caesar and over Jesus' authority itself. When I consider the context of this Gospel narrative from Mark, I imagine an almost exasperated, deeply troubled, somewhat fearful and undoubtedly physically weary Jesus finding all the incessant questioning to be increasingly tedious *and yet*, the clarity and the graciousness of his response ought leave us in no doubt of its singular importance for us today.

If we want to be true disciples:

1. We put our trust in God.
2. We put that trust into action by loving our neighbours unconditionally as ourselves.

You see, I believe we can only love one another as neighbours if we see each other above all else, as absolute equals in the image and likeness of God. Our respective race, gender, sexualities, age, status, etc. are of utterly secondary and much lesser importance. What matters, in fact ALL that matters, is our human capacity to simply be kind, hospitable, compassionate, generous, unconditionally loving—to love God and our neighbours, just as God has always loved us.

Bible Study
24 September 2002
The Most Reverend Ian George

Exodus 34:14–16

(for you shall worship no other god, because the LORD, whose name is Jealous, is a jealous God). You shall not make a covenant with the inhabitants of the land, for when they prostitute themselves to their gods and sacrifice to their gods, someone among them will invite you, and you will eat of the sacrifice. And you will take wives from among their daughters for your sons, and their daughters who prostitute themselves to their gods will make your sons also prostitute themselves to their gods.

Deuteronomy 7:3–4

Do not intermarry with them, giving you daughters to their sons or taking their daughters for your sons, for that would turn away your children from following me, to serve other gods. Then the anger of the LORD would be kindled against you, and he would destroy you quickly.

Leviticus 19:33–34

When an alien resides with you in your land, you shall not oppress the alien.

The alien who resides with you shall be to you as the citizen among you; you shall love the alien as yourself, for you were aliens in the land of Egypt: I am the LORD your God.

Deuteronomy 24:17–22

You shall not deprive a resident alien or an orphan of justice; you shall not take a widow's garment in pledge. Remember that you were a slave in Egypt and the LORD your God redeemed you from there; therefore I command you to do this. When you reap your harvest in your field and forget a sheaf in the field, you shall not go back to get it; it shall be left for the alien, the orphan, and the widow, so that the LORD your God may bless you in all your undertakings. When you beat your olive trees, do not strip what is left; it shall be for the alien, the orphan, and the widow. When you gather the grapes of your vineyard, do not glean what is left; it shall be for the alien, the orphan, and the widow. Remember that you were a slave in the land of Egypt; therefore I am commanding you to do this.

Ezra 10:44

All these had married foreign women, and they sent them away with their children.

Isaiah 42:1–4

Here is my servant, whom I uphold, my chosen, in whom my soul delights; I have put my spirit upon him; he will bring forth justice to the nations. He will not cry or lift up his voice, or make it heard in the street; a bruised reed he will not break, and a dimly burning wick he will not quench; he will faithfully bring forth justice. He will not grow faint or be crushed until he has established justice in the earth; and the coastlands wait for his teaching.

1 Corinthians:13

If I speak in the tongues of mortals and of angels, but do not have love, I am a noisy gong or a clanging cymbal. And if I have prophetic powers, and understand all mysteries and all knowledge, and if I have all faith, so as to remove mountains, but do not have love, I am nothing. If I hand over my body so that I may boast, but do not have love, I gain nothing. Love is patient; love is kind; love is not envious or boastful or arrogant or rude. It does not insist on its own way; it is not irritable or resentful; It does not rejoice in wrongdoing, but rejoices in the truth. It bears all things, believes all things, hopes all things, endures all things. Love never ends. But as for prophecies, they will come to an end; as for tongues, they will cease; as for knowledge, it will come to an end. For we know only in part, and we prophesy only in part; but when the complete comes, the partial will come to an end. When I was a child, I spoke like a child, I thought like a child, I reasoned like a child; when I became an adult, I put an end to childish ways. For now we see in a mirror, dimly, but then we will see face to face. Now I know only in part; then I will know fully, even as I have been fully known. And now faith, hope, and love abide, these three; and the greatest of these is love. (All Bible references from NRSV)

Questions for Discussion Groups

1. Why is there ambivalence in the Hebrew scriptures about the stranger?
2. Is your nation gripped by that ambivalence today?
3. Is your province of the Anglican Communion gripped by that ambivalence?
4. How do we set up boundaries? consciously? unconsciously?
5. How does our church set up boundaries?
6. What do we do, as members of the Anglican Communion, to eliminate such boundaries?
7. To what extent is our church resistant to the elimination of such boundaries?

Day 1

The theme for ACC-12, you will remember, is "That you may have life". The final two bible studies come from the viewpoint of the Migrant and Refugee Network.

The ancient Hebrew, we are told, had a deep ambivalence towards the stranger. The Old Testament amply demonstrates that. On the one hand the Hebrew was driven by a deep concern for an identity maintained by the call of God to be holy, to be a holy people. The Purity Code which resulted is a very exclusive one and you will note the first passage on the bible study list from Exodus 34, "for you shall worship no other God, because the Lord, whose name is Jealous, is a jealous God." And it goes on, "you shall not make a covenant with the inhabitants of the land, for when they prostitute themselves to their gods and sacrifice to their gods, someone among them will invite you, and you will eat of the sacrifice. And you will take wives from among their daughters for your sons." (Exodus 34:14–16) There is a deep fear of integration and assimilation there. And the Deuteronomy 7 passage reiterates the same theme. (Deut. 7:1–4)

Over the centuries there was a great deal of religious syncretism and inter-marriage with foreign women. And we all know the remarkable strength and courage of Solomon with the vast array of wives he managed to maintain!

After the return from exile the Purity Code reasserted itself with a rigid return to fundamentals under Josiah. That tiny passage from Ezra 10 speaks volumes. "All these had married foreign women, and they sent them away with their children." (Ezra 10:44) What happened to those wives and children? Where did they go? Who would receive them? Based upon our experience of the last few decades we can make a fair guess. Just as in our own day (when 80% of all refugees are women and children) their fate is exploitation, rape, hunger and hopelessness.

Ann Rolf, a Jewish novelist from the United States, has written that "beneath the text of Ezra and Nehemiah we can hear the children of the exiled wives calling for fathers who have disowned them. We can hear the women, the women who disrobed and gave their bodies in trust as a result of this exclusion who are now alone in the night wandering in a no man's land between the nations, betrayed and abandoned because of an accident of birth. We cannot shut our ears to the weeping." She might well have said, 'wandering in a no **woman's** land between the nations'.

At the basis of this rejection is fear. Fear of the alien and the influence that they bring: fear of strange and misunderstood religious traditions. So Jewish identity is hedged about by boundaries, which give special religious and commercial advantages to the Jew. The kosher rules are still with us, and are rules within rules.

Such severe boundaries are not confined to the Jewish people or the Jewish nation. A former Human Rights Commissioner in Australia has said that since the European settlement of our country Australians have been dominated by two great obsessions. The first is that we want to lock everybody up. We are doing that extremely well with asylum-seekers in breach of our commitment to the United Nations Conventions to which we are a signatory. The second great obsession is our fear of the stranger who is going to come over the horizon and steal "our" land!

Religious boundaries were at the core of many of the recent tragedies in the Balkans as they are today in the Holy Land. Sri Lanka and Sudan are ravaged by civil war largely engendered by racial, economic and religious boundaries.

But in fairness there is another side to the Jewish experience. The passages from Leviticus 19 and Deuteronomy 24 illustrate the other side of the coin. "The alien who resides with you shall be to you as the citizen among you, you shall love the alien as yourself, for you were aliens in the land of Egypt" (Leviticus 19:34). And Deuteronomy 24, "You shall not deprive a resident alien or an orphan of justice; you shall not take a widow's garment in pledge. Remember that you were a slave in Egypt and the LORD your God redeemed you from there" (Deut. 24:17)

Those passages remind us of the way the classical middle-eastern tradition of hospitality was taken so seriously in Jewish communities. The Book of Ruth, of course, is another constant reminder. The Hebrews were to remember to look after the stranger and the alien for a special reason, "for you were strangers in the land of Egypt." The ambivalence which the Jewish communities experienced is a common phenomenon in today's world. The United States and Canada, like Australia, once famous for their generosity to refugees, are hardening their arteries and their boundaries. I mentioned the other day in presenting the Migrant and Refugee Network report that the US quota for refugees for this year is supposed to be 70,000 people. Richard Parkins (who runs the Episcopal Church department in this area) says that they expect fewer than 17,000 people are likely to be received. This is all a result of our fears since September 11, 2001.

Our Anglican Church, with others, is engaged in a vigorous battle with the Canadian government trying to prevent them from tightening their borders and boundaries against those in need as a result of the quest for security in the wake of September 11, 2001.

We turn now to the prophets and I have given you one small passage from Isaiah (42:10–12) Isaiah is perhaps the first to see the God of the Hebrews as the God of all nations: a God whose constant will is to bring justice to the whole of creation. These days we tend to talk about "human rights" more than "justice". Hugh McCallum is a Canadian journalist who has written on the role of the churches in the genocide in Rwanda and about the humanitarian responses of the church in the west. He asks the question, "Do we really seek justice?" His response is, "We did what we have always done. We tried to help the victims rather than stop the victimisation." This provides us with our starting point for any discussion of our attitudes to the marginalised, the deprived, the lost and, in this context, refugees and migrants, displaced persons and asylum-seekers. How we respond to them is a mirror of our ambivalence: our concern for purity, exclusivism or inclusivism.

So we go on to St Paul in that much loved passage from 1 Corinthians 13, which I would suggest needs to be read in conjunction with chapter 12. That reminds us of our constant and prior obligation of love. St Paul reminds us elsewhere that perfect love casts out all fear and that is the kind of love we are given by God in Jesus Christ, the kind of love we are expected to express in our individual and corporate lives. That is the love which we are called to offer Bishop Rhia when he cries out, "I would rather die in my homeland than live elsewhere as a refugee."

That is the kind of love we are called to express when we look in the eyes of the Sudanese women in the Kakuma Refugee Camp who asked me why the Anglican Church doesn't really care about them because even the Muslims bring in special food for their people to celebrate their festivals.

Refugees are a very special group of people for whom we need, and to whom we need, to offer life. We have heard from Jenny, we have heard from Sally and we have heard from our good friend Bishop Fernando from Sri Lanka about the plight of so many other disadvantaged and marginalised people. Refugees and displaced persons are now throughout our world, God's world, in pandemic proportions.

Let us pray.

"Almighty and loving God, guide us through your Holy Spirit as we open your holy word and hear your call to stand with the marginalised, the rejected, the lost and the outcast, with all of whom you stand, through Jesus Christ our Lord."

Bible Study
25 September 2002
The Most Reverend Ian George

Luke 7:36–50

One of the Pharisees asked Jesus to eat with him, and he went into the Pharisee's house and took his place at the table. And a woman in the city, who was a sinner, having learned that he was eating in the Pharisee's house, brought an alabaster jar of ointment. She stood behind him at his feet, weeping, and began to bathe his feet with her tears and to dry them with her hair. Then she continued kissing his feet and anointing them with the ointment. Now when the Pharisee who had invited him saw it, he said to himself, "If this man were a prophet, he would have known who and what kind of woman this is who is touching him—that she is a sinner." Jesus spoke up and said to him, "Simon, I have something to say to you." "Teacher," he replied, "Speak." "A certain creditor had two debtors; one owed five hundred denarii, and the other fifty. When they could not pay, he cancelled the debts for both of them. Now which of them will love him more?" Simon answered, "I suppose the one for whom he cancelled the greater debt." And Jesus said to him, "You have judged rightly." Then turning toward the woman, he said to Simon, "Do you see this woman? I entered your house; you gave me no water for my feet, but she has bathed my feet with her tears and dried them with her hair. You gave me no kiss, but from the time I came in she has not stopped kissing my feet. You did not anoint my head with oil, but she has anointed my feet with ointment. Therefore, I tell you, her sins, which were many, have been forgiven; hence she has shown great love. But the one to whom little is forgiven, loves little." Then he said to her, "Your sins are forgiven." But those who were at the table with him began to say among themselves, "Who is this who forgives sins?" And he said to the woman, "Your faith has saved you; go in peace."

Matthew 25:31–46

"When the Son of Man comes in his glory, and all the angels with him, then he will sit on the throne of his glory. All the nations will be gathered before him, and he will separate people one from another as a shepherd separates the sheep from the goats, and he will put the sheep at this right hand and the goats at the left. Then the king will say to those at his right hand, 'Come, you that are blessed by my Father, inherit the kingdom prepared for you from the foundation of the world; for I was hungry and you gave me food, I was thirsty and you gave me something to drink, I was a stranger and you welcomed me, I was naked and you gave me clothing, I was sick and you took care of me, I was in prison and you visited me.' Then the righteous will answer him, 'Lord, when was it that we saw you hungry and gave you food, or thirsty and gave you something to drink? And when was it that we saw you a stranger and welcomed you, or naked and gave you clothing? And when was it that we saw you sick or in prison and visited you?' And the king will answer them, 'Truly I tell you, just as you did it to one of the least of these who are members of my family, you did it to me.' Then he will say to those at his left hand, 'You that are accursed, depart from me into the eternal fire prepared for the devil and his angels; for I was hungry and you gave me no food, I was thirsty and you gave me nothing to drink, I was a stranger and you did not welcome me, naked and you did not give me clothing, sick and in prison and you did not visit me.' Then they also will answer, 'Lord, when was it that we saw you hungry or thirsty or a stranger or naked or sick or in prison, and did not take care of you?' Then he will answer them, 'Truly I tell you, just as you did not do it to one of the least of these, you did not do it to me.' And these will go away into eternal punishment, but the righteous into eternal life."

Luke 10:25–37

Just then a lawyer stood up to test Jesus. "Teacher," he said, "what must I do to inherit eternal life?" He said to him, "What is written in the law? What do you read there?" He answered, "You shall love the Lord your God with all your heart, strength, and with all your mind; and your neighbor as yourself." And he said to him, "You have given the right answer; do this, and you will live."But wanting to justify himself, he asked Jesus, "And who is my neighbor?" Jesus replied, "A man was going down from Jerusalem to Jericho, and fell into the hands of robbers, who stripped him, beat him, and went away, leaving him half dead. Now by chance a priest was going down by on the other side. So likewise a Levite, when he came to the place and saw him, passed by on the other side. But a Samaritan while travelling came near him; and when he saw him, he was moved with pity. He went to him and bandaged his wounds, having poured oil and wine on them. Then he put him on his own animal, brought him to an inn, and took care of him. The next day he took out two denarii, gave them to the innkeeper, and said, "Take care of him; and when I come back, I will repay you whatever more you spend." Which of these three, do you think, was a neighbor to the man who fell into the hands of the robbers?" He said, "The one who showed him mercy." Jesus said to him, "Go and do likewise."

Galatians 3:28–29

There is no longer Jew or Greek, there is no longer slave or free, there is no longer male and female; for all of you are one in Christ Jesus. And if you belong to Christ, then you are Abraham's offspring, heirs according to the promise. (All Bible references from NRSV)

Questions for Discussion Groups

1. What do you understand to be the range of attitudes to the stranger in the culture into which Jesus found himself born?
2. How did he respond?
3. What techniques did he use?
4. For what are we accountable to God in relation to the stranger and other marginalized and needy people?
5. How can we exercise compassion in the global community as the Anglican Communion?
6. How can we hear from the victims?
7. How should we be seeking to influence government and community attitudes?

Day 2

Yesterday we were focussing upon the Hebrew experience with strangers and Hebrew ambivalence towards them. We were looking at the boundaries the Hebrew people set up to protect their holiness and hence their identity.

Today we come to the time of Jesus and immediately we find ourselves plunged into the Purity Code. It is alive and well: the community of merit is still with us.

Luke (7:36–50) tells us that one of the Pharisees invited Jesus to eat with him. But there is a sense in which the Pharisee did this out of curiosity. Simon the Pharisee had not even offered Jesus, as his guest, the customary water for washing his dusty feet. He certainly offered him no welcome kiss nor anointed his head. Clearly they were not brothers in the faith in the terms of Psalm 133.

But Jesus is shown, by Luke, to be at his customary work of breaking down these boundaries and aligning himself with the marginalised, the deprived and the rejected. "The woman is a sinner", we hear. As we might say, "that covers a multitude of sins". But she is humble, repentant and seeking forgiveness.

Simon declares that Jesus is no prophet because he obviously cannot see the kind of woman she is. We are reminded of the woman at Jacob's Well who declared that Jesus was a prophet because he could see through exterior appearances. Now this woman is rejected by Simon the Pharisee. Jesus is only less suspect to a degree, a degree of separation.

Jerome Mary has described the Purity Code as the orderly system whereby people perceive that certain things belong in certain places at certain times. Purity is the abstract way of indicating what fits: what is appropriate and what is in place. Purity is a cultural map which indicates a place for everything and everything in its place. It sounds extraordinarily Anglican to me.

The Purity Code establishes clear boundaries of separation. Gentiles, of course, were on the outer, but so were tax gatherers, lepers and prostitutes, to name a few. Jesus makes a particular point of associating with those who are outcast and unclean. Remember the lepers, the menstruating woman, the prostitute, the physically handicapped, the demon-possessed, the tax collectors and Gentiles.

Jesus challenges rigidity over fasting, Sabbath observance and ritual washing. He must have aroused deep fears when he said, "there is nothing outside a person that by going in can defile, but the things that come out are what defile." (Mark 7:15) The acquisition of merit through the purity code is irrelevant. It cannot lead to salvation. Only the Grace of God can help. In most of his parables Jesus challenges all these boundaries. The best known of course is the parable of the Good Samaritan which we have this morning. Someone in our Bible study group said we should do more to hear the voice of the victim. This parable is the parable par excellence where the voice of the victim is crucial. Of course, the victim was left in the gutter half dead and when he resumed consciousness he was no doubt so astounded by the generosity of the Samaritan that he was rendered speechless!

It would not be surprising for Jesus to have turned the question "Who is my neighbour?" on its head by asking a question in return, something like "Why don't you ask the victim?" or "Why don't you ask the rejected or marginalised or outcast?" or even "the crucified?"

As in Jesus' conversation with the woman at the well, it is clear that he regards Jewish boundaries as essentially obsolete. I have given you Matthew's parable of the Great Assize. (Matt. 25: 21–46) We are told that our neighbour is not only anyone in need, but extending such love in action is the same as doing it to Jesus himself. Failing to do so is the same.

These parables must have left Jesus' hearers absolutely speechless. As John Dominic Crossan says, "Jesus is taking sides with human beings in a concrete situation where the existing politico-religious structure has dehumanised people." And he goes on to say the point is not that one should help the neighbour in need. Rather the metaphorical point is that the Kingdom of God breaks abruptly into human conscientiousness and demands the overturn of prior values, closed options, set judgements and established conclusions.

It is disturbing to think we are accountable to Jesus for how we respond to the marginalised, including refugees, both as individuals and as church. A few months ago a man came to see me. He had been a senior guard in one of the detention centres our Australian Government has built to contain the asylum seekers who arrived in unseaworthy boats on our northern coastline. This man has had a nervous breakdown. He told me that he could cope with the various demonstrations, the pleas and the stories of the adults in the Woomera Detention Centre, but when the children began sewing up their lips to go on a hunger strike, he became totally unnerved. He was suddenly sensitised and so became accountable.

I think we are called to be similarly sensitised. We are all called to loving compassion to suffer with those in need. To suffer with a woman I met in the Gaza Strip when it was a refugee camp. She sent her small boy out to buy some milk. He never returned. He never returned because he picked up a small stick, which an Israeli soldier interpreted as a weapon and so shot him. He did not die immediately, but was taken to an Israeli hospital and his mother was denied permission to move out of the Gaza Strip to see him. I can still hear that woman's wailing.

As St Paul reminds us in Galatians, we are all one in Christ, but we are also all one with the rest of God's creation. We are all wrapped up in the same bundle of life. Walter Brueggeman says compassion constitutes a radical form of social criticism for it announces that the hurt is to be taken seriously. That the hurt is not to be accepted as normal or natural, but as an abnormal and unacceptable condition for humanness.

There is no limit to what we could do as the Anglican Communion in this area if we were determined to do so. May God help us get our act together. Only God can help us because we all have our ways of excluding the unlovely and the uncomfortable even amongst those who are not marginalised.

The *South China Morning Post* this very morning gives us a classic example of the way in which governments around the world are using September 11, 2001, to incorporate into their legislation all kinds of provisions against sedition, treason and terrorism. Many of us fear such measures will be used harshly against comment which is unfriendly to the government.

We are essentially conservative, as Anglicans. We talk about justice, but not when it endangers our own peace or good order. It was Paul you remember who battled against the conservatism of the Jerusalem Christian establishment. We need Paul's courage in a world riddled by caste, class, boundaries, exclusivism and rejection. In most places of the world only the church is left to ask the questions. We ask the questions, but we ask the questions that they may have life. Let us pray:

> Almighty and loving God,
> guide us through your Holy Spirit
> as we open your Holy Word
> and hear your call to stand with the marginalised,
> the rejected, the lost and the outcast,
> with whom you stand in Jesus Christ, our Lord.

ACC-12 Bible Study Groups

Group 1

Leader

Mrs. Margaret Bihabanyi	Rwanda
The Revd Damien Nteziryayo	Rwanda
Bishop Martin Nyaboho	Burundi
Archbishop Michael Peers	Primates Standing Committee
Bishop Josias Sendegeya	Rwanda
Miss Joyce Tsongo	Congo

The Revd Basimaki Byabasaija (deceased) from Congo was to have been a member of this Group.

Group 2

Leader

Canon Michael Burrows	Ireland

Bishop Samuel Azariah	Pakistan
Archdeacon Winston Halapua	Aotearoa, New Zealand and Polynesia
Bishop Richard Harries	England
Bishop Petrus Hilukiluah	Southern Africa
Archbishop Peter Kwong	Hong Kong
The Revd Dr. Susan Moxley	Canada
Archbishop Livingstone Mpalanyi-Nkoyoyo	Uganda
Mr. Bernard Turner	West Indies
Mandy Tibby	Christian Conference of Asia

Group 3

Leader

The Revd Govada Dyvasirvadam	South India
Canon Job Bariira-Mbukure	Uganda
Ms. Judith Conley	U.S.A.
Archdeacon Kay Goldsworthy	Australia
Archbishop Bernard Malango	Primates Standing Committee
Mr. Martin Parvez	Pakistan
Miss Candace Payne	West Indies
Dr. Stephen Toope	Canada
Bishop David Vunagi	Melanesia
Professor Whatarangi Winiata	Aotearoa, New Zealand and Polynesia
The Revd David Bolen	Roman Catholic Church

Group 4

Leader

Canon Lovey Kisembo	Uganda
Archbishop George Carey	England
Mr. Saw Si Hai	Myanmar
The Revd Samuel Koshiishi	Japan
Mr. Warren Luyaben	Philippines
Mr. John Rea	Scotland
Bishop Catherine Roskam	U.S.A.
Mr. Daniel Taolo	Central Africa
Bishop Hector Zavala	Southern Cone

Group 5

Leader

Bishop Bolly Lapok	South East Asia
Mr. Roger Baboa	Papua New Guinea
Mrs. Jolly Babirukamu	Uganda
Mr. Nicholas Casie-Chetty	Sri Lanka

Dean John Moses	England
Mr. Antonio Ortego Reybal	Mexico
Bishop David Silk	Australia
Canon Maureen Sithole	Southern Africa
Bishop James Tengatenga	Central Africa
Metropolitan Nikitas	Ecumenical Patriarchate

Group 6

Leader

Mrs. Joyce Ngoda	Tanzania
Archbishop Peter Akinola	Nigeria
Mr. Robert Fordham	Australia
Bishop Michael Lugör	Sudan
The Revd Robert Sessum	U.S.A.
Mr. Richard Thornton	North India
Miss Kate Turner	Ireland
Mr. Luis Valleé	Central America
The Revd Dr. Harald Rein	Old Catholic

Group 7

Leader

Mrs. Lenore Parker	Australia
Chief Goodwin Ajayi	Nigeria
Canon Mauricio de Andrade	Brazil
Professor Adrian De Heer-Amissah	West Africa
Mr. Bernard Georges	Indian Ocean
Bishop Carlos López-Lozano	Spain
Bishop Gerard Mpango	Tanzania
Mr. Ghazi Musharbash	Jerusalem and the Middle East
Archdeacon Christopher Potter	Wales
Bishop James Terom	Primates Standing Committee

Group 8

Leader

Canon Elizabeth Paver	England
Mr. John Chang-Jin Chong	Korea
Bishop Riah Abu El-Assal	Jerusalem and the Middle East
Bishop Michael Ingham	Canada
Mr. Amos Kiriro	Kenya
Archdeacon Ezekiel Kondo	Sudan
Professor George Koshy	South India
The Revd Sunil Mankhin	Bangladesh
Archdeacon David Okeke	Nigeria
Archdeacon Margaret Vertue	Southern Africa
The Revd David Gill	World Council of Churches

Group 9

Leader

Canon Robert Thompson	West Indies
Bishop Simon Chiwanga	Tanzania
Mr.Is-Hag Kodi Kodi	Sudan
The Revd Enos Pradhan	North India
Miss Sylvia Scarf	Wales
Bishop Peter Sugandhar	South India
Bishop Joseph Wasonga	Kenya
Ms. Fung Yi Wong	Hong Kong
Bishop Joseph Mar Irenaeus	Mar Thoma

Resolutions of the Twelfth Meeting of the Anglican Consultative Council

Contents

Resolution 1. A World Fit for Children

This Anglican Consultative Council, in response to the United Nations Special Session on Children (May 2002) and the International Decade For a Culture of Peace and Non-violence for the Children of the World (2001–2010):

1. calls on churches of the Anglican Communion, ecumenical partners, faith communities, Governments and Non-Government Organizations to support the United Nations Convention on the Rights of the Child by advocating and, where possible, initiating the following:

   a) considering of the interests of children in building a world free from war, exploitation, abuse and violence;

   b) providing affordable and accessible healthcare for all children with a particular emphasis on HIV/AIDS prevention;

   c) protecting the environment for this and future generations;

   d) ending the vicious cycle of poverty, including promoting transparency in expenditure and cancellation of the debt that impedes progress for children;

   e) providing free and quality education that includes education for life including lessons in understanding, human rights, peace, acceptance and active citizenship;

   f) engendering a real and effective commitment to the principle of childrens' rights in all sectors of society, including participation in religious, civic and political structures; and

   g) promoting active and meaningful participation of children in planning, implementing, monitoring and evaluating all matters affecting the rights of the child.

2. encourages the churches of the Anglican Communion to promote a culture of non-violence that values love, compassion and justice and that rejects violence as a means of solving problems;

3. encourages Anglican churches to work at diocesan and parish levels to provide worship and study resources that relate both to current world conflict situations and to the theological and Biblical questions involved in the development of a culture of peace and non-violence;

4. requests that each member church of the Anglican Consultative Council report action taken to ACC-13.

Resolution 2. HIV/AIDS

This Anglican Consultative Council:

1. receives the report on HIV/AIDS and expresses its appreciation for it and the leadership of the Most Revd Njongonkulu Ndungane, who has been tasked to lead the Communion's efforts in this regard;

2. affirms the Primates Statement on HIV/AIDS issued in April 2002, at the meeting of the Primates in Canterbury, and commends its widest possible circulation through the churches of the Anglican Communion;

3. encourages the churches throughout the Communion to make awareness of HIV/AIDS a priority, and to undertake gender-sensitive education and information programmes to alert and protect their respective communities and nations;

4. urges each church of the Anglican Communion to develop and adopt a plan of action in response to the HIV/AIDS pandemic by ACC 13, and report on what has been achieved;

5. applauds the efforts of the Council of Anglican Provinces in Africa (CAPA) to co-ordinate and lead AIDS ministry response across sub-Saharan Africa;

6. recognises and endorses those efforts, both within government and private sector on the continent to Africa, to develop vaccines and make life-saving treatments available to all people living with AIDS;

7. thanks the Compass Rose Society for its pro-active leadership and financial support in launching the All-Africa Anglican Conference on HIV/AIDS in Boksburg, South Africa in 2001, and acknowledges the outstanding leadership of the Archbishop of Canterbury, the Most Revd & Rt Hon Dr George Leonard Carey, for his inspired and courageous leadership in bringing the Anglican Communion to an awareness of this unfolding catastrophe;

8. extends gratitude for the financial and technical resource efforts of the international donor community and faith-based charities in supporting and sustaining HIV/AIDS programme efforts within the Anglican Communion, which educate, build capacity to respond, and alleviate suffering around the world;

9. calls upon the churches of the Communion to support and assist with church resources, human and financial, and provide technical assistance in meeting the challenges of this pandemic to bring about a generation without AIDS;

10. requests that the Secretary General of the ACC establish an ACO-managed Anglican Communion AIDS Fund.

Resolution 3. Patents

This Anglican Consultative Council:

1. views with concern the increased levels of exclusion and marginalisation of the world's most vulnerable peoples as a result of the changes in the application of international patent law, in that:

    a) patents on medications, particularly those related to HIV/AIDS are making antiviral agents inaccessible in parts of the world where their availability is critical; and

    b) the practice of applying for patents on genetic and biological materials means that the developing nations are finding it increasingly difficult to maintain control over their own genetic and biological resources.

2. recognising that patent rights are intended to protect legitimate commercial needs and interests, invites member churches of the Anglican Communion:

    a) to engage in advocacy within their jurisdictions and co-operation with each other to ensure that ongoing changes to patent law both at national levels, and at the level of international trade agreements (GATT—General Agreement on Tariffs and Trade/TRIPS—Trade Related Intellectual Property Rights Agreement) protect the needs and interests of vulnerable populations and of developing nations;

    b) to avail themselves of the resources of the Consultant for Ethics at the Anglican Communion Office to support this work;

    c) to communicate their activities to the ACC through the office of the Consultant for Ethics.

Resolution 4. World Summit

This Anglican Consultative Council, following the recent World Summit held in Johannesburg, South Africa:

1. supports actions in the five key areas identified by the Summit, namely water and sanitation, energy, health, agricultural productivity, and biodiversity and ecosystem management;

2. adds its voice of concern and support to those calling for a renewed and committed international approach to the control of those processes which increase global warming and affect climate change;

3. urges each member church of the Anglican Communion to celebrate the Sunday nearest to 1st June, World Environment Day, as

Environment Sunday in order to raise environmental awareness across the Communion.

Resolution 5. Funding for Disease

This Anglican Consultative Council, noting the continuing debt burden faced by African countries and being advised that debt relief could release an estimated US $10 billion for the provision of desperately-needed medications for the treatment of HIV/AIDS, malaria, tuberculosis and cholera, calls on nations and institutions to which African countries are indebted to find ways of relieving them of their debt in order that the money so released can be applied to the purchase of medications and treatment of disease on the continent.

Resolution 6. Debt Burden

This Anglican Consultative Council notes with satisfaction that there is movement with the World Bank and the International Monetary Fund that may offer some positive relief to the most heavily indebted countries; nevertheless, in view of the fact that the debt burden continues to cripple the economies and aspirations of the developing world, reaffirms its commitment to the campaign for debt relief and for a review of the conditions imposed on debtor nations.

Resolution 7. Bigotry and Hate Crimes

This Anglican Consultative Council:

1. asks member churches to give increased attention to the implications of heightened bigotry and hate crimes against those designated as people of colour, indigenous peoples, and peoples of religions and ethnic origins or races other than one's own who are currently migrating from their own countries, including refugees and asylum seekers;

2. requests the Anglican Peace and Justice Network and the Anglican UN Observer to prepare an overview of international implications of increased hostility and tension directed in many countries towards people of other religions, ethnic origins, colour and nationalities and to report to the Joint Standing Committee of ACC and the Primates;

3. states clearly that there should be no outcasts in our churches.

Resolution 8. L'Arche

That this Council:

1. receives the report concerning the ministry of L'Arche presented by Jean Vanier and the Rt Revd Roger Herft;

2. commends the prophetic ministry in mutual service expressed in L'Arche communities across the world;

3. notes the changing structures of L'Arche;

4. recognises the appointment of Rt Revd Roger Herft, for a period of six years from July 1999, to the International Church Leader's Group as the Anglican Representative, and encourages Bishop Herft to report as appropriate to the Joint Standing Committee of the Primates of the Anglican Communion and the Anglican Consultative Council;

5. encourages Bishops and Provinces within the Anglican Communion to interact with, and be supportive of, L'Arche communities within their regions;

6. gives gracious thanks to God for the faithful obedience of Jean Vanier and expresses its prayerful support to L'Arche as it continues to offer a model of mutual ministry.

Resolution 9. International Anglican Family Network

This Anglican Consultative Council affirms the developing work of the International Anglican Family Network and urges all African Provinces and members to support the pilot consultation on Violence in the Family to be held in Africa early in 2003.

Resolution 10. Refugee and Migration Network

This Anglican Consultative Council:

1. receives the report of the Refugee and Migrant Network;

2. notes the current and imminent refugee, displaced peoples and asylum seeker situation; that there are at least 22 million refugees and 50 million displaced persons in the world today;

3. affirms the right of all refugees to return to their country of origin;

4. gives thanks that:

   a) most provinces have now appointed contact persons for the Network

   b) nearly half the provinces have appointed an annual Sunday to be observed as Refugee Sunday;

5. notes the burden borne by neighbouring countries and dioceses in areas where unstable conditions prevail;

6. asks the bishops of every province to ensure that programmes of education of their priests and people relating to these matters are made available and to encourage their use;

7. asks the people of every province to pray for those who are refugees, displaced peoples and asylum seekers throughout the world, pray for

change for the better in situations which cause such mobility of peoples, and pray for those who work to help them;

8. recognises the enormous potential which exists within the Anglican Communion for effective action for mutual support in prayer, advocacy, material support and education;
9. encourages every diocese in the Communion to take whatever local action is possible in the care of refugees and asylum-seekers and their resettlement;
10. notes the difficulties with communication experienced by the Network;
11. notes that the Network has not met since 1992;
12. encourages the Network to meet during the next eighteen months.

Resolution 11. UN Observer and Environment Network

This Anglican Consultative Council:

1. receives the UN Observer's report presented to the Council;
2. adopts the resolutions suggested in the report and letter (Annex IV) as its own, namely:
   a) asks all churches of the Anglican Communion to place environment care on their agenda;
   b) asks all Anglicans to make their own personal commitments to care for God's world, respecting all life, for "the Earth is the Lord's and all that is in it" (Psalm 24:1);
   c) establishes the Anglican Environmental Network as an official network of the Anglican Communion; and,
   d) endorses for immediate action, the declarations of the Anglican Congress to the United Nations and to the Anglican Communion.

Resolution 12. Inter Anglican Standing Commission on Mission and Evangelism

This Anglican Consultative Council Resolves:

1. to receive with thanks the Interim Report 'Travelling Together in God's Mission' from the Inter Anglican Standing Commission on Mission and Evangelism (IASCOME);
2. to give thanks for the successful Nairobi Consultation for Provincial Mission and Evangelism Co-ordinators 'Encounters on the Road'; to receive the report of that Consultation; to encourage dissemination

of its report and to support plans for a follow-up conference, funded outside of the budget of the ACC;

3. to look forward to and pray for the Mission Organisations Conference planned for February 2003;
4. to take note of action taken on matters remitted to the Commission;
5. to note that comments on the Primates Strategic Working Party on Theological Education have been sent direct to that working party;
6. to encourage the Commission to develop its mandate, reflection and work particularly in the areas of:
   - Leadership Training and Formation for Mission
   - Islam and Islamisation
   - Developing Anglicanism: A Communion in Mission
   - The Journey to Wholeness and Fullness of Life
   - Justice Making and Peace Building
   - Evangelism
7. to circulate the interim report to provinces, other Commissions and networks and more widely for comment and discussion.

Resolution 13. Legal Advisors Network

This Anglican Consultative Council welcomes the establishment of a Network of Anglican Legal Advisors which will:

1. produce a statement of principles of Canon Law common within the Communion;
2. examine shared legal problems and possible solutions;
3. provide reports to the Joint Standing Committee of the Primates Meeting and the Anglican Consultative Council as the work progresses.

Resolution 14. Colleges and Universities of the Anglican Communion (CUAC)

This Anglican Consultative Council recognises The Colleges and Universities of the Anglican Communion (CUAC) as a Network of the Anglican Communion.

Resolution 15. Inter Anglican Standing Commission on Telecommunications

This Anglican Consultative Council:

1. endorses resolution 15 of the Joint Standing Committee of the Primates of the Anglican Communion and the Anglican Consultative

Council supporting the formation of an Inter Anglican Standing Commission on Telecommunications;

2. expresses its gratitude to Trinity Grants Program, New York for its generous financial support of the new Commission for the initial three year period, with a possibility for renewal for a further two years.

Resolution 16. Inter Anglican Liturgical Consultation

This Anglican Consultative Council:

1. awaits a survey by the Inter Anglican Liturgical Consultation of practice in relation to the elements of Holy Communion in the churches of the Anglican Communion, and of the reasons given for any departure from dominical command; and
2. requests that the results of such a survey be presented to the Joint Standing Committee upon completion.

Resolution 17. Francophone Network

This Anglican Consultative Council:

1. receives with gratitude the report of the Executive Council of the French Speaking Anglicans around the World;
2. recognises the Executive Council of the French Speaking Anglicans around the World as a Network of the Anglican Communion.

Resolution 18. Interfaith Initiatives

This Anglican Consultative Council:

1. welcomes the interfaith initiatives of the Archbishop of Canterbury;
2. endorses the agreements concluded at Al-Azhar Al-Sharif (An Agreement for Dialogue between the Anglican Communion and Al-Azhar Al-Sharif), and Alexandria (The Joint Alexandria Declaration of the Religious Leaders in the Holy Land);
3. calls on the member churches of the Communion to continue to pray for the success of these interfaith dialogues and future initiatives.

Resolution 19. African Union

This Anglican Consultative Council recognises and supports the efforts of the newly created African Union to bring about a cessation of hostilities and a sustaining of peace on the African continent by enhancing the economic prosperity of the countries of Africa.

Resolution 20. Sudan, Burundi and Congo

This Anglican Consultative Council:

1. a) urges the government of Sudan to return to the peace negotiations in Machakos, Kenya;

   b) urges the government of Sudan and the SPLM/A to agree on a comprehensive cease fire leading to a just and durable peace in the Sudan;

   c) urges all churches of the Anglican Communion to note with concern the plight of all involved in the conflict, in particular the Christian community and in general citizens in the Sudan (and those who are refugees outside Sudan) who are suffering from the result of over 20 years of civil war;

2. a) notes with concern that Burundi and the Democratic Republic of Congo continue to be trouble spots with major loss of life;

   b) urges the leaders on all sides of these conflicts to sit together to bring about peace;

   c) calls for all hostilities and bloodshed to stop;

   d) asks all churches of the Anglican Communion to continue praying for and being in solidarity with, the populations of these countries.

Resolution 21. Israel/Palestine

This Anglican Consultative Council:

1. notes with increasing concern the continuing instability and violence in Israel/Palestine and the resulting economic and social disadvantage in vulnerable groups and communities, as well as the widespread destruction, fear, injury and loss of life in the area;

   a) believes that the best way to achieve longer-term security and a lasting basis for peace is for each side to recognise the legitimate aspirations, rights and needs of the other;

   b) condemns all violence against civilians;

   c) whilst recognising the legitimate right to its own defence, believes that the present conduct of the State of Israel has raised the level of threat to Palestinians and thus escalated the violence, with its consequent threat to the security of all families and individuals within the State of Israel;

d) calls upon the Israeli Government and the Palestinian Authority, as well as individual politicians, religious groups and community leaders, to find a way of breaking the spiral of revenge violence by entering into a new joint formal process of negotiation, based on international, religious and humane values of truth, forgiveness and reconciliation, in order to move towards genuine peace, justice and stability in the area;

e) calls upon the Israeli Government to implement UN resolutions 242, 338 and 194; and supports resolution V.20 of the 1998 Lambeth Conference;

f) urges the member churches of the Anglican Communion and associated agencies to find new ways of supporting collaborative projects between Israeli and Palestinian, Jewish, Muslim and Christian individuals and groups;

g) assures the people of Israel/Palestine of its prayers for peace; that its prayers will be offered in the name of God who calls us all to a greater love for each other, our neighbours, those who are strangers to us and our enemies.

Resolution 22. Korea

This Anglican Consultative Council:

1. commends the strong leadership of the Anglican Church of Korea (ACK) within the ecumenical community of Korea for its efforts to seek reconciliation of North and South;
2. notes the visit of the Nippon Sei Ko Kai and the Episcopal Church of the USA to Seoul, prior recommendations from the Peace and Justice Network to the ACC, and resolution 24 of ACC-11;
3. encourages the Secretary General to make an official visitation on behalf of the ACC to the Korean peninsula, to support the work of the ACK towards reunification.

Resolution 23. Iraq

This Anglican Consultative Council:

1. welcomes the proposed return of UN Weapons Inspectors to Iraq;
2. calls on the government of Iraq to comply fully with UN resolution 687;
3. believes that, on present evidence, military action against Iraq is not morally justified;
4. calls, subject to reports from UN Weapons Inspectors, for sanctions,

except for materials that could be used for weapons of mass destruction, to be lifted.

Resolution 24. Solidarity with ECUSA Position on Iraq

This Anglican Consultative Council affirms its solidarity with the position taken by the Episcopal Church, USA, in June 2002, in opposing unilateral military action against Iraq by the United States, and with the view expressed by the Presiding Bishop in his statement of 6 September 2002, that:

1. war holds the prospect of destabilising the Middle East and we will all be better served to see our national energies and resources expended in resolving the Israeli/Palestinian conflict, such that Israel finds security and peace with its neighbours and Palestinians achieve statehood;

2. military action would surely inflame the passions of millions, particularly in the Arab world, setting in motion cycles of violence and retaliation, further straining tenuous relationships that exist between the United States and other nations;

3. the United States has the opportunity to express leadership in the world by forging a foreign policy that seeks to reconcile and heal the world's divisions and reflect its values and ideals by focussing upon issues of poverty, disease and despair, not only within the US but throughout the global community of which it is a part.

25. Death Penalty

This Anglican Consultative Council:

1. commends the section entitled "Death Penalty" in the 2001 Anglican Peace and Justice Network Report;

2. endorses in particular the statement that "theologically we believe that the death penalty is immoral and outside of God's chosen realm";

3. urges the member churches and their Primates to maintain pressure for the total abolition of the death penalty, in countries with democratically-elected governments as well as other regimes.

26. Inter Anglican Standing Commission on Ecumenical Relations

This Anglican Consultative Council welcomes the reports of the first two meetings of the Inter Anglican Standing Commission on Ecumenical Relations and commends the Commission for its comprehensive work to date; and reminds member churches of the role this Commission has to advise and support national and regional ecumenical initiatives, as envisaged by resolution IV of the Lambeth Conference of 1998.

Resolution 27. 75th Anniversary of the Bonn Agreement

This Anglican Consultative Council notes that 2006 will be the 75th anniversary of the Bonn Agreement which established full communion between the Old Catholic Churches of the Union of Utrecht and the Churches of the Anglican Communion, and encourages the Anglican-Old Catholic Co-ordinating Council and the member churches of the Anglican Communion to seek ways to celebrate this milestone in our ecumenical relations

Resolution 28. Anglican-Roman Catholic Relations

This Anglican Consultative Council:

1. welcomes the statement *Communion in Mission* and the accompanying action plan resulting from the international meeting of Roman Catholic and Anglican bishops in May 2000 in Mississauga Canada;

2. welcomes also the establishment of the International Anglican-Roman Catholic Commission for Unity and Mission which will oversee the preparation of a Common Statement and which will take other steps to further growth towards unity in mission;

3. expresses its gratitude to the Archbishop of Canterbury and Cardinal Edward Cassidy for their efforts in bringing about this new development in Anglican-Roman Catholic relations and encourages member churches to give support to this new stage on the journey to full visible unity between the Roman Catholic Church and the Anglican Communion.

Resolution 29. Anglican-Lutheran International Working Group

This Anglican Consultative Council:

1. welcomes the report of the Anglican-Lutheran International Working Group *Growing in Communion*;

2. commends the report for study and follow-up by the Inter Anglican Standing Commission on Ecumenical Relations at its next meeting;

3. approves the establishment of an Anglican-Lutheran International Commission with membership and mandate as set out in paragraph 170 of *Growing in Communion.*

Resolution 30. Inter Anglican Theological and Doctrinal Commission

This Anglican Consultative Council:

1. notes with approval the method adopted by the Inter Anglican Theological and Doctrinal Commission (IATDC) in engaging dioceses,

centres of theological education, and individuals in a dialogue concerning the nature and sustaining of communion;

2. endorses the Commission's present plan of work; and

3. encourages members of the ACC to help promote responses to the next phase of the IATDC study within their own Provinces.

Resolution 31. Stipends and Pensions in Developing World

This Anglican Consultative Council:

1. is reminded that the churches in the developing world have long relied on the member churches in the developed world for sustenance and support;

2. notes with approval the stated commitment of churches of the developing world to become financially self-supporting within an interdependent Communion;

3. recognises nonetheless that the provision for adequate stipends and pensions for clergy and provincial staff remains a major problem for the churches in the developing world;

4. supports the initiative of African provinces to commence a regional process to address these issues at a meeting to be held in Nigeria in 2004;

5. commits itself to finding ways to provide technical assistance to the churches in the developing world in capacity building and training in investment methods, as well as seeking direct financial support to enhance and develop more stable stipend and pension provisions in these churches and refers this matter for priority attention of the upcoming Mission Agencies Conference.

Resolution 32. Endowment for the Anglican Communion

This Anglican Consultative Council meeting reiterates resolution 8 of the meeting of the Joint Standing Committee of the Primates of the Anglican Communion and the ACC in 2000 and greets with pleasure the intention of the Compass Rose Society to raise funds for an endowment for the work of the ACC in its many and varied aspects and resolves to work with the Compass Rose Society towards that end.

Resolution 33. Anglican Communion Sunday

This Anglican Consultative Council:

1. urges each province of the Anglican Communion to identify a day which will be Anglican Communion Sunday, the purpose of which will be to raise awareness of and celebrate the Anglican Communion;

2. invites churches to take a second offering on that day to be made available to the Anglican Communion Office for additional funding for, or special purposes within, the Inter-Anglican Budget.

Resolution 34. Province-wide and Communion-wide Consultation

This Anglican Consultative Council, being concerned about a range of matters of faith and order which have arisen since we last met, and having in mind the constant emphasis on mutual responsibility and interdependence in the resolutions of successive Lambeth Conferences, from the call in 1867 for "unity in faith and discipline . . . by due and canonical subordination of synods" (1867, IV) to the call in 1998 for a "common mind concerning ethical issues where contention threatens to divide . . ." (1998, IV 5 (c)) calls upon:

1. dioceses and individual bishops not to undertake unilateral actions or adopt policies which would strain our communion with one another without reference to their provincial authorities; and

2. provincial authorities to have in mind the impact of their decisions within the wider Communion; and

3. all members of the Communion, even in our disagreements to have in mind the "need for courtesy, tolerance, mutual respect and prayer for one another" (1998, III.2 (e)).

Resolution 35. Anglican Gathering 2008

This Anglican Consultative Council:

1. welcomes the work of the Feasibility Group for an Anglican Congress in 2008;

2. in the light of Resolution 14 of ACC-11, requests the Archbishop of Canterbury to give consideration to ways in which such a Congress might be held "in association with the next Lambeth Conference" in Cape Town in 2008;

3. requests the Feasibility Group to continue until the time of the meeting of the Joint Standing Committee of the Primates of the Anglican Communion and the Anglican Consultative Council in February 2003; and

4. further requests the Inter Anglican Finance Committee to release funds from the interest in the Lambeth Conference Account for any necessary expenses.

Resolution 36. More Representative Lambeth Conference

This Anglican Consultative Council:

Whilst recognising the value of past Lambeth Conferences,

1. encourages the Archbishop of Canterbury to consider the participation of clergy and lay people in future Conferences, and therefore
2. invites the Archbishop of Canterbury in consultation with ACC to appoint a working party to explore the possibility of a more representative gathering.

Resolution 37. Future Alterations to the Schedule of Membership of the ACC

This Anglican Consultative Council:

Resolves to amend the Constitution as follows: In the third line of clause 3 (a) delete the word "Council", and insert the words "Standing Committee".

Resolution 38. Membership of the Anglican Church of Tanzania on the ACC

This Anglican Consultative Council, noting with pleasure the growth of the Church in Tanzania, resolves, subject to the assent of the Primates, that the Church of Tanzania should be transferred from Category (c) to Category (b) of the Schedule of the Constitution.

Resolution 39. Co-opted Members of the Anglican Consultative Council

This Anglican Consultative Council, noting there will be four vacancies for Co-opted Members for ACC-13, resolves to delegate to its Standing Committee the appointment of Co-opted Members.

Resolution 40. Limitation of Liability

This Anglican Consultative Council welcomes the progress that has been made towards reconstituting the work of the Council within the framework of a limited liability company as directed by ACC-11 Resolution 6 (d); and authorises the Standing Committee to establish such a body in accordance with legal advice and to transfer to such a body all the Council's assets and liabilities in due course.

Resolution 41. Constitution of the Anglican Consultative Council

This Anglican Consultative Council:

1. asks that the Standing Committee appoint a committee to review the Constitution and By-Laws of the ACC, and to report to the Standing Committee;
2. asks that the Standing Committee circulate such proposals for amendment to the members of ACC in advance of ACC-13.

Resolutions 42. Finance and Budget

This Anglican Consultative Council:

1. receives the report of the Inter Anglican Finance Committee, and
2. adopts the budget for 2003.

Resolution 43. Prayers and Greetings

This Anglican Consultative Council sends its greetings and assurances of prayer to the following:

The Bishop of Rome, His Holiness Pope John Paul II, with prayers for his apostolic, evangelical and ecumenical ministry among all Christians, and with thanks for the growth towards *Communion in Mission* between the Roman Catholic Church and the churches of the Anglican Communion;

The Ecumenical Patriarch, His All Holiness Bartholomeos I, with prayers for the apostolic Church of Constantinople, and with thanks for the long-standing fraternal relationships between the Orthodox churches and the churches of the Anglican Communion;

The General Secretary of the Lutheran World Federation, the Revd Dr Ishmael Noko, with thanks for stimulating and challenging our thinking as a keynote speaker from our sister Communion of Lutheran Churches;

The Most Revd Joris Vercammen, Archbishop of Utrecht, and the Most Revd Dr Philipos Mar Thoma for ensuring the presence of representatives from Churches in Communion, The Revd Dr Harald Rein and Metropolitan Joseph Mar Irenaeus, who have made visible our unity in Christ;

His Eminence Metropolitan Nikitas, Orthodox Archbishop of South East Asia; the Revd Donald Bolen of the Pontifical Council for Promoting Christian Unity; the Revd Dr David Gill who represented the World Council of Churches; and Ms Mandy Tibbey of the Christian Conference of Asia with thanks for accompanying our meeting and enriching our fellowship as ecumenical partners.

Resolution 44. Resolutions of Thanks

This Anglican Consultative Council thanks God for the ministry of so many whose dedication and service have enabled the Council to do the work of the Church:

For our President, the Most Reverend & Right Honourable Dr. George Carey, for his Grace's faithful service of eleven years in office, and on this special occasion of his Grace's impending retirement from office in October 2002, to express our heartfelt gratitude for his personal commitment, clear proclamation, pastoral compassion and involvement in the daily life of the Council which constantly inspires the Church, and this Council wishes his Grace and Mrs. Carey a happy and fulfilling retirement.

For the invaluable presence of members of the Primates' Standing Committee the Most Reverend Bernard Amos Malango, the Most Reverend Michael Peers, the Most Reverend Rowan Williams, the Most Reverend Peter Kwong and the Most Reverend Z. James Terom.

For our Archbishop of Canterbury-designate the Most Reverend Rowan Williams, whose presence at the Opening Ceremony was deeply appreciated.

For our Chairman, the Right Reverend Simon Chiwanga, whose wisdom and experience have been a grace and strength to us and we wish him and Mrs. Chiwanga a happy and fulfilling retirement after eighteen years of faithful and dedicated service and enormous contributions to the Council.

For our Vice-Chairman, the Most Reverend John Paterson, whose steady hand has guided the work of the Council and we continue to look to him for his embracing and wise leadership.

For the Secretary General, the Reverend Canon John L. Peterson, whose enthusiastic presence encourages us, and indefatigable efforts in connecting members of the entire Anglican Communion family unites us, as one body in close fellowship in Christ. This Council is deeply grateful for his significant contribution to the Anglican Communion and this ACC-12 says fond farewell to the Secretary General whose term of service as Secretary General will expire by December 2004.

For the Design Group led by the Most Reverend John Paterson, assisted by Mr. John Rea, Canon Maureen Sithole and Ms. Wong Fung-Yi, who enabled us to diligently discharge our responsibility to the theme and the agenda.

For the Inter-Anglican Finance Committee, chaired by the Most Reverend Robin Eames, assisted by the Most Reverend Peter Akinola, Ms. Judith Conley, Mr. Ghazi Musharbash and Ms. Wong Fung-Yi for their conscientiousness and insights on financial matters.

For the Nomination Committee led by Mr. John Rea, assisted by the Most Reverend Peter Akinola, Ms. Lenore Parker and the Reverend Margaret B. Vertue who helped us discern our future leaders.

For the Resolutions Committee, led by the Reverend Robert Sessum, assisted by the Reverend Canon David Hamid, Mr. Bernard Georges, Ms. Sylvia Scarf, Mr. Bernard Turner and Ms. Wong Fung-Yi who helped us express our minds and priorities clearly.

For the Bible Studies in connection with the ministry of NIFCON presented by the Right Reverend Kenneth Fernando; in connection with the ministry of the Family Network, by Dr. Sally Thompson; in connection with the ministry of the Peace and Justice Network by Dr. Jennie P. Te Paa; in connection with the ministry of the Refugee and Migrant Network by the Most Reverend Ian George, which challenge us in our Christian walk and for the Bible Group Leaders: Mrs. Margaret Bihabanyi, Canon Michael Burrows, the Reverend Govada Dyvasirvadam, Canon Lovey Kisembo, the Right Reverend Bolly Lapok, Mrs. Joyce Ngoda, Mrs. Lenore Parker, Canon Elizabeth Paver and Canon Robert Thompson led by the Very Reverend Dr. John Moses who initiated animated discussions.

For the presentation by the United Nations Observer of the Anglican Communion Archdeacon Taimalelagi Fagamalama Tuatagaloa-Matalavea of our mission, ministry, opportunities and vision of service at this unique international organisation.

For the presentation by the Reverend Canon Eric Beresford on Ethics and Technology and for his diligent work in networking on these issues.

For the worship team, led by the chaplains, the Reverend Paul Gibson and the Reverend Andrew Chan, and the organists, Mrs. Jannie Chau, Mr. David Cooper and Ms. Alice W. S. Chan, who directed our hearts and minds in common prayer; and for the Reverend Paul Gibson's presentation on the International Anglican Liturgy Consultation.

For the Communications team, led by Canon Jim Rosenthal, assisted by the Reverend Paul Kwong, Canon Margaret Rodgers, the Reverend Dan England, Mr. Robert Tong and Mr. Christopher Took who enabled us to speak to the world both in paper and on our web-site.

For the executive assistant to the Secretary General, Mrs. Deirdre Martin; the co-ordinator of the meeting Ms. Marjorie Murphy; the Secretariat headed by Mrs. Veronica Elks and assisted by Mr. Matthew Davies; the Treasurer Mr. Andrew Franklin, assisted by the Reverend Dorothy Penniecooke; and for the Travel officer, Ms. Lynne Butt; the IT technician, Mr. Ian Harvey and for conference room IT support, Mr. Christopher Took, for their dedication and skills in serving the Council.

For the Legal Adviser, the Reverend Canon John Rees, for his counsel and assistance on legal and constitutional matters and his in-depth presentation and helpful sharing of the development and substantive agenda of the Legal Advisers' Network.

For the Director of Ecumenical Affairs, The Reverend Canon David Hamid, for assisting the ACC with its ecumenical and doctrinal agenda and this Council offers its best wishes to the ministry of the Reverend Canon David Hamid as Suffragan Bishop of Europe from October 2002.

For the Archbishop of Canterbury's staff the Reverend Canon Dr. Herman Browne, Mrs. Gill Harris-Hogarth and Miss Fiona Millican for assisting the Archbishop.

For the Reverend Gregory Cameron, Chaplain to the Archbishop of Canterbury-designate, the Most Reverend Dr Rowan Williams, for assisting his Grace.

For our partners in full Communion:
The Right Revd Joseph Mar Irenaeus—Mar Thomas Syrian Church of Malabar
Professor Harald Rein—the Old Catholic Churches of the Union of Utrecht for enriching the life of the Council with insights from their churches.

For our ecumenical partners:
The Reverend David Gill—World Council of Churches
The Reverend Donald Bolen—Roman Catholic Church
Ms. Mandy Tibby—Christian Conference of Asia
The Reverend Dr Ishmael Noko—General Secretary of the Lutheran World Federation
The Most Reverend Metropolitan Nikitas—Orthodox Church
whose encouraging greetings and presence reminded us of the Church beyond the Anglican Communion.

For our speakers and presenters:
The Most Reverend Dr Peter Kwong on "How Hong Kong Sheng Kung Hui faces challenges to the Church";
The Right Reverend Kenneth Fernando on the Network for Interfaith Concerns (NIFCON);
The Most Reverend Ian George on the Refugee and Migrant Network;
The Reverend Canon Ted Karpf on the HIV/AIDS pandemic;
The Reverend Dr Ishmael Noko on "A Global Overview of the Challenges Facing the Church";
Dr. Sally Thompson on the Family Network;
The Reverend Isamu Koshiishi on the Urban Network;
Miss A. Candace Payne on the Youth Network;
Dr. Jennie Te Paa on the Peace and Justice Network;
The Reverend Canon Ogé Beauvoir and the Reverend Emmanuel Adekola on the Telecommunication Network and the Reverend Canon Ogé Beauvoir on the launch of the Anglican Web Portal and the proposed Francophone Network;
Canon Maureen Sithole on the Women's Network and Anglican Gathering, and the Inter Anglican Standing Commission on Mission and Evangelism with Ms. Marjorie Murphy;
and for the Panel Responses from the Right Reverend Kenneth Fernando, the Most Reverend Ian George, Dr. Sally Thompson and Dr. Jennie Te Paa, who, each in their turn, informed and challenged us on the pressing issues before the Church.

For our hosts:
This ACC is pleased to place on record its profound thanks to the Province of Hong Kong Sheng Kung Hui for the warmth of its welcome, the magnificence of its hospitality, the generosity of its people and the lavish attention given to every detail of our visit and meeting. Our corporate sense of gratitude cannot readily be reduced to words, however effusive—so just a heartfelt thank you, in particular, to the Most Reverend Dr. Peter Kwong, the Right Reverend Louis Tsui, the Right Reverend Thomas Soo, the Reverend Dorothy Lau, the Reverend Andrew Chan and the Reverend Paul Kwong; the Very Reverend Christopher Phillips, clergy, congregations, organist, choir master and choir of St John's Cathedral for the Opening Service on 15th September 2002; the Reverend Chan Hin Cheung, clergy, congregation, organist, choir mistress and choir of Holy Trinity Church for Sunday Service on 22nd September 2002; the Reverend Ian Lam, clergy, congregations, organist, choir master and choir of St Mary's Church for the Closing Service on 25th September 2002.

For the volunteers from the Hong Kong Sheng Kung Hui Province.
Local Organising Committee:
Adviser: the Most Reverend Dr Peter Kwong, Local Liaison: the Reverend Dorothy Lau, the Reverend Andrew Chan, the Reverend Paul Kwong, Programme Group: Mr. Willy Ngai, Mrs. Judy Chua, Mr. Joseph Man, Local Tour Group: Miss Sally Law, Miss Michelle Lin, Press & Protocol Group: the Reverend Paul Kwong, Mr. Andrew Kwong, Mr. Lai Man, Mr. Patrick Wong, Conference Helpers: Ms. Sally Law, Miss Angel Ko, Ms. Paulie Lam, Ms. Nancy Tse, Mr. Chow Sai Chung, Ms. Tse Yim Fong, Ms. Sandy Yuen, Ms. Heidi Chun, Hospitality Group: Ms. Michelle Ng, Services: the Reverend Andrew Chan, the Reverend Frankie Lee, Mr Peter Koon, Local Staff Member: Mr. Chan Kwok Wai, Mr. Frankie Chow, Mr. Stephen Chung, Mrs. Lindy Ho, Ms. Victoria Kwan, Mr. Simon Lee, Mr. Tsui Kam Tong, Ms. Phoebe Wong, Mr. Wong Pui Leong.

Hospitality, Meeting and Programme: 50
Opening Eucharist: 60
Closing Service: 60
Welcome Dinner: 50
Musicians: 10
Cultural Night: 50

Local Churches/Schools/Service Units visited:
St John's Cathedral, Holy Trinity Church, St Mary's Church, Crown of Thorns Church, Church of the Ascension, HKSKH Ching Shan Primary School, HKSKH Yat Sau Primary School, HKSKH Tung Chung Integrated Services.

Students/Service Users involved:
Eucharist: 100 (including Scouts, St. John's Ambulance, etc.).

Welcome Dinner:
Kindergarten Students: 30, Primary School Students: 100, Secondary School Students: 350, Seniors and Housewives: 50 Primary School Students: 40

For members whose last meeting was ACC-12: the Right Reverend Robert Silk (Australia), the Right Reverend Michael Ingham (Canada), the Right Reverend Richard Harries (England), the Reverend Samuel Koshiishi (Japan), the Right Reverend Joseph Wasonga (Kenya), Engineer Antonio Ortega Reybal (Mexico), Chief Godwin O. K. Ajayi (Nigeria), Mr. Warren Luyaben (Philippines), the Right Reverend Josias Sendegeya (Rwanda), Mrs. Margaret Bihabanyi (Rwanda), Mr. John Rea (Scotland), the Right Reverend Bolly Lapok (South East Asia), the Right Reverend Badda Peter Sughandar (South India), the Reverend Govada Dyvasirvadam (South India), Canon Maureen Sithole (Southern Africa), the Right Reverend Hector Zavala (Southern Cone of America), the Right Reverend Michael Sokiri Lugor (Sudan), Mr. Is-hag Kannidi Kodi Kodi (Sudan), the Most Reverend Livingstone Mpalanyi-Nkoyoyo (Uganda), Ms. Judith Conley (United States of America), Professor Adrian DeHeer-Amissah (West Africa), Mr. Bernard Turner (West Indies), Mr. Nicolas Casie Chetty (Ceylon); Mrs. Lenore Parker (co-opted), Mr. Ghazi Musharbash (co-opted), the Reverend Lovey Kisembo (co-opted); for their dedication and commitment to the work of the wider Anglican Communion.

For the interpreters, Ms, Nicole Rochon, Ms. Ghislaine Chabanol and Mr. Jean Damascene who opened the meeting to Spanish and French speakers.

For the YMCA Salisbury staff, and all who assisted in the chapel, plenary hall, dining room, the bible study suites, the corridors, shepherding us to the correct venues, the amenities and facilities rooms.

For the members whose last meeting was ACC-12 for their dedication and commitment to the work of the wider Anglican Communion.

The Last Word

—THE RIGHT REVEREND RICHARD HARRIES, BISHOP OF OXFORD

How to Decide What is Doctrine

ACC members meeting in Hong Kong from 14 September until yesterday were greeted by the news that one of the members from Congo had been hacked to death, and the other was in hiding. At the opening ceremony, in which each province had its own banner, the one from Congo was wreathed in a black band.

There have been other sombre reminders of the harsh realities of the world in which we live. The Revd Ted Karpf, who heads the Archbishop of Cape Town's campaign on HIV/AIDS, gave a desperately moving presentation of the world situation. Up to 50 million people now suffer from HIV/AIDS; in South Africa, 3,000 people a day are dying from the disease, the same number as were killed on 11 September. Life expectancy in Botswana is now 37, in contrast with Hong Kong, where it is 81.

Such figures can make one despair. Yet they can also impel action, and there were a good number of examples of churches trying to bring something of the care of Christ to a diseased world—not with a sense of superiority, but in solidarity with it. As Ted Karpf emphasised: "Our Church has AIDS"—10 million Anglicans will die.

In South Africa and Uganda, the Church is active in education programmes on AIDS prevention, as well as succouring those who are isolated. In Africa, it is individual Christians who are responding at a personal and family level. One delegate told me that she was from "a typical African family". She explained that her three sisters and her brother-in-law had all died of AIDS. The result was that, in addition to her own three children, she had brought up and educated five others, as if they were her own.

One positive story is that of Hong Kong itself. This small, new province has a major programme of social care, partly in partnership with the government. It runs integrated social services units—200 of them, and more than 100 schools.

Bishop Peter Kwong revealed himself to be a man of extraordinary foresight and leadership in the way he has helped the Church make the transition from British to Chinese rule. Hong Kong itself is a remarkable example of human drive, ingenuity, and a multiplicity of skills co-operatively used. Despite the economic downturn, its Church also has this dynamic character.

Although the ACC is concerned with problems of the world and how the Churches might best respond to them, inevitably there were some internal matters. The Archbishop of Canterbury proposed a motion that dioceses should not undertake unilateral actions without reference to their provincial authorities, and these should bear in mind the impact of decisions on the wider Anglican Communion.

In response, the Bishop of New Westminster in Canada, the Rt Revd Michael Ingham, together with the Chancellor of the diocese and the Archbishop of the province, made an unofficial presentation on the process whereby the diocesan bishop has now agreed to sanction same-sex blessings.

It is clear that they went through a very careful consultative process. Yet this process brings out starkly the different relationships of the diocese to the province and the national Church in different parts of the world. In Canada, it is up to the diocese to decide its policy, unless either the province or the National Synod has the will to pronounce. The precedents are to leave it to the diocese. So neither the province nor the National Synod pronounced on same-sex blessings.

A legal commission set up by the diocese of New Westminster stated that a blessing is not a sacrament, and thus it falls within the jurisdiction of the diocesan bishop whether to authorise such blessings. But this raises further questions about what counts as a doctrinal matter and, crucially, who decides—diocese, province, national Church or the Anglican Communion (in so far as its mind can be discerned through the Lambeth Conference and other instruments of unity).

One of the Anglican instruments of unity is the Archbishop of Canterbury himself, and Dr. Carey was attending his last ACC. Here, as in so many other parts of the Communion, his ministry has been warmly appreciated. As one delegate put it: "You have shown us what Evangelical defiance is all about. You have stood up in the Sudan and so many other places of suffering and conflict for Christians."

Another instrument of Anglican unity, the Lambeth Conference, was also the subject of a resolution. Dr. Williams, when he takes up office, will be presented with two options. One is for an Anglican Congress; the other is for a very different, more representative, kind of Lambeth Conference, each diocesan bishop bringing a priest and lay person from their diocese.

The original motion on this contained the phrase "a more synodical gathering". But the idea of Anglican synod sent a tremor through some quarters; so this was amended to “a more representative gathering”.

I look forward to the day when the Lambeth Conference evolves in that direction. The ACC and the Primates’ meeting could also change into more of a standing committee of such a Lambeth Conference.

Reprinted with kind permission from *Church Times,* 27 September 2002
www.churchtimes.co.uk

Directory of Provincial Secretaries of the Anglican Communion

The Anglican Church in Aotearoa, New Zealand & Polynesia
Mr. Robin A. I. Nairn
General Secretary/Treasurer, The Anglican Church in Aotearoa, New Zealand & Polynesia
P.O. Box 885, Hastings, NEW ZEALAND
Street Address: 204N Warren Street, Hastings, New Zealand
Office: +64 (0)6 878 7902
Fax: +64 (0)6 878 7905
E-mail: gensec@hb.ang.org.nz

The Anglican Church of Australia
The Reverend Dr. Bruce Norman Kaye
General Secretary, The General Synod, Anglican Church of Australia
P.O. Box Q190, Queen Victoria Post Office, Sydney, New South Wales, 1230, AUSTRALIA
Office: +61 (0)2 9265 1525
Fax: +61 (0)2 9264 6552
Email: gsoffice@anglican.org.au *or* bnkaye@anglican.org.au
Web: www.anglican.org.au/nco

The Church of Bangladesh
Mr. Albert Achintya Samadder
Hon. Provincial Secretary, Church of Bangladesh
St Thomas' Church, 54 Johnson Road, Dhaka-1100, BANGLADESH
Office: +880 (0)2 711 6546
Fax: +880 (0)2 711 8218
Email: cbdacdio@bangla.net *or* cmcy@bdmail.net

Igreja Episcopal Anglicana do Brasil
The Reverend Canon Maurício José Araújo de Andrade
General Secretary, Igreja Episcopal Anglicana do Brasil
Caixa Postal 11 510, Porto Alegre, RS 90870 970, BRAZIL
Office: +55 (0)51 3318 6200
Fax: +55 (0)51 3318 6200
Email: m_andrade@ieab.og.br
Web: www.ieab.org.br

The Episcopal Church of Burundi
The Reverend Pascal Bigirimana
Provincial Secretary, The Episcopal Church of Burundi
BP 2098, Bujumbura, BURUNDI
Office: +257 224 389
Fax: +257 229 129
Fax: +257 21 91 72

The Anglican Church of Canada
The Venerable James B. Boyles
General Secretary of the General Synod,
600 Jarvis Street, Toronto, Ontario, M4Y 2J6, CANADA
Office: +1 416 924 9199
Fax: +1 416 924 0211
Email: jboyles@national.anglican.ca

The Church of the Province of Central Africa
The Reverend Albert Chama
Provincial Secretary,
P.O. Box 22317, Kitwe, ZAMBIA
Office: +260 2 096 90
Fax: +260 2 224 778
Email: cpca@zamnet.zm *or* albertchama@hotmail.com

Iglesia Anglicana de la Region Central de America
The Reverend Hector Monterroso
Provincial Secretary,
19 Ave. 8-64, Zona 15, Vista Hermosa I., Guatemala City, GUATEMALA
Office: +502 (0)2 369 0669
Fax: +502 (0)2 369 0669
Email: iarcahfm@terra.com.gt *or* iarcahfm@hotmail.com

Province de L'Eglise Anglicane Du Congo
The Reverend Molanga Botola
Provincial Secretary, Province de L'Eglise Anglicane Du Congo
P.O. Box 25586, Kampala, UGANDA
Street Address: BP 798, Bunia, Republique Democratique Du Congo CAC—Bunia, PO Box 21285, Nairobi, KENYA
Office: +256 41 273 817
Fax: +256 41 343 497
Email: eac-mags@infocom.co.ug

The Church of England
Provincial Secretary,
Church House, Great Smith Street, London, SW1P 3NZ, ENGLAND
Office: +44 0207 898 1360
Fax: +44 0207 898 1369
Email: synod@church-of-england.org

Hong Kong Sheng Kung Hui
The Reverend Andrew Chan
Provincial General Secretary,
1 Lower Albert Road, Central, Hong Kong, PEOPLE'S REPUBLIC OF CHINA
Office: +852 2526 5355
Fax: +852 2521 2199
Email: gensec@hkskh.org *or* office1@hkskh.org
Web: www.hkskh.org

The Church of the Province of the Indian Ocean
The Reverend Emile Victor Rakotoarivelo
Provincial Secretary,
Box 8445, Tsaralalana, 101, Antananarivo, MADAGASCAR
Email: eemdanta@dts.mg

The Church of Ireland
Mr. Denis Reardon
Chief Officer and Secretary,
Church of Ireland House, Church Avenue, Rathmines, Dublin, 6, REPUBLIC OF IRELAND
Office: +353 (0)1 497 8422
Fax: +353 (0)1 497 8792
Email: chief@rcbdub.org

The Nippon Sei Ko Kai (The Anglican Communion in Japan)
The Reverend Lawrence Minabe
General Secretary,
65-3 Yarai Cho, Shinjuku-Ku, Tokyo, 162-0805, JAPAN
Office: +81 (0)3 5228 3171
Fax: +81 (0)3 5228 3175
Email: general-sec.po@nskk.org

The Episcopal Church in Jerusalem & The Middle East
The Venerable Ian Young
Provincial Secretary,
P.O. Box 22075, Nicosia, 1517, CYPRUS
Office: +357 22 671 220
Fax: +357 22 674 533
Email: georgia@spidernet.com.cy

The Anglican Church of Kenya
Mrs. Susan Nzisa Mumina
Provincial Secretary, The Anglican Church of Kenya
P.O. Box 40502, Bishops Gardens, Nairobi, KENYA
Street Address: CPK, Language School Building, Off Bishop's Road, Nairobi, Kenya

Office: +254 2 714 752
Office: +254 2 714 753
Fax: +254 (0)2 714 750
Email: ackenya@insightkenya.com *or* amurage@ackenya.org

The Anglican Church of Korea
The Reverend Chae-Yul Kim
General Secretary, The Anglican Church of Korea
3 Chong Dong Chung Ku, Seoul 100-120, REPUBLIC OF KOREA
Office: +82 (0)2 738 8952
Fax: +82 (0)2 737 4210
Email: anck@peacenet.or.kr *or* abgw@lycos.co.kr

The Church of the Province of Melanesia
Mr. George S Kiriau
General Secretary,
P.O. Box 19, Honiara, SOLOMON ISLANDS
Office: +677 20470 / 21892
Fax: +677 210 98
Email: gkiriau@comphq.org.sb
Web: http://melanesia.anglican.org

La Iglesia Anglicana de Mexico
The Reverend Jose Manuel Sonora
Provincial Secretary, La Iglesia Anglicana de Mexico
Calle La Otra Banda #40, San Angel, 01090 Mexico, DF, MEXICO
Office: +52 (0)5 550 4073
Office: +52 (0)5 616 2490
Fax: +52 (0)5 616 4063
Email: ofipam@adetel.net.mx *or* msonoram@correoweb.com
Web: www.iglesia-anglicana-mexico.org.mx

The Church of the Province of Myanmar (Burma)
Mr. Kenneth Saw
Provincial Secretary,
140 Pyidaungsu Yeiktha Road, Dagon PO 11191, Yangon, MYANMAR
Office: +95 1 246 813
Fax: +95 1 251 405

The Church of Nigeria (Anglican Communion)
The Venerable Ranti Odubogun
General Secretary,
Episcopal House, P.O. Box 212, AD CP, Abuja, NIGERIA
Street Address: Episcopal House, 23 Dovale Street, WUSE Zone 5
Office: +234 9 523 6950
Email: abuja@anglican.skannet.com.ng

The Church of North India (United)
Dr. Vidya Sagar Lall
Provincial Secretary,
CNI Bhawan, Post Box No 311, 16 Pandit Pant Marg, New Delhi, 110 001, INDIA
Alternate contact for the Right Reverend Zechariah James Terom, Moderator of the Church of North India.
Office: +91 (0)11 373 1079
Office: +91 (0)11 373 1081
Fax: +91 (0)11 371 6901
Email: sagar@cnisynod.org
Email: gscni@ndb.vsnl.net.in
Web: www.cnisynod.org

The Church of Pakistan (United)
Dr. Aziz Gul
Secretary General, The Synod, Church of Pakistan
Mission Compound, Daska, Dist Sialkot, PAKISTAN
Office: +92 (0)4341 5104

The Anglican Church of Papua New Guinea
Mr. Martin Gardham
National Secretary, Anglican Church of Papua New Guinea
Box 673, Lae, Morobe Province, PAPUA NEW GUINEA
Office: +675 472 4111
Fax: +675 472 1852
Email: acpng@global.net.pg

The Episcopal Church in the Philippines
Dr. Andrew Tauli
Provincial Secretary,
Provincial Office, P.O. Box 10321, Broadway Centrum, 1112 Quezon City, PHILIPPINES
Office: +632 722 8460
Fax: +632 722 8481
Email: ecpnational@edsamail.com.ph *or* a2t2@pacific.net.ph
Web: http://episcopalphilippines.net

L'Eglise Episcopal au Rwanda
The Right Reverend Josias Sendegeya
Bishop of Kibungo,
BP 2487, Kigali, RWANDA
Office: +250 514 160
Office: +250 514 161
Fax: +250 514 160
Fax: +250 6504
Email: peer@rwandate11.rwanda1.com

The Scottish Episcopal Church

Mr. John Stuart
Secretary General, Scottish Episcopal Church
21 Grosvenor Crescent, Edinburgh, EH12 5EE, SCOTLAND
Office: +44 (0)131 225 6357
Fax: +44 (0)131 346 7247
Email: secgen@scotland.anglican.org

Church of the Province of South East Asia

Datuk Robert Jacob Ridu
Provincial Secretary, Church of the Province of South East Asia
c/o P.O. Box 347, Kuching, Sarawak, MALAYSIA
Street Address: McDougall Road, 9300 Kuching, Sarawak
Office: +60 (0)82 472 177
Fax: +60 (0)82 426 488

The Church of South India (United)

The Reverend G. Dyvasirvadam
General Secretary, CSI Synod Secretariat
P.O. Box 688, Royapettah, Chennai-600 014, INDIA
Street Address: 5 Whites Road, Royapettah, Madras 600 014, India
Office: +91 (0)44 852 1566
Office: +91 (0)44 852 4166
Fax: +91 (0)44 852 3528
Email: csisnd@md3.vsnl.net.in *or* csi@vsnl.com

The Church of the Province of Southern Africa

The Reverend Canon Luke Luscombe Lungile Pato
Provincial Executive Officer, Church of the Province of Southern Africa
16-20 Bishopscourt Drive, Claremont, 7708, SOUTH AFRICA
Office: +27 (0)21 761 2531
Fax: +27 (0)21 797 1329
Email: cpsa-peo@mweb.co.za *or* lukep@mweb.co.za

Iglesia Anglicana del Cono Sur de America

The Reverend Enrique Lago
Provincial Secretary,
Iglesia Anglicana de Chile, Oficina Diocesana, José Miguel de la barra 480, Oficina 205, Casilla 50675, Santiago, CHILE
Office: +562 638 3009
Fax: +562 639 4581

The Episcopal Church of the Sudan

The Very Reverend Ezekiel Kondo
Provincial Secretary, The Episcopal Church of the Sudan
P.O. Box 604, Khartoum, SUDAN
Office: +249 11 762 964
Fax: +249 11 762 962
Email: ecsprovince@hotmail.com

The Anglican Church of Tanzania
Dr. R. Mwita Akiri
Acting General Secretary, Church of the Province of Tanzania
P.O. Box 899, Dodoma, TANZANIA
Office: +255 026 232 1437
Fax: +255 026 232 4565
Email: cpt@maf.org *or* akiri@maf.or.tz

The Church of the Province of Uganda
The Reverend Canon Dr. Tom Tuma
Acting Provincial Secretary,
P.O. Box 14123, Kampala, UGANDA
Office: +256 (0)41 270 218
Fax: +256 (0)41 251 925
Email: coups@uol.co.ug *or* counet-ps@Mukla.gn.apc.org

The Episcopal Church in the USA
The Reverend Canon Patrick Mauney
Director of Anglican and Global Relations, & Provincial Secretary
The Episcopal Church Center, 815 Second Avenue, New York, NY, 10017, USA
Office: +1 212 716 6223
Fax: +1 212 983 6377
Email: pmauney@episcopalchurch.org

The Reverend Rosemari Sullivan
Executive Officer and Secretary of the General Convention,
The Episcopal Church Center, 815 Second Avenue, New York, NY, 10017, USA
Email: rsullivan@episcopalchurch.org

The Church in Wales
The Reverend Robert Paterson
Secretary, The Council for Mission & Ministry
39 Cathedral Road, Cardiff, CF11 9XF, WALES
Office: +44 (0)29 2034 8200
Fax: +44 (0)29 2038 7835
Email: marerskine@cmm.nildram.co.uk
or rosemaryrichards.cmm@churchinwales.org.uk
Web: www.churchinwales.org.uk

Mr. John M. Shirley
Provincial Secretary, The Church in Wales
39 Cathedral Road, Cardiff, CF11 9XF, WALES
Office: +44 (0)2920 231 638
Fax: +44 (0)2920 387 835
Email: johnshirley@churchinwales.org.uk

The Church of the Province of West Africa
Mr Nat N. Stanley
Provincial Secretary, The Church of the Province of West Africa
Bishopscourt, P.O. Box 8, Accra, GHANA
Office: +233 (0)21 663 595
Office: +233 (0)21 662 292
Fax: +233 (0)21 669 125
Email: cpwa@gppo.africaonline.com.gh

The Church in the Province of the West Indies
Mr. Idris G. Reid
Provincial Secretary, The Provincial Secretariat
Church House, P.O. Box N-656, Nassau, BAHAMAS
Office: +1 242 322 3015/6/7
Fax: +1 268 462 2090
Email: ireid@bahamas.net.bs *or* cpwi@bahamas.net.bs

The Church of Ceylon
Mrs. Mary Thanja Peiris
Provincial Secretary,
368/3A Bauddhaloka, Mawathe, Colombo 7, SRI LANKA
Office: +94 1 684 810
Office: +94 1 696 208
Fax: +94 1 684 811
Email: diocol@eureka.lk

Iglesia Episcopal de Cuba
The Right Reverend Jorge Perera Hurtado
Bishop of Cuba,
Calle 6, No 273 Vedado, Havana, 10400, CUBA
Office: +53 (0)7 32 11 20
Office: +53 (0)7 31 24 36
Fax: +53 (0)7 333 293
Email: episcopal@ip.etecsa.cu
Web: http://cuba.anglican.org

Archbishop of Canterbury's Enthronement Sermon

–The Most Reverend and Right Hon. Rowan D. Williams, Archbishop of Canterbury

Canterbury Cathedral, Thursday, 27 February 2003

It's sometimes been said that if someone came up to you in the street and whispered, 'They've found out! Run!', nine out of ten of us would. We nearly all have secrets that we don't want exposed—even if they are quite trivial in the cold light of day—and that phrase tell us a lot, the cold light: we don't want to be under the kind of detached scrutiny that threatens and diminishes us, sitting under a bare light bulb being interrogated. So when it looks as though our secrets are about to be revealed, we easily panic and run.

More seriously, there are secrets too that are terrible for us and others to face because they have to do with pain we can't cope with, abuse, enforced silence, secrets that others make us keep. To feel that the truth is to be revealed before we have the resource to live with it is humiliating and frightening. Again we might properly shrink from this. But secrets are also fascinating. If someone came up to you in the street and whispered, 'Go to such and such an address and you will be told the secret of your real identity', most of us would feel at least a flicker of temptation to go and find out. We never knew there was such a secret, a life we have never known—but what if there were?

The gospel reading we've just heard [Matthew 11:25–30]is about knowing and telling secrets, discovering a truth not everyone sees. In one way, nothing is hidden: Jesus has just been talking about what happens to the local towns that have seen his miracles and heard his words and yet haven't changed. It's as though the people in these towns haven't realised there is any mystery about who Jesus is; they look at what he does and they listen to what he says, yet they treat it as something they can think about at arms' length, an interesting phenomenon that has nothing really to do with how they live and die. And Jesus rounds on them and says, 'I don't want your idle curiosity, I don't want your patronage. There is a secret that you haven't a clue about—and the ones who know that secret are the ones who don't try to protect themselves by staying at a safe distance.' And he might equally round on us, in what used to be called 'Christendom' in the West, and say, 'You have seen everything, the truth has been displayed, and yet you too react with boredom or polite curiosity. It's all a bit too familiar,' he says. 'Perhaps it's time for you to listen to some strangers.'

'You have hidden these things from the wise and intelligent', says the Lord, from those who make the kind of sense we can cope with. We must turn to the children; the exhausted; the ravaged and burdened and oppressed—they know the secret. Unless we know that we need life, we'll be baffled; but we hate admitting our lack, our poverty. It's the really hungry who can smell fresh bread a mile away. For those who know their need, God is immediate—not an idea, not a theory, but life, food, air for the stifled spirit and the beaten, despised, exploited body.

But what is this food, this life? Here's the deeper secret. To Jesus is given the freedom to give God's own life and love; and that life and love is bound up with knowing God the source of all as one who in giving life to his children holds nothing back, whose life is poured into the willing heart of Jesus so that Jesus can give it to the world. 'All things have been handed over to me by my Father'. So wherever Jesus is, God is active, pouring out his gift, inviting our response. And this means we can't know fully who God is and what God gives unless we are willing to stand in the same place as Jesus, in the full flood of the divine life poured out in mercy and renewal. It's only in the water that you can begin to swim.

We learn painfully quickly that we cannot hold our own there by our own strength; it is Jesus's gift in life and death and resurrection that makes it possible for us to stand with him, breathing his breath, his Spirit. Without the gift of the Spirit, we couldn't survive the presence of that absolute Truth, that unfading light which is God. And if we're not seeking to stand where Jesus is, all our talk about God remains on the level of theory; nothing has changed. On the Day of Judgement, says Jesus, looking back at the towns where he has ministered, the people who are in trouble are those who have seen everything and grasped nothing; who know everything about bread except that you're meant to eat it.

The one great purpose of the Church's existence is to share that bread of life; to hold open in its words and actions a place where we can be with Jesus and to be channels for his free, unanxious, utterly demanding, grown-up love. The Church exists to pass on the promise of Jesus—'You can live in the presence of God without fear; you can receive from his fullness and set others free from fear and guilt'. And, as with all secrets, people will react with a mixture of that fascination and alarm we began with. Here is the secret of our true identity—we are made to be God's children and to find our most profound freedom in surrender to him. We only become completely human when we allow God to remake us. Like the conservationist in the art gallery, God works patiently to remove the grime, the oil and dust of ages, and to let us appear—as we say—in our true colours. Wonderful, yes; but it means also that God will lay bare all the ways we hide from him and each other, all the sad and compromised and cowardly things we do to stop ourselves being human. 'They've found out! Run!' But, says Jesus, gently and insistently, we must stay. In the unsurpassable words that George Herbert puts into Our Lord's mouth, 'You must sit down, says Love, and taste my meat'. Truth looks terrifying; but taste and see. You will find that Truth is indeed the bread of life.

But it's still pretty frightening. Once we recognise God's great secret, that we are all meant to be God's sons and daughters, we can't avoid the call to see one another differently. No one can be written off; no group, no nation, no minority can just be a scapegoat to resolve our fears and uncertainties. We cannot assume that any human face we see has no divine secret to disclose: those who are culturally or religiously strange to us; those who so often don't count in the world's terms (the old, the unborn, the disabled). And this is what unsettles our loyalties, conservative or liberal, right wing or left, national and international. We have to learn to be human alongside all sorts of others, the ones whose company we don't greatly like, the ones we didn't choose, because Jesus is drawing us together into his place, into his company.

So an authentic church has a difficult job. On the one hand, it must be constantly learning from the Bible and its shared life of prayer how to live with Jesus and his Father; its life makes no sense unless we believe that the secret Jesus reveals to those hungry for life is the very bedrock of truth. The Church can't believe and say whatever it likes, for the very sound reason that it is a community of people who have been changed because and only because of Jesus Christ. I am a Christian because of the change made to me by Jesus Christ, because of the gift of the Holy Spirit, which gives me the right to call God 'Abba, Father'; what other reason is there?

But then there is a further dimension. Living in Jesus's company, I have to live in a community that is more than just the gathering of those who happen to agree with me, because I need also to be surprised and challenged by the Jesus each of you will have experienced. As long as we can still identify the same Jesus in each other's life, we have something to share and to learn. Does there come a point where we can't recognise the same Jesus, the same secret? The Anglican Church is often accused of having no way of answering this. But I don't believe it; we read the same Bible and practise the same sacraments and say the same creeds. But I do believe that we have the very best of reasons for hesitating to identify such a point too quickly or easily—because we believe in a Jesus who is truly Lord and God, not the prisoner of my current thoughts or experiences.

But it is this that gives us the freedom and the obligation to challenge what our various cultures may say about humanity. If all we have to offer is a Jesus who makes sense to me and people like me, we have no saving truth to give. But the truth is that we are given the joy of speaking about one who is the secret of all hearts, the hidden centre of everything—and so one who comes to us always, yes, as a stranger, 'as one unknown', in

Albert Schweitzer's words, but also as the one that each person can recognise as 'more intimate to me than I myself'. This is why the Christian will engage with passion in the world of our society and politics—out of a real hunger and thirst to see God's image, the destiny of human beings to become God's sons and daughters come to light—and it must be said also, out of a real grief and fear of what the human future will be if this does not come to light. The Church has to warn and to lament as well as to comfort.

So when Christians grieve or protest about war, about debt and poverty, about prejudice, about the humiliations of unemployment or the vacuous cruelty of sexual greed and unfaithfulness, about the abuse of children or the neglect of the helpless elderly, it is because of the fear we rightly feel when insult and violence blot out the divine image in our human relations, the reflection to one another of the promise of Jesus in one another. And anything that begins to make us casual about this is one more contribution to obscuring the original image of God in us, another layer of dust and grime over the bright face of Jesus Christ.

What we need to learn is the generosity that comes from true and proper confidence in the secret shared with us. We need to be confident that we are created: that we exist because God has freely called us into life so that God's joy may be shared. In this confidence, we know that our human task is to answer that call in every moment, shaping our lives as a response to God's voice. We need to be confident that we are redeemed: that God has acted once and for all in Jesus Christ to halt us in our slide towards self-destruction and has opened to us the possibility of life that is animated by nothing less than God's life. In this confidence, we know that our human task is to be thankful, to respond to God with noisy praise and silent adoration. And we need to be confident that we are being transfigured: touched by God's Holy Spirit, we have been decisively changed and endowed with something of God's liberty. In this confidence, we know that we are not prisoners of the world, we can make a difference by God's grace, and can share in the work of uncovering afresh the hidden face, the life-giving secret.

Can we, then, as a Church—in this diocese, in Britain, in the worldwide Communion—discover such confidence? Yes; but only if our foundation is that sense of being told our secret, our real identity, by Jesus; only if we come to him as the one who alone can satisfy the hunger of human hearts. 'You must sit down, says Love, and taste my meat. So I did sit and eat'.

Today is a time to reflect with you all about the character of the ministry that I'm taking on; but as I try to do this, I find it's not possible to think how I can minister the living bread of Christ unless I first seek to become clearer about what I long to see in the Church in which I shall be ministering. After all, it is God in the midst of God's people who will enable me to minister—not any programme or manifesto, not any avalanche of projections. So the most significant question I can ask myself in your presence about the work ahead is 'What do I pray for in the Church of the future?'

Confidence; courage; an imagination set on fire by the vision of God the Holy Trinity; thankfulness. The Church of the future, I believe, will do both its prophetic and its pastoral work effectively only if it is concerned first with gratitude and joy; orthodoxy flows from this, not the other way around, and we don't solve our deepest problems just by better discipline but by better discipleship, a fuller entry into the intimate joy of Jesus's life. When we have become more honest about our hunger and our loss, we shall have a fuller awareness of what that joy is; and as that joy matures, we shall have a fuller sense of the depth of our need. And so it goes on, the spiral of discovery, moving deeper into the radiant mystery of Christ.

About twelve years ago, I was visiting an Orthodox monastery, and was taken to see one of the smaller and older chapels. It was a place intensely full of the memory and reality of prayer. The monk showing me around pulled the curtain from in front of the sanctuary, and there inside was a plain altar and one simple picture of Jesus, darkened and rather undistinguished. But for some reason at that moment it was as if the veil of the temple was torn in two: I saw as I had never seen the simple fact of Jesus at the heart of all our words and worship, behind the curtain of our anxieties and our theories, our struggles and our suspicion. Simply there; nothing anyone can do about it, there he is as he has promised to be till the world's end. And nothing of value happens in the Church that does not start from seeing him simply there in our midst, suffering and transforming our human disaster.

And he says to us, 'If you don't know why this matters, look for someone who does—the child, the poor, the forgotten. Learn from them, and you will learn from me. You will find a life's work; and you will find rest for your souls; you will come home; you will sit and eat.'

Pastoral Letter from the Primates of the Anglican Communion

THE PRIMATES OF THE ANGLICAN COMMUNION SENT THIS PASTORAL LETTER TO ALL BISHOPS, CLERGY AND PEOPLE OF OUR CHURCHES, WITH THE DESIRE THAT IT BE READ OR DISTRIBUTED AT PUBLIC WORSHIP ON THE FEAST OF PENTECOST, 2003.—"I HAVE CALLED YOU FRIENDS." (JOHN 15.15)

United in Common Prayer and Witness

To our sisters and brothers of the Anglican Communion: Greetings in the name of our Lord Jesus Christ and in the joy of the Holy Spirit.

We met as Primates of the Anglican Communion in Gramado, Southern Brazil from 19th to 26th May 2003, at the invitation of the Igreja Episcopal Anglicana do Brasil, to bring before God our common life as the Anglican Communion and to take counsel together on the life of our churches. Five Primates were unable to be with us, and we prayed especially for the Archbishop and people of the Hong Kong Sheng Kung Hui, facing the difficulties of the SARS situation.

We gathered first and foremost in a spirit of common prayer and worship, listening for the voice of God as revealed in the Holy Scriptures and manifested in the lives of our communities. We give thanks to God for what was shared among us — for the welcome of the Brazilian Church; for the music and worship led by local Christians; for the Bible studies led by the Archbishop of Canterbury, Rowan Williams; for the theological reflections by Dr Esther Mombo and Professor David Ford; and for the stories of witness and Christian discipleship from across the Anglican Communion.

In particular, we listened to stories of the growth of our churches in mission, of the creation of new dioceses and provinces and of the fruits of discipleship. They reflect the richness of our diversity across the globe, and the abundant resources of the Gospel to address all people in all situations.

We heard accounts of how many people, including faithful Anglicans, have faced extreme situations of natural disaster, disease, the threat of terrorism, social unrest, war and its aftermath. We were moved by stories of Christian witness:

- in Sudan, where the Episcopal Church faces the huge challenge of helping to transform a culture of war to a culture of peace;

- in other African nations, such as Burundi and the Congo, where despite war, death and disease, the Anglican Church is courageously expanding its mission in circumstances of deprivation and hardship;

- in the Holy Land, where we are saddened by the unbroken chain of violence but encouraged by some recent signs of progress towards a resolution of the Israel-Palestine conflict;

- in Afghanistan and Iraq, where the humanitarian crisis is in many ways worse than before the recent conflicts, and where we see a need for greater United Nations involvement in repairing the damage;

- in some island states in the Pacific, where the Anglican Church is playing a peacemaking role in conditions of great political instability and corruption.

We thank God for the courage and wisdom that he has given in these situations, and affirm our solidarity with all who face alienation, persecution or injustice. We are mindful of those who live out their Christian faith as small minorities within their societies.

We give thanks for our life together in the Anglican Communion, for the way in which churches of the Communion support one another and, in particular, for the contribution which the Episcopal Church (USA) continues to give to many provinces across our Communion. We send our brotherly greetings to George and Eileen Carey, with thanksgiving for all they achieved in their ministry among us.

We rejoice in the fellowship we share with other churches and denominations, at the same time recognising that any true ecumenical endeavour has to be built on the mutual recognition and respect which we must accord each other as fellow members of the Body of Christ.

Our Work Together

We take to heart the words of Dr Esther Mombo, who urged us to "talk to each other rather than about each other". We welcomed our brother in Christ, Rowan Williams, to his first meeting with us as Archbishop of Canterbury. We listened to him as he shared some of the priorities for his ministry. As reflected in the agenda of our meeting, these are:

- Theological education, which is facing different kinds of crisis in all provinces;

- The continuing engagement of our churches with HIV/AIDS;

- The nature of communion itself and, in particular, how we might be drawn together and renewed in an Anglican Gathering.

Theological Education

It is our conviction that all Anglican Christians should be theologically alert and sensitive to the call of God. We should all be thoughtful and prayerful in reading and hearing the Holy Scriptures, both in the light of the past and with an awareness of present and future needs.

We discussed what basic standards of theological education should be provided for and expected from all members of the Church. All regions face major challenges in this area, particularly in the provision of resources in non-English speaking provinces, and we considered how these should be met.

We recognise that there is a distinctive Anglican approach to theological study. This is reflected not only in the way our worship and liturgical life express our belief, and in our attention to Scripture read in the light of tradition, but also in our respect for exploration and experiment.

Theological education in the Anglican Communion honours each local context and, at the same time, calls us together into communion and mutual accountability. Therefore, though we wish to develop common standards of theological education worldwide, we value the uniqueness of the work of the Holy Spirit in each place.

Supportive of the Archbishop of Canterbury and, with him, convinced of this need, we affirm and encourage the work of the Anglican Communion Task Group on Theological Education.

HIV/AIDS

We pondered the impact of the HIV/AIDS pandemic on our lives and in our communities and provinces as we shared our experiences and sorrows. HIV tears at the very fabric of our nations and homes. We admitted that the "Body of Christ has AIDS".

Adhering to the teachings of the Church, we determined to engage more deeply in challenging cultures and traditions which stifle the humanity of women and deprive them of equal rights. We agreed that our greatest challenge is to nurture and equip our children to protect themselves from HIV, so that we can fulfill the vision of building a generation without AIDS.

AIDS is not a punishment from God, for God does not visit disease and death upon his people: it is rather an effect of fallen creation and our broken humanity. We were reminded at our meeting that Christ calls us into community as friends so that we might befriend others in his name. In that spirit, we resolved to build on what has already been achieved and to re-commit our efforts, prayers and support for all who are living with, and dying from, the effects of HIV/AIDS.

Our Shared Communion in Christ

As Primates, we believe that the 38 provinces and united churches in the Anglican Communion are irrevocably called into a special relationship of fellowship with one another. We thank God for our common inheritance of faith, worship and discipleship — an inheritance which has sustained our journey as one Christian family, and in which we have been united in our proclamation of the Gospel.

We recognise that all churches, and not just Anglicans, face challenges in applying the Gospel to their specific situations and societies. These challenges raise questions for our traditional teaching and understanding — questions which require of the Church a careful process of thought and discussion in order to discover a way forward that is true to our inheritance of faith in Christ and to our duty as Christians to care for all people.

Recalling the Virginia Report's exhortation that we should strive for "the highest degree of communion possible with tolerance for deeply held differences of conviction and practice" (Report of the Inter-Anglican Theological and Doctrinal Commission, 1997, chapter 1), we are committed as Primates:

- to the recognition that in each province there is a sincere desire to be faithful disciples of Christ and of God's Word, in seeking to understand how the Gospel is to be applied in our generation;

- to respect the integrity of each other's provinces and dioceses, acknowledging the responsibility of Christian leaders to attend to the pastoral needs of minorities in their care;

- to work and pray that the communion between our churches is sustained and deepened; and to seek from God "a right judgement in all things" (Collect of Pentecost).

Human Sexuality

We take seriously the duty laid upon us by the Lambeth Conference 1998 to monitor ongoing discussion of this matter and encourage continued study and reflection in the context of common prayer and worship. We are grateful to the Archbishop of the West Indies, Drexel Gomez, for taking forward our discussion on matters of sexuality by introducing the booklet "True Union in the Body?", which fruitfully illuminated our study. We are also grateful to Presiding Bishop Frank Griswold for drawing our attention to the Report of the Theology Committee of the House of Bishops of the Episcopal Church (USA) on this issue. We commend the study of both documents.

The question of public rites for the blessing of same sex unions is still a cause of potentially divisive controversy. The Archbishop of Canterbury spoke for us all when he said that it is through liturgy that we express what we believe, and that there is no theological consensus about same sex unions. Therefore, we as a body cannot support the authorisation of such rites.

This is distinct from the duty of pastoral care that is laid upon all Christians to respond with love and understanding to people of all sexual orientations. As recognised in the booklet "True Union", it is necessary to maintain a breadth of private response to situations of individual pastoral care.

Anglican Gathering

We discussed the proposal for an Anglican Gathering of lay and ordained people, drawn from all parts of our Communion, which could be held in association with the next Lambeth Conference.

There would be significant financial costs, but we firmly believe that such an event would offer the Communion an important opportunity to renew its life, witness and mission together. The Archbishop of Cape Town, Njongonkulu Ndungane, has offered to welcome a Gathering and the Lambeth Conference in Cape Town , which has the facilities for such events. We encouraged the Archbishop of Canterbury to move ahead with planning for the Gathering in 2008. This would be an occasion for celebration, learning and the deepening of our communion.

Invitation to Prayer

Having been renewed in the fellowship of our meeting, we invite Anglicans everywhere to pray with us. In his Bible studies, the Archbishop of Canterbury spoke of the joy we have as friends of God in Christ. "Jesus' joy is given to us", he said, "so that we might become nourishing to one another, nurturing and feeding one another in the Body of Christ." It is this vision of the rich blessings to be found in the fellowship of Christ's Body that inspires us.

Give thanks to God for the vibrant life of the Brazilian Church; for the diversity of the Anglican Communion, with its 75 million Christians, witnessing in 164 countries in a thousand languages; and for the faithful and courageous witness of Anglicans as they seek to bring God's love into situations of hardship, danger and despair. Pray that, by the power of the Holy Spirit, the Anglican Communion may everywhere be a faithful witness to what God has done in Christ, and to the abundant fullness of life to which he calls us.

The fire of love which binds together the Father and the Son be shed abroad in our hearts by the ministry of the Holy Spirit, and renew us in our lives and in our discipleship; and the blessing of God Almighty, the Father, the Son and the Holy Spirit, be among you and remain with you always.

Sermon by the Archbishop of Canterbury in Brazil

TEXT OF THE SERMON PREACHED BY THE ARCHBISHOP OF CANTERBURY AT A CELEBRATION FOR THE UNITY OF THE PEOPLE OF GOD WHICH WAS HELD IN GRAMADO, BRAZIL, ON SATURDAY 24 MAY 2003

What is it that Jesus Christ gives us? And what is it that we are to give to the world? Jesus answers us in today's gospel, in the clearest possible way. He gives us glory; and what we are given, we must share. Certainly, he gives us forgiveness, life, confidence, the promise of eternal rest in God - but in this passage from John's gospel, he sums it all up in the word 'glory', because what he longs to give us is ultimately just what the Father gives him. It isn't a very easy word to translate or understand for many people these days. We associate glory with fame or success - and Jesus on his way to a humiliating and dreadful death is obviously not someone who possesses that kind of glory. Instead, he speaks, a few verses later, of a glory given by the Father before the world was made. And the picture conjured up for us is of a radiant light streaming from the Father, reflected without any loss or inequality in the face of the Son. The Son, who becomes human for us in Jesus, never turns from the Father, and so never loses that radiant light; Jesus in his life on earth never loses it - though it is only for a moment, at the Transfiguration, that his face literally shows this eternal light. And if we keep ourselves turned to Jesus, then that same light is reflected in our faces, and it lights up the world around.

The relationship between Jesus and God his Father is the foundation for this radiance; and so, obviously, the relation between Jesus and us is what makes the light travel still further. But what is important in this gospel passage is that it is also the relationship between us as Christians that makes the light shine that causes the glory to radiate. When we are turned to Jesus, glory is reflected - St Paul says just this in II Corinthians. But when we are turned to each other the same is true. The glory given by Jesus is given so that we may become one; and this implies that it is when we are one with each other that the glory shines out for others.

To turn to Christ is in practice always to turn to each other. Conversion is always conversion to one another if it is truly and fully conversion to Jesus. And when we are 'turned around' like this, glory becomes visible. The Church is a place of glory when we see each other face to face and give thanks - like Jacob meeting Esau in the Genesis story: Esau welcomes and forgives his brother, and Jacob says, 'Truly, your face is like the face of God to me'. One of the great joys of belonging to a worldwide communion is that we can always encounter fresh and challenging contexts in which the Christian and Anglican tradition has come alive, and we find the glory of God in the face of the stranger. We have experienced it in our meeting as Primates; we experience it as we receive your welcome, dear friends. We trust that in these meetings and welcomes, glory will appear: the world will see how our faithful gazing at each other in gratitude and delight makes room for God's own light to be reflected.

When that light is reflected, the landscape changes. Isaiah's prophecy speaks of the desert bursting into flower; the glory of the Lord appears in the glory of the actual physical surroundings - not difficult to understand in our surroundings here. When God's light shines on our world, it becomes infinitely more precious; we cannot in such a light believe that the world is there to exploit and ruin. This great country has had its share of tragedy in the exploitation both of the natural world and of human beings - sometimes both together as in the ravaging of the rain forests which has put so much life, human and non-human, at risk. And when God's light shines on the human faces around us, we cannot treat them as having no interest for us; wherever the light falls, there we see the possibility of a life reflecting God. So there we see yet another face which we must look at with gratitude and hope. This is the foundation of all the work done with those whom the world wants to forget; and it is a real proclamation of the gospel when we hear of the work done by your local churches with the forgotten and those without voices, the indigenous peoples and those who live in the favelas. The Brazilian Church , as we have learned, is one that has given to the poor a degree of loving support out of all proportion to its size, and we wish you every strength and blessing in this work. We pray that glory may dwell in this land, as the eighty-fifth psalm puts it.

But we must return to what we do together as a communion, as Primates and people together. Jesus tells us in the gospel reading why our unity matters. Unless we are looking gladly and faithfully at each other, the glory we are given will fail to appear. That does not mean that we don't sometimes have the responsibility of calling each other to turn back to Jesus when it is difficult to see that the brother or sister is turning, to face the Lord, as fully as could be. And this is a service we must ask of each other: tell me when you see me turning from Jesus, when the glory that comes from looking at him has become invisible. Yet, even when we argue, rebuke and find ourselves in deep and painful division, the basic responsibility remains: to keep looking, to refuse to be turned away from the brother or sister for whom Christ died; to look in hope, until the radiance begins again to appear.

Our Christian calling is to renew the face of the earth, by the Spirit's power. By looking in love at the world and one another, we somehow allow glory to come to light - so that the non-believer may find their own awareness of the world mysteriously changed by the way the Christian neighbour looks at it. 'How can I learn to see what you see?' the neighbour asks, if we are living and looking as we should. God calls us to be at every level the agents of transformation - in a ruined and exploited natural environment, of deep divisions and much poverty, and in a Church whose communion can be undermined by fear or suspicion.

You cannot spend half a day in this country without realising that here the guitar is inseparable from the human voice! So I think of the poem by the American writer Wallace Stevens about 'The Man with the Blue Guitar':

They said, You have a blue guitar,

You do not play things as they are.

The man replied, Things as they are

Are changed upon the blue guitar.

Things as they are, with human beings left to themselves, so often seem shadowed by death and cruelty. But we have been given another song to sing, we, the ransomed of the Lord returning to Zion with singing. As we sing what we have learned from Jesus, things as they are changed. Glory dwells in our land, the glory that the Son shares with the Father in the Holy Spirit.

Amen.

Report published for ACC 2003